*Torture in the
National Security Imagination*

Torture in the
National Security Imagination

Stephanie Athey

University of Minnesota Press
Minneapolis
London

Chapter 1 was originally published as "The Terrorist We Torture: The Tale of Abdul Hakim Murad," in *On Torture,* ed. Tom Hilde (Baltimore, Md.: Johns Hopkins University Press, 2008), 87–104. Portions of chapter 3 are adapted from "The Torture Device: Debate and Archetype," in *Torture: Power, Democracy, and the Human Body,* ed. Shampa Biswas and Zahi Zalloua (Seattle: University of Washington Press, 2011), 129–57. Portions of chapter 5 are adapted from "The Torturer's Tale: Tony Lagouranis in Mosul and the Media," in *Iraq War Cultures,* ed. Cynthia Fuchs and Joe Lockard (New York: Peter Lang, 2011), 160–77.

Copyright 2023 by the Regents of the University of Minnesota

All rights reserved. No part of this publication may be reproduced, stored in a retrieval system, or transmitted, in any form or by any means, electronic, mechanical, photocopying, recording, or otherwise, without the prior written permission of the publisher.

Published by the University of Minnesota Press
111 Third Avenue South, Suite 290
Minneapolis, MN 55401-2520
http://www.upress.umn.edu

ISBN 978-1-5179-1327-4 (hc)
ISBN 978-1-5179-1328-1 (pb)

A Cataloging-in-Publication record for this book is available from the Library of Congress.

The University of Minnesota is an equal-opportunity educator and employer.

This book is for my mother and my father, for my brilliant sisters and brothers—Kris, Al, Michelle, Mary Beth, Dave, and Jana—and for Isla and Keenan.

Contents

Acknowledgments	ix
Prologue: "A Nasty Business" in the Public Press	xi
Introduction: U.S. Torture, Prisons, Police	1
1. Anecdote: Abdul Hakim Murad and Torture in Four Dimensions	31
2. Rationale: The Refashioning of Colonial Violence—Roger Trinquier, Jean Lartéguy, and Edward Lansdale	57
3. Archetype: Mistaking the Plurals of Torture	99
4. Technique: The Waterboard Spectacle	121
5. Perpetrators: Sabrina Harman, Tony Lagouranis, and Crafted Confession	159
6. Networks: Deploying the Salvador Option	189
Epilogue: Complicity	215
Notes	225
Index	303

Acknowledgments

This book is the product of many hours given over by generous minds, all of whom lent critical suggestions, conversation, and insight at important stages. Portions of this work were previously published in early versions, with the significant dialogue, encouragement, and support of Darius Rejali, Andy Nathan, Tom Hilde, and Cindy Fuchs.

I am grateful to J. Paul Martin and the Center for the Study of Human Rights at Columbia University for providing a key setting for research. I also wish to acknowledge the work of Alexandra S. Moore and Elizabeth Swanson, who have championed critical scholarship on human rights, narrative, and culture. They invited me into projects and several dynamic forums that enriched this work. Sharp and attentive readers improved the ideas and articulation at several points. In addition to those already mentioned, these include Wendy S. Hesford, Lisa Lynch, Lisa Gitelman, Lydia Sampson, Amy Bracken, Lean Sweeney, Jared del Rosso, and Patricia Roy. The careful attention and guidance of Doug Armato and Zenyse Miller of the University of Minnesota Press improved the whole.

A special thank you goes to filmmaker Jeff Stephens for his interest and collaboration. His breadth of reading and love of detail made for animated conversation on many of the fine points and key figures in this book. Likewise, I have benefited enormously from colleagues who have drawn me into dimensions of teaching and learning that have deepened this effort: Jesse Tauriac, Charlotte Frazier, Tessa LeRoux, Liz Hartmann, Karin Raye, Sarahbeth Golden, Halliday Piel, Denny Frey, James Perry Jr., Alanis Perez-Rivera, and Nicholas Shelley. I thank as well Susan Farrell and the many students whose insight, experience, and outrage have left an imprint on these pages.

There are many other personal and professional debts to recognize. I thank María del Refugio López Cruz for her partnership, ingenuity, and teachings. I am indebted to the goodwill, endless humor, and companionship of bright minds toiling with their own projects, all of whom lent energy and support to mine: Cynthia Becker, Hortense Gerardo, Eloy Martinez, and Grete Viddal. Throughout my time with this project, I have been energized by the political fire, inspiration, and creativity of the magnificent Magdalena Gomez, Jim Lescault, Fred Ho, and Ximena E. Mejía. Finally, I owe a special thanks to Lisa Gitelman for smarts, kindness, and steady and generous example; to Ximena for wisdom, loving persistence, and willingness to challenge everything; to Daniel Cooper Alarcón for wit, recommendations, and unyielding friendship over distances; and to Lean Sweeney for critical feedback, dialogue on all things, and for forging my connection to John, Amelia, and Arthur, who keep me loving the journey.

Prologue

"A Nasty Business" in the Public Press

> We put an emphasis on due process and sometimes it strangles us.
> —Richard Thornburgh, former attorney general

In a society where torture is both common and illegal, what provokes its debate?

In the case of torture during the twenty-first-century United States, the speculative press launched the topic immediately and enthusiastically six days after September 11, 2001. In this, the press led the public as well as the executive branch. It instigated debate before the U.S. government implemented its war on terror, before President George W. Bush's Office of Legal Counsel issued pronouncements on "obsolete" elements of the Geneva Conventions, before that counsel set about redefining severe pain and torture, and before a Department of Defense team assembled the set of aggressive protocols, spaces, and personnel that, in early 2002, physically crippled Guantánamo captive Mohamad al-Qahtani and drove him insane.[1] Feature stories, news analyses, and commentaries emerged rapidly in publications like the *New York Times*, the *New Yorker*, the *Wall Street Journal*, the *Washington Post*, *Newsweek*, *Time*, and *Atlantic Monthly*, where they continued to appear over a number of years. Just a few of the article titles that appeared from September 2001 to the end of 2003 illustrate why it is useful to call these contributions speculative: "How Far Americans Would Go to Fight Terror," "Seeking a Moral Compass while Chasing Terrorists," "Security Comes before Liberty," "Time to Think about Torture," "Agonizing over Torture: Can Deliberate Hurt Be Justified in Times of Terror?" "No Tortured Dilemma," "A Nasty Business," "Should We Torture Qaeda Higher Ups?" "Making Terrorists Talk: America Doesn't Use Torture to Get Information Out of Terrorists; Perhaps We Just Need to Use the Magic Word: Mossad," "Make Them Talk," "Interrogation School—30 Techniques—Just Short of Torture; Do They Yield Much?" "The Torturer's Apprentice," "Torture, Tough or Lite: If a Terror Suspect Won't Talk, Should He Be Made To?" "Psychology and Sometimes a Slap: The Man Who Made Prisoners

Talk," and "The Dark Art of Interrogation: The Most Effective Way to Gather Intelligence and Thwart Terrorism Can Also Be a Direct Route into Morally Repugnant Terrain; A Survey of the Landscape of Persuasion."[2]

This outpouring considered the nature and potential of torture in limiting, even fanciful, ways. What is more, peculiar tendencies in the initial speculation became common features of the larger public conversation on torture as it expanded over years. These patterns motivated the inquiry that became this book.

A few elements were striking from the outset. First, for instance, the press "debate" was circular. It spread quickly but retained a kind of symmetry. Certain questions preoccupied the U.S. press and academic class, and still do: Does torture work? Should we or shouldn't we torture? Is this or isn't this torture? These questions are trip wires, set to spring circular debates—ever ready, easily triggered, and inexhaustible.

Second, the speculative press debate was influential and set important parameters on thought. Both participants who favored harsh treatment and those who opposed it reached for a common set of images and assumptions. They struck narrative postures, anointed experts, and circulated anecdotal evidence, terminology, and unexamined propositions that were taken up and repeated in other arenas. Legal opinions and scholarship by elite lawyers including Alan Dershowitz and Sanford Levinson directly borrowed from the speculative press. This press speculation gathered an even wider audience; indeed, military interrogator Tony Lagouranis, who admitted to torturing captives in Mosul, Iraq, cited the impact of the speculative news on his thinking and self-concept.[3]

A third observation about this trend: the speculators brashly claimed the word "torture" and reveled in Hollywood idioms, like brass-knuckled or making them talk. Stories divided into types. The first to appear I call Hypothetical. These should-we-or-shouldn't-we surveys presented torture as an urgent dilemma suddenly on the public mind when, in fact, close reading shows that it was the writer who proposed the subject. These were followed by two strands I refer to as Historical and Heart of Darkness, which are purportedly more grounded in the real. While these strands were clearly rooted in habits of colonial writing and thinking, a subject taken up in the Introduction, they drew no connection to ongoing abuses or familiar torture histories, even when those were reported in the very same pages and news outlets. For instance, in 2001 and 2002, while journalists and jurists like Alan Dershowitz purported to broach torture as an unspeakably new idea whose time was right, Ehab Elmaghraby, Javaid Iqbal, and many others were subjected to flashlight rapes and beatings at the Metropolitan Detention Center in Brooklyn. They were among more than 1,200 resident immigrants swept up after September 11, 2001, and held at a site where sexual terror was rampant and captured on camera.[4] Likewise, in 2002, the last New York police assailant in the torture of Abner Louima was finally retried and sentenced. Louima was a Haitian immigrant raped and battered by a set of New York police officers in the 1990s. Papers in both the 1990s and 2002 forthrightly called this police torture. As the press speculated, high-ranking torturers from El Salvador's history of government death squads were reportedly living comfortably in Miami, despite being known to have received financial and weapons support from the United States. From France in 2002 came reminders of widespread military torture and terror over half a century earlier in the Algerian anticolonial struggle: General Jacques Massu died, a man infamous for his command of the Battle of Algiers, and General Paul Aussaresses published memoirs that drew outrage for defending widespread torture in that war. As speculative news on the topic of torture grew, attempts to try Chile's infamous Pinochet and notorious Serbian perpetrators were also in the news, and all the while, investigative journalist John Conroy continued his lonely, dogged reporting on the ongoing, obstructed prosecution of Chicago's Area 2 police torture team, led by Jon Burge.[5]

Had the speculative, hypothetical writing across 2001 to 2003 engaged any of these highly publicized examples of torture practice unfolding in the press, it would have found several well-documented cases with bearing on torture's purported effectiveness, a chief concern of the debate. Better, it might have forced different questions about the core functions at work and the powerful social networks that organize and protect torture, as well as the local, professional, financial, political, and even geopolitical incentives and dynamics so visibly central to the examples from El Salvador, Chile, and Serbia; the police tortures of Chicago and New York; and the rapes in Brooklyn's Metropolitan Detention Center.

A fourth aspect of this press attention is this. Over three years, 2001 to early 2004, across dozens of outlets, speculation on hypothetical torture became big news while actual torture in the war on terror was overlooked or misnamed. Striking evidence of the torture of U.S. captives was ignored in Afghanistan, in many regions of Iraq, in the prisons of rendition allies, and in what would become known as CIA black sites. While speculative torture in the war on terror became a scintillating news commodity, only seven meager *investigative* stories on "detainee treatment" appeared across the same period, and the treatment was pointedly not termed torture.[6]

These investigative pieces warrant a look. One of the first investigative stories ran on March 11, 2002, in the *Washington Post*, "U.S. Behind Secret Transfer of Terror Suspects." Writers Rajiv Chandrasekaran and Peter Finn describe in some detail the cases of eight persons who had been subject to extralegal arrest and rendition to a third country.[7] Their discussion of U.S. responsibility is frank:

> Since Sept. 11, the U.S. Government has secretly transported dozens of people suspected of links to terrorists to countries other than the United States, bypassing extradition procedures and legal formalities, according to Western diplomats and intelligence sources. The suspects have been taken to countries, including Egypt and Jordan, whose intelligence services have close ties to the CIA and where they can be subjected to interrogation tactics—including torture and threats to families—that are illegal in the United States, the sources said. In some cases, U.S. intelligence agents remain closely involved in the interrogation, the sources said. "After September 11, these sorts of movements have been occurring all the time," a U.S. diplomat said. "It allows us to get information from terrorists in a way we can't do on U.S. soil."

The *Washington Post* returned to the topic nine months later, on December 26, 2002.[8] Sources spoke to Dana Priest and Barton Gellman of "take down teams" made up of "a mix of military special forces, FBI agents, CIA case officers and local allies." Once terror suspects are en route to their detention facility, soldiers "aim to disorient and intimidate them." On arrival, captives face "softening up" by military police and Special Forces "who beat them up and confine them in tiny rooms," where prisoners are "blindfolded and thrown into walls, bound in painful positions subjected to loud noises and deprived of sleep." This technique is called stress and duress. Officials acknowledged withholding medication and sending captives to countries that use torture, where U.S. personnel were said to observe or offer the questions and receive transcripts.[9]

The point: In early 2002, all the elements of torture that would be received with shock in 2004—the revelations concerning U.S. behavior at Abu Ghraib in Iraq—were already in the news and the public eye, along with the basic elements of rendition practice and black sites. Nevertheless, this reporting vanished without follow-up stories. Protests and documentation by Amnesty International and Human Rights Watch that warranted investigative reporting went unpursued. What is more, even early in 2004, the government's own near acknowledgment of torture set off no storm of curiosity. A one-paragraph press release issued on January 16 indicated in colorless language an investigation into detainee abuse by military personnel at a "coalition facility." Only four newspapers and three networks offered cursory reports on the release.[10] Not until a cache of participant photographs of that abuse from Abu Ghraib prison were broadcast on CBS in April 2004 would investigative reporting on torture really take off.[11] As it did, the speculative debate persisted.

That Spot Where We Could Go to Pressure

How did speculation on torture become a big story at a time when reporting of actual torture received scant attention?

Polling suggests that a sea change took place in the relationship between the news media and the public in the immediate aftermath of September 11. News consumption was at an all-time high. Polls in the week after the attacks found that 98 percent of those surveyed were following terrorism news closely, and 83 percent said they were following very closely.[12] By October 21, PEW Research Center for the People and the Press found that 94 percent of respondents were following the news closely, with 78 percent claiming to do so very closely.[13] The public was riveted. October saw a prevailing media "obsession with endlessly reporting and debating the *potential* for biological, chemical and nuclear warfare in the wake of 9-11." Some journalists acknowledged the guilty "good fortune" inherent in the uptick in readership, and a few wondered aloud at their own role as "unwitting accomplices" in terror, as Robert J. Samuelson put it, or "merchants of fear."[14]

The speculation on torture that began in September gathered momentum in this context of news anxiety and addiction. When news broke on October 4 that an unknown terrorist had sent anthrax by mail to celebrity news anchors and Capitol Hill legislators, the number of stories devoted to anthrax and other potential biochemical terrors jumped tenfold. Anthrax killed two postal workers, and several others were critically poisoned. Military strikes on Afghanistan began October 7.[15]

The Hypothetical brand of speculation found its legs in this moment and changed from a form that surveyed public mood to one that surveyed its own selected so-called experts. In an October 21 story in the *Washington Post*, "Silence of Four Terror Probe Suspects Poses Dilemma for FBI," Walter Pincus seemingly bridges the gap between speculation and event coverage. He reported investigators were "increasingly frustrated" at four suspects, noting "civil liberties may have to be cast aside if they are to extract information about the Sept. 11 attacks and terrorist plans." "It could get to that spot where we could go to pressure," says an unnamed agent, "where we won't have a choice, and we are probably getting there."[16] The article got an immediate response. Various letters to the editor followed that week, and the story was picked up internationally. The *Australian Times* captured the gist in its title: "Stymied FBI Looks to Torture." U.S. publications weighed in on the FBI "frustration."[17] Readers see the FBI already at the end of its resources only thirty-five days into the war on terror. Who were the men who moved the unnamed source to contemplate torture? Three of the four were particularly worrisome, yet allegations against all four are provided in one quick sentence; fewer than a hundred words of the eleven-hundred-word story are devoted to the men.[18] Although their silence fueled speculation on torture lasting months, five years later, the government had determined their silence was warranted. Three never had anything to say. The fourth, arrested a month before September 11, was Zacarias Moussawi, who had said all he could. He eventually pleaded guilty in civilian court to terrorist conspiracy as a member of al-Qaeda.

Surprisingly, the three said to be of critical concern to the FBI included Nabil Almarabh, a Boston cabdriver, who was rounded up immediately after the terror attacks, jailed, and spent eight months in solitary confinement. He was denied access to a lawyer and in 2003 was charged only with credit card fraud and deported to Syria.[19] The two men deemed the greatest threat were hapless Indian Muslims, who were denied a lawyer and held for a year. Arrested on a train on September 12, with box cutters, hair dye, and $5,000 in cash, they too were denied lawyers and made detailed complaints of mistreatment while in U.S. custody.[20]

In 2001, however, with so few words devoted to the suspects, what remains matters. Pincus notes the illegality of torture under U.S. law, then explores the possibility of whether the United States could "let it happen." One former FBI source stands against torture but notes there would be an important difference in using drugs "to try to get critical information when facing disaster, and beating a guy till he is senseless." That the drug, sodium pentothal, is illegal and discredited as a truth drug received no mention. Also considered were "pressure tactics, such as those employed occasionally by Israeli interrogators to extract information." "Another idea," Pincus reports, "is extraditing the suspects to allied countries where security services sometimes employ threats to family members or resort to torture."

Pincus established a pattern that will be followed. Hypothetical pieces now sought out experts in a few fields and anonymous sources, no longer the public and never torture survivors. For example, David Cole, then of Georgetown University Law Center and described as a "firm supporter of civil liberties," offered, "If there's a ticking bomb, it's not an easy issue, it's tough."[21] Former attorney general Richard Thornburgh spoke more generally still: "In the aftermath of Sept. 11," he said, "legally admissible evidence in court may not be the be-all and end-all. . . . We put emphasis on due process and sometimes it strangles us."[22]

One week later, in a *Newsweek* issue entitled "Protecting America," Jonathan Alter made a sensation of Pincus's factoid on silent men with "Time to Think about Torture."

> OK, not cattle prods or rubber hoses . . . not here in the United States, but *something* to jump-start the stalled investigation. . . . Right now, four key hijacking suspects aren't talking at all. Couldn't we at least subject them to psychological torture, like tapes of dying rabbits or high-decibel rap? (The military has done that in Panama.) How about truth serum. . . . Or deportation to Saudi Arabia, land of beheadings. . . . Some people still argue that we needn't . . . but they're hopelessly "Sept. 10"—living in a country that no longer exists.[23]

Alter waxes facetious, grim, and nostalgic. He summons specious distinctions that will become stock elements of the arguments to come: torture to prevent terror is wise, but torture to convict on past crimes is out of bounds. So-called psychological torture can be distinguished from physical torture and is a measure less brutal.[24] Torture here in the United States is unseemly, but torture abroad is inevitable. And this: "It's a new world, and survival may well require old techniques that seemed out of the question." The concise and poetic logic of Alter's formulation—new threats require new methods or new thinking—was devised in the 1950s, when even these methods were neither new nor discarded.

The week of Alter's piece, the *New York Times* highlighted its seismic effect on human rights organizations and the news media, listing additional features on the viability of torture that ran in many outlets, including Fox News, CNN's *Crossfire,* and *Slate* online.[25] The rash of Hypothetical commentary that followed for over a decade often repeated these false but fundamental distinctions, and rebuttals at times left these unchallenged. For debaters, the exchange provided a tool through which to frame war imaginatively and to strike postures that aligned one among peers: to wax patriotic or to burnish progressive credentials. It developed its own rhythms. At first, rapidly, the torture debate courted sensation with a supposedly taboo topic and pointed to its own daring or high dudgeon. Later, participants passionately defended or denounced the U.S. administration's clear involvement in torture during the war on terror. The conversation on torture slowed with the election of a new president and administration in 2008; interest in the public and academic press truly waned after 2014, with the declassification of the Senate Select Committee intelligence report on enhanced interrogation by the CIA. That report served as a convenient bookend on an episode that many were eager to shelve.[26]

However, as the public speculation and debate unfolded and after, so did U.S. torture practice in its everyday spaces of detention, confrontation, and confinement.

Introduction

U.S. Torture, Prisons, Police

In 2003, a story in *U.S. News and World Report* quietly noted that the Commerce Department had waived restrictions for sixty U.S. manufacturers, allowing exports of thumbscrews to thirty-nine countries the State Department had censured for torture.[1] Thumbscrews—and thumb cuffs—were designated by the U.S. Commerce Control List that year as "specially designed implements of torture," part of category number 0A982. The classification also included finger cuffs and spiked batons. A look at the Commerce Department's annual exports shows that such items continue to be manufactured and special waivers continue to be granted.[2]

Mainstream news reports on the subject are extremely rare, so it might come as a surprise to learn that there exists a manufacturing and export category entitled "specially designed implements of torture." In learning these details, there comes the risk we might fixate only on the implements: the thumbscrews. (Why do these even exist? What else is on that list?) Or we might focus on the U.S. regulatory effort to stop certain exports. (At least some places cannot have spiked batons!) To indulge either reflex—highlighting the instrument or separating a U.S. "here" from some distant "there," the nasty places where markets for torture tools exist—is to fall prey to classic misdirection and patterns in thinking about torture that are nearly a century old.

No device is necessary for torture, of course; human ingenuity ensures that any device can be used to produce severe pain and suffering, both mental and physical. In addition, given the inevitable flow of all goods across any border, and given that all the items listed are made and sold within the United States, the ban may function simply to designate which countries torture and which do not—a distinction that exists only in the imagination. In the early 2000s, this dry, regulatory language reflected a premise found in the livelier routines of public discussion surrounding torture. Standard public refrains positioned the United States at a spatial but also temporal remove from torture in the world, measured in a kind of civilizational time, as if torture happens in places where people are caught in errors of the past, places revisiting a history of violence, or places manifesting violence due to a particularly chaotic or tragic cultural circumstance, like corrupt governance or sectarian war. This continues to be the case. The implicit distinction between "here" and "there" permeates all levels of torture talk, regulation, denunciation, and debate in the United States. However, it is just one of many inherently colonialist features of common thinking on torture, dividing civilized from uncivilized and what some term "liberal" from "illiberal" forms of violence. The U.S. license to torture remains bound up with the nation's self-image and its pride of civilizational place.

These and other stubborn patterns in public discussion of torture contrast starkly with facts that the Commerce regulations make plain. State torture is an integrated global and local undertaking that involves many people, profits, and purported benefits. Professional ties, routines, and incentives, after all, connect those who oversee the design, marketing, sales, and investor dividends in torture implements. Federal employees and lobbyists guide the conversations each year that determine which goods to label "specially designed for torture" and which to not. Other employees read the waiver applications from manufacturers and issue permits allowing export, including goods sent to Cambodia and Estonia in 2001, Iraq and Tajikistan in 2013, and Colombia and Syria in 2015.

Although this book touches at least in part on some of the most provocative moments in the U.S. media outpouring on torture between 2001 and 2014, when the war on terror and the U.S. invasion of Iraq focused peak news attention on the subject, it is a reckoning with something more. In that period, both advocates and detractors of torture reached for a common set of images and assumptions even as they disagreed. Beyond the moral or practical justificatory frameworks that seemed to be at odds in that debate, opponents' presentations of torture and salient concerns were regularly aligned. That presentation differed greatly from what has been captured by ethnographic and sociological studies, spectator and survivor accounts, human rights monitors, and medical reports for decades: that state torture is a collaborative undertaking that is driven by social functions and putative benefits.

For this reason, the book steps away from the framework of debate entirely to examine instead what I term the national security imagination, a shared reservoir of presumption, image, and orientation in which torture remains inextricable from imperial imaginings. That national storehouse captures a kind of social imaginary on what torture is, what it looks like, where it comes from, and why it exists. A social imaginary, as that term is used in sociology and cultural studies, describes a body of shared understandings that transcend conscious thought yet manifest in real policy and institutions, shaping human interpretation and action.

Within that universe of shared understandings about national security, key assumptions that pertain to torture circulate, for instance, about the torture techniques or implements that we debate and regulate, or concerning the perpetrator we scrutinize and revile. Particular features like these are embedded in that security vision of torture and work like a series of hooks. They snag our attention or ire, making it a challenge to look beyond them. So too premises attach to this vision that typically, as with any social imaginary, go unexamined. These and other elements became focal points that steered the 2001–14 U.S. conversation, and they still shape our thinking on violence. Today, the crafted role of torture in that security imagination promotes torture practice because it also works, first, to rationalize the union of torture and American empire, and second, to obscure the relation between the community-building, race-making violence of domestic tortures and that of torture performed in the name of national security. The book offers a historical, political, and cultural explanation for these shared preoccupations, aiming to reject them and foreground instead an alternative understanding of state torture we can easily find in regulations on thumbscrew manufacture and sale. While the details of the Commerce Control List would undoubtedly stir interest in the tool or technique used to torture, what if the national imagination on torture focused instead on a fact that has been visible all along? This is the fact that human, material, professional, and procedural networks engineer state torture, and the practice thrives because it has carved out social functions and benefits.

The professional networks of the Commerce Department point to another claim of this book. Just as, on the one hand, an economically and politically supported calculus assembles, trains, and incentivizes the workers who will coordinate and label the violence, so does, on the other hand, a societally supported economic, racial, and gendered calculus mark out the large populations who will be targeted for state torture.[3] Moreover, U.S. torture work at home and abroad are interdependent and daily operations; they are far from separate things. In detailing how features particular to the vision of torture in this century were actually devised in the last, the book proposes a large conceptual switch. We need to unseat a common perception of state torture as an incident or an act perpetrated by a torturer. Instead, we need to recognize it as a collaborative, compartmentalized, and networked process that assembles and stratifies communities and resources.

In 2001, the public had many opportunities to see state torture in just this way—as a standard process by which the United States manages populations, maintains colonial relations of power, and defines threat. Three efforts to confront U.S. state torture at the time illustrate this well. For one, just days before the attacks of September 11, seven members of the U.S. Congressional Black Caucus were in Durban, South Africa, at the World Conference against Racism to denounce the role of U.S. terror and torture in political suppression. Their report to the U.N. high commissioner on human rights, Mary Robinson, documented activities of the Federal Bureau of Investigation counterintelligence program COINTELPRO, infamous for surveillance, infiltration, torture, and harassment of civil rights organizers. Targets included American Indian Movement figures like Dennis Banks and Russell Means as well as civil rights leaders Martin Luther King Jr. and Malcolm X; military-style attacks were coordinated on Black Panther activists. The latter included the federal, state, and local forces that ensured the murder of Fred Hampton in Chicago, or the federal, Louisiana, and California police who convened in New Orleans for the torture of Harold Taylor, John Bowman, and Ruben Scott.[4]

In another September 2001 instance, the place of torture was visible in the U.S. criminal justice system. Richard Devine, the state's attorney of Cook County, Illinois, offered to reduce the death row sentences of four men, provided they dropped their long-standing claims of police torture. Devine had offered deals like this before to prevent Chicago police from testifying in court on torture routines. He was one of a number of city and state employees who obstructed investigation into over two decades of systematic torture of African American residents conducted by a dozen officers.[5]

Throughout 2001, the South Dakota State Training School, a juvenile detention center in Plankinton, was the subject of a suit on behalf of children tortured there.[6] In a notorious holdover from two centuries of federal American Indian boarding schools, Native youth were penalized for speaking Lakota and held in the lockdown unit, which saw the worst abuses. For example, "one young girl from the Pine Ridge Reservation had been held in a secure unit within the facility for almost two years, during which she was placed in four-point restraints and made to 'spread eagle' on a cement slab for hours at a time. She was also kept in isolation for days and even weeks and pepper-sprayed numerous times."[7] A national report found Native youth, who comprise only 1 percent of the U.S. youth population, are 70 percent of the youth committed to the federal system as minors. They comprise 31 percent of youths committed as adults.[8]

Each of these reports from 2001 points back to a history of U.S. torture as an engine of misogynist racial and political terror. They also foreground issues that would fuel the Movement for Black Lives, the mass protest of immigration bans and detention, and other activism across the first three decades of the twenty-first century. What were taken by some in 2001 to be distinct crises or phenomena (the newly emerging war on terror; racialized political surveillance; public order policing; burgeoning detention and punishment regimes) were in fact united by torture. They continue to be. Torture remains a routine way of enacting racial difference and colonial dominance through the work of collective containment and suppression.

Yet when the U.S. news and public speculated on torture in 2001, a mere six days after the terror strikes of September 11, the press raised torture as an extraordinary weapon—a means, perhaps, of communal protection entirely divorced from its homeland racial and colonial uses, both past and present. This omission, in a passionate torture debate that grew over a decade and a half, was matched by the participants' own inability to see the symmetry in pro and con stances, or to recognize that symmetry as a failure of debate itself, even a mode of complicity with torture. As conversation grew on what the mainstream press named torture, participants with opposing views reached for the common set of images, assumptions, and obsessions; these headline each chapter of this book. Bundled into these obsessions were and are untenable premises, unquestioned conceptual divides, and false oppositions: civilized versus barbaric, interrogation versus detention, geopolitical versus domestic, psychological versus physical, torture versus police brutality.

These patterns are easily traced across news features and commentary from 2001 to 2004 in the *New York Times*, the *Wall Street Journal*, the *Washington Post, Newsweek, Time, U.S. News and World Report, Atlantic Monthly*, and the *New Yorker*. Even after 2004 and the appearance of photos of U.S. torture of Iraqis at Abu Ghraib prison, these same obsessions riveted national media and activist attention. From mid-2004 to 2014, when the Senate issued the declassified, truncated version of its intelligence report on the CIA's "enhanced techniques," the same narrative hooks and presumptions concerning torture radiated with a surprising persistence across a range of legal and academic scholarship, Senate hearings, State Department and Defense Department cables, and documentary film.[9] Even in careful and durable scholarship that argued in small or large part against some of these folkloric obsessions, there was often an unwitting retreat—momentary or prevailing—to stylized concepts and vehicles for argument common to that social imaginary.

The twenty-first-century result was less a contentious debate than the echo of a carefully developed tradition of evasion that would attempt to part company with mass terror and the domestic branches of torture practice. The book identifies two contrasting stages in the U.S. adaptation and development of that tradition. The first stage I consider occurs as settler tortures rooted in colonial race making, labor exploitation, or policing terror were refined in domestic expansion, then refashioned as technical systems of imperial and racial surveillance in the Philippines. In a second stage, discourse about torture was reinvented in midcentury counterinsurgency theory as the United States joined Europe in suppressing anticolonial independence struggles. The obsessions we know today arose in the latter phase as deliberate fabrications—professional lore carefully spun around torture across the late 1940s to the 1960s, as the idea of national security emerged as a conceptual field.[10] That fabrication departed in structured, methodical ways from torture in practice. Mid-twentieth-century counterinsurgents and a growing set of security professionals sought to make the racialized, gendered structure of torture invisible while reinventing it for public consumption as a purportedly limited and technical tool, a necessary weapon in their story of defense against terrorism and subversion.

Presented in the 1950s, therefore, as something rare and preventive, a matter of expertise and special finesse, torture was reconceived as an intimate and existential contest of wills between two opponents. Early counterinsurgency theorists played their part in popularizing this idea, as did journalists, publishers, and spies. Proponents and their heirs began to isolate and present elements of the larger torture process, reducing torture to a matter of individual suffering, to the particular technique, to the perpetrator, or to the anomalous incident. Nonetheless, the practice of torture continued to target large numbers for terror and violence, and the broad racial, sexual, colonial, and social functions of torture practice persisted. Interest, collaboration, and competition in security through terror assembled new transnational academic, economic, and governmental networks that channeled prestige, equipment, and operational skill to geopolitical and neocolonial ends at home and abroad.

Put another way, state torture, like race, is a foundational player in the peacetime social order that the United States takes to be security, and has been from the beginning. Yet a growing national security stance and imaginary was crucial to the advance of a post-1947 phase of racial capitalism. "Security" came to signify a particular global and social order. "Counterinsurgency" as a coinage lent a technical cachet to neocolonial capitalist warfare and urban policing. In the guise of national security, "torture" signaled expertise and a brand of white supremacist restraint even as it purported to offer a nonracist, intelligence-based solution to terror. This vision of torture as a minimalist, specialist tool of security was among the most powerful tropes in that shared security vision. It deliberately cut ties between the community-building, race- and gender-making functions of domestic and colonial tortures on the one hand, and that of torture said to be in the name of national security on the other. Nevertheless, the methods of counterinsurgency and torture, whether abroad or at home, embraced mass racial terror and police power.[11]

To make this case, each chapter of this book showcases a fundamental fixation—a hook, as it were—surrounding torture in this social imaginary. Together, these fundamental fixations let us train a historical lens on some of the strangest moments and most appalling silences in the twenty-first-century public debate, from the should-we-or-shouldn't-we-torture, does-it-or-doesn't-it-work debates to the activist waterboard challenges and reenactors, from the media fascination with perpetrators and eclipse of survivors to the anger over secret memos and the hand-wringing over torture on entertainment TV. At every step of this debate-like spectacle, key elements of this torture lore did what they were designed to do over half a century before: they privileged the Anecdote (chapter 1); insisted on a security Rationale for torture, no matter the facts (chapters 1 and 2); defined "torture" through a recurring Archetype (chapter 3); and fixated, then split hairs, on regulating the particular tool or Technique (chapter 4). Torture talk foregrounded the Perpetrators (chapter 5) instead of survivors, and in looking so defiantly away from team-based torture practice and its everyday functions, it normalized domestic tortures both past and present. To counter the national security vision of torture, chapters 4, 5, and 6 use examples from across these years to identify key dimensions of torture as a networked practice: the pace, coordination, and details of its violence; its organizational setting; and its social functions. These dimensions bring to the fore the spectators and commentators, the communal energy of violence, and the teams and target groups necessary to a mass undertaking, including equipment suppliers, contractors, bureaucrats, university researchers, and profiteers.

Chapter 6, which addresses Networks, demonstrates these networked and social dimensions are legible, not hidden, using the case of the U.S. Salvador Option that envisioned, then built, financial, procedural, and interpersonal networks supporting Shi'ite death squads in the Iraq war. While details were available in funding bills and the press, against the raucous landscape of the U.S. media debate, the human networks that sponsored U.S.–Iraqi death squads gained less attention. Ironically, those death squads broadcast tortured confessions as entertainment on U.S.-sponsored Iraqi TV. Transnational violence networks hummed along throughout the debate, quietly yet publicly shaping ISIS and the new Iraq.

The remaining sections of this introduction will, first, lay out the book's definition of torture and its role in terror; second, indicate key literatures and interventions, including the social functions of torture; and third and last, offer a means to understand a social imaginary on national security in historical, practical, and theoretical terms.

Torture and Terror

According to the 1984 U.N. Convention Against Torture (CAT), torture is "severe pain or suffering, whether physical or mental, intentionally inflicted on a person" by a public official or with the "instigation, consent or acquiescence" of some "other person acting in an official capacity." The convention condemns severe pain and suffering for "such purposes as" obtaining information, confession, punishment, suspicion, intimidation, coercion, or discrimination of any kind. This prohibits a broad range of state violence.[12] At the same time, the convention also invites the distinction between torture and "legal" pain and suffering: "[Torture] does not include pain or suffering arising only from, inherent in or incidental to lawful sanctions."[13]

State torture is a political act and is condemned by convention. Definitions of torture are therefore political in themselves and come under considerable interpretive pressure from all sides. As Danielle Celermajer has said, the very word "torture" comes with "a moral inflection and motivational force."[14] This force can be instrumental in the fight against certain coercive practices.[15] For instance, successful efforts to articulate rape as a method of torture by activists and legal scholars across the 1980s and 1990s demonstrate this contest over interpretation, as does the evolving conversation on torture and sexual and gender-based violence.[16] Importantly, the 1984 U.N. CAT binds states to prevent, prosecute, and punish not only torture but also a wider range of coercive pain and suffering that falls short of torture. Called cruel, inhuman, and degrading treatment or punishment, or CIDTP, both are "absolutely and universally prohibited, with no exceptions or justifications."[17] No matter how a state might attempt to limit the definition of torture, treatment approaching torture is also barred.

Modern states use many modes of violence to cement their power and regulate people. Torture and CIDTP are among them. As John T. Parry notes, to hold torture as especially egregious and categorically apart from the "larger mosaic" of state violence is to make these other forms mundane, to normalize them in comparison.[18] To elevate torture in this way also isolates violence from its context in a way that, I argue, supports torture. It is better instead to specify the role torture plays without making it special. To identify the relationship of torture to that mosaic pushes us to see how and when it complements or anchors other forms of violence in the state repertoire. Parry's term "mosaic" is useful because torture is always an ensemble player, and unlike terms such as "continuum of violence" or "spectrum," it implies no objective ranking or scale among these forms. This challenge to make visible the specific and productive work of torture in confrontation, confinement, and policing violence does inevitably question the legitimacy of these and other coercive practices.

This book adopts that U.N. CAT definition, and like it, it identifies torture by its impact on persons—pain and suffering—not on the techniques used to inflict it. This aspect matters for two reasons. First, arranging methods on an objective spectrum or scale of suffering, least to most severe, becomes impossible in this view. Only those experiencing the suffering in a particular time and place would be able to judge. Second, in this definition, I emphasize the coordinated environment and organization essential to produce severe pain and suffering, because as the book hopes to demonstrate, that social context, as well as the number of subjects and accomplices involved, are often eclipsed. To this end, I consider torture to consist of severe pain and suffering, mental and physical, inflicted on captive bodies by state agents for any purpose and by any means, including through a coordinated environment; a process of domination; and the manipulation of time, space, gravity, the senses, or other psychic and biological needs. Captive persons include those who cannot safely walk away from streetside stops or questioning by security forces, or from other extracustodial violence.[19] In other words, whether state torture occurs in a raid, in a local jail, during a street corner confrontation, or in a secret offshore installation, and whether severe pain and suffering, physical or mental, is induced by hypothermia, a chokehold, rape, electroshock, sensory assault, isolation, forced standing, the enemas that the United States termed "rectal feeding," or none of these, a collaborative process is at work. A network of human actors identifies and targets a marginalized population, apprehends representative subjects, coordinates their environment and their pain, and justifies their misery, communicating terror broadly and translating that terror and justification into a particular distribution of economic, political, and social resources.

To understand this, we must consider torture as productive; it creates not only pain but also terror. Terror is a political strategy aimed at spreading fear and managing its effects.[20] Psychiatrist and survivor of torture Dr. Carlos Alberto Arestivo describes torture as a "structured process of destruction" with two simultaneous functions. First, all physical, psychological, and social factors "that hold the survivor to her existence in the world are systematically attacked." He refers to this as an attack on the subject's "social body," capturing the way torturers and subjects are embodied and understand themselves, their place in the world, and the suffering they inflict or experience through those social contexts, relationships, ideas, and practices that came before them.[21] Second, torture "aims to have a psychosocial effect through the commotion that it produces when a member of a determined social group is captured and tortured." He explains, "The logic of creating a climate of fear, through persecutions, detentions, torture, exile and even death itself is to seek the destruction of the entire social network that has given rise to trust and solidarity between people."[22] In the attack on its subjects as social bodies, torture is inseparable from the terror it projects beyond those subjects—capable, he says, of paralyzing societies. Like Arestivo, Kristian Williams remarks that the social product of torture is "not truth but terror. Its strategy is . . . political intimidation."[23]

Marnia Lazreg goes further and specifies the role of torture within the larger mosaic of state violence. She formulates an exact relationship between torture and terror in her study of French torture during the 1954–62 war in Algeria. Lazreg documents widespread use of several forms of torture under multiple commanders in multiple regions. When terror is the strategy, she argues, torture is essential, noting, "Terror needs torture to magnify its impact."[24] Although torture and terror feed on and substitute for each other, they are analytically distinct, because "without torture, terror would lose its capacity to sustain fear and silence in its victims." Torture is therefore essential as a "terror multiplier." In the Algerian war for independence, torture not only terrorized in its own right but also magnified four common, related acts of terror: disappearance, summary execution, reprisal, and rape. Torture seldom occurred without rape, she writes, and disappearances, executions, and reprisals seldom occurred without torture.[25]

Torture might be ubiquitous in practice, but it need only be exemplary to have the terror-multiplying effect that controls behavior broadly—that is, torture the few, control the many. Torture does not elicit immediate preventive information, but torture—even a credible threat of torture by agents of the state—is an engine of fear and complicity in peacetime or war. When the U.S. logic of organization embraces terror, torture is not an excess or an accidental by-product but rather a central feature.

Key Literatures and Theoretical Intervention

Historical patterns in the United States confirm that a logic of domination by terror can organize peacetime existence and civil institutions as well as military. The long history of racial capitalism in the United States has been anchored by terror, and terror anchored by torture. Torture has never been incidental to the enterprise of security, as security has come to be understood in the United States. Instead it has been a foundational, structural element of misogynist racial terror and race making, and it does productive social work.

This claim unsettles popular understandings of torture. Michel Foucault's influential *Discipline and Punish* had circulated widely by the late 1970s. He held that public torture in Europe had transformed across the eighteenth and nineteenth centuries in favor of prisons (and what he termed their "trace of torture"). Several historians of the 1970s and 1980s followed this premise and trajectory, detailing the career of torture in Greek, Roman, and European law as a creature of judicial proof that diminished in use over time.[26] Yet torture practice was clearly maintained and invigorated for a variety of uses in European colonial frontiers of the eighteenth and nineteenth centuries. As empires expanded and contracted, voices that condemned the "barbarity" of torture's violence also argued that scenes of suffering and torture played an instructive role in the development of the education and moral sentiment of the "civilized."[27] Humanitarian opposition to torture reinforced a false divide between civilization and torture, an opposition we cling to still.[28] In contrast, other scholars argue that torture has been at the foundation of Western notions of truth, democratic life, and judicial processes since classical Greece.[29] The United States is not alone in this respect, and Darius Rejali's influential *Torture and Democracy* traces the evolving methods and stark persistence of torture in the United States and other liberal democracies, France, Britain, and Israel. Torture does not undermine or unmake the civilized world; rather, it is a piece with that world and constitutes it.[30] This is not to say it is a necessary piece of that world; nor must we accept it.

Still, much work by historians of human rights, scholars of torture, and journalists still presumes that across the long history of torture, public attitudes in the West have moved decidedly against torture and that it has been progressively condemned and eliminated, as I note in chapter 3. This notion holds power because it contains a certain liberal-humanist, self-congratulatory common sense, one that presumes history is a process of rational enlightenment, human betterment, and social progress. Support for this perspective might be drawn from the proliferation of torture-monitoring organizations as well as global human rights campaigns and conventions emerging since 1972. The perspective is countered, however, by findings that torture remains prevalent globally and changes form to evade detection.[31] Even so, leaning on a narrative of progress, torture in the twenty-first-century U.S. war on terror was met as if it were anomalous, even new.

I take a different view. State torture in the United States is a colonial legacy with a corporate future. Torture persists because it has carved out productive social functions. Rather than a progressive prohibition against torture, the United States—like other democracies and world powers—has attempted to distribute torture in space, harnessing its social work while tucking it into alternative vocabularies (e.g., brutality, restraint, order) and relegating torture to certain neighborhoods, or to internal populations, select institutions, or prisons, or to certain client states or external theaters of operation.

That spatial and situational distribution of torture in the United States today has an undeniably racial character. Torture is written deeply into legal and racial codes, and U.S. history provides clear examples of torture as a tool of racialization, spatial confinement, and expansion of state power via "civilizing" and "democratizing" efforts at home and abroad.[32] It is therefore useful to see U.S. torture as a tangled root system feeding at least three crisscrossing veins of historical violence: first, in colonizing expropriation of land and labor through massacre, removals, enslavement, lynching terror, purges, and internments; second, in raids, public order policing contexts, border regimes, detention, and prisons; and third, in U.S. imperial wars, cold war client states, and counterinsurgencies. These lines are mutually supportive and continue to engender and feed twenty-first-century violence.

Historically, these interdependent branches of state torture practice were in fact all tied to robust social, economic, and political functions. Torture served as the fulcrum and terror the lever of a colonial economy in the Americas. The emerging settler economy of the north, south, and west rested on theft of Indigenous land and internment and sale of Native Americans, just as profits depended on African capture and the ongoing exploitation of African American labor and reproductive power over generations.[33]

Details here are useful. European settlers—recruited by joint stock companies with the backing of government armies—installed themselves in foreign areas with the intent to wrest land from its occupants. In North America, the ostentatious violence with which settlers made good on that intent—banding together as rangers and routinely targeting and killing Indigenous men, women, and children; destroying towns, fields, and food stores—shocked the Native American allies who sometimes fought by their side.[34] The for-profit collaboration of private anti-Indian rangers and colonial governments in such total war forged what military historian John Grenier has called America's "first military tradition and thereby part of a shared American identity."[35] It also spurred a trade in Indigenous slaves and support for expansion, expropriation, and control of Native populations via Catholic missions and Protestant "praying towns." All of these methods of conquest involved excruciating modes of capture, assault, and military or religious discipline and confinement. The infliction of severe pain and suffering in the process of capture and confinement of Indigenous populations marks the institutionalization of the reservation system as well as American Indian boarding schools.[36] Likewise, all manner of torture and sexual terror integral to the maintenance of the slave economy has been well documented by the survivors and by historians since. The motivational force of such depictions figured largely in the campaign to abolish that system.[37]

Torture is pervasive in historical accounts of settlement and development of the nation. From those accounts, we can draw four important themes relevant to the current study. First, I emphasize U.S. torture's deeply colonial frame and functions because torture has been a consistent, but never the only, element of that campaign of colonization, and the descendants of original inhabitants are still in a contest for their land, rights, sacred artifacts, culture, and resources.[38] Second, across this history, powerful local institutions of government and commerce collaborated in the violence producing domestic, peacetime terror. Third, these endeavors also enlisted and deputized the violence of private actors who sought access to economic and political resources and social benefits through this work, such as land, money, prestige, influence, or other property. Fourth, for much of this history, state violence, including torture, served an undisguised supremacist social function, to appropriate resources for settlers and to build, defend, and maintain a racial, economic, and geopolitical order through elimination or subordination of a part of the population.

Thinking historically, it is not necessary to point to an example of torture in every campaign of terror in order to identify and acknowledge the everyday role torture played in establishing and maintaining the racial economic order. It is important to see the devastating multigenerational impact of the enterprise on the one hand, and on the other to see the very personal and professional benefits for those involved at the local level at every step. These purported benefits are both gratuitous and instrumental.[39] Patrick Wolfe's description of "race in action" suits torture and its local, "visceral force" well: "fear, hatred, rapine, violence, callousness, cruelty are the essence of race or we overlook the point."[40]

Modern institutions, like those noted above in the torture examples from September 2001—the FBI, or the systems of corrections in Chicago or Plankinton, S.D.—emerged from that early template for public–private collaboration in terror that on the one hand secured personal reward, and on the other ensured racial-economic and patriarchal dominance. U.S. policing emerged from early white slave patrols in the South, and in the North from the pressure exerted by commerce to contain immigrant and working-class "disorder," to institute wage labor, and to punish "vagrancy."[41] Like the anti-Indian rangers and slave patrollers, domestic police and private accomplices were allowed significant license for violence against these targets for subordination. After emancipation, white communities were backed by business and government when they enforced their own place in the racial-economic order through lynching tortures or expulsion of entire African American populations. Following a pattern of public participation laid down by the earliest settlers' anti-Indian removals, new generations engineered terror, torture, and massacre to accomplish anti-Chinese, anti-Japanese, anti-Black, and other ethnic and racial purges, plundering land and businesses with the explicit or tacit support of the state.[42]

With the exception of those writing histories specific to U.S. torture, most authors leave torture unnamed among the standard mechanisms at work in such terror or in the violence of confrontation, capture, and confinement. It demonstrates that the meaning and presence of torture in this story, while increasingly documented, has not been sufficiently theorized. For instance, a substantial literature exists on the history of the police and policing as embodiments of state violence citing political theorists like Mark Neocleous. Often Neocleous is clear about the enormous range of police discretion without identifying torture per se, noting that "the police have the power to take control of the body and the property of the suspect to the utmost degree."[43] Following this lead, the body of scholarship on police power rarely names or articulates the requisite place maintained for torture in the police and corrections tool kit. Torture is there most often by implication only, left to lurk under the rubric of discretion or the mandate of discipline.

Like the work on police power, key works on counterinsurgency theory or practice (e.g., Khalili, Owens) are often elliptical on the place of torture, at best indicating a correlation of torture and this global mode of detention, war, and governance.[44] In the same vein, two important ethnographic and historical works (Siegel, Schrader) study the U.S. international police training efforts conducted through the Office of Public Safety (OPS) from 1962 to 1974. They emphasize the interdevelopment and reciprocity among U.S. military, paramilitary, and policing methodologies. Congressional commissions, think tanks, and personnel coordinated methods and funding, ensuring that counterinsurgency was not only a global security preoccupation but also a U.S. domestic undertaking.[45] However, although torture practice cultivated through OPS has been the subject of other work (e.g., McCoy, Langguth), discussion of torture is less prominent in Schrader's excellent history, and it is something handled delicately through the perspectives of OPS personnel themselves in Seigel's work.[46] Rather than a flaw in their research, these choices in part reflect an accurate understanding that discussions of torture are inflammatory and can easily derail a thesis bent on discussing something more. Yet it leaves readers with a vision of torture as something excess or extra, not basic to the enterprise. Herein lies the importance of Marnia Lazreg's effort. Her *Torture and the Twilight of Empire* is unique in the care taken to distinguish torture first among an array of methods of terror, and second in its particular role as a terror multiplier.

Important writing on U.S. policing, corrections, state violence, and race has not focused on torture, investing the weight of argument instead in articulating the transition from U.S. slavery to urban ghettoization and then to mass incarceration as sequential cornerstones of the U.S. racial state (Wacquant, Alexander, Gilmore), or calling for the abolition of police or prisons (Davis, Gilmore, Kaba).[47] Within African American studies, there is an important debate that holds explicit accounts of violence and pain can reinforce a racialized "pornography of violence." That sensationalized display of Black suffering can rob African Americans of agency and dignity even as it can exacerbate white indifference.[48] Laurence Ralph enters that conversation from an important angle.[49] In *The Torture Letters,* Ralph subjects decades of systemic torture by a team of officers within the Chicago police and Cook County to an anthropological analysis. He concludes that the use-of-force continuum that guides police training and judgment ensures that police mistreatment and harassment grow inevitably into racial suppression, torture, and death.[50] Torture and the use-of-force continuum reinforce a racial caste system and disproportionately injure and kill those in the bottom caste.[51] Officers who closed case after case through torture were rewarded, and standard work routines allowed torturers in particular to excel and rise in law enforcement.[52]

Ralph is explicit about torture in order to articulate its particular role in the mosaic of state violence, as well as its organizational persistence and function. Like Ralph, prison and police abolitionist Mariame Kaba illustrates the strategic power of naming and explicit speech, saying, "Stop pretending you don't know about the violence of policing and the violence of prisons. You know that basically when we send people to prison, we're sentencing them to judicial rape. You're aware of that enough at 12 years old to make jokes about people getting locked up and getting raped."[53]

Naming torture becomes all the more important in light of the thesis advanced here: that the national security enterprise and imagination distort our conversations on torture in specific ways. Within that imaginary, torture is posed uniquely as an excess or tool linked to interrogation, warfare, and international policy. Torture at work domestically is customarily euphemized as something else—brutality, excessive use of force, abuse. Or it may not register as a domestic issue at all. Border and citizenship regimes permit vast agent discretion and must be understood through the lens of torture practice.[54] Detention is a standard step in the U.S. immigration process, with on average of 200,000 people in immigration detention each year all over the United States. Immigrants bring close to 30,000 torture claims under the U.N. CAT convention to immigration court annually.[55]

There is a deeper issue than the failure to name torture, however. The absence of a clear discussion of torture as an underpinning of policing, confinement, and counterinsurgency as well as of our larger sense of security suggests that we have yet to adequately account for torture as a productive means. We need to track the role it has played practically and imaginatively in different manifestations of racial and social control. In addition, the relation of torture to other pillars of the racial caste system—racial terror, mass supervision, confinement—demands that those of us working on torture position ourselves relative to the growing movement to end policing and prisons.[56] For instance, Jared Sexton and Elizabeth Lee faulted the responses to the U.S. torture of prisoners at Abu Ghraib prison in Iraq that fixed blame on one corrupt administration or chain of command. Echoing Ruth Gilmore, they noted that the entire range of capture, captivity, immobilization, and confinement are fundamental state functions we deem legitimate; historically and today, they remain primary (and bipartisan) features of Black containment and social control. To contest torture abroad—but not the roundups and confinement in the United States at their most basic level—is to naturalize the preconditions of torture. "Once the body has been seized in these ways, the necessary conditions for any subsequent brutality have already been met."[57]

Legal scholar Dorothy Roberts also makes this connection between "the long history of racialization by torture" and the prison and policing abolition movement.[58] Moreover, she is careful to extend the number of sites at issue: "Torture has been an accepted technique of racialized carceral control. The nation's public schools, prisons, detention centers and hospitals serving poor people of color are marked not only by stark inequalities but also by dehumanizing bodily neglect and abuse."[59] She adds: "The female incarceration rate has grown twice as quickly as the male incarceration rate over the past few decades, and black women are twice as likely as white women to be behind bars."[60] The violation and confinement of "wayward" or "criminal" Black and brown, queer, nonbinary, and transgender persons as well as sex workers have served for decades to communicate the racial-patriarchal order to be secured.[61] The fact that prisons and torture also affect white persons does not change the racist design or function, because "prison is and always will be a tool to preserve capitalist inequalities, which are most acutely felt through racism (what a number of people call racial capitalism)."[62]

Absent a strong alliance with the prison abolition enterprise, work on torture prevention, like that on prison reform—both urgently necessary—can become a mode of analytical retreat. We do not eliminate torture in order to perfect a system of apprehension, captivity, and confinement or the racist imperative it serves. As Angela Y. Davis notes, "As important as some reforms may be . . . frameworks that rely exclusively on reforms help to produce the stultifying idea that nothing lies beyond the prison. Debates about strategies of decarceration, which should be the focal point . . . tend to be marginalized when reform takes center stage."[63]

In sum, work against torture cannot set it apart or elevate torture as especially egregious in order to distinguish itself from the abolitionist struggle. Nor can antitorture work focus on sweeping political or economic logics alone. While an accounting of torture and terror in securing racial capitalism is essential, acknowledging that fact only prepares us to look at the specific functions of torture in specific cases. Danielle Celermajer suggests that to see everyday "torture inflicted in countless locations around the country" as an explicit state program "is to misunderstand the phenomenon."[64] For one, as she notes, political logics are not realized at the apex of the state but rather are embedded in material arrangements and organizational values. The people embedded in those arrangements are subject to a thicket of systems and dynamics that is local, cultural, and interpersonal.

To review, then, the book identifies the reach of torture within the national security imagination in order to counter it with three related claims. First, torture has never been incidental to the enterprise of security, as security has come to be understood in the United States; instead, it has been a foundational, structural element of misogynist racial terror and race making. Second, torture thrives because it does productive social work for local persons, communities, and organizations. Third, although that work is neither necessary nor acceptable, creating routines and social arrangements that supplant and cease performing that work will depend on our ability to grapple with torture's functional relationship to a society reliant on human capture and containment. We need to know the specific role played by torture in specific settings. Confronting torture demands more than our acknowledging that torture is "rooted in everyday practices and taken for granted ways of making sense of the world."[65] It also requires a new set of questions about its productive functions.

The next section outlines productive functions and some necessary questions. It is followed by a section that describes national security as a taken-for-granted way of making sense of our world—a social imaginary.

Social Functions of Torture

Even though it is empirically, demonstrably evident that torture shatters lives and communities, jeopardizes security, and corrupts civic institutions, one question recurs. Does it work? This has been answered amply in the past, repeatedly in the present, and always resoundingly in the categoric negative.[66] Torture does not supply intelligence. Yet torture works effectively to achieve many things, and to understand this, we need to move beyond the claims of torturers. Torture practice thrives, as explicit policy or not, because it has carved out social functions and benefits that operate locally and at large. It is time to stop asking "Does it work?" and to ask instead, "What work does it do"?[67]

I emphasize that this argument foregrounds the productive social work of torture to disrupt the familiar perception that torture arises as an excess tied to interrogation and is somehow a feature of security. To make its social work visible, the book formulates the social elements and functions in the following way.[68]

1. **State torture is a process, not an incident.** It is one form through which humans ritualize dominance, causing severe psychological and physical pain and suffering through deliberate ongoing manipulation of the captives' environment more often than through any single application or apparent technique of violence. That is, in addition to or alongside any dramatically detectable application of physical violence, humans accomplish torture through physical settings, routines, and conditions that turn the tools of space, gravity, time, and the senses against other

human bodies. These manipulations alone can be debilitating, even fatal. They work in concert as a process, and although they are not often considered techniques of physical torture, they are.

2. **State torture is team based, collaborative, and plural.** Human teams collaborate to torture and through it to terrorize groups, debase groups, and dominate groups (all plural). The physical settings, routines, and conditions that are a piece with the captives' suffering are collaboratively designed and maintained. Within the groups most directly privy to the collaborative process of violence—among them its subjects, perpetrators, and observers—the ritual uses and group energy of torture generates, severs, reinforces, or remakes interpersonal bonds, distinctions, competitions, and hierarchies, thereby serving immediate communal and social agendas as well as institutional functions.[69] These plural, group elements deserve emphasis because they are particularly prone to obfuscation or misunderstanding. Torture is often rendered in thought problems as well as in seemingly evidentiary accounts as a matter affecting only a specific individual, as addressed in chapter 3. While on occasion a state agent may torture a subject in seeming isolation, there are always more subjects, and the social and organizational context in which that behavior was incentivized, conducted, and typically kept quiet was one populated with silent accomplices, reluctant witnesses, and blinkered proceduralists pressured to sweep conduct deemed exceptional under a carpet of necessity or routine. Moreover, the work of torture would be impossible to sustain or deny without a variety of transnational, technical networks for transportation and supply, or the practical, professional interagency networks and the host of interpersonal ties and obligations they represent, including the teams of lawyers, medical experts, spectators, and apologists necessary to state torture.

3. **State torture is local.** For the humans who design and use it, torture is local in meaning and function. It is a practice that survives by improvisation and local innovation, feeds on group-based apprenticeship and competition, and is taught through anecdotes and observation.[70] Torture enacts subjugation and

cultivates allegiance. To do so, it exploits local idioms, materials, spaces, and cultural meanings for its particular power to debase. In Arestivo's terms, torturers tailor their destruction to social bodies, attempting to scramble or disintegrate their subjects' hold on local markers of personhood, autonomy, collectivity, status, gender, sexuality, race, rank, and so on. Sexual violence and racist-misogynist terror are omnipresent and are engines of this work that upend learned understandings of status, dignity, and belonging in macabre ways.

The reverse is also true. Even as severe pain and suffering marks and marginalizes certain bodies and destroys social ties, it forges or assigns new communal identities for perpetrators, their witnesses, bureaucrats, and other accomplices. It does so in specific ways that serve local community agendas, such as improved organizational reputation for efficiency, community well-being, projections of authority, or status. Communal identities are often accompanied by what are perceived as personal or professional rewards or benefits, such as confirmation of racial or hypermasculine position or dominance (or alignment with that dominance). Torture enacts religious, linguistic, or cultural superiority. Benefits can also be realized materially; professional promotions or recognitions may be issued, for example. For this reason, terror can permeate daily institutional environments that otherwise seem functional and to some professionally acceptable, even optimal, depending on to whom the perceived benefits and the harms accrue.

Because identities are built and subjugation ritualized through the suffering of representative subjects, in this book, I refer to torture as a community-building, identity-forging work that marks out subordinations in arenas like citizenship, gender, sexuality, race, religion, and language.

4. **State torture works beyond the local.** By targeting, debasing, and discrediting representative subjects, those who torture simultaneously terrorize and cast suspicion on larger populations while legitimizing their own power. Torture is therefore extraordinarily effective in targeting many communities at once, and targeting them differently. It effectively projects safety, power, authority, intimidation, and subordination simultaneously, and

it assigns identities intended to organize societies at large. Such distinctions may be political, racial, religious, linguistic, economic, ethnic, sexual, gendered, or more.

In considering the social work of torture, one must consider all of this—the process, the plurals, the local uses, the community building and destroying, and beyond. If torture is one among many forms of violence, then why this form, in this instance? What does the practice enable or accomplish (professionally, interpersonally, erotically, emotionally) for a team of perpetrators and witnesses over the short and long term? How do the modes of verbal abuse and suffering injure, discredit, silence, disempower, and kill the subjects over the short and long term? More broadly, what does torture communicate, and to whom? How does it bind, divide, and serve the communities that sponsor the practice? How does it serve those who imaginatively debate it? How does it terrorize, divide, silence, and alter the behavior and status of those who fear they may be targeted as a result?

No pretense to interrogation or forced confession is necessary to these social functions. Yet when historically, demonstrably, the human, social work of state torture has forced compliance or false confessions, those confessions dutifully contribute to this work. They then undermine or further support social distinctions, allegiances, divisions, hierarchies, or identities. State torture, as both latent threat and action, plays a role in legitimizing state power, targeting would-be threats, and generating terror to construct or attempt to maintain a social order, to allot services and political and economic resources, and to control spaces in which people live and through which they move.

National Security Imagination

This view of torture as a social instrument contrasts with the presumptions and preoccupations circulated about torture in the episodes described in this book. Nevertheless, those preoccupations concerning torture make up one, but not the only, consequential pillar of a national security imagination that coalesced in the mid-twentieth century along with the national security state. This section offers historical, theoretical, and practical grounding to understand this.

First, let's put a powerful contemporary imagining of torture against one from the past. In 2002, Office of Legal Counsel attorney John Yoo notoriously crafted a narrow definition of torture, thereby expanding the range of pain and suffering that could purportedly be legally inflicted on detainees. But Yoo's claim was more dramatic. He restated it frankly in an interview: "Congress doesn't have the power to tie the President's hands in regard to torture as an interrogation technique. . . . It's the core of the Commander-in-Chief function. They can't prevent the President from ordering torture."[71] As the legal memo has it, "Any effort to apply Section 2340A [prohibiting torture] in a manner that interferes with the President's direction of core war matters as the detention and interrogation of enemy combatants thus would be unconstitutional."[72]

By positing torture at the "core," in a world with permanent security concerns, Yoo situates torture as a prerequisite to executive power; it is both a foundation and a necessary fulcrum. Neither the pinnacle of power nor the power of last resort, torture creates the leverage necessary for all manner of other powers to rise and expand. War cannot be fought without torture at the president's command. French commander Roger Trinquier's influential 1960s handbook on counterinsurgency and torture, *Modern Warfare,* could not have been plainer. Nearly forty years before Yoo took the spotlight, Trinquier's thinking found many enthusiasts among the U.S. military, national security staff, and others with their eyes on Vietnam, as I discuss in chapter 2.[73] Yoo's peculiar presentation of torture as a creature of security, for good or for ill, and the contemporary ideas bound up with that vision are widespread. How can this be?

The conceptual and logistical blueprint of what the United States has come to understand as national security was engineered under President Truman in 1947, in the wake of the mammoth 1946 congressional report on the 1941 Pearl Harbor air attack. As Douglas Stewart writes, the possibility of "sneak attack" transformed the U.S. view of time, space, and vulnerability and made "security" the top goal of policy.[74] It displaced a broader sense of national interest—say, in a dynamic competitive economy; in a well-educated populace; in diplomatic influence and collaboration; in global public health; or through information and misinformation. Instead, the notion of national security centered on some key understandings: the U.S. military must maintain permanent readiness and preeminent strength; economic and scientific resources should coordinate to that end; the citizenry must remain alert and committed to God and country; and a capacious surveillance-intelligence net—both inside and outside of U.S. borders— was required to ensure each of these capacities and commitments.[75] As a result, the 1950s and 1960s saw the rise of "a network of several hundred high-level military, intelligence, diplomatic and law enforcement officials within the executive branch who are responsible for national security policymaking."[76]

That commercial and bureaucratic enterprise continues to expand. Only ten years after September 11, a *Washington Post* "landmark study," Top Secret America, "identified 46 federal departments and agencies engaged in classified national security work. Their missions range from intelligence gathering and analysis to war-fighting, cyberoperations, and weapons development. Almost 2000 private companies support this work, which occurs at over 10,000 locations across the US and many outposts outside. The sizes of their [classified] budgets and workforces . . . are enormous—a total annual outlay of around $1 trillion and millions of employees."[77]

We have come to refer to this vast hive of professional, institutional, legal, political, and commercial arrangements as the national security state. It is not hard to see those arrangements both generate and rely on a certain state of mind, one in which the acquisition of agency turf and resources has become an important end in itself.[78] As Douglas Cassell notes, when it comes to U.S. national security, "internalized values and priorities become a force on their own."[79] The term "groupthink" is often ascribed to a kind of insularity that leads decision-making astray in tight-knit teams or administrations. However, in time, national security thinking, as some call it—that set of internalized and often unspoken values—sprawled just like the bureaucracy, even outstripping it. The extent of its public reach, power, and longevity as a social imaginary requires a better explanation and theoretical footing.

Social Imaginaries

Philosopher Cornelius Castoriadis uses "social imaginary" to describe the realm of human ideas, values, perceptions, and principles that support and interpret human action. These spheres, the imaginary and the material, are mutually constituting and responsive. Far from ephemeral, inconsequential, or pretend, such shared ideas and perceptions influence material arrangements, just as those material arrangements feed perceptions and ideas. Social theorist Charles Taylor elaborates on the social imaginary as the often unarticulated yet nonetheless "common understanding that makes possible common practices." It is that stratum of understanding, conveyed in images, metaphors, stories, maxims, and the fabric of associations, that constitutes our accepted ways of making sense of the world and interacting with others daily. Like a software operating system, a social imaginary runs continuously in the background, explaining why it makes sense to do something this way and not that, and what data are worth tracking and what are not. It is the medium or platform through which work is conducted, an often tacit schema without which certain social behaviors, undertakings, and rituals would seem arbitrary.[80]

Social imaginaries are not universal or fixed, of course; they are culturally and historically specific constellations of ideas and images in which some concepts and beliefs, at a transitional moment, were leveraged into dominant modes of thinking and being. In the welter of such a transitional moment, alternative concepts and understandings—of, say, national well-being or global integration—are either rejected or simply neglected.[81] In other words, at that transitional moment, there were, and therefore still are, other available ways to organize our thinking.

The late 1940s and 1950s were one such moment in the United States. Amid the maneuvering and ferment around decolonization struggles, new international bodies and geopolitical realignments, nuclear armament, economic restructuring, and so on, a collection of reconfigured ideas and relationships congealed around the notion of security. On the one hand, these ideas reframed U.S. warfare. On the other hand, they resulted in extreme social regulation of civilians via order and disorder, or crime.

These newer configurations adapted older colonial, racial, and gendered features of U.S. state power and surveillance in the face of ongoing resistance to that racial formation. Integral to these changes was a reorganization of racial logics intent on preserving the interlocking gendered–racial hierarchies while minimizing the visual impact of white supremacy conveyed via mass media and resetting its rhetorical justifications.[82] Governmental structures, economic logics, and public practice were reorganized in ways we now see as characteristic of the cold war era and beyond—for example, the rapid expansion of overt and covert executive functions or innovations in global communications and surveillance technology, tested in attempts to control or eliminate nonwhite or insufficiently white or "wayward" populations at home.[83]

By identifying a national security imaginary, we can see how markedly different functional operations are linked—operations like, say, law-and-order policing, military operations, and border control. These systems and bureaucracies are distinct; they are subject to different bureaucratic structures, legal regimes, trends in technology, funding, and management. However, they are "culturally connected and embedded," framed by a shared understanding of what defines the millions presumed bound together as one nation, what or who merits securing, what or who constitutes a threat, and why it makes sense to use force instead of other means to achieve certain goals.[84]

As a conceptual lens, a social imaginary reminds us that the answers to these questions manifest in popular preferences and dispositions that reach well beyond security decision-makers. Among the shared and characteristic orientations of that security imagination are the following:

- A tendency to amplify a continuing sense of public threat, crisis, and emergency, which in turn affirms and nurtures current security spending arrangements.[85]
- A strongly racialized and gendered lens used to identify a supposed threat and to escalate the security postures deemed appropriate to meet it.[86]
- A receptive stance toward assistance from private actors when they affirm a racialized, gendered narrative of threat (e.g., private corporations, citizen militias, or vigilantism).[87]
- A strategic preference for force, spatial and carceral modes of containment, and the latest technological solutions.[88]
- A strong obligation to protect capitalist growth, ensuring the expansion, not simply the stability, of infrastructure, markets, and private accumulation.
- An appetite for surveillance and data collection and storage that outstrips the capacity for data analysis.[89]
- Significant investments in the physical, social, and behavioral sciences, as well as the humanities and the arts, as military and paramilitary instruments.[90]

These and other orientations constitute a shared cultural and conceptual field animated by public participation, not official pronouncement. These interests and dispositions circulate in media analyses, political theater, activist campaigns, fictional drama, institutional storytelling, and the symbolic language of patriotism and success. Agents of the security apparatus and members of the public alike consume and contribute to that cultural production. It shapes their self-concept and relationships. Both classified documents and public policy are inspired by it.[91]

As a conceptual tool, social imaginaries therefore call attention to culture as interactive, innovative, and reiterative, making it an important field for intervention. Observing differing U.K. and U.S. responses to terrorism, Cassell points to the impact of certain British cultural tendencies and distinct U.S. sensitivities: "Culture joined law and geopolitics to condition the respective responses" that were shaped and reinforced by "differing legal institutions and contrasting geopolitical positions." These ideas and tenets, "invoked over time, endlessly remarked upon and repeated by multiple voices, legislatures, courts, media and the academy—and confirmed by government practice . . . became self-perpetuating factor[s] in [their] own right."[92]

The chapters that follow engage exactly this range of public voices as they came together to discuss torture in the 2000s and 2010s. The understanding of torture they manifest, its function, its practice, the anodyne thought problems we still summon to discuss it, the metaphors, the iconic images, even the clichés—all these came easily to hand at the time because they are embedded in a larger national security constellation of ideas and beliefs. These understandings of torture will doubtless recirculate long into the future unless disrupted and replaced. Individuals and groups may challenge or alter these understandings, of course, but as Celermajer points out, a shift in imaginary requires an alteration in understandings that is shared.[93]

Yoo's vision of torture provides a good example here. One can reject Yoo's formulation and maintain that executive torture can only ever undermine the nation's safety, and many have. Many have also taken aim at the ticking time bomb hypothetical as a fiction beloved by philosophy professors and security advocates. However, to stop there is still to imagine state torture as if it were a security option or excess, good or bad, consisting of an act, incident, or technique used to extract valuable information from individuals—something that, by its nature, can be stopped once identified and criminalized in law.[94] To step free of the security imagination, we must grapple with how often torture is discussed in this containable and stylized way. In contrast, as in the case of device manufacturing and Commerce Department controls, we could discuss torture as a form of interorganizational exchange and commerce among perpetrators, functionaries, and profiteers. Or, as in the case of the Chicago police department and the Cook

County state attorney's office, one could imagine torture as a management strategy enlisting terror to accomplish organizational goals and access personal benefits. Or, as in the case of juvenile justice facilities in South Dakota and the American Indian boarding schools that preceded them, we could present torture as an intensely social, collaborative process that recruits teams and targets groups in order to enact caste—racial, gendered, economic, and political domination—locally and broadly. This takes us far from torture as a tool of security; it forces us to see it as a mode of social organization.

Outline

Chapter 1, "Anecdote," makes detailed reconsideration of the story of Abdul Hakim Murad, a Pakistani terrorist subjected to torture in 1995 by the Philippine National Police at the behest of the FBI. Murad's story became the favorite post-9/11 anecdote summoned to demonstrate that torture works. Like other torture anecdotes, it stands as a crafted delivery mechanism for the ubiquitous national security rationale: the claim that torture was a last-resort attempt to acquire lifesaving, preventive information. Yet the facts of Murad's ordeal demonstrate otherwise. They also serve in a practical way to distinguish four dimensions of torture: organizational setting, torture practice (e.g., details of coordinated violence and suffering), verbal rationales surrounding it, and social functions at work. These dimensions are necessary to analysis that steps out from under the shadow of the national security imagination.

Chapter 2, "Rationale," pursues the national security rationale as an old construction and begins with colonial modes of violence and control used by the United States in the Philippines during the war from 1898 to 1902 and under U.S. occupation. The chapter follows that trajectory to the 1950 U.S. interventions in the Philippines as counterinsurgency reinvented the discourse on torture. Three masters of the anecdote at midcentury illustrate the evolution of the rationale and the vision behind it: Roger Trinquier, Jean Lartéguy, and Edward Lansdale. That evolution was joined to a structural expansion of violence networks and markets and the collaboration—governmental, private, and academic—in support of security by terror and torture.

Chapter 3, "Archetype," points to an iconic image of torture that emerged from the mid-twentieth-century military and intelligence revisionists. In this iconic image, torture is an intimate and existential battle of wills, a one-on-one interrogation either bent on destroying the one or on saving the other and the world he holds dear. The archetype shapes the early 2001–5 news writing, legal writing by prominent patrons and critics of torture, and antitorture polemics, including Amnesty International's early campaigns, Elaine Scarry's treatise on torture from the 1980s, and contemporary scholars who critique her work. The cases of survivors Ehab Elmaghraby and Javaid Iqbal highlight how legal and moral accountability recedes when torture does not fit the archetypal mold.

Chapters 4 and 5 contend with twin obsessions at the heart of the Archetype. Chapter 4, "Technique," considers the fascination with the waterboard that built to public outcry and a media frenzy in 2007, complete with a host of activist performances and reenactment videos that saturated political conversation and popular entertainment. Scrutiny of that technique and others—as they appear in investigative news, secret memo, activism, and dramatic film—reveals a common story of the citizen's relation to state power. The chapter contrasts attention to the waterboard against that devoted to survivors and forms of torture accelerating over the same period: extraordinary rendition and the collaborative manipulation of detention environments. Both require extensive legal, logistical, and economic arrangements: networks.

Chapter 5, "Perpetrators," examines the unique allure or awe with which the public regards the Perpetrator. It discusses the media coverage of Tony Lagouranis and his torture confession and memoir, *Fear Up Harsh*, as well as the testimony of Sabrina Harman in the Errol Morris documentary on Abu Ghraib. Survivor Ali Naser filed a criminal complaint against Lagouranis for subjecting him to stress positions, strobe, audio, and dogs in a Mosul shipping container. The chapter provides theoretical and comparative context from South Africa, Brazil, Chile, and Argentina, where survivors and journalists disrupt media formats to redress the undeniable difference in quality and kind of attention granted perpetrators.

Chapter 6, "Networks," returns us to the logistics, professional relationships, agencies, and systems that incentivize and sustain the process of violence. An effort that U.S. administration officials dubbed the Salvador Option was implemented in Iraq, where Department of Defense officials, contractors, and administrative personnel knowingly assisted and protected torture and death-squad activity by Iraqis. The collaborative, compartmentalized networks that linked U.S. money and personnel to those death squads received near-total disregard, even when those death squads broadcast tortured confessions as entertainment on Iraqi TV. The U.N. special rapporteur on torture called in 2013 for an inquiry into U.S. responsibility. Such torture networks are, as this one was, highly legible once we step away from the security imaginary and turn attention to them.

The Epilogue takes up the ways attention to torture networks and the national security imagination must alter understandings of public complicity. The example of organized survivors confronting the impact of torturer-psychologists and their collaborators in the American Psychological Association suggests strategies for interrupting our material and imaginative support for torture.

1

Anecdote

Abdul Hakim Murad and Torture in Four Dimensions

> The preponderance of reports seems to weigh against its effectiveness.
>
> —On anecdotes of torture, Intelligence Science Board 2006 report

> At least 98 detainees have died while in U.S. custody in Iraq or Afghanistan. At least 45 detainees died in U.S. custody due to suspected or confirmed criminal homicides. At least eight people were tortured to death. At least 69 of the detainees died at locations other than Abu Ghraib. At least 51 have died [in the two years] since . . . the abuses at Abu Ghraib [first documented in January 14, 2004].
>
> —*Command's Responsibility*, Human Rights First 2006 report

The Tale of Abdul Hakim Murad

In 1996, the Southern Federal District Court of New York would hear the case of Abdul Hakim Murad. Murad had been building bombs in Manila with two accomplices.[1] When caught by the Philippine National Police (PNP) in January 1995, he was held for three months while the PNP conducted "tactical interrogation." They released him to the FBI in April. Murad and his defense claimed the confession had been obtained through prolonged and systematic torture during that time. The allegations of torture were carried in the international news surrounding his trial. Exactly what the tactical interrogation had included became Judge Kevin Thomas Duffy's problem to resolve.

In the motion to suppress, the defendant presented his account of what I will call torture practice. Although Murad's defense concentrated only on a list of methods that comprise his treatment, the term "torture practice" in this book will refer to the entire ensemble of conditions, actions, and privations that are established collaboratively to cause subjects severe pain and suffering while in custody. Torture in practice is always more than a list of methods or contacts with captive bodies. Because torture attacks human bodies—their rhythms and senses; their mooring in social values and networks that give their lives meaning—the actual torture practice or conduct of violence includes not only the network and team of perpetrators and observers but also the settings, temperature, timing, phase and duration of custody, and violence, as well as actions and privations.[2]

Judge Duffy confronted details. The defense said Murad had been held blindfolded and subjected to rape and threats of rape as well as dragging of his body back and forth across his cell; cigarette burns on his genitals, hands, and feet; electroshock, drowning, force-feeding with liquid, beatings that broke bones, and the "denial of proper sustenance." On the basis of an investigation they published in 2000, two Filipina journalists added to this list the application of ice to his body.[3] The judge heard testimony from two psychologists who examined Murad, and he listened to audiotape of the first interrogation by the PNP, which the defense said held the sounds of Murad undergoing a "drowning procedure." One psychologist concluded Murad had been tortured; the second found possible indications but could not conclude with certainty.

Judge Duffy made a finding of "no torture" and noted his belief that the first expert, a woman, had been fooled by Murad. The judge allowed that the sounds on the tape were "suspicious," but they could not serve as sufficient proof. He further stated that physical positions Murad described in his motion to suppress were impossible, and for this and other reasons, the defendant's statement itself was incoherent and "not credible." For example, wrote the judge, Murad's hands could not have been shackled behind him while men pinned him on his back and held down his arms; nor would torture and care for his wounds have proceeded simultaneously, as Murad claimed. (In these assertions, the judge divulged a limited understanding of torture practice.) Finally, Judge Duffy held that even if Murad's confession had been assembled over three months' time under uncertain or brutal conditions, the confession was repeated "freely" to an FBI agent as they left the Philippines during the five-hour transfer flight to the United States. With this reasoning, Judge Duffy held Murad's confession admissible.

The court was wrong, and both the FBI and the PNP knew it. In an informal U.S.–Philippine arrangement, Murad had been held for months and tortured in the Philippines in order to make a case for U.S. courts. Tapes of the PNP's tactical interrogations had been transmitted to the FBI during Murad's time in Manila. On cross-examination, FBI agent Frank Pellegrino said he had visited with the PNP "frequently" during Murad's ordeal.[4] It was Pellegrino who took the confession "freely" offered by Murad in flight. In both the FBI partnership and the judge's finding, torture was met with accommodation by the U.S. civil institutions.

Five years later, in the immediate aftermath of the September 11, 2001, attacks, gruesome aspects of Murad's torture were accepted as fact and repeated; a score of journalists in the U.S. press discovered in him the very embodiment of the ticking time bomb terrorist. In ways nearly incredible, Murad's ordeal was remade as a highly versatile torture anecdote and circulated widely in the United States to support torture after 2001. It fed a speculative debate concerning torture, which I set in context in the prologue.

While the 2001 press devoted to Murad made no mention of his trial or the court's original finding of "no torture," it did affirm Murad's torture even as it attached grossly inaccurate conclusions to selective aspects of his ordeal, added variations, and further obscured the reasons his case was historically significant.[5] Seen in context, Murad's efforts, plots, and contacts in the mid-1990s were in fact forging financial, familial, and geographical networks that shaped the logistical routines of a nascent al-Qaeda. Murad's experience and the FBI–Philippine relationship of 1995 also foreshadowed one Bush-era response to al-Qaeda, a program called extraordinary rendition that would capture suspects and fly them to a network of torture allies. The 1995 FBI–PNP partnership should also point us back to a century-long history of U.S.–Philippine collaboration during which torture became integral to security, policing, counterinsurgency, and intelligence in the Philippines—terms not to be taken at face value and histories to be taken up in chapter 2.

The Anecdote, however, is both a staple of torture discourse in the national security imagination and a pillar of torture practice. Refashioned as a torture anecdote, the 2001 press version of Murad sidestepped and even clouded historical curiosity. Instead, extraordinarily simplified and revised, stripped of any U.S. involvement, sustaining a series of conflicting details but with all the trappings of a good story, the quick mention of Murad's case in 2001 and 2002 became the most prevalent example on offer of how, its proponents claimed, torture works efficiently to produce necessary, lifesaving, terror-preventing information from terrorists. I will refer to this claim—that torture is used for last resort, lifesaving, preventive intelligence—as the national security rationale, or simply the security rationale for torture. The torture anecdote serves as a compelling delivery system for this rationale and a set of related premises.

To think more deeply about the form and function of torture anecdotes is to better recognize them for the targeted fictions that they are; to see how they serve to deflect complex thinking on torture; to take a pseudo-empirical role in debate; and to deliver a cagey security rationale. The chapter has three sections. The first weighs the U.S. press writing on Murad against its conflicting source material. It offers a case study in the speed and power of torture myth making where the myth is spun from local materials ill-suited to demonstrate its claims. The section follows the construction of the tale to call attention to all such anecdotes; they share the same powerful, folkloric rise and play a common role in supporting torture.

Second, the chapter contrasts the anecdote closely with the torture practice that confronted Murad in the Philippines. The practical elements that have been altered or omitted in the retelling from one decade to the next point to dimensions of torture that public conversation on torture tends to contradict, obscure, and avoid. This is not inadvertent. These basic details of his ordeal are at odds with the national security rationale, the lifesaving, preventive intelligence justification that the anecdote is meant to affirm.

The chapter's third section uses Murad's case as a guide to distinguish four interacting dimensions of torture necessary to analysis: torture discourse; torture practice; torture's organizational setting; and torture's multiple social functions. That framework helps free us from the security rationale to ask what was at stake in Murad's torture if not national security? What work did torture do? A closer look at these four dimensions in Murad's case directs us to the variety of social functions that state torture supports. Collaboration in state torture and misrepresentation served the local Philippine police, the FBI, and the judiciary, as well as journalists and commentators of 1996 and 2001. This multilevel collaboration also prepares us to inquire more deeply into the mid-twentieth-century making of the security rationale for torture in chapter 2.

Inventing Murad

In his controversial response to the 9/11 attacks, media-savvy author and legal scholar Alan Dershowitz appeared frequently on news outlets arguing that to limit torture, we must authorize it in special cases. In 2002's *Why Terrorism Works,* he confronts the reader with this "empirical reality": "The tragic reality is that torture sometimes works, much though many people wish it did not. There are numerous instances in which torture has produced self-proving thoughtful information that was necessary to prevent harm to civilians."[6] Instead of "numerous instances," however, Dershowitz gives us only one: the case of Pakistani terrorist Abdul Hakim Murad and his "plot to knock down 11 or 12 commercial airliners flying over the Pacific and a plot to kill the Pope."[7]

Dershowitz's reliance on Murad was hardly novel. For years after September 11, without even cursory investigation of the circumstances surrounding Murad's torture, his case received virtually uncontested repetition in news and in arguments by influential legal voices such as Dershowitz—who cited Murad frequently in television appearances and in print—as well as Richard Posner, Sanford Levinson, and David Luban.[8]

In these arguments on torture, Murad is made to answer the question "Does torture work?" In the idiom of this debate, the question is not in truth about torture but a question that positions the writer or speaker among peers. One's willingness to engage the question is paramount. "Does torture work?" is a question that tests one's ability, purportedly, to contend with hard realities and jettison dubious queasy moralities. The question separates the sturdy thinker who has done real-world homework from the willowy idealist lost in a daydream. Yet notice the question is in fact half formed.[9] Does torture work . . . to do what precisely? What is being debated? Does it achieve that thing better than . . . what exactly? Does it do that thing better than a multileveled, well-coordinated police investigation? Better than rapport-based interrogation?

The shortened, overly simplified, and suggestive question "Does torture work?" is a rhetorical prop designed to conjure fear-based hypothetical scenarios yet somehow retain the cachet of hard reality. It is designed to wither objections and be answered in the affirmative with a single anecdote. Murad's case was designed to be that anecdote. For example, the long, verifiable record of the role of state torture in destabilizing institutions and jeopardizing security apparatus is an imminently practical, not moral, objection to its use. Of this ruinous track record, Philippine history is a good but not singular example, as I discuss in chapter 2. Yet a focus on "Does torture work?" makes a practical examination of history and broad social impacts irrelevant to the necessity for pragmatism concerning an urgent (hypothetical) threat. No matter the number of practical objections or the debilitating and wasteful impacts tied directly to torture, torture must remain a ready tool if but even one case demonstrates that it can produce lifesaving information. To engage the half question "Does torture work?" is to concede to irrational terms of argument and to grant outsize weight to a single (always disputable) anecdote.

Consider the background. When Abdul Hakim Murad, a Pakistani, was arrested in the Philippines in 1995, he was already a licensed commercial pilot who had received his flight training at a number of U.S. schools. He was a naive but determined recruit of terrorist bomber Ramzi Yousef, a man born in Kuwait to Pakistani-Palestinian parents. Murad and Yousef were in Manila together experimenting with bombs and detonators that could bring down one or more flights originating in Asia and heading to the United States. Accounts of Murad's plot alternately claim he was targeting two, ten, eleven, or twelve planes at one time. Murad's vague intentions and the conflicting claims made about them are an important part of the story.

The men's collaboration indirectly touched many important players. Their financial officer, Wali Khan Amin Shah received funding channeled through an Islamic charitable organization run by Osama bin Laden's brother-in-law. Ramzi Yousef was nephew to Khalid Sheikh Mohammed, the man credited with the design that became the September 11, 2001, strikes. Yousef already was well known in the United States as a principal actor in the successful bombing of the New York World Trade Center's garage in 1993, killing six people and wounding more than a thousand.

According to plan, Murad was to assemble a liquid bomb beneath his passenger seat and set its timer during the first leg of a flight; he would deplane on layover and repeat the process on a second aircraft. The bombs would be timed to explode together during the transpacific segment of each flight. The process could be repeated on multiple planes; the timers could be set hours, even days, ahead. Yousef dubbed this scheme *bojinka*, "loud bang."[10]

In Manila by December 1994, he had made a dry run at *bojinka* by planting a device on a Philippines Airlines flight. The explosion killed one passenger. Soon after, and only five days before Pope John Paul II paid a high-security visit to Manila in January 1995, a chemical fire in the Manila apartment they had stocked with bomb-making components drew police attention. Murad was arrested and the plot foiled by Philippine investigation; his two accomplices were identified. Both were soon taken. The CIA and FBI were notified, and the FBI assembled a case that convicted Yousef, Murad, and Shah in New York in 1996.

In the immediate wake of the attacks in 2001, the PNP made sure the FBI got the blame for failure of vision. They pointed out the FBI had known for six years that terrorists with a connection to a notorious bin Laden associate, Khalid Sheikh Mohammed (Yousef's uncle), were developing a vision of attack by passenger airline. More than a few voices in the United States and international press now insisted Murad's case was a warning that went unheeded. Other reporting hailed him as an intelligence success. This is because Murad experienced prolonged and systematic torture in the custody of the PNP and intelligence service. Arrested January 7, 1995, Murad was held until mid-April. During months of tactical interrogation, he confessed to several plots.

Although Judge Duffy flatly dismissed the notion, the Philippine authorities acknowledged his torture. In 1996 as well as today, they claim their work on Murad was a great success. Two Filipina reporters verified PNP torture in *Under the Crescent Moon: Rebellion in Mindanao,* published in 2000. In their book, Marites Vitug and Glenda Gloria draw on declassified PNP and FBI intelligence reports as well as courtroom testimony from the 1996 trial. Reference to the book is important because *Under the Crescent Moon* is cited repeatedly in 2001 and after by U.S. commentaries that showcase Murad's torture, yet also ignore or suppress important elements of the story Vitug and Gloria try to tell. From partial accounts in the speculative press, Murad's story takes wing. Its very ubiquity becomes self-confirming.

Recounting Murad

Reading the post-9/11 stories on Murad together, one can see exact or nearly exact repetitions, the kind that arise when papers and lawyers crib from each other. What is remarkable, however, is the amount of variation and conflict in the writing on Murad. Puzzling contradictions of fact are allowed to stand without question, including the number and kind of targets under attack, whether the pope was ever one of them, and whether an aircraft crash attack on a U.S. building was ever planned.

A sense of these conflicts is conveyed by reading across several sources that describe a plan to explode two U.S. passenger planes (Vitug and Gloria)—or ten planes simultaneously or eleven (Winik, Fainaru) or twelve (Wren). Stories suggest that Murad planned to assassinate the pope by disguising himself as a priest, kissing the pope, and detonating explosives hidden under his cassock (Winik). In one version, police found a cassock in his apartment (Francia); in another, police found a phone message from a tailor working on a cassock (Brzezinski). However, both the FBI FD-302 report and Vitug and Gloria note Murad rejected assassination entirely. The plan instead was to detonate three bombs along the pope's parade route, hoping to incite "worldwide panic" and kill onlookers. The Joint Congressional Inquiry into intelligence failures before 9/11 found that the plan to assassinate the pope and to dive a plane were "only at the 'discussion' stage and therefore not included" in the indictment for conspiracy. The 9/11 Commission reinforced this view, finding only "casual conversation" regarding crashing a plane with "no specific plan for execution." Even so, this plot to crash a plane was widely reported, albeit in conflicting versions: Murad would fly a private Cessna into the CIA headquarters (Brzezinski, Fainaru, Dershowitz). Or he would use a large commercial jet (Borger). The plane would be filled with explosives (Brzezinski, Dershowitz) or nerve gas (Winik), or it would dive into the Pentagon, not the CIA, or into a nuclear plant (Wren).[11]

Even more baffling, several reports portray these obviously disparate plots as a single unified scheme. They do so even when the journalist's own version of the unified scheme would make the sequence impossible because Murad would need to commit suicide twice (suicide-bombing the pope, then flying into CIA headquarters, for instance).[12]

Which portions of which plots were underway exactly, and which were foiled by torture? The claims made for Murad's torture are specific—namely, his torture "produced self-proving thoughtful information that was necessary to prevent harm to civilians."[13] Given the well-known correlations between false confession and duress, let alone false confession and torture, it is surprising that no reporting registers the discrepancies. This is not to deny that a plot was active but rather to ask at what point would this proliferation of conflicting accounts merit attention in itself? Why does it not raise a shade of doubt around the validity of the confessions, the utility of torture, or at least the reporting's reliability?

But there are greater problems than clarity at stake. Rather than a tale that grows suspect through error or cemented through repetition, there seems to be a more dynamic echo and distortion at work. This is the making of lore and a familiar feature of torture discourse in the national security imagination.[14] From story to story, aspects of Murad's physical ordeal, his arrest, and his plans are amplified and embroidered; other details are recast or removed.

What emerges is a purpose-driven parable, one that reinforces favorite premises and comes packaged with all the suspense, horror, and didactic zeal of a good story. Instead of flat affect and passive construction, we routinely get an action vignette steeped in the language of noir nostalgia. Doug Struck introduces the story of Murad's torture into the post-9/11 news stream in a September 23, 2001, *Washington Post* report.[15]

> Murad would not talk. Handed over to intelligence agents, he taunted them. That didn't last. "For weeks, agents hit him with a chair and a long piece of wood, forced water into his mouth and crushed lighted cigarettes into his private parts," wrote journalists Marites Vitug and Glenda Gloria in "Under the Crescent Moon," an acclaimed book on Abu Sayyaf. "His ribs were almost totally broken and his captors were surprised he survived."
>
> An investigator intimately knowledgeable of the investigation confirmed the torture, but gloated that it was Murad's fears of Jews that finally broke him. "We impersonated the Mossad," he said, referring to the Israeli intelligence service. "He thought we were going to take him to Israel." Murad told all.
>
> One of Murad's two roommates in Apt. 603 was a young Kuwaiti chemical engineer named Ramzi Ahmed Yousef, who had helped him plan the 1993 explosions at the World Trade Center, he said. They were in Manila to make a bomb to kill the Pope. One of them would hide it under a priest's robes, and try to get close enough to kiss the pontiff as the bomb went off.
>
> The next part of the plan was to bomb American airliners. The device on the Philippine airliner was a dry run, he said. Murad had earned a commercial pilot's license, and told investigators he had planned to fly a plane into the CIA headquarters.

Murad's plans are harrowing, and the terse phrasing that opens and closes the scene of violence confirms the power of torture: "Murad would not talk." "Murad told all."

Struck supplements *Under the Crescent Moon* with a new anonymous source. Deemed credible despite his "gloating" delivery, the source introduces a detail not found elsewhere: impersonating the Mossad. It is reprised in Jay Winik's *Wall Street Journal* piece, "Security Comes before Liberty."

In 1995, a little-known operative, Abdul Hakim Murad, was arrested in the Philippines on a policeman's hunch. Inside Murad's apartment were passports and a homemade bomb factory—beakers, filters, fuses and funnel; gallons of sulfuric acid and nitric acid, large cooking kettles.

Handed over to intelligence agents, Murad was violently tortured. For weeks, according to the book "Under the Crescent Moon," agents struck him with a chair and pounded him with a heavy piece of wood, breaking nearly every rib. . . . Even then, he remained silent. In the end, they broke him through a psychological trick. A few Philippine agents posed as members of the Mossad and told Murad they were taking him to Israel. Terrified of being turned over to the Israelis, he finally told all. Then and only then.

And what a treasure trove of information it was. . . . One wonders of course, what would have happened if Murad had been in American custody.[16]

Winik, a historian, kicks up the drama and insinuates the moral: U.S. squeamishness about torture would have sacrificed information and lives. Other stories will be more forthright, saying in the wake of September 11 terror attacks, Americans must take a page from the Filipino playbook.

Embedded in the anecdote is the security justification it affirms: in this emergency, torture saved lives. Once that is delivered, one finds an ensemble of five premises begin to cohere around it. First, although the work of investigation is not named or explored, the anecdote implies that torture works better than investigation. Second, the coverage contrasts U.S. and Filipino methods. The anecdote aligns the writer's community with civilized superiority, while primitive, developmental derogatives collect around the Filipinos. The gist: torture is alien to the contemporary United States; it is not thoroughly integrated into police work, domestic systems of punishment, or international security relationships.[17] The premise offers colonial order and explanation, splitting an "us" from a "them." As Peter Maass writes in "Torture Tough or Lite: If a Terror Suspect Won't Talk, Should He Be Made To?": "In many countries, terrorism suspects like Mr. Murad rarely receive the local equivalent of the Miranda rights; instead, they are tortured."[18]

The third standard premise that adheres to the rationale concerns psychological methods and is served up by the Mossad story. Its explicit function is to reinforce a bogus distinction between psychological and physical torture. In the process of torture, no matter the techniques, the two are simultaneous and cannot be disentangled. In the prologue, I discussed *Newsweek*'s widely read November 5, 2001, essay "Time to Think about Torture," by Jonathan Alter. He too uses Murad to state a lesson plainly: "Some torture clearly works." Yet he suppresses details of the extreme physical assault entirely. "Philippine police reportedly helped crack the 1993 World Trade Center bombings (plus a plot to crash 11 U.S. airliners and kill the Pope) by convincing a suspect that they were about to turn him over to the Israelis."[19]

Alter proposes the United States permit such psychological torture, including immersion in the high-decibel sound of crying babies or suffering animals. Yet to focus on the putatively psychological, his argument ignores the burned genitals and broken ribs. Peter Maass, too, takes up the Mossad lesson: "Mr. Murad, who feared Jews as much as he hated them, quickly spilled the beans." He quotes "a prominent terrorism expert": "You've got to engage in this psychological game. Not just pain but wearing him down physically and spiritually." Here is the too common suggestion that "wearing him down physically" is not truly physical but more properly psychological in nature. In fact, psychological tactics are also physical. They impact the body and senses; they take place under conditions in which the body is captive and intentionally distressed, subjected to ongoing physical and mental deprivation, suffering, and violence.[20]

The sensory deprivation and high-decibel auditory assaults that intrigue Alter (and were practiced on war on terror detainees in Afghanistan, Guantánamo, and Iraq) demonstrate this illusory divide between psychological and physical stressors. That illusion falls apart once again in an alternate version of the Mossad story. Journalist Peter Lance tells us extreme hunger seemed a more powerful motivation to "talk" than the "fear and hatred of Jews." Denied food for a long period, Murad is taunted with a Big Mac and fries. In this account, he remains unmoved by a choice between extradition to the Americans or the Mossad, but he speaks up when the interrogators begin to walk out with the food.[21] In these anecdotes, the possibility of a purely psychological method becomes charged with a talismanic quality, suggesting a magic line between psychological and physical, when in truth there is only wishful thinking. Matus's *Daily Standard* piece asserts the distinction between U.S. and Philippine methods and contrasts psychological and physical torture in a single headline: "Making Terrorists Talk: America Doesn't Use Torture to Get Information Out of Terrorists. Perhaps We Just Need to Use the Magic Word: 'Mossad.'"[22]

A fourth premise common to anecdotes is the notion that graphic detail in the anecdote provides enough of an empirical grace note to authorize all the writer's conclusions. Most stories cannot resist publishing explicit details of the torture, but these are selected and showcased differently in each account. The broad ramifications of this graphic logic are laid out in chapter 4, but in an anecdote like this one, the effect is that we seem to look right at the act of torture with all its repugnance and horror. Even so, certain forms of violence are omitted—electroshock, rape, burns to the genitals, force-feeding, starvation, drowning—perhaps because those tactics smack of the group sadism and debasement that make an interrogation rationale seem less plausible.

This type of empiricism works for jurists Dershowitz or Posner or Levinson; Murad is positioned as a foothold in the real, a point of sturdy leverage from which one quickly pushes off into gross generalization or pure speculation. No one did more to peddle the parable of Murad than Alan Dershowitz. In writing, he offers the story in nearly the same ubiquitous stylized form seen so far and concludes "there can be no doubt" that torture sometimes works—hence the increasing weight borne by Murad builds to Dershowitz's colossally uninformed assertion: "It is precisely because torture sometimes does work and can sometimes prevent major disasters that it still exists in many parts of the world and has been totally eliminated from none."[23]

The fifth and final premise carried with the torture anecdote is that this stand-in for worldly knowledge of torture, the brief and graphic exhibition of Murad's violation, initiates the reader into a community. Here it is a community of the "morally serious," to use a phrase Levinson invokes often. "Whether lawyers or simply citizens," he writes, when "we" see Murad's ordeal, we know that torture is repugnant and also pragmatic—that is, provided we look no further into its conditions of possibility and its effects.[24] This is community building and positioning through torture discourse.

All torture anecdotes operate in this formulaic and folkloric manner, and all fall apart under scrutiny. The anecdote par excellence that followed Murad's was a predictable parallel. The torture of Khalid Sheikh Mohammed, known as KSM, furnished this new material. The uncle of Murad's coconspirator, Ramzi Yousef, Mohammed is referred to often as the mastermind of 9/11. KSM was captured in 2003 and underwent prolonged torture by CIA handlers on international soil. From 2007 on, the story of how KSM cracked under a single technique, CIA waterboarding, replaced

Murad as the empirical demonstration that torture works. The anecdotes and arguments surrounding KSM's torture, its results, and their value are just as ambiguous, fanciful, and conflicting. The teller recanted the claim in 2010, but not before Kathryn Bigelow's feature film script for *Zero Dark Thirty* (2012) presented a version of this anecdotal success as a key plot point.[25]

The fantastical knots tied out of the Murad or KSM anecdotes are also index to the wider group of speculative news stories that emerged immediately after September 11. The manufacture of Murad only leveraged a public discourse on torture in which these five premises were already in play, and in fact ubiquitous: (1) torture works better than investigation, (2) torture is alien, not integrated into the social organization of the civilized United States, (3) psychological techniques are not physical, and vice versa, (4) graphic displays of injury or techniques offer empirical knowledge of torture, and (5) one enters the community of the morally serious when one contends with real cases where torture worked (for security). A serviceable torture anecdote confirms these in a concise and contagious tale. Let's look beyond the tale.

Assessing Torture Practice in Murad

The actual conduct of violence in Murad's case—the network and team; the conditions, timing, phases, and durations; the actions and privations surrounding torture practice—confounds the favorite premises of the Murad parable. Were Murad not so satisfying in his narrative incarnation as ticking time bomb terrorist, his case might have motivated writers in 2001 to a more thorough and responsible use of original sources and the back file of their own newspapers, where reporting on Murad's trial appeared in 1996.

Timing and torture. The claim that torture was an urgent race-against-the-clock affair is belied by the circumstances and the long duration of Murad's torture. Philippine authorities explained, "What was at stake was the life of the Pope."[26] Yet the pope came and went within the first nine days of his ordeal. Murad was tortured systematically and continuously over three months' time.[27] Moreover, the January 7 interrogation tape that suggests a drowning procedure indicates torture was a first approach on the day of his capture, not a last resort.[28] Nor is torture a means to an end, a practice that stops when the talking begins. January and February transcripts and intelligence reports suggest Murad was "cooperating" from the start but nonetheless was tortured for a long period.[29] As a common ritual of detention, torture and talking proceeded in tandem until his April release to the FBI.

Investigation and torture. An additional problem for the claim that this torture prevented imminent terror lies in the fact that the terror plots, whatever they were in actuality, were routed at the moment Murad was arrested. At that time, the Manila apartment that served as the cell's bomb-making laboratory was shut down, and receipts and the like at the site led to two accomplices. Shah was arrested five days later, and Yousef was arrested February 7.[30] Although plotters and weapons were quickly in hand, torture continued in grossly ingenious ways for two months more.

Of course, officials could not have known that the plots were scuttled completely on the first day. But within two days, by January 9, the U.S. State Department acted on the Philippine knowledge of a threat to airlines traveling to and from East Asia, and the Federal Aviation Administration ordered increased security.[31] Moreover, stories that attribute the break in the case to torture flatly ignore the evidence said to be found in Murad's apartment. In addition to bomb-making equipment and information that led to coconspirators, a computer there was said to hold photos and aliases, airline names, flight numbers, and timer detonation settings. With this wealth of detail, airline security foiled the Bojinka plot promptly—but they could have done so even if Murad, accomplices, and bombs were not also soon in hand. The prosecution opened Murad's 1996 trial declaring the computer held the best evidence, "the whole story" in fact—something patently not true of confessions drawn from Murad's torture. If the evidence at the scene was what the police said it was, then the swift use of routine investigative tools could have delivered (and indeed did deliver) more useful intelligence more quickly than the tools of torture.[32]

Police credibility I: Blame the Mossad. One irony of torture discourse in the security imagination is that torturers are asked to attest to the success of their own practice. This is not unique to Murad's case, and these are the very individuals who have the most at stake in asserting the value of their methods. That one admits to torture poses no problem of credibility. It is against the mass of physical evidence acquired at Murad's capture, for instance, that his torturers are asked to speak to the relative "efficacy of torture" and detention over several months. Members of the torture team who are allowed to vouch for the urgent necessity of their approach, often face no questions on this apparent conflict of interest.

In this light, we ought to reconsider the "gloating" anecdote of the Mossad that becomes a stock element of the story: "We impersonated the Mossad. . . . He thought we were going to take him to Israel." The claim combines braggadocio and self-justification, and torturers are known to indulge in both, depending on the audience. Argentine subject Jacobo Timerman writes of his own torturers' tendency to exaggerate when recounting the very procedures he had just endured.[33] John Conroy's excellent comparative look at torture by Israeli, English, and U.S. police demonstrates that torturers routinely blame others for worse behavior; that is, it is a torturer's commonplace to attempt to neutralize accusations of atrocity by contrasting their more "humane" techniques with the extreme methods supposedly used elsewhere.[34] In the terms of the torturer's boast, the listener is meant to understand that, in comparison to the Mossad, the gross violence of the Filipino perpetrators was nothing. Given that this detail is divulged years later by a Philippine official belatedly claiming credit for working over Murad, it would be no surprise to find the Mossad ruse was actually a tale invented for the reporter.

Police credibility II: Planted evidence. It would be a mistake to place total faith in the evidence found at the apartment while investing with skepticism only the confessions forced by torture or the words of the torturers themselves. As with the conflicting confessions, there are conflicting reports of materials found at Murad's apartment. Unconscionably, all recent accounts of Murad omit the fact that the Philippine police invented evidence, falsified reports, and memorized testimony for court concerning evidence on the scene. This fact is available in press coverage of the 1996 trial and in *Under the Crescent Moon.* During that trial, two Philippine officers unexpectedly testified that they had manipulated evidence under orders. They surprised the defense, who were already planning to argue that the files in the laptop computer had been "altered and changed consequentially" by the PNP.[35] The episode highlights what reporters in 1996 or in 2001 might have pursued (but did not), just as it throws into question the reliability of the police sources on the matter of the torture, on the forced confessions, and the links between torture and myriad other forms of corruption. If torture is permitted under professional pressure to make a case, then what is not?

U.S. collaboration in torture. Vitug and Gloria remind their readers that torture was systematized in the Philippines under Ferdinand Marcos as a means to force criminal suspects to incriminate themselves, and torture has remained a tool of the judicial system. What they find unique about Murad's case was that he was not Filipino. They suggest the potential for international repercussions had previously spared foreigners such severe assault.

However, the international implications of Murad's capture were clear from the outset and would have weighed in favor of aggressive treatment, not against it. More importantly, the Philippine police knew the United States was offering a $2 million reward for tips on Ramzi Yousef, Murad's accomplice. The CIA and the FBI were informed at the time of Murad's capture, and "a team of intelligence agents flew in from Washington."[36] Murad's interrogators in Manila received frequent visits from FBI agent Frank Pellegrino, a fact Agent Pellegrino confirmed on cross-examination during the trial.[37] Nonetheless, it is likely that, as his sworn testimony states, Pellegrino never asked to see Murad during those visits, and did so in order to deny knowledge of torture with some credibility. Nonetheless, the FBI received audio of Murad's ongoing tactical interrogation, and an American voice can be heard asking questions during some of these taped sessions.[38] U.S. personnel and agencies were no rarity in the Philippines of the 1990s. Manila had long served as the main station for the CIA in Southeast Asia, and U.S. military and State Department officers as well as civil sector agencies had been involved in police, intelligence, and military joint operations and training for decades. The Filipinos covering the Murad story stress that the PNP understood the working relationship: "The U.S. realized . . . it was in their best interest to have all information extracted from Murad, by all means possible, in the Philippines. 'They preferred we did the dirty job for them,' says a Camp Crame official."[39]

In 1996, Judge Duffy and court reporting on Murad did consider the possibility of a U.S.–Philippines collaboration in torture, if only to dismiss it. However, the post-2001 writing on Murad obscures the FBI's role entirely in order to contrast ineffective U.S. methods of interrogation with urgent lifesaving techniques embraced by Filipinos. Although the story changes, what remains consistent in 1996 and 2001 is a denial of U.S. knowledge and involvement in torture.

The PNP of the 1990s had earned its reputation for violence—a reputation of which the FBI would have been aware. As the U.S. State Department, the military, and intelligence agencies have known for decades, torture and corruption in the PNP are endemic, and action against it has been halting.[40] In the case of Murad's torture, key figures who credited themselves with participation in his treatment, such as Alberto Ferro and Rodolfo "Boogie" Mendoza, advanced to higher posts in the organization. As the nature of commentary on Murad in 2001 and after demonstrates, their resort to torture actually won them praise for international cooperation in the fight against terrorism, even though their torture practice and the outcomes were wholly inconsistent with the national security rationale.

Congressional investigations of the 1970s and 1980s tell us the United States knew much more. During the Marcos regime, the United States itself trained this generation of Filipino officers in "inappropriate" and extralegal measures. Such training relationships do not make for puppets and masters; they do make for convenient allies as well as leverage and complicity, maintaining networks that enable bad behavior and benefit by it rather than end it. What the United States learned from the training has mattered as well. From the beginning of the twentieth century, when the United States added island colonies to its colonized Native American "domestic dependent" nations, and through to the twenty-first-century joint operations against Abu Sayyaf and southern Moro separatists, the Philippines has been an important workshop for torture as a centerpiece of U.S. imperial power.[41]

State Torture in Four Dimensions

The PNP and later the U.S. press invoked national security to justify Abdul Hakim Murad's severe physical torture, claiming it was a lifesaving effort on behalf of the pope, then on behalf of airline passengers whose flights were cleared within a day. Evidence and investigation foiled the plot; the torture was accomplishing a variety of other things. To this point in the chapter, his tale and its garrulous tellers have illustrated the perverse utility of torture anecdotes for delivering the national security rationale for torture and its companion premises: Torture works better than investigation, and it is alien not integral to social arrangements in the "civilized" United States. Physical torture is separate from and worse than so-called psychological torture, and to display graphic details of torture is to offer empirical evidence of this. A final premise: merely to engage the security value of torture—whether to support or to refute that value—positions one in a serious moral community.

Torture anecdotes typically unravel in just this way under examination, yet the security rationale itself somehow deflects scrutiny.[42] When debunked in one case, it remains ready to attach to the next case, and the next. Worse, as Murad's case illustrates, despite the urgency implied and facts to the contrary, security can be claimed as the rationale before, during, or after the violence of torture. Once assigned, the security pretext for torture can persist despite nonsensical contradictions and particulars that undermine the rationale's very lifesaving, last-resort claim. Even torture detractors find themselves responding to its terms. Whether agents of the state believe there is an emergency or not, or whether those agents believe torture can produce intelligence or not, the security rationale works handily to block our view of torture's group dynamics and productive work.

This section, then, turns to two questions. First, how do we begin to identify that productive work? Second, how do we discredit the rationale and question its premises without discounting the powerful role this vision of torture plays in our history and society?

Distinguishing four practical dimensions of state torture can help with both. These are torture practice, organizational setting, torture discourse, and social functions. These dimensions provide an analytical framework, although in reality, they overlap and are interdependent in important respects; as we have seen with Murad, they need have no connection to the rationale offered for torture. They not only discredit the tenacious rationale but also enable us to look past the national security imagination and ask what work torture does. Importantly, they help us see how social functions unrelated to security pervade each of torture's other dimensions: discourse, practice, and organizational setting. Murad's case is a good example because it provides a lens on each dimension.

Torture practice. The first sections of this chapter have laid out what is known about the group that put Murad through a lengthy process of torture. In considering the practice, we have considered the actual conduct of violence in Murad's case—the network and the team; the conditions, timing, phases, and durations; the actions and privations surrounding torture's practice. His torture and detention continued for three months, and the PNP worked in collaboration with the FBI to coordinate logistics, settings, transcripts, spectators, and conditions of confinement.

Organizational setting. This dimension has been outlined by political scientist Darius Rejali and mapped by professor of sociology and social policy Danielle Celermajer. Let's first consider their work in some depth and then apply it to Murad. In *Torture and Democracy,* Rejali writes that attention to context highlights "elements of empirical cases that may be missed otherwise." The details of how torture happens serve as an "important check on misleading or overly general accounts of why torture happens."[43] In a similar vein, Danielle Celermajer has argued that prevention of torture requires closer attention to the why, especially the interagency and organizational worlds in which torture occurs. She notes that when considering violence "from the perspective of those inflicting it, one finds that it has meanings embedded in their everyday practices and ways of dealing with the distinctive work world they occupy."[44] Situational analysis removes no responsibility from individuals for their actions and choices. Instead, it specifies the local structures and systems that influence and give shape to the environment in which humans choose. For Celermajer, "it is permissive or authorizing contexts rather than either the individual disposition or the explicit demands of superior officers that best explain the persistence of violations."[45] Rejali emphasizes the same; context does not cause torture, but it may allow torture to be used then excused, or hidden under another name. Rejali details three institutional "models" from which "torture may arise" in democracies: the juridical model, the civic discipline model, and what Rejali names the national security model and I will call the emergency model.[46] In each model, he notes an enabling social pact at work between the public and the organization. I will expand on these pacts and underscore social functions in these settings.

The juridical model refers to a judicial system that overvalues confessions and may also allow preventive or incommunicado detention. In such a system, key organizations—the security forces and justice system—may seek shortcuts to rigorous investigation and analysis in a quest for clear results—meaning convictions. Rejali observes torture for confession is strongly associated with systems that allow extensive periods of detention without charge and arrest. Because juries have been proven to give weight to confessions even when the judge instructs them not to, manipulated confessions close cases quickly and improve conviction records even when evidence is unavailable or elements of evidence contradict the confession. Twenty-seven percent of DNA exonerations involve innocent persons who confessed.[47] Quick, tortured confessions serve the organization because they have a social function: convictions can boost public confidence. Confessions reassure the public that police detain (only) the guilty; or, in a corollary assumption, confessions indicate that the guilt of persons appearing marginal, suspicious, or "of notorious reputation" will show itself under sufficient pressure.[48] In an organizational context that incentivizes (forced) confessions, there are benefits. Prosecutors, police, courts, and a broad enough sector of the public may find reasons to disregard shortcuts around the law out of desire to see criminal classes punished or crime contained.

Yet when it comes to torture, perceived benefits are actually harms. Rejali points to what is lost in such a juridical context. With a premium placed on confession, the police's investigative capacity degrades, in turn cultivating a permissive legal system and detention regime. Overreliance on confession also leads to imprisoning and executing the innocent. In the juridical model, police, juries, courts, and the public join in a common effort to show results, but at a price. The incentive to cover up mistakes grows exponentially.

Civic discipline is Rejali's next organizational context for torture. "Because neighborhoods want civic order on the streets whatever the cost," police or private security may use violence simply to mark certain persons, behaviors, dress, or locations as unacceptable. Extrajudicial violence—beatings, chokeholds, rough handling, stun equipment, pepper spray—sends a message. Rejali writes that violence of this kind functions as a nuanced "civic marker": "It is conferring identities, shaping a finely graded civic order. It reminds lesser citizens who they are and where they belong."[49] The social pact at work in this case is that the public will disregard state violence that occurs on roadsides, public settings, doorsteps, or homes when (marginalized) persons are pulled aside, questioned, or delayed by police or security. When delayed, people are obliged to comply, even though not in a space of formal custody.

In the U.S. context, Rejali's model of torture as a civic marker has clear applications to racial and economic caste made and maintained through public order policing, immigrant detention, or prison settings. As discussed in the introduction, in these settings torture is justified as discipline or an effort to communicate authority by establishing a pecking order. No crime or confession need be at stake; there is no urgency, simply the agents' perceived duty to keep marginalized persons to their supposed place in the social order through displays of physical power. Torturing some alerts everyone in the social hierarchy of their status and the dominance of the institution and its workers. It signals the intent (and ability) to preserve that hierarchy with arbitrary and extralegal violence. Although it is sometimes publicly conceded that treatment amounting to torture occurs within our state institutions, these instances are considered an excess on the part of isolated perpetrators. Other language thus substitutes for the term "torture"— abuses, police brutality, unnecessary cavity search, rape, assault.

To expand further on Rejali's model, one can consider torture's impact as a civic marker to be a powerful social function on the streets, one that is too often perceived as a benefit. As noted in the Introduction, white communities and institutions have worked with public order policing in the United States historically to enact the violence of civic discipline. Work that emerged in law reviews of the 1990s began to question effectively the racial encoding implicit in legal standards of "reasonable fear," "suspicious activity," or "disorderly behavior" when it is reported by the public or acted on by the police.[50] In application, these legal standards have protected police and citizens who report, harass, and violate persons seen as marginal.[51] Over the decades, the concentration of disciplinary policing in minoritized neighborhoods and the racially disproportionate impacts have been spotlighted by direct action movements like the Movement for Black Lives, Department of Justice investigations, and public dissent (e.g., profiling, traffic stops and searches, disparately harsh sentencing, Taser use, injury, or death). This is all testimony to the power of extrajudicial torture, violence, and surveillance to organize and stratify public and residential life by race, gender, income, mental health status, and more. Torture transmits terror and sends distinct messages, threatening and subordinating some while reassuring others. But again, these perceived benefits are actually grievous harms that cripple both persons and entire societies. When a society defines groups and subordinates them by violence, then that society weakens its own institutions and expends enormous social, psychological, and economic resources to block, contain, waste, or otherwise exploit the energies, accomplishments, leadership, participation, and ingenuity of the subordinated classes.

The last organizational context Rejali describes is the emergency model in democracies. The work of institutions charged with security—including the police, the military, border control, and contractors—is authorized, funded, and monitored by legislatures, courts, and the press and therefore the public. However, these services are managed by security bureaucrats positioned to identify an actual or perceived emergency and execute responses. Those leaders can claim special knowledge or expertise, and, as in the case of Murad, may seize on the ever-ready security rationale or myths surrounding torture to overrule, ignore, or undermine safeguards against it. In the face of this, groups that monitor the police may be "unwilling or unable to stop the turn to torture."[52]

The models Rejali outlines—juridical, civic discipline, emergency—do not encompass all organizational settings for state torture. Nor do the models themselves justify, explain, or cause the torture that occurs within them. However, these descriptive models indicate how institutional environments mediate and influence the interactions of organizations and teams. As Celermajer argues, individuals embrace for themselves the logic, definitions, and aims of the organization and navigate its routines. They are acting and choosing, but those choices are mediated through the organizational and societal understandings of their place and position in that world.

Here we return to the slippery national security rationale and its claim that torture is necessary to obtain lifesaving, preventive information. Notably, a putative claim to emergency or security is used to explain or excuse torture occurring in any of Rejali's three models. For example, within days of the September 11, 2001, attacks, a new level of civic discipline was underway, backed by the security rationale. At least 1,200 members of marginalized groups, minoritized ethnic or religious communities, shop and restaurant owners, documented and undocumented migrants, and U.S. resident immigrants were rounded up without charge and held at facilities like the Metropolitan Detention Center in New York. Surveillance video there captured widespread sexual assault and beatings of people who had no relationship to terrorist activity and were by no means being interrogated.[53] There are elements of all three of Rejali's organization models involved here—juridical, civic discipline, emergency—but only one rationale. The torture practice in no way squared with a claim of national security. Instead, the violence enacted social divisions and stratifications, signaling a desire to maintain a particular social order.

If we return to the organizational setting in the case of Murad, we see we have to account for the interaction of all these models—juridical, civic discipline, emergency—transnationally. Inside the PNP and the FBI, there were codes of behavior and routines of communication; collaborations, caseloads, and procedures worked out over long histories; and ongoing professional dynamics, resource pressures, and conflicts. The 1995 to 1996 U.S.–Philippines collaboration in Murad's capture, tortured confession, and trial offers a potent demonstration of how the U.S. legal system has incrementally integrated the use of torture, not banned it. In Murad's trial, Judge Duffy applied his skepticism to elements that did not align with his vision of torture: the security vision. He doubted the ability of torturers to contort a physical body as described and their willingness to care for Murad as they tortured him. Duffy also cast doubt on the objectivity of expert psychological testimony. He might have directed skepticism instead toward the inordinate length of time Murad spent in Philippine hands, the involvement of FBI agent Pelligrino during that period, the track record of the PNP and torture, and the history of U.S.–Philippine organizational collaboration in torture. He might have acted when police admitted in court to presenting false evidence. Any one of these interventions could have cast doubt on the confession and vigorously discouraged tortured confessions in his courtroom and maybe others in the future. The judge could have made the prosecution rely on an apartment full of material evidence that linked coconspirators and outlined the plot. Given the PNP's reputation, the intensive FBI collaboration and visits, and the shared interrogation transcripts, the U.S. voice audible on the interrogation tapes, and the psychological examiner who found indications of torture, the more patent and tenable conclusion is that the Philippine authorities tortured Murad over an extended period with U.S. knowledge. They did so not to elicit preventive information but rather to build a case for U.S. courts.

Murad's torture saved no lives but served in court—a pattern replicated by the FBI when it has sought to establish other cases of terrorism. Allegations of torture posed problems in 2000, when three of the four defendants brought to trial for the 1998 embassy bombings in Kenya and Tanzania argued that they had signed confessions only after physical coercion in Pakistan and Kenya under the supervision of the FBI.[54] Despite public and scholarly emphasis on the CIA's post–September 11 program of secret torture, Murad's case shows that the FBI should not be exonerated so easily.[55] These are also reminders that despite the attention given extraordinary rendition in the early twenty-first-century war on terror, the practice had a long backstory, and such relationships remain ripe for exploitation today. Transnational torture relationships continue in manufacturing and commerce, as do tacit routines of noninterference with the torture practice of allies or proxies (see chapter 4). We have looked at organizational settings and the actual torture practice; there are two more dimensions of state torture we need to consider.

Social functions. The social dimension of torture is rarely considered and speaks to the interpersonal, generative, and productive functions of torture for particular participants within the organization, as well as to the functions of the torture for the organization, the state, the press, and wider society. The discussion above of intersecting organizational settings details many of these social functions, noting that perceived benefits and social pacts are damaging to many in the short and long term. Beyond the organizational level, different group and interpersonal dynamics are likely present in the practice of torture itself, at the level of those most closely involved in the violence and its coordination. These would comprise another set of social functions or benefits and harms. For example, for the FBI and U.S. prosecutors, the torture of Murad forced, rehearsed, and shaped a confession. For the Filipinos, however, it showcased their hard-nosed work ethic and international security cooperation with the United States. Moreover, Murad's torture enabled participants to vie for promotion, media attention, or status among rivals in the PNP; it also allowed the PNP to believe they might receive the $2 million cash incentive the United States offered for information leading to Ramzi Yousef. (The PNP learned later that police and intelligence services were not eligible.)

Finally, for members of the general public who became aware of it, Murad's violent ordeal sent a dual social message. Petty criminals, Muslims, and marginalized residents of Manila could believe they were under watch, just as other persons and transatlantic passengers could believe their lives and social hierarchy would be tended by police violence or FBI expertise. These are terror effects that stratify and sustain social order. These social and professional benefits were not accidental. Nor were the institutional, interorganizational, and geopolitical benefits unanticipated by either the FBI or the PNP.

Torture discourse. We have spent some time in this chapter following a range of discourse. This dimension encompasses more than the rationale. Official explanations for torture arrive with a swarm of additional language: court reporting, judges' findings, legal argumentation, news speculation, anecdotes, imagery, refutation, apologia, activist campaigns, and more. Rationales are just part of a larger discourse that precedes and surrounds the violence.

The four-dimensional analytical framework helps us see that torture discourse can operate with little relation to the practice, organizational setting, and social functions at work in those dimensions. Just as the framework insists we look for social functions in each dimension, it draws attention to the social functions of the discourse itself. The din of conversation around Murad and his torture generates social benefits and incentives for those who take part. Journalistic routines easily accommodated the security rationale. Those who spun the Murad anecdote and the larger speculative debate on torture in 2001 received professional and public attention. Even six to ten years after his torture, U.S. journalists and jurists were still unable to apply skepticism, analysis, or history to the case. Nonetheless, they ignored conflicting information and borrowed the anecdotes of others without further consideration. They amplified an anecdote to debate torture with a measure of moral seriousness. The folkloric work of torture anecdotes substituted for both logic and history in just this way to better circulate the security rationale. The wealth of conflicting information in Murad's story demands attention, as do the unreliable narratives that emerge from torture and the fantasies that surround it. The thicket of misinformation generated by torture, police corruption, and carefully crafted routines of deniability is made denser by the disparate motives and mixed agendas of U.S. agencies and Philippine officials. It is made denser still by reporting. Whether it arrives in the form of rumors, rationales, rules, protests, or hairsplitting legal distinctions, it is the tradition of torture discourse indebted to the security imagination to distract from the social functions that drive torture and to invite civic institutions to accommodate torture in its local, peacetime domestic uses.

• • •

This chapter on Abdul Hakim Murad participates in torture discourse, with the intent to call attention to those social functions and emphasize the role of the national security imagination, its torture rationale, and the premises that travel with it. For instance, once our attention is drawn to it, it is obvious that anecdotes and widespread press speculation on torture would do the work of imagining the terrorist we torture as well as the torture itself. But another chief product of torture discourse conducted in the speculative press was the palpable sense of moral community it deliberately crafted, and the speakers' efforts to position themselves within it. The recurring debate on torture surely imagines the terrorist and torture, but also the community that will authorize and benefit from it, or end it. What is true of writing on Murad, then, is true of the larger conversation. In elaborating a concept of the terrorist we torture, what is at stake is a vision of security and wishful self-definition on a national scale.

It is possible to debate the role of torture in security without ever posing questions about other functions of torture, or the torture debate itself. The first sections of this chapter have followed the course of a single anecdote to illustrate the perverse utility of all torture anecdotes for keeping that vision alive. This final section has used the complexities surrounding Murad's torture to use four interacting dimensions of state torture as a framework to push us beyond the rationale and its vision. Torture's practice, organizational setting, discourse, and multiple social functions are all dimensions that reinforce the kind of situational analysis urged by institutional detail (Rejali) and a broader ecological diagnosis of torture (Celermajer). Yet the framework places new emphasis on social functions of torture in each of the other dimensions. In particular, this chapter on Murad has tracked the operation of torture discourse as it neglects or misrepresents those social functions while undertaking social agendas of its own.

It is not enough to simply debunk the security rationale in specific cases. The case of Murad and the four-dimensional framework forces us to see all the argument as a performance in its own right, accomplishing more than mere denial, refutation, or condemnation. The conversation on torture as an excess or necessity of national security projects a vision and enlists relationships; it mobilizes and divides communities. The national security vision for torture normalizes domestic terror used for civic discipline, for marking caste, for keeping order.

The next chapter takes up the colonial ingredients of that vision and follows their transformation into national security torture at mid-twentieth century in the global context of counterinsurgency. Twenty-first-century examples foreground the security relationships and markets for force that this vision feeds. They demonstrate how this security representation continues to undergird a particular understanding of empire and obscure the work of torture in domestic racial terror and containment.

2

Rationale

The Refashioning of Colonial Violence—
Roger Trinquier, Jean Lartéguy, and Edward Lansdale

> Excessive force may not be a frequent event for any specific police officer or department, but it is on the menu of potential responses.
> —John T. Parry, *Understanding Torture*

> Potential violence . . . is the essence of their power.
> —Micol Seigel, *Violence Work*

The previous chapter examined the story of Abdul Hakim Murad as a classic torture anecdote. This chapter looks to national security rationale at the heart of such anecdotes and identifies it as an old construction, part of the imperial invention of torture as national security in the middle of the twentieth century.

The first section opens with early colonial methodologies of violence and control that were used by the United States in the Philippines during the war from 1898 to 1902 and in the first decades of its U.S. occupation. U.S. voices disagreed about those methods, including torture, but they projected a common understanding that torture was a method of racial domination at home and abroad. The section points up three intertwined aspects of violence in U.S. colonial practice: first, the combined use of surveillance, torture, and terror; second, the control of space; and third, the appropriation of racialized science. All three of these tools have roots in domestic racial terror. The same practices were retained and expanded in what Western powers began to term "counterinsurgency warfare" at the midpoint of the twentieth century. Despite the clear continuities between colonial warfare and counterinsurgency practice, including torture, the theorists at midcentury dubbed the enterprise counterinsurgency and radically altered the discourse on torture as an attempt to distinguish colonial terror from their neocolonial brand of domination.

The second section, therefore, examines how novel arguments around torture developed and circulated in the work of three influential practitioners and purveyors of counterinsurgency, two French and one American: Roger Trinquier, Jean Lartéguy, and Edward Lansdale. This depiction is a composite construction that is bound up in a set of ideas: the future of warfare, torture's expert and minimal use, its existential and interrogational purpose. It aimed to insulate torture from the facts of its practice: the mass use of torture and the race- and caste-based terror at its heart.[1] Lansdale, a former adman turned spy, served as U.S. "advisor" to the Philippines during the midcentury Huk rebellion. He offers insight into U.S. applications of counterinsurgency. This section concludes with twenty-first-century news, policy by the executive branch, and military reports that reprise the midcentury depiction of national security torture.

The final section of this chapter turns to specific developments in counterinsurgency previewed in the discussion of Lansdale. Among those developments are the assignment of terror and its violence to specific forces, units, or locals that work in tandem with a more scrupulously "humane" military or unsullied advisory staff. This structural shift to compartmentalization is important to note, as are the expanding global networks that assembled professional communities around the promotion of terror and torture. Proliferating security networks and the growing sensibility surrounding torture in that security imagination carefully connect skill in operations, academic prestige, and market forces. In the U.S. case, these networks also bring the policing model of counterinsurgency back to its roots in racial terror.

From Colonial Legacy to Counterinsurgency

This section follows an early twentieth-century to midcentury trajectory, from the U.S. war and colonial violence in the Philippines to the U.S. counterinsurgency there against the Huk rebellion from 1946 to 1954. It illuminates two aspects. First, the colonial-era press, policy makers, and politicians in the United States disagreed over the viability of retaining an imperial stake in the Philippines, but they articulated a common understanding that state violence was needed to achieve the twin goals of racial subordination and economic advancement. They used plain language to connect torture and terror to white supremacy, and they highlighted the clear kinship between torture and terror in the Philippines and the lynching and massacres used to subordinate and racialize African American and Native American populations.

Second, the U.S.–Philippine war and colonial government innovated new paramilitary policing structures, thereby creating dimensions of executive power that would continue to extend and support the era of national security and counterinsurgency in the late 1940s and 1950s. A significant innovation was the imperial police force established in 1901, the Philippine Constabulary (P.C.). It became "the first U.S. federal agency with a fully developed covert capacity" and served as a precursor to the FBI and Office of Naval Intelligence and eventually the CIA.[2] The P.C. refined wartime methods in the racialized context of occupation, where security came to mean defense of the colonial government and its agendas from the dissident populace.

Colonial Violence

As had the arguments for continental expansion from the 1830s to the 1890s, the U.S. call for overseas expansion worked from a straightforwardly racial and civilizational paradigm. In the lead-up to war, paternalistic discourse had pointed to ghastly Spanish tortures in the Philippines as grounds for invasion in support of Filipino "liberty."[3] In the Philippines, the United States sought coaling stations for U.S. ships, military bases, and economic influence sufficient to ensure a point from which to project power across Asia for years to come.[4] Newspapers of the time promoted annexation as a means to "keep China open to our goods" and enforce that access with a military arsenal "nearer to China than the port at San Francisco or Hawaii." White dominance was a clear part of this equation. Some argued the islands might make a good home for the "surplus Negro population" of the U.S. South "to prevent negro domination there . . . and do away with . . . competition of Southern negro labor with the white labor of the North." This solution might even make "American negroes, the ultimate secondary rulers, under the necessary white supervision."[5]

Once Spain ceded the islands to the United States in 1898, the United States confronted a well-organized independence movement that continued the military struggle. The Filipinos' political and military sophistication forced proponents of ongoing U.S. rule to revise older homegrown racial stereotypes. Altered constructions assigned a different level of racial advancement to Spanish-speaking Catholic Filipinos than to Filipinos of "un-Christianized tribes." This lent some nuance to what Senator and Harvard historian Henry Cabot Lodge called, "Asiatic indifference to life with the Asiatic treachery and Asiatic cruelty."[6]

General Arthur MacArthur, among others, observed the popular strength of the Filipino independence struggle, remarking on the "almost complete unity of action of the entire native population." He concluded unity lay in the racial nature of the people and guerilla warfare. "The adhesive principle comes from ethnological homogeneity," he stated, "which induces men to respond for a time to the appeals of consanguineous leadership, even when such action is opposed to their own interests."[7]

References to the "new" and "unknown" abounded, often characterizing a racial type, a fighting tactic, and a terrain all at once. Of the Philippines, one veteran wrote: "Uncle Sam's cohorts . . . saw in everything something new, strange and utterly incomprehensible. . . . The enemy existed unseen in the dripping jungle, in the moldering towns and in the smoky clearings on the hillsides . . . the enemy was not to be found. But they existed nonetheless."[8] A commissioned officer who had served in the regular army from 1899 to 1905 used similar racialized terms steeped in newness, unknowability, and deceit to characterize the people and excuse the water torture used against them:

> A great majority of *insurrectos* . . . adopted guerilla tactics, wearing no uniform, hiding their rifles when it suited their convenience to appear friendly. The "water cure" was the only answer to this policy. Brutal yes. . . . In a country where the boys and women fight with the same weapons as the men, and where quarter is neither given nor expected, stern measures are necessary.[9]

Despite the "new, strange and utterly incomprehensible" enemy, the techniques put to work by the United States in the Philippines were old and long familiar from use in internal U.S. racial suppression and continental expansion. U.S. forces in the Philippines used torture as exemplary violence, reprisals, and executions. They destroyed or contaminated food supplies; conducted massacres of hundreds; and "reconcentrated" civilian populations, relocating them by the thousands to what were called concentration camps.[10] Indeed, throughout the nineteenth century, the United States had used similar means to secure commercial dominance and territory through population removal, lynching, terror, and massacre that targeted Native Americans and African Americans as well as Spanish-speaking communities and Asian immigrants in the West and Pacific Northwest. These tactics all reappeared in the Philippines. A two-way traffic in personnel and methods, from the United States to Philippines and back again, reinforced the kinship. Twenty-six of thirty U.S. generals in the Philippines were veterans of the U.S. Indian wars of expropriation.[11]

One torture in particular drew attention to the islands. The coyly macabre term "water cure" referred to an infamous feature of U.S. action there— the kind of drowning and stomach pumping Murad endured there a century later and discussed in chapter 1. In the Philippine context, the water cure applied equally to the practice of cutting off air by dunking or drowning subjects, or to the practice of pumping the stomach full of water, then applying sharp weight to the distended stomach.[12]

Debating violence. Given the kinship in practice and function between militarized terror in the Philippines and domestic modes of so-called frontier justice and race repression, it is no coincidence that Herbert Welsh, a wealthy, white advocate in the late-century Indian Rights movement, began publishing letters from U.S. soldiers attesting to atrocities in his Philadelphia weekly, *City and State*.[13] Anti-imperialists called for a congressional inquiry on the basis of continuing reports of water torture, massacres, and forced removals.[14]

Sociologist Christopher Einolf has documented and parsed the 1902 Senate and media debate over torture, finding in it "strong domestic norms against torture."[15] However, I read the debate differently. The U.S. press and political class did hold an animated debate over the level of atrocity permissible in war and race conflict. Witnesses called to Lodge's Senate committee testified that the water cure was in common use in the Philippines, that superior officers knew it, and that they did not try to prevent it.[16] In response, senators argued over atrocity and its presumed impact on white soldiers, on Filipinos, and on U.S. honor itself. However, the debate was primarily a means to position oneself against opponents, to stand for or against ongoing U.S. administration of the islands, for or against the economic and geopolitical value of expansion.

The Senate debate invoked the term "torture" as a flexible rhetorical category only, a moral cudgel used liberally to disgrace the opponent, no matter the position. The debate reflected the basic fact that state torture takes many forms and serves many social and institutional purposes. Participants shared no common sense of what torture means or the purpose it serves. On the occasions when the use of torture was said to be connected in some way to obtaining information or supposed evidence of ammunition or rifles, this protean rationale swam in a sea of other explanations, including vengeance, "punishment," leverage to "obtain the unwilling service of a guide," "a method of conducting operations," and what one senator described as a racial superior's "almost involuntary practice [of] inhuman conduct" when he confronts an inferior race in combat.[17] The elements of the twenty-first century's national security rationale—torture for preventive information—had yet to coalesce.

Moreover, senators and newspapers in 1902 freely compared violence at home to torture abroad. There was good reason for this. Both stateside lynching terror and water torture on the islands used public display of terror to target insubordinate behavior, dissent, and rivals (be they Filipino politicians or Memphis business owners).[18] Drawing the parallel between home and abroad sharply, pro-imperialists in the Senate held that torture in the Philippines was the only effective response to Filipino savagery; they argued that the water cure was no different than domestic cruelties used against the "Negroes of the South," including the "sand cure," with Senator Pritchard of North Carolina describing the latter as "the victim having his face crushed into the ground to stifle his cries while he was being beaten to intimidate him politically."[19]

In reply, an anti-imperialist Democrat from South Carolina, Senator Ben "Pitchfork" Tillman, declared the "sand cure of the South to be mild compared to the outrages in the Philippines," with lynching more merciful than torture in the islands, noting, "When we get ready to put a negro's face in the sand, we put his body there too."[20] Senator Simmons of North Carolina added it was only manly to refuse Black rule in the Southern states.[21] Only four years earlier, Wilmington, North Carolina's largest city and a mixed-race community that once boasted Black aldermen, police, and magistrates, was the site of a devastating white supremacist coup and massacre.[22] Tillman agreed, noting that "lynchings will continue so long as fiends rape wives and daughters" and to keep white society free of "Negro domination."[23] In response, senators who favored expansion argued Philippine atrocities were tied to a higher purpose.

A similar set of parallels drawn to wars on American Indians emerged when news broke of the massacre on the island of Samar led by Major Littleton Waller. When Senator Patterson of Colorado denounced the massacre, he was reminded that he had supported the slaughter at Sand Creek in 1876, where massacre of Native American men, women, and children was followed by the "revolting" mutilation of their bodies.[24] Unperturbed, Patterson said he supported the violence because native peoples had attacked homes and holdings of white settlers. In contrast, the Samar massacre was unconscionable because white men had attacked first.[25] Methodist Bishop Thoburn expressed the opposite view in the press: "We have held the American Indians by force for centuries and we have stronger claim upon the Filipinos . . . [who] have fallen to us as the fortune of war."[26]

This debate, then, affirmed that torture practice at home or abroad had multiple manifestations and social functions. It also demonstrated that whether senators or editorials or activists defended or disparaged U.S. atrocities abroad, all affirmed the rightness of white racial and economic supremacy and agreed that extreme violence may be necessary to secure it. The Black press was of course a telling exception to this rule; it too highlighted the kinship between domestic torture and torture overseas. The Washington *Colored American* held: "It is all right to investigate the water cure in the Philippines, but we should not meanwhile forget the sand cure in North Carolina." Other African American papers insisted that the battle against stateside tortures and voter suppression ought to take precedence. Speaking to the Afro-American Council in Washington, D.C., journalist, suffrage backer, and antilynching crusader Ida B. Wells-Barnett declared African Americans should oppose expansion until the government chose to protect them at home. In contrast, the *Indianapolis Freeman* saw expansion as an opportunity to demonstrate "Negro" citizenship: "We are to share in the glories or defeats of our country's wars, that is patriotism pure and simple."[27] With important exceptions, leading white suffragists and Women's Temperance Union advocates supported imperialism if it would eventually assist their own campaigns in the States—that is, if "civilizing" meant granting Filipina suffrage, even before far less deserving Filipino men.[28]

Decades later, the makers of counterinsurgency theory deliberately countered this sense that state torture took a variety of forms and served many functions. They offered instead a stylized and singular image of torture and its function. Key counterinsurgents would also strip explicit reference to race subordination and terror from their portrait of torture.

Violent practice—imperial police. The domestic wrangling over the water cure and the sand cure in 1902 faded as the United States took up occupation and governance. In the war and after, the United States borrowed from the European template for colonial control.[29] But in this distant political and legal environment, the United States created a distinctive paramilitary mechanism, the Philippine Constabulary, to fight lingering insurgents and construct a state. Its mission embraced violence as a necessity of race subordination and political control. Three methods will demonstrate. The first is a commitment to a trio of tools for direct coercion: surveillance, terror, and torture. Second is the control of space as a mode of domination. Third is the application of "modern" science in efforts to racialize, intimidate, and control. The P.C. portfolio of coercion included many other direct tactics that work in concert with surveillance, terror, and torture—for example, infiltration, disruption, harassment, and arbitrary enforcement—but I highlight the relevance of this trio and their interaction. As noted in the Introduction, and in the words of Marnia Lazreg, torture gives terror its force; it is a necessary terror multiplier.[30]

The United States created the Philippine Constabulary during the war; it was made up of a small number of native troops headed by American officers. It remained a predominantly white force for two decades, adding Filipino personnel only by slow increments.[31] As the war was declared over in 1902, insurgents were relabeled as brigands, effectively depoliticizing their claims. Colonial reorganization of Philippine society began.[32] With national duties ranging from public works to policing to the conduct of war, the P.C. was charged with coercion as well as ensuring public sanitation and building roads.[33] This broad but unified mission incorporated violence in clear racial terms. The first chief of the P.C., Henry T. Allen, pointed to the semisavagery of the population to underscore the intimate relationship between race, violence, and civic development: "Education and roads will effect what is desired, but while awaiting these, drastic measures are obligatory. . . . The only remedy is killing and for the same reason that a rabid dog must be disposed of."[34] In another recommendation to West Point, Allen wrote the "only rational policy" to control messianic movements in 1903 would be to "kill off leaders and enlighten the masses."[35]

Policing on the U.S. mainland at this time had no such centralized national capacity, but local forces were known to use torture under colloquial phrasing like "the third degree" and to partner with public and private lynchings in both North and South, as well as purges of mixed-race communities.[36] The P.C. emerged differently. McCoy's work emphasizes that this colonial entity developed outside of U.S. constitutional constraints. The P.C. learned from the Filipino guerillas' skill in counterintelligence and covert organizational structures. They developed several forms of coercion and covert capacities, including informants, political infiltration, provocation, and disinformation.[37] A secret service under Commander Harry H. Bandholtz became versed in "the wearing of disguises, fabricating disinformation . . . [and] recruiting paid informants and saboteurs." They also "monitored the press" and "carried out periodic assassinations."[38]

Torture was integral, not accidental, to the terror the P.C. used to project power, suppress rebellions, stifle speech, and dominate wider populations. The water cure and other tortures and abuses were outlawed in 1903. Yet the P.C. continued to use torture and other methods of terror to crush ongoing rebellions, to cultivate politicians, and to partner with business: "Armed resistance was met with mass slaughter. . . . Nationalist agitation was contained through suffocating surveillance, and labor agitation crushed by arbitrary arrests and agent provocateur operations."[39] From 1901 to 1907, both the army and the P.C. used torture and suppression in Samar, Batangas, and Cavite.[40] In an institutional pattern well known to policing and paramilitaries, torture and abuses provoked legitimation crises.[41] When in 1905 torture and other outrages in Cavite province drew an outcry in the Manila press, political expedience pressed the P.C. to purge upper ranks and temper the outright racism of its leadership.[42] Torture remained in the P.C. arsenal, but as elections for a new indigenous national assembly neared in 1907, their colonial administrators were eager to lessen the attention it drew.

In the colonial context of suppression, leaders placed great importance on state control of information and surveillance. The Division of Military Information at Manila formed during the war in 1900, and within a year, it had introduced an inspired breadth to the types of information now deemed necessary to fight opponents.[43] Military information had once only referred to strategic and tactical information on opposing fighters—things like their firearms, numbers, equipment, and movements. Now the P.C. acquired an appetite for the collection, analysis, and transmission of a vast array of data on Filipinos, "compil[ing] dossiers on thousands of individuals" as a means to extort allegiance.[44] The targets for surveillance expanded to include all levels of civilian life, political activity, and individual behavior in households as well as offices, including individual finances, commercial economic activity, personal communications, ideology, and civilian supporters.[45]

The new value placed on micro-level surveillance for extortion and suppression in the Philippines was met with a growing communication infrastructure. This boasted the latest advances in the technology of identification, classification, and data management. By 1905, the P.C. commanded "an intelligence office, transport office, 172 wagons, 65 boats, medical service with ten hospitals, 7300 troops, and a network of 400 telegraph and telephone offices communicating over 4200 miles of copper wire."[46] Alfred McCoy describes the Philippine achievement as a blueprint for perfection of American internal and external state power: "a surveillance state that used its information controls to terrorize Filipinos, intimidate Americans, and deny the U.S. Congress news about the policies implemented in its name."[47]

Intimate surveillance and copious records on (racial) behavior and threat were assisted by science. The reach of the P.C. was essential to conducting the first census in the islands, the data from which was interpreted to distinguish racial types among Filipinos. A similar mandate drove an anthropology lab located in Bilibid prison where they collected photographic images and plaster busts of the "vast diversity of racial 'types'" for analysis and later display at the 1904 Louisiana Purchase Exposition.[48] In another instance, advances in bacteriology spurred an extensive public health apparatus that developed alongside the P.C. and made use of its coercive power.[49] Victor Heiser, who served first as director and then as commissioner of health from 1902 to 1928, declared it an era in which "the microscope supplanted the sword, the martial spirit gave place to the research habit."[50] In truth the microscope and sword worked in tandem and shared a clear racial agenda. According to Heiser, "the Philippines may be considered to-day as a laboratory where an experiment with important bearings on the 'race problem' is being conducted."[51] Warwick Anderson described the obsessive collection of fecal samples. In the year 1909, for example, the Manila Bureau examined over seven thousand fecal samples, almost all from Filipinos.[52] The work "demonstrated" the source of tropical disease lay not, after all, in the racial susceptibility of whites or the climate, but in the Filipinos themselves.[53] Like the financial and behavioral detail collected in P.C. dossiers, this lab data was bureaucratized as racial knowledge and racial difference, and hence authority.

Control of civic space and surveillance of private lives was also bolstered by racialized science. One decade earlier, control was asserted through mass removals and reconcentration camps. Now, this racist interpretation of lab findings squared with the P.C.'s directive for civic development and underwrote an intensive regime of sanitary laws, inspection, and coercion that reconstructed all areas of Filipino life. Heiser claimed "almost military power" to contain an "innately unhygienic" people.[54] Filipino markets were a "foci of infection."[55] An ambitious redesign of civic space and public markets was accompanied by more intimate inspection of the personal hygiene of shop owners, including fingernails. In the same way, sanitary squads were empowered to conduct house-to-house inspections, remove the sick, and isolate those carrying infection. Says Heiser, "We had to invade the rights of homes, commerce and parliaments."[56] A fervor arose for displaying and instituting model privies. Inspection teams could forcibly disinfect persons, their homes, their surroundings—and in some cases entire districts.[57]

Across these decades, then, the P.C. acquired the license and structural capacity to modulate, varying the form and intensity of violence and selecting among techniques that included torture and murder. Armed with this array of regulations and coercive powers, the P.C. by 1908 was breaking political movements from within and containing lower-class dissidence.[58] Rivalries in business could be managed through summary deportation. Selective enforcement of "crime" worked to cultivate or quash political power.[59] Torture and terror served all manner of suppressive political and social functions and helped enforce internal regional, racial, and economic hierarchies. In the Philippines, these capacities were emboldened by the colonial and racialized lens the U.S. applied to daily interactions, permitting great breadth in surveillance targets, in the collection of intimate data, and in levels of violence that would likely have been impossible without a premise of Filipino racial inferiority.[60]

A good share of the P.C.'s racist paradigm, techniques, and personnel transferred to the U.S. mainland and are reflected in the scope and operations of the FBI, the Office of Naval Intelligence, the CIA, and military intelligence units that evolved in the decades to come.[61] The P.C. eventually reorganized under the name Philippine National Police (PNP) and continued as a paramilitary force with political power. The PNP, of course, is the agency that collaborated with the FBI in the torture of Abdul Hakim Murad, discussed in chapter 1. Since the 1990s, the PNP tactical portfolio has continued to include torture as terror (e.g., displaying tortured corpses in public, known in the Philippines as salvaging); manipulating elections; conducting economic and political sabotage; suppressing public demonstrations; suppressing armed separatist movements; eliminating political opponents; funding propaganda; indulging violent vigilante operations and extrajudicial killings; and finally, operating vice or kidnapping syndicates with intentions as varied as reaping profit or seeding chaos.[62]

The PNP has remained a critical arm of executive power and the preferred means to guide Philippine independence for American ends. From the colonial period onward—which is to say, well before, during, and after the atrocities of the Marcos dictatorship (1972–86)—the P.C. and military, for reasons of their own, opened the door, decade by decade, to U.S. aid, advisors, security doctrines, and covert operations, thereby curbing local threats to the U.S. global order posed by communist guerillas, student demonstrators, or Islamic insurgents. Roland Simbulan of the University of the Philippines observes: "Activities in [the CIA's] Manila station have never been limited to information gathering. Information gathering is but a part of an offensive strategy to attack, neutralize and undermine any organization, institution, personality or activity they consider a danger to the stability and power of the United States."[63]

This first section of the chapter has argued that the colonial era spoke plainly on the racial motives of suppressive violence, and to that end forged a flexible alliance among direct coercion via surveillance, terror, and torture, the regulation of space, and seemingly scientific efforts to minutely record and racialize subject populations in the Philippines. This alliance would come also to characterize, even define, the era that embraced national security and counterinsurgency decades later. While colonial methodologies persisted in counterinsurgency and racial terror continued to anchor its logic of domination, the language of counterinsurgency underwent significant transformation. The next section tracks a deliberate revision in the way torture was described. The now-pervasive national security rationale for torture, and the package of ideas surrounding it, was one result.

Counterinsurgency

This section argues that despite its humane rhetoric, counterinsurgency theory was formulated alongside widespread use of torture as terror in warfare. Counterinsurgency adapts the tactics of colonial warfare to colonial governance, conducting both at once, in a way demonstrated by the P.C. Counterinsurgents added a compelling argument on torture that proved transitional, eventually attaching torture, along with companion assumptions, to security in the public imaginary. With the counterinsurgent depiction came an entire sensibility well beyond the ticking time bomb hypothetical. They suggested torture could be made new, minimized, and adapted to the single purpose of interrogation and thereby professionalized. Depending on the forum, they pried it loose from explicit references to race but preserved its racial inflection. The development and circulation of this altered representation of torture is, as with other aspects of counterinsurgency rhetoric, an exercise in humane branding for an era of decolonization. As a result, one could argue torture was a terrible approach to security without severing its connection to the idea of security or these companion assumptions. To demonstrate, three practitioners who effectively shaped popular consciousness as well as policy in the 1950s and 1960s are discussed here. First I consider Roger Trinquier and several of his French colleagues from the war of Algerian independence; second is novelist Jean Lartéguy; and third is the ubiquitous CIA interloper and U.S. advisor in the Philippines, Edward Lansdale. The section concludes with the legacy of their depiction and arguments as they are sustained in twenty-first-century U.S. news and policy statements.

Terror had proved an effective method of suppression and control in colonial wars beyond the Philippines. The Boer war in South Africa, the wars of conquest in the Americas, the anti-Indian wars of expropriation of the northern and westward U.S. frontier, the French conquest of Indochina, modes of British occupation in the restive western and northwestern frontiers of India—all served as models for imperial powers in the late 1940s and 1950s who found their colonial rule challenged.[64] All have been termed counterinsurgencies in retrospect.

Yet the energy exerted to name it counterinsurgency and promote it as a distinct theoretical and tactical formulation in the 1950s is important.[65] Rebranding has since become a commonplace of this form of war.[66] Groundwork was laid in 1952–53 in what the French first dubbed a theory of revolutionary war. Veterans of French Indochina sized up Mao's success in China and reflected on their own failing attempt at suppressing guerilla warfare in Indochina. A variety of officers carried on the conversation in military journals, until by 1956, "revolutionary" or "counter-revolutionary warfare" had become the predominant frame of reference among both French politicians and military men bent on suppressing the Front de libération nationale (FLN) in Algeria.[67] The term "counterinsurgency" gained currency as French, British, and U.S. proponents learned from each other. It had reached public circulation by the early 1960s.[68]

Under this name, counterinsurgents codified a transnational theory of warfare built on colonial tactics. However, they attuned theory and doctrine to an era of humanitarian international diplomacy and the cold war. As the United States, France, and other Western powers committed to suppress rebellions in client territories, they were also deeply engaged in post–World War II dialogues that reconstructed Europe, organized new international bodies, and added instruments to govern warfare.[69] For its part, anticolonial rebellion increasingly adopted the terminology of self-determination. In 1955, delegations from twenty-nine countries, most newly independent, laid bold claim to these international instruments at the watershed Bandung Conference, called to promote Afro-Asian cultural and economic cooperation and to oppose colonial or neocolonial occupation by any nation.[70]

In effect, counterinsurgents at midcentury rescripted their own imperial motivation for maintaining broad control of political leaders, populations, and economies in overseas territories. The theory suggested that Soviet and Chinese influence underwrote "subversive elements" everywhere.[71] "Local" settler populations and amenable natives in regions claimed by Europe now represented fragile outposts of Western civilization vulnerable to communism. A humane quality entered the discourse, emphasizing that these wars were "population-centric." Militaries must shoulder civic development projects as well as weapons to "win hearts and minds," lest local populations throw their support behind the armed resistance. Humane postures, aid, and inducements were backed by punishments—that is, surveillance, terror, and control of basic life needs to ensure loyalty.[72] One twenty-first-century proponent proudly referred to the counterinsurgent's philosophy as "armed social work," saying it encompasses "community organizing, welfare, mediation, domestic assistance, economic support—under conditions of extreme threat requiring armed support."[73]

Along with humane rhetoric and armed social work, enthusiasm for "psychological warfare" was part of the mix. Believers held that anthropologized forms of "crowd science" and cutting-edge psychology could assist control of the local "population" and manipulate or sabotage the enemy.[74] Like other racialized science, it lent authority to superficial understandings of history and culture, as it reduced economic and political struggles to a matter of personality. Depoliticizing the rebellions it sought to suppress, counterinsurgency theory also collapsed distinctions among forms of armed resistance, whether popular or peasant movements, whether moderate or radical, whether for land reform, economic justice, cultural rights, national sovereignty, or more.

This reorganization in discourse at midcentury did not limit the available tools of suppression; it made them stronger. In a similar way, Truman's

1947 national security doctrine and legislation reorganized executive military, diplomatic, and surveillance hierarchies and relationships as the United States altered ideological and rhetorical postures from offense to defense.[75] However, renaming the Department of War as the Department of Defense, for instance, did not curtail any of its offensive capacity; in fact, the structural reorganizations underway created more flexible and expansive powers. The same would be true of counterinsurgency. The very last section of this chapter will discuss the structural expansion and professional networks beneath the humane rhetoric.

There were many dedicated to promoting the theory of counterinsurgency. Among these were a soldier, a novelist, and a spy: Roger Trinquier, Jean Lartéguy, and Edward Lansdale. As writers, public figures, and highly influential conduits, two significantly reimagined torture and its use for public consumption. All remained in sync with old methods of colonial terror and torture while they were at pains to promote the whole undertaking as new.

Trinquier: Specialist in Modern Warfare

French lieutenant colonel Roger Trinquier's writing has been especially influential in U.S. military discourse and popular culture. His methods came to the attention of Americans in 1951 as he successfully implanted paratroopers to cultivate anticommunist guerilla groups deep inside Vietminh territory. Trinquier was invited to visit U.S. antiguerilla training centers in Korea and Japan, and U.S. officers, like Edward Lansdale, traveled to observe French tactics in Indochina.[76] Presidents Truman and Eisenhower followed the struggle in Indochina closely, and by 1953, the United States bore 70 to 80 percent of its cost.[77] When the French fell decisively at Dien Bien Phu in 1954, the armed struggle for independence in Algeria escalated.

Assigned to Algeria in late 1956, Trinquier worked under General Massu, where he served with a tight-knit group of colonels, many of whom had experienced warfare and captivity in Indochina. Among these men were Antoine Argoud, Yves Godard, and Marcel Bigeard.[78] The French applied torture as an engine of terror. A study by sociologist Marnia Lazreg, as discussed in the Introduction, found torture to be unabashed and systemic under multiple commanders in many regions of Algeria. It functioned as performative terror, intimidation, destabilization, exemplary "justice," punishment, reprisal, and entertainment.[79] In a critical year for the war, these men were charged with eliminating terrorists from the town of Algiers and "pacifying" the surrounding region. In 1956–57, they implemented meticulous control of urban and rural space to do so, using surveillance, torture, and terror on a massive scale.

The lessons Trinquier gleaned from Indochina and Algeria became his book *Modern Warfare,* issued in French in 1961. His formulation and rationale for torture are important for two reasons. First, his rendering of French torture in Algeria contrasts starkly and strategically with the historical record. He represented torture as a limited, modern, and necessary tool. Second, his writing was particularly influential in France and the United States, where it found its way into revisions of military doctrine and popular culture alike.[80] Translated into English in 1964 for military training in Vietnam, *Modern Warfare*'s rationale for torture was noted in the U.S. press:

> In a recent book . . . Col. Roger Trinquier describes terrorism as the principal weapon of what he calls modern warfare. It is warfare without uniforms, silent, deadly, stalking: the thrown bomb, the attack in the night. . . . In 1957 French paratroopers . . . eliminated terrorists from the city of Algiers. But they did it with . . . "cold ferocity" and the employment of torture, "the particular bane of the terrorist."[81]

The reviewer identifies two important threads in Trinquier: the new era and torture. He predicts that although the U.S. use of torture in Vietnam is unlikely, "the first American schoolchild killed by a terrorist bomb may challenge this restraint."[82]

Trinquier's writing emphasizes the new epoch and measures progress in weapon technology, which now includes nuclear armaments. He posits a mythic era "lost these many centuries" when physical combat or torture was off-limits:

> The increasing power of weaponry, which places distance between combatants, is also abruptly bringing them together. Once again, they will confront one another on a clearly defined field, and will rediscover the physical contact lost these many centuries. Immense armies will no longer simultaneously invade a vast battlefield. War will be a juxtaposition of a multitude of small actions. Intelligence

and ruse, allied to physical brutality, will succeed the power of blind armament.[83]

As he erases recent colonial histories from view, he preserves the Eurocentric and linear trajectory of civilization and superiority founded on such conquest. His text also removes the explicit reference to the enemy's racial duplicity, inferiority, and suppression so common in European and U.S. rationales and accounts of war before and during World War II. This erasure is part of a larger recalibration in the rhetoric of race in the period.[84]

Despite this, Trinquier's formula tacitly ushers in a primitive. Military men confront a "new enemy," one at odds with modernity, one without honor. This new combatant, "the terrorist," refuses to risk death and face it. He offers a series of parallels to demonstrate. "The aviator knows antiaircraft shells can kill or maim him," and the infantryman faces "the rifle, the shell, or the bomb," but the new enemy hides among a civilian population. This has forced militaries, yet again, to advance their techniques. "If the terrorist tells what he knows very well. If not, specialists must force his secret from him. Then, as a soldier, he must face the suffering, and perhaps the death . . . inherent in his trade and in the methods of warfare that, with full knowledge, his superiors and he himself have chosen."[85] The torture lost to history in this rendering is here reintroduced as the weapon of specialists against a dishonorable foe. It corresponds to other advancing technologies of the battlefield. With each advance from land to air, the battlefield changes too. Detention becomes a battle space in its own right. There the pain and risk of combat occurs face to face.

For Trinquier, torture in custody is not a moral or immoral choice. It is the enemy's due. As he seems to limit the use of torture to interrogation, he offers compelling symmetry: The enemy's atavism must be matched by the specialist's superior skill and intelligence. But torture is not yet after lifesaving, preventive information. The problem is an atavistic foe; the solution is torture.

Anticipating the publication of the English-language version in 1963, Bernard Fall introduced Trinquier to war college students with a terse summary. Fall, a Jewish Austrian who fought in World War II and joined the French resistance at age twelve, highlights Trinquier's parallels:

> When you are in the infantry your bane is the machine gun and the enemy tank. When you are in the air force, you are going to get

shot down by flak or rockets. When you are in the Navy it is going to be torpedoes or a mine. And when you are in revolutionary war, you are going to get tortured. And if you are in the revolutionary war business, you might as well reconcile yourself to it, or quit.[86]

Trinquier's scenario holds a powerful symbolic logic that has stayed with us, as it did with Fall: Traditional weaponry has always given way to new weapons and methods. Now, faced with a new era, older tactics must give way to torture—an advance that requires expertise. Torture is a strategic necessity, a weapon of combat to win war. Trinquier writes: "A problem confronts us: Will we in *modern warfare* make use of all necessary resources to win, as we have always done in the traditional wars of the past and as we at present envisage doing when we construct nuclear weapons?" To force his point, he invokes the French loss to English bows and arrows in 1346. Let no one's notion of honorable combat bar torture; the stakes are existential.[87] "If like the knights of old, our army refused to employ all the weapons of *modern warfare*. . . . We would no longer be defended. Our national independence, the civilization we hold dear, our very freedom would possibly perish."[88] For any disturbed by bloody "combat" in detention, Trinquier offers the comfort of "science": "The interrogators must always strive not to injure the physical and moral integrity of individuals. Science can easily place at the army's disposition the means for obtaining what is sought. But we must not trifle with our responsibilities."[89] He warns against shirking and cites military strategist Carl von Clausewitz: "To introduce into the philosophy of war itself a principle of moderation would be an absurdity."[90]

In keeping with his stress on advancing technologies, Trinquier gestures to a "science" of painless torture used for interrogation. This remains whimsical even today.[91] Although objects of intense study over the 1950s and on, neither Nazi experimentation nor U.S. military and CIA inquiries into drugs, sensory manipulation, or paranormal sensibility yielded avenues to information any more effective than isolation or a beatdown. However, those efforts did capture popular interest and cast an aura of science and scientific competition around work on torture, mind control, and psychological warfare. That aura of science has been retained as folklore in torture discourse. Trinquier's text evoked this lore and circulated it.[92]

In *Modern Warfare,* Trinquier only speaks to torture explicitly in detention. However, he hints at the role terror must play in securing the cooperation of civilians in the streets and villages. It is the barest suggestion of a familiar method: the strict control of space for surveillance, terror, and torture. Because "the inhabitant in his home is the center of the conflict," he has no choice but to "participate in [his] own protection" in the form of constant, mutual surveillance. Tight neighborhood grids and strict block-to-block organization of civilian wardens and informants must form "a vast intelligence network, which ought to be set up, if possible, before the opening of hostilities."[93] Fear binds the population to the military cause: "We may always assure ourselves of their loyalty by placing them within an organization it will be difficult to leave once admitted."[94] Civilians may be treated as the enemy: "Anyone found away from his home at night is suspect and will be arrested and interrogated."[95] He continues: "The people will be manhandled, lined up, interrogated, searched. Day and night." The committed will be "compelled to intern prisoners under improvised, often deplorable conditions."[96]

Modern Warfare was published after the Algerian war was decidedly over. It is Trinquier's justification and manifesto, but not his alone. He had refined his stylized presentation of torture and his argument in the company of many others over the course of his career. Widespread torture in Algeria spurred public outcry in France, and he and other military apologists wrote in that atmosphere. Elements of the picture painted in *Modern Warfare* appear in interviews, journals, and books published by other French officers—men who in fact modeled torture in a variety of ways under commands in Algeria. In 1974, Colonel Antoine Argoud, Trinquier's colleague in the Algiers region and eventual chief of staff to Massu, offers a rationale with the same symmetry of opponents, technology, battle space, and weaponry:

> Torture is an act of violence just like the bullet shot from a gun, the [cannon] shell, the flame-thrower, the bomb, napalm or gas. Where does torture really start, with a blow with the fist, the threat of reprisal, or electricity? Torture is different from other methods in that it is not anonymous. The shell, the bomb, gas are often blind. Torture brings the torturer and his victim face-to-face. The torturer at least has the merit of operating in the open. It is true that with torture the victim is disarmed, but so are the inhabitants of a city being bombed, aren't they?[97]

Like Trinquier, Algeria veteran David Galula exerted influence on U.S. counterinsurgency practice. Galula described his own methods in a 1963

RAND Corporation publication.[98] Galula exhorts warriors to humane treatment and indicts the French press for its "campaign against 'tortures' (in my view 90 percent nonsense and 10 percent truth)."[99] He refers to torture as "police work," an implicit acknowledgment that although coercion in detention is beneath a military man, it is a routine policing practice. Unlike Trinquier, he offers illustrations of what he calls "pressure": men and women forced to stand, several persons bound closely together in wine tanks, or as individuals "kept in a large wine drum open at both ends and laid horizontally on the ground."[100] He takes more time describing the "oven system" he approved: locking a man in a bakery oven covered with soot while threatening to fire it up. "Within 10 minutes Amar was screaming to be let out and he says he's ready to talk now." To test the method, Galula had himself locked in: "It was of course dark and silent as a grave inside, psychologically very impressive but otherwise quite harmless." In describing his oven system, Galula offers logic that parallels Trinquier's rationale.

> I wish to make myself clear to the reader on this score. Insurgency and counterinsurgency are the most vicious kind of warfare because they personally involve every man, military or civilian, on both sides, who happen to be in the theater. No one is allowed to remain neutral and watch the events in a detached way . . . The police work was not to my liking but it was vital therefore I accepted it. My only concerns were (1) that it be kept within decent limits, and (2) that it not produce irreparable damage to my more constructive pacification work. Being an amateur in the field, I wanted to stay in complete control and not be led by still more amateurish subordinates. As for moral twinges, I confess I felt no more guilty than the pilot who bombs a town knowing of the existence of, but not seeing, the women and children below.[101]

Trinquier's *Modern Warfare* neither acknowledges nor justifies the diverse modes and uses of torture common among his fellows in Algeria, including public and exemplary torture, sadistic sexualized group displays of dominance, or beatdowns at the point of capture or in detention yards. The archives of the storied battle in Algiers in 1957 demonstrate pacification of the city was achieved through terror and torture, including a tightly cordoned city quarter, overwhelming military force, coerced informants, mass detention, disappearances, and murder. In the city of Algiers, the percentage of townspeople tortured is staggering.[102] Vast and systematic torture produced terror but not information; the few cases that claim it did are ambiguous and secondhand—they are, in effect, torture anecdotes.[103] This is detailed in arrest and torture warrants, commander memoirs, and soldier testimony. Elsewhere, torture was to assist "the creation in the population of a new mindset favorable to our cause."[104] Many Algerian informants were converted in torture centers. In Algiers, Godard, Trinquier and Léger "turned" an impressive set who would infiltrate the Casbah.[105]

Trinquier's depiction of torture bears no recognizable connection to its actual use. He produced an image and argument for wide consumption. In his depiction, torture in custody was a limited and necessary technology, equivalent to armaments, assisted by science that was wielded by specialists. He makes no claim that lifesaving information will result. His volume was translated widely into Spanish and English.

Lartéguy: Mythographer of Algiers

It was war correspondent, decorated soldier, and novelist Jean Lartéguy, the pseudonym of Jean Pierre Lucien Osty, whose nostalgic fiction of the Algerian struggle, *Les Centurions,* refined the security rationale for broader public consumption and invested it with the power to save the populace.[106] This proved its strongest dramatic formulation. Lartéguy became an influential mythographer of the French paratrooper mind-set; his novel sheds light on Trinquier and other counterinsurgents who were reimagining torture and its security rationale. Lartéguy is also credited with creating the first fictional depiction of the ticking time bomb scenario.[107] There is reason to believe versions of this trope designed to motivate radical experiments on mind control circulated in U.S. Navy intelligence circles in 1951.[108]

The Centurions held immense appeal. It sold over 400,000 copies in France in two years and won praise from both the military and the literary establishment.[109] It was adapted as Hollywood's *Lost Command* in 1966, and it is still recommended for its lessons on counterinsurgency. Among the twenty-first-century promoters is General Stanley McChrystal, commander of the U.S. counterinsurgency effort in Afghanistan during 2009–10. McChrystal studied the book in 1974 at West Point. Of it, he states, "My notes served as a cautionary primer for the challenges I'd later see emerge time and again. The lands, languages, uniforms and personalities were different—but the themes and emotions were constant."[110] Another fan, General David Petraeus, onetime commander of U.S. ground forces in

Iraq and Afghanistan, also praises the lessons in Lartéguy's tale. Petraeus, an admirer of French general Marcel Bigeard, one of the characters fictionalized by Lartéguy, read the book as a young man and pursued a correspondence with Bigeard that lasted until 2010. The real-life Bigeard earned a reputation for murder in detention. The gruesome coinage "Bigeard's shrimp" referred to corpses that collected in the sea near his post.[111]

Lartéguy's *Centurions* reads at times like a novel of manners about class politics in France and at times like a tract on Basque cultural pride, or a satire of the elite aspirations of the French settler-overlords in Algeria. It is also a primer on revolutionary warfare and a preposterously lusty bodice ripper. One reviewer likened the book to the "adventures and torments of seven modern musketeers."[112] A more disparaging review notes, "It is difficult to keep track of who is who and it is impossible to care."[113] Lartéguy's characters are composite portraits, each a blended homage to young French colonels closely involved in the battle of Algiers—Trinquier, Bigeard, Argoud, Godard, and others who, like centurions, kept barbarians from the gates of the "Greco-Latin-Christian civilized world."[114] But more like masterless samurai than musketeers, they lament the end of empire and honor. They wish for a cause—any cause—more worthy than French decadence, the civilization of "the Frigidaire and the bidet."[115] As racial heirs to that civilized world, these characters were humane by nature, but when imprisoned by the Vietminh, they saw revolutionary war and its tactics up close: "Our *bourgeois* conception of honor we left behind us in Indo-China."[116] They must adapt: "I don't like massacres and I don't like torture," said one, but "if we want to win this war we have to shed all sorts of conventions."[117] Terror is required. "The population . . . will veer towards the stronger side, that is to say the one they fear the most."[118]

The ambitious and tireless Colonel Raspeguy, a likely composite of Bigeard, Trinquier, and Argoud, sums up. Modern warfare calls for two armies:

> One for display, with lovely guns, tanks, little soldiers, fanfares, staffs, distinguished and doddering generals and dear little regimental officers . . . an army that would be shown for a modest fee on every fairground in the country.
>
> The other would be the real one, composed entirely of young enthusiasts in camouflage battledress who would not be put on display but from whom . . . all sorts of tricks would be taught. That's the army in which I should like to fight.[119]

One army for display, one for tricks. Lartéguy's heroic commandos are the second army, and torture is a trick learned in Asia, where mindless Asiatic communist "termites" slither in mud, a "hive of sexless insects [that] seemed to operate by remote control . . . a kind of central brain which acted as the collective consciousness."[120]

The blatant racism of Lartéguy's novel clarifies what Trinquier avoids. With noses described as hooked and flat, racial types abound; characters embody the life-force of Africa or celebrate the sexual passions born in war—one in which beautiful Arab terrorists and Vietnamese spies cannot resist rugged French warriors. Brave paratroopers confront the "lawless nationalism of the Arab" and their "looting and rape, in fact everything that endowed this war with its powerful attraction for the primitive creatures."[121]

Lartéguy makes clear the racist logic for torture that Trinquier conveyed with subtlety. The problem of modern warfare is one of dishonorable opponents—that is, racialized others rejecting colonialism, civilization, and capitalism. The modern solution, therefore, is face-to-face torture, bloody reprisals, and executions. After many hundreds of pages, the final chapter treats one climactic night when officers and soldiers must take on the "police work"—the work of torture. Lartéguy portrays three episodes of torture, each perpetrated by a different member of the team. These set pieces lend narrative drive to Trinquier's hypothetical pairing: civilized specialist versus now blatantly primitive opponent. He ups the emotional urgency of torture, locates it in the battle space of interrogation, and grants it the structure of an anecdote.

In the first set piece, the character of Boisfueras operates with cold detachment and uses a field telephone to electrocute the FLN leader and extract a single address. Once torture "works," they murder the subject.[122] In the second set piece, Major Glatigny is distraught. A woman he admired is with the enemy. His interrogation becomes rape that transmutes into shame, but together, they also experience the first real passion either has ever known: "I love you and I hate you . . . you've raped me . . . and I want you to start all over again." Between tumbles, Aicha draws Glatigny maps, one to a drop point for detonators, another to a factory that holds twenty-seven bombs ready to be planted. Torture works.[123]

The final set piece features a divided perpetrator. Esclavier confronts a dentist who has hidden fifteen bombs around Algiers that are set to explode as shops open, at 9:00 AM. Esclavier and his father were subjected to torture by the Gestapo, and he swears to his Arab captive he will not use it. This episode foregrounds a clock on the mantel, and should the reader miss the point, the sequence mentions the clock, the time of day, or ticking seventeen times in nine pages. Ultimately, manly rage moves him to violence. His settler girlfriend calls: her father has been murdered by rebels, the farm set afire. He tortures; torture works. The bombs are located and disarmed, lives are saved, and Esclavier, the broken torturer, leaves the scene to take refuge and breakfast with his lover.[124]

The novel's potent formulation of state torture as a matter of ticking necessity and heroic drama has exerted imaginative force over the structure of entertainment plots and policy debates for decades. Both Trinquier and Larteguy achieve an anecdote-like crystallization of argument in their depictions of torture, and they use the portrait to convey an entire ensemble of ideas about security: a new era, racial dominance, civilizational necessity, interrogation, and professional efficiency. Larteguy takes the standoff between specialist and primitive and fuses it to torture for preventive lifesaving information.

Lansdale: Free World Machiavelli

The national security argument for torture was crafted succinctly by Trinquier and its rationale rendered dramatically by Larteguy. The work of CIA agent and Air Force lieutenant colonel Edward Lansdale in the Philippines and Vietnam played a leading role in translating his French colleagues' practice into an American idiom and ideology.[125] He exuded a U.S. brand of can-do counterinsurgency that continues to characterize its U.S. promoters today.

Like other midcentury counterinsurgents, Lansdale urged humane treatment of civilians by the Philippine military, and at its side, he developed specialized terror teams made up of local people to do the dirty work. As both Trinquier and Larteguy have shown, humane rhetoric is a paradigmatic tool of counterinsurgency, disguising the paternalist racism and violence of terror and torture wielded for U.S. or European ends.[126] Lansdale, for his part, played up terror in his memoir, but he kept torture apart from his public writings. What matters here is that torture and terror were squarely linked in the tool kit of the experts he observed and aligned himself with, and both torture and terror swim around him in the types of anecdotal legend he himself used to promote counterinsurgency.

Historian Max Boot's 2018 *New York Times* bestseller redeems and elevates Lansdale as an "American-style Lawrence of Arabia." In *The Road Not Taken: Edward Lansdale and the American Tragedy in Vietnam*, Boot honors an exemplary humanitarian warrior-prophet who, unheeded, urged "empathy as a powerful tool of U.S. policy."[127] Lansdale's personal mythology lives on in tomes such as this.[128] This is owing to his own flair for propaganda and to his role in some of the most charged undertakings in U.S. history. Lansdale moved from an advertising career in Los Angeles into the Office of Strategic Services during World War II, and in 1948, he was stationed in the Philippines.[129] An agent of the CIA, Lansdale appeared there undercover as an adjunct of the U.S. Agency for International Development. He won notoriety in the 1950s for his work to suppress the Huk rebellion and to install a new Philippine executive.[130] This stint was followed by a similar assignment in Vietnam. He was later tasked to assassinate Fidel Castro and sow chaos in Cuba.[131]

In the Philippines, Lansdale pioneered a distinctive combination of gonzo primitivism, guerilla tactical teams, and a civil infrastructure for propaganda and disinformation.[132] As with Trinquier, Lansdale's expertise required an implicitly primitive opponent. He took an anthropological interest in native psychology and rural folk music, and he was known for his deep friendships with the Filipino men he trained and the political figures he advised, funded, and put in office. These friendships may have been genuine, but Lansdale's personal appeal cannot be separated from the paternalism and ample U.S. financing that he represented. Moreover, both Lansdale and his assistant, Colonel Charles Bohannan, were steeped in racialized, colonialist retentions, heirs to the anthropology of race practiced in the Philippines' Bilibid prison in the early 1900s.[133]

Like Trinquier, Lansdale believed the complexity of modern warfare demanded new approaches, a tool kit he referred to as psywar. For Lansdale, psywar meant small groups of elite warriors with the license to influence everything—elections, battles, public health. His methods did not shy from mutilation, murder, the display of bodies, economic sabotage, and other forms of violence and disruption designed to anchor terror. In particular, he liked to exploit what he believed to be "native superstitions." He prized macabre episodes, which he termed "practical jokes" and described as "low humor."[134] As the next examples show, the jokes he describes are difficult to separate from exhibitionist sadism. They strongly suggest one measure of success in his mind was the pleasure an operation inspired in the covert team.

Historian Jonathan Nashel recounts one episode meant to impress teams with the importance of torture. Coming upon Filipino soldiers who had severed the head of a Huk captive, Lansdale took the head and questioned it with shouts and slaps "until the soldiers thought he had lost his mind."[135] As this moment illustrates, Lansdale knew well that psychological warfare was a performance for three distinct audiences: first, the local Filipinos or Huk guerillas they battle; second, his team of operatives, who absorb the object lesson or perpetrate the "practical joke"; and third, the wider audience and network he would build: politicians, intelligence operatives, and military personnel who hear the tale, make policy, and direct the funding.

In all this, Lansdale was himself a master of the uncorroborated anecdote.[136] In one case, Lansdale's team generated rumors of a vampire and then captured and killed a man by draining blood through a puncture wound in the neck. They displayed the corpse for his Huk comrades to find. By Lansdale's account, when the Huks found the body, superstitious horror immediately dispersed the enemy from that region. In another, Lansdale recounted a midnight graffiti operation to paint images of a single glowering eyeball on doors in a Huk village; this quickly became known as the Eye of God campaign. Although he offered the only account of its impact on "natives," this anecdotal success was elevated as a model at the renowned 1962 RAND Corporation symposium on counterinsurgency as a way of "defeating an enemy 'on the cheap.'"[137] After rigging a Philippine election through massive disinformation and terror, his CIA after-action report records his advice to Filipinos: "We passed them information on the techniques of sabotage and 'accidental' murder: 'kill a few and you don't have to kill thousands.'"[138]

In the telling, Filipinos were always terrified in a specifically primal way, hoodwinked by even the most unlikely tactics. In these accounts, Lansdale frankly failed to credit Filipinos with extensive experience in American-inspired terror and racism; nor did he grant them rational responses. It is hard to imagine the Filipinos would believe an assault on their ranks was the work of a vampire, for instance, not a U.S.-sponsored assassin. After all, Filipinos had used precisely this kind of deception against the United States since the century began.[139]

Nonetheless, Lansdale's personal anecdotes entered spy lore and military manuals, affecting the next generations of cold war warriors and counter-insurgents. Exploits in terror were excerpted from his memoir and included as instructional material in 1976 Army Pamphlet 525-7-1 and other army training manuals.[140] Lansdale approved. He hoped for the day a school for politics would train "skilled free world leadership" with "a good political textbook . . . a sort of U.S. version of *The Prince*."[141] Lansdale no doubt considered himself a free world Machiavelli, one who coached Filipinos on murder in democratic elections.

These figures—Trinquier, Lartéguy, and Lansdale—bear comparison. Lansdale's writing, like that of novelist Lartéguy, magnifies men with nerve and cunning who save the world, but Lansdale indulges no melancholy over the collapse of French rule. In its place, Lansdale projects enthusiasm for an empire on the rise and a firm belief in imposing "freedoms" in the form of U.S.-directed political and economic dependence. He combined ideological certainty and grandiose self-concept with a developmental racism. Nashel writes that while he was "outraged" by the political corruption and the gross economic inequalities Lansdale saw in the Philippines, the economic roots of the Huk struggle eluded him.[142] As is characteristic of the counterinsurgency model and practitioners like Trinquier and Lartéguy, Lansdale depoliticized his opponents' struggle and failed to see the U.S. hand in that plight.[143]

To this point, this section has argued the emerging national security view of torture was a composite, one freighted with a set of ideas. Torture was ostensibly race-free, but it was clearly inflected with racial and imperial supremacy, driven by intelligence, and a matter of expertise. Trinquier was forthright about torture while fraudulent in its depiction. He remained mute on its mass use. Lartéguy clarified the race supremacy that separates Europeans' purportedly reluctant use of terror and torture from that of Asians and Arabs. As a novelist, he dramatized what we now know as the security rationale for torture in a compelling way. Lansdale offers no explicit rationale for any of it, demonstrating instead that murder and torture have their rightful place in this warfare as tools of terror deployed by an elite few.

Wielding the National Security Rationale Today

The national security rationale and the depiction of torture that developed in Trinquier, Lartéguy, Lansdale, and others across the 1950s and 1960s has gained ground since and saturated the public conversation on torture today. The newness of the war and the enemy, and therefore putatively new approaches to interrogation, have become as timeworn as any part of this discourse. It recurs in news, policy statement, legal opinion, military reports, and memoirs.

Over the years, journalism has channeled the melodrama and intrigue of war correspondent and novelist Lartéguy. During the U.S. counterinsurgency in Vietnam, William Tuohy provided a "war is hell" template that still characterizes twenty-first-century war reporting. Chapter 6 will highlight its role in accounting for U.S. torture in Iraq. In 1965, Tuohy's *New York Times* piece presents torture and the ensemble of ideas it attaches to national security first and foremost. Headlined "'War Is Hell and, by God, This Is One of the Prime Examples'; A Big 'Dirty Little War,'" it leads with what is "new," quoting a U.S. soldier: "This is not so much a dirty war as a different war." Next, General Maxwell Taylor, ambassador in Saigon, remarks, "This whole war is a matter of intelligence." Tuohy continues: "Intelligence, or more simply information, is a vital commodity. . . . It explains much of the terror and torture inflicted by both sides."

> South Vietnamese troops have behaved brutally too. Anyone who has spent much time has seen the heads of prisoners held under water and bayonet blades pressed against their throats. . . . victims have had bamboo slivers run under their fingernails or wires from a field telephone connected to arms, nipples or testicles. Another rumored technique is known as "the long step." The idea is to take several prisoners up in a helicopter and toss one out in order to loosen the tongues of the others.[144]

Tuohy tells the reader U.S. soldiers are repelled by the approach: "No soldier in the world has been more loath to adopt the bloody tactics of revolutionary warfare than the average senior U.S. officer." He repeats this often: "Few American military advisers would sanction such brutality." But U.S. soldiers show enthusiasm:

> Assassination teams are "sanitation" squads who take pride in their work. "I'm a great believer in getting the guys responsible for the war," says an American who has been trained to clean up. . . . "I believe in bribing guards to assassinate their officers, buying them off, working through their relatives, putting prices on their heads, sowing suspicion in every way. . . . Too many think our job is only to kill Cong," he notes, "but ultimately it is to convert them."[145]

Tuohy describes "revolutionary warfare tacticians" who, like Larteguy's heroes, are committed to their "art": "This specialist is one of the handful of Americans in Vietnam practicing the arcane (some call it 'black') art of revolutionary warfare." The language of black ops, black arts, and black warriors runs through the piece, suggesting a modern hero with a medieval allure, someone engaged in "loosening tongues" and "working through their family."

Tuohy ushers in Trinquier's formula: civilized specialist plus implicitly primitive double. Although Tuohy explicitly states that a "war for intelligence" was the root of the torture, in war reporting especially, the latent primitive provides a gateway for contradictory but time-honored colonial rationales for torture. Soldiers and journalist blend the national security rationale seamlessly with older colonial excuses:

> **Vietnamese culture.** "Assassination is what the peasant understands."
> **Torture and terror mirror the opponent's primitive savagery.** "Vietnamese on both sides hold primitive animistic beliefs . . . responsible for macabre brutality." "It is a war fought by Asian standards." "They have no concern for human life."[146]
> **Torture educates.** A "U.S. specialist" explains: "One act will be understood by 95 percent of the villagers concerned."[147]

Tuohy's short piece achieves the woeful ambivalence and ultimate inevitability that Larteguy developed over hundreds of pages: "The gospel as taught at Fort Benning is often inappropriate in the villages of Asia."

Policy makers wield the national security rationale a bit differently than journalists. The enemy is tacitly primitive. The Bush administration rhetoric in 2001–2 defined al-Qaeda and the Taliban as a new enemy made up of bearded zealots without uniforms, driven by premodern goals, organized by tribes, and living in the caves of Afghanistan. Lead White House counsel Alberto R. Gonzalez formulated a legal statement accordingly using the exact terms of the security rationale:

> The war against terrorism is a new kind of war. It is not the traditional clash between nations adhering to the laws of war. . . . The nature of the new war places a high premium on other factors, such as the ability to quickly obtain information from captured terrorists and their sponsors in order to avoid further atrocities against

American civilians, and the need to try terrorists for war crimes such as wantonly killing civilians. In my judgment, this new paradigm renders obsolete Geneva's strict limitations on questioning of enemy prisoners.[148]

New enemies and a new kind of war require new methods of gathering lifesaving preventive information. Gonzalez's opinion arrived as U.S. detention in Guantánamo prepared for its first arrivals.

Military interrogator Chris Mackey and his team loaded captives onto that first plane to Guantánamo on January 10, 2002. Stationed in Kandahar, Afghanistan, forty years after Trinquier, Mackey echoes his melodramatic detention face-off and its import:

> This is a story about the war in the shadows, of battles the public never sees. Most of the time, they take place inside a dusty tent or a dank cell, furnished with little more than a table and a couple of chairs. There are no bullets flying or bombs dropping. They are battles of psychology and intellect, of will instead of weaponry.... They are dramatic . . . because of the threat we face.... Success depends on discovering the enemy's intentions before it is too late. And in this new war, the most crucial weapon in the American arsenal may be the ability of a relative handful of "soldier spies" to get enemy prisoners to talk.[149]

Mackey's team innovated and excused an extended sleep deprivation program, a variation on the relay interrogation and "sweating" torture that produced confessions for Soviet show trials and known to U.S. policing in the 1920s as "the third degree."[150] His team called it monstering.

Two years and a series of homicides in detention later, the Department of the Army Inspector General contended with torture's aftermath. A 2004 report took a system-wide review of U.S. military detention centers and 125 cases, citing ninety-eight confirmed incidents of "murder, assault, wrongful death, and abuse" across Afghanistan, Iraq, and Guantánamo Bay. "The Army is in a new and unique operational environment stemming from the need for immediate tactical level intelligence coupled with the significant numbers of non-traditional combatants/detainees encountered."[151] New war, new enemy, new approach. The report found no systematic cause for homicides, concluding that the enemy had created a "new battlespace" and these incidents were the result.

The non-linear nature of the battlespace and missions dependent on human intelligence made administrative processing a secondary priority to intelligence exploitation of detainees. This had additional second- and third-order effects on accountability, security, and reporting requirements for detainees. Detaining individuals primarily for intelligence collection or because of their potential security threat, though necessary, presented units with situations not addressed by current policy and doctrine.[152]

Torture and murder in custody were inadvertent second- and third-order by-products of a new kind of war.

Without a doubt, in tangible ways, armed conflicts are unique.[153] However, to invoke the newness of an enemy or of war for intelligence has become schtick, and one that rationalizes terror. The formula invokes epic complexities and ascendant resolve, all of which require that the rules on torture be bent. Torture as intelligence, torture as security, continues—tacitly or manifestly—to align the targets with barbarity (or disorder or crime), the better to justify the colonial status of a people and region and, as an additional benefit, to showcase the counterinsurgent's advancement.

Torture and the Entrepreneurial Way of Peace and War

Elizabeth Gilbert's work dubs counterinsurgency the "entrepreneurial way of war."[154] However, counterinsurgency also functions as a form of governance at home, a way of doing what we call peace. This third and final section of the chapter makes explicit the intimate relationship of torture and counterinsurgency. Next it takes up the twentieth-century professional networks formed around torture and terror in peacetime and war. Both steps help us center state torture, the developing security imaginary that supports it, and its community-building work into the twenty-first century.

Torture and Counterinsurgency

Across the twentieth century and into the present, U.S. counterinsurgency has been consistently attended by torture and profiteering—a seeming contradiction, considering its population-centered, humane rhetoric and the development programs it promotes. That contradiction leads the public and even its own practitioners to believe the presence of torture to be merely incidental, a bug that can be eliminated with a technical fix. Other observers and critics note the correlation of torture and counterinsurgency but have found the operational relationship between the two either difficult or unnecessary to articulate.[155] It is important to articulate.

Torture is an engine of terror, not intelligence, and it serves a variety of other social functions. Counterinsurgency combines colonial warfare and colonial governance, rebranding itself for eras when colonial relationships and military occupations are not in vogue. The last century and this one have seen it institutionalized as governance (in the United States and elsewhere), in military alliances, and in war.[156] Its goal is to anticipate and suppress resistance with force. In so doing, typically, it generates the resistance it fears. Its method therefore is to economize on the most explicit violence using "armed social science"—that is, the armed management of populations through terror and social inducements. Both are administered through the control of space and access to life needs. As David Galula articulates bluntly, to generate more fear in the population than one's opponent is to ensure widespread cooperation.[157] Torture is exemplary and integral to this framework; it is the consort of terror, the essential terror multiplier.

Since the 1950s, the securitization of the U.S. has been manifested through very different institutions and organizational histories and cultures. Taking counterinsurgency in war and peace as an example, and at the risk of oversimplifying the larger, more complicated bureaucratic effusion that is national security, I will foreground some themes to challenge the understanding of torture as security that emerged with it. These themes open each paragraph below. In this telling, and moving from the mid-twentieth century to the twenty-first, I take torture from this story's margins to the center. This is not to suggest state torture is an abstract actor in its own right, or the most significant or heinous human undertaking at work. It is not. Instead, this is to counter the sense that torture is incidental, a bit player, a second- or third-order by-product in a story with otherwise moderate or respectable intentions.

Evolution and Infrastructure in the Delivery of Violence

Lansdale was by no means the sole or most important player in these developments, but he serves as a convenient marker of the growing operational networks and communities that assembled around the promotion of terror and torture over the second half of the twentieth century. Across three decades of U.S. cold war intervention around the world, Lansdale was witness to rapid institutional and budgetary growth in the national security apparatus and in the global reach of its mind-set. In the midst of competing players, philosophies, and agendas, Lansdale helps shed light on two shifts in the structural evolution of U.S. violence practice that might otherwise seem abstractly bureaucratic affairs, even at times inevitable. In contrast, the human energy that worked to assemble these professional communities marks these developments in national security as intentional, handcrafted, and, importantly therefore, open to change.

In the case of the first structural shift underway, Lansdale's work modeled a kind of compartmentalized strategy for the delivery of terror that became characteristic of future U.S. counterinsurgency efforts at home and abroad. In the neocolonial Philippines, Lansdale's counterinsurgency involved the Filipino military in humane civic action and conventional combat engagements, while Lansdale, and advisors like him, funded and built teams of local commandos that did not shrink from infiltration and assassination in the enemy's camp. For U.S. audiences, the arrangement put a Filipino face to all the decision-making and terror, no matter the battle space, be it detention, guerilla action, or elections. In this, Lansdale's work is a clear endorsement of Lartéguy's two armies working in collaboration, one for display and one for tricks. But Lansdale now represented a third, an army of first world military advisors and funders: U.S. advisors, unconventional commandos, and conventional military. This chain promoted the appearance that U.S. action was at root humane and detached and that torture and terror were things incidental, even originating overseas, and in no way integral to counterinsurgency. This kind of compartmentalized network for violence went on to underwrite the collaboration of the United States and the Philippines in funding, equipment, and operational planning for years to come. Historian Alfred McCoy describes the Filipino attitude to this compartmentalized violence work: "Since the 1950s, American analysts have usually separated overt aid, developmental and military, from covert operations, ignoring or minimizing the CIA's role in the conduct of U.S. foreign policy. From a Filipino perspective, these two aspects appear fused in a unitary application of American power."[158] This compartmentalized construction creates deniability for U.S. audiences and funders but also illustrates the next point: extended professional networks become necessary to state torture.

This, then, is the second structural shift. Lansdale, and others, brought promotional verve to build global networks that would support counterinsurgency, and consequently torture and terror. The last half of the twentieth century saw a host of opportunities and incentives to professionalize, brand, and market torture and terror. These help us think about the evolution of the national security imaginary.

Enthusiasm for counterinsurgency brought together a global constellation of state and corporate funders as well as an array of military and intelligence personnel with practical experience fighting rebellions in Palestine, Ireland, Burma, Algeria, the Philippines, and more. The coordination of efforts, loose at first, drew resources and created institutes that sponsored and convened such activity, such as the RAND Corporation.[159] Lansdale's personality and skill in public relations "made him a natural pole of attraction for the counterinsurgency dignitaries of allied nations."[160] McClintock observes that "congressmen, journalists and publishers concerned with the United States' posture in the Cold War" met with Lansdale. He proved a vital clearinghouse and point of transfer across this network, traveling widely, distilling lessons, swapping tales and information on tactics. Lansdale channeled practitioners and true believers to publisher Frederick Praeger, who produced "a virtual counterinsurgency library within a few years."[161] The influential 1964 English translation of Trinquier's *Modern Warfare* was among these.

Lansdale's work building the U.S.–Philippines relationship served as a model strategy for U.S. geopolitics. By 1954, as the Huk rebellion was stifled: "U.S. forces had girded the globe with seven mutual-defense treaties, 33 military aid agreements and 300 overseas military bases backed by 2.5 million troops."[162] But sensitive to the anti-imperialist dynamism of the time, U.S. foreign policy was trading in its old military terminology. A humanitarian tenor was preferred, and the notion of global policing was elevated. For example, in 1961, as President John F. Kennedy initiated the diplomatic and developmental mission of the Peace Corps, he also formed a high-level task force called the President's Special Group on Counterinsurgency. He named Lansdale a member.[163] This group created the OPS, the Office of Public Safety. Funding came under the humanitarian mantle of the State Department's Agency for International Development but control was placed with the CIA.

Keeping the Peace

As Vietnam ensured a protracted military engagement with counterinsurgency, the OPS elevated alliances with "civil police" and "police-type organizations." According to one National Security Agency memo, the latter were to "include paramilitary forces . . . [who] have as a primary mission the maintenance of internal security."[164] New efforts sought to convey a civilian character, embracing "internal security"—a euphemism for suppressing dissent—and "technical services," a bureaucratic, neutral-sounding way to say equipment and training in methods of violence.[165] Together, the OPS, the CIA, and the military created exportable advisory teams, manuals, and curricula for police training in the Philippines and other parts of Asia and Latin America. The United States founded training institutes for foreign officers inside the United States and Panama.[166] Robert Komer, early recruit to the CIA, National Security Council staff member, and eventual engineer of the notorious counterinsurgency action Operation Phoenix in Vietnam, argued, "The police program is even more important than Special Forces in our global C-I effort." It also posed as a more cost-effective and civilian-type embodiment of counterinsurgency.[167]

The OPS is a good example of how surveillance, torture, and terror became fused with security in both concept and practice. The P.C. had expanded these tactics for suppression and governance in the colonial era. Trinquier's lessons from Algeria endorsed this coercive trio, specifying that surveillance grids and numerous informants were best set up "before the opening of hostilities."[168] Allied police-type forces would now be able to do just that. To populations in the United States and abroad, support for policing in allied nations was promoted as humanitarian and professionalizing. Security was said to be safety, policing, and protective. In practice, these relationships were deemed a critical countermeasure against "subversives" and political instruments for U.S. military and CIA concerns.[169] Internal CIA documents described these as "American programs to create and exploit foreign police forces, international security services, counterterror squads overseas."[170] Historians have been clear that through this global apparatus, "U.S. officials, OPS and CIA associated with security forces who tortured and terrorized" Latin American societies.[171] The CIA was also clear. Course and training materials specifically addressed "training regarding use of sodium pentothal compound in interrogation, abduction of adversary family members . . . prioritization of adversary personalities for abduction, exile, physical beatings and execution." Mail-order materials advised readers on "executions, beating, abduction of families, bounties, truth serum, execution."[172] Congressional investigations of the 1970s and 1980s made conclusive links between torture training by the CIA and Latin American perpetrators. A later Clinton-era Intelligence Oversight Board affirmed that the training manuals, syllabi, and methodologies from 1960 to 1991 had been "inappropriate."[173] Disturbed by OPS activity, Congress formally disbanded it in 1974, but its activities were continued through the State Department's Drug Enforcement Agency and elsewhere.[174]

Meanwhile, in the United States, the fervor for counterinsurgency, and thereby surveillance, torture, and terror, had already returned to its roots in homeland racial terror. As a century of U.S. involvement in the Philippines illustrates so well, the U.S. international and domestic experience fed each other and evolved together. The global networks building counterinsurgency and developing the OPS, even many of the same personnel, spawned a domestic counterpart. The Law Enforcement Assistance Administration (LEAA) was the financial hub created by a larger crime control bill in 1968, part of the federal response to the high-profile antiwar and antiracist urban rebellions of the mid-1960s. This became one important financial motor driving the U.S. corrections and incarceration boom of the second half of the twentieth century, with devastating impacts on racially marginalized Americans.[175] In ideology and design, the LEAA built on the OPS experience and transferred the spirit and tactics of counterinsurgency toward the category of crime. Eight billion federal dollars flowed into U.S. state and local policing from 1968 to 1982.[176]

All this activity must be considered from a market standpoint. The creation of operational networks for violence was fully joined to the enterprise of assembling and circulating expertise around violence. Conferences, task forces, and reports were vital to the manufacture of "technical expertise." Of the term "technical," Seigel writes it multiplied around these policing relationships to convey specialized knowledge—a proven way to ward off critics.[177] Expertise then translated into political and financial support. Giving expertise a tangible form—events, manuals, courses, programs, credentials—legitimated the enterprise, authorized experimentation, and marshaled prestige.

Prestige returns us to a market perspective, where the security imagination animates the material infrastructure, and vice versa. All these endeavors established new markets with their own sets of rules, a phenomenon that emerged around torture, policing, and counterinsurgency in this period and that has grown to what scholars call "the markets for force."[178] This market has been found to be self-perpetuating; it is constantly producing new experts, new kinds of threats, and new equipment. The ever-increasing supply drives a perceived need for protection.[179]

Expansion of the security market and the security imagination are intertwined; they feed each other. The sensibility surrounding torture expertise in that security imagination provides an excellent example. Across the 1960s and 1970s, the United States did not, as some have argued, become an expert on torture or a "universal distributor" of a specialist style of modern, scientific, or psychological methods. But it could establish schools and market itself that way, both within the United States and abroad.[180] Between 1962 and 1974, the OPS "provided $337 million in training, equipment, and advisors to Third World police."[181] Alongside that investment, the United States traded on the false notion that special techniques in torture and terror existed and could be taught (and therefore mastered and controlled). We see the same notion percolating in Roger Trinquier's suggestion that "science can easily place at the army's disposition the means for obtaining" intelligence by force.[182] This relation of security imaginary to security market was realized as well across 2002 to 2009, as the CIA invested heavily in two psychologists and the illusion of expertise they brought to enhanced interrogation techniques in the war on terror, a subject touched on in the epilogue.[183]

The rise of professional violence expertise internationally bound the networks for equipment and training to those in research, experimentation, and publishing. But these torture networks failed to render violent strategies more humane, scientific, or "effective." It monetized them. The false aura surrounding such knowledge and tactics was commodified for export and branded France or the United Kingdom, Mossad, KGB or CIA, military special forces, or U.S. Office of Public Safety. The aura enhanced these organizational brands; policing relationships became a flexible currency through which the United States attempted to purchase cold war allegiance throughout Southeast Asia and Latin America. They allowed the United States to access developing markets and align with governments, stabilizing both for investment.

The symbiosis between security market and security imagination also points up a variety of social functions that torture serves. Government contracts stimulated industries in purportedly professional equipment for torture, terror, crowd control, and surveillance. These industries and transnational ties multiplied career paths for researchers, contractors, and consultants. However, the local roots and social functions of torture and violence never disappeared. Allies and client states have always known how to manipulate U.S. security relationships to their own ends.[184] Paramilitary forces respond to the internal politics, goals, and vendettas of their own ruling elites—that is, until those forces choose to usurp the role of ruling elite entirely. The founding of new teaching institutions, courses, and diplomas all offered local military and paramilitary alumni practitioners elevated status. When special training is limited to a few, it creates by intention an elite team with a reputation for rare knowledge and skills—and license to do what others cannot.

Making War

Ever-expanding civilian markets for "keeping the peace" through surveillance, torture, and terror in the United States and elsewhere have a counterpart in state and corporate mobilization for full-scale war. This dimension includes sizable mobilization of U.S. public, military units, private security firms, trainers, and equipment to support police or militaries of the target country. The entrepreneurial way of war has kept remarkable faith with colonial methods of terror. Three colonial-to-counterinsurgency continuities introduced in the first half of this chapter appear clearly in the twenty-first-century counterinsurgencies in Afghanistan and Iraq: first, an ongoing commitment to the role of surveillance, torture, and terror; second, domination through the elaborate control of space; and third, an appropriation of scientific authority to racialize, intimidate, and stratify.[185]

Surveillance, torture, and terror. Structurally, the colonial P.C. developed this work along with its civic development efforts under a centralized agency. Midcentury counterinsurgents, however, met armed resistance with more clearly demarcated roles for local paramilitary special forces, commandos, or police versus the standing military. Contemporary engagements continue this partitioned strategy for the delivery of violence. The results project an imaginary divide between the host nation's institutions and personnel and the United States' funding, military, and advisors. In peace or war, the compartmentalized strategy hides culpability in torture and terror. During war in Iraq, for example, military regulations prohibited U.S. personnel from participating in torture, but they also prohibited them from stopping torture by the Iraqi commandos who patrolled by their side, as I discuss in chapter 6. The United States depended on at least 100,000 mercenaries in Iraq who were subject to still different guidelines.[186] Detentions and torture continued to target enormous numbers, not just exemplary terrorists.

Control of space. As in the colonial era, later twentieth- and twenty-first-century applications of counterinsurgency strategically transform civic, economic, and residential space in the name of security. The United States, local governments, and the military still collaborate to divide and reorganize rural zones as well as urban areas, and they construct a variety of camps and prisons for mass detention.[187] In this way, the quest for information lends an apparent purpose to cycles of terror that become ends in themselves. Rolling raids, indiscriminate mass searches, assaults, arrests, injuries, or wrongful deaths in and out of custody—these are modes of violence that map and lock down a space and its inhabitants, establishing surveillance, gatekeeper checkpoints, and rules of movement.[188] Control of space enforces multiple lines of dominance to divide populations. Some people are homogenized as the population that can be won through economic incentives and fear (intimidated, humiliated, and pacified); others are designated enemies or collaborators and are detained, degraded, killed, and tortured by the tens of thousands.[189] Through control of space, access to basic life needs can be stratified and controlled.

Racialized, militarized science. Where colonial enterprise in the Philippines once aligned itself with bacteriology, anthropology, and sanitation, and where midcentury counterinsurgency embraced a Lansdale-style psychological warfare fueled by racism, recent versions continue the colonial obsession with intimate data collection. New technology, the prestige of scholarship, and the language or techniques of scientific fields help classify, stratify, and dominate populations. For example, the military effort to map and control urban and rural space was renamed in 2008 as human terrain mapping. Human terrain teams embedded anthropologists in Afghanistan and Iraq to develop "ethnographic intelligence."[190] This incarnation quietly dissolved in 2015, but the accretion of intimate microknowledge continued (e.g., biometrics, heat signatures) to design, detect, and multiply "cultural" and kinship divisions, select human targets, and reorganize civic space.[191] Racialized knowledge has legitimized forms of pain and suffering in the battle space of detention.[192]

The hearts-and-minds, whole-of-government, or nation-building approach that U.S. counterinsurgents embrace continues to function under humanitarian rhetoric and often explicitly in the name of democracy and freedom. However, the outcomes have more surely won freedom for international corporate investment, reproduced U.S. models for business, and undermined fragile local institutions by routing judicial consequences, cash flows, contract approvals, and accounting around those same local institutions. The results have made regions dependent on long-term economic support as well as on terms for security, training, and investment set by the United States.[193]

Philippine Harms

A record of torture outcomes for the Philippines and the United States offers a coda appropriate to this chapter, one that once again dispels any belief in a security vision of torture. Alfred McCoy writes that as a home for institutionalized torture, the Philippines was particularly lethal, with the number of torture survivors and dead in the 1970s surpassing those of Latin American torture regimes of the same era.[194] The Philippines also demonstrate the corrosive effects of institutionalized torture, corruption, and excessive force. As happened in France and Brazil, torture in the Philippines became a destabilizing element within the Philippine police as well its army. In the post-Marcos Philippines, democracy struggled against these same security forces for a solid footing, facing more coup attempts in the 1980s than any country in the world. In 1986 alone, Corazon Aquino's government survived five coups led by a set of rebel colonels who sustained an underground resistance until 1992.[195] In that year, the government offered a structured reconciliation: the Philippine Constabulary fused with regular police units to form the Philippine National Police, and an amnesty deal for right-wing military torturers, death squads, and PNP quelled the coups. As Amnesty International documented, that deal also allowed the rise of perpetrators in the police and surveillance structures.[196] In 1997, the year after the Philippine National Police invented a portfolio of evidence and false testimony for a U.S. court and cooperated with the FBI to prepare Abdul Hakim Murad's confession by torture, human rights monitors reported that Philippine police actions accounted for 1,074 of the human rights violations. Only eighty-one were attributed to the Armed Forces.[197] Murder of hundreds of "drug personalities," kill lists, and capture for ransom were common methods of police operation under the Philippine war on drugs, which was at its height in 2016–18.[198] Torture and abduction have remained tools of suppression since, and the 2022 election of Marcos's son, Ferdinand "Bongbong" Marcos Jr., to the presidency had academics and activists anticipating a return to his father's brutal methods.[199]

• • •

Torture as security, which is to say torture as expert interrogation, is itself a product of the last century. Whether for it or against it, scholars and the public easily associate torture with the need for intelligence, and thanks to Trinquier's portrayal and those like it, we imagine torture as a creature of interrogation. Thanks to Lartéguy and those like him, we see it as an excess in the urgent quest for lifesaving intelligence. We take comfort when official statements reject torture and urge humane treatment. Sincere or not, they are obligatory. We fail to focus on the mass use and daily social, economic, and organizational functions of torture.

This security imagining of torture strikes a deep a chord. Like any compulsive behavior or ritual learned to dispel fear, torture as security has its high priests and true believers, even its anecdotal miracles. Chapter 1 of this volume argued that such anecdotes do not bear up under scrutiny. This chapter has tracked a handful of dubious portrayals, which were concocted by the torturers themselves to distort its mass use. They reimagined torture in a way now central to the national imagination. Their portrayals too were packaged in anecdotes and passed down as lore.

Like all social imaginaries, the national security imagination is made of deeply sedimented layers. Imaginaries develop through transitional arguments that erupt in key moments and reject some available ideas while elevating others; Trinquier, Lartéguy, and Lansdale represent such arguments. As Meili Steele puts it, "transitional arguments urge us to shift the way we understand packages of ideas, images and principles . . . [The arguments] are not necessarily historically accurate or without considerable ideological baggage."[200] Across the 1950s and 1960s, this imagining of torture began to radiate a field of explanation that reinterpreted but did not limit the pervasive use of torture as terror. It eventually accomplished an imaginative shift of Copernican proportion. It placed interrogation at the dramatic center of a coercive universe around which all forms of state torture then seemed to revolve. In due course, it has developed such gravitational pull that it draws into its explanatory orbit every other state incident of gratuitous group-based violence against unarmed persons. Although the discourse bends our attention to the individual, the practice ensures individuals are violated en masse. Information is said to be the root of torture, not terror and not social functions or social control. Yet within the United States, fundamentally and profoundly, torture has been an integral form of race making, social stratification, and community control.

3

Archetype

Mistaking the Plurals of Torture

In 2001, Ehab Elmaghraby was a New York restaurant owner and Muslim immigrant who had lived in the United States for thirteen years. He was apprehended, along with hundreds of Muslim and Arab immigrants, in the days after September 11, 2001, and held in the Metropolitan Detention Center in Brooklyn, New York. Jailed until 2003, he was among many who were charged only with financial crimes unrelated to terrorism and finally deported. Upon release, Elmaghraby and fellow inmate Javaid Iqbal filed suit against the U.S. government. Among other things, they charged they were subjected to kicking and punching until they bled and "multiple unnecessary body-cavity searches, including one in which correction officers inserted a flashlight into [Elmaghraby's] rectum, making him bleed."[1] Theirs was not an isolated case. A Department of Justice review later denounced assaults at the Brooklyn facility during that period, many of them caught on videotape. The Department Inspector General's 2003 report on the detention center found "widespread abuse of noncitizen detainees." On February 28, 2006, the *New York Times* announced that the U.S. government agreed to pay $300,000 to settle with Elmaghraby.

Rape in detention, which the *New York Times* described in Elmaghraby's case as an "unnecessary body cavity search," qualifies as torture. Torture, according to United Nations convention, involves acts by persons who, as agents of the state or with the acquiescence or at the instigation of the state, inflict severe pain or suffering, whether physical or mental, on persons in custody. Rape is a routine form of torture, and historically, a search is a common alibi for rape.[2] Yet although a rape in a New York detention center by corrections officers falls well within the definition of state torture, the location, perpetrators, and act itself place it in a universe of similar violations that the United States is accustomed to recognize as police brutality or abuse rather than torture. This chapter hopes to show the preference in wording is more than euphemism or careful language crafted to evade prosecution—although of course it is both of these. The choice is also indicative of the ways many in the United States imagine torture—what they have come to believe torture is and is not.

That belief affects the meaning of the experience for those who survive and those who die, the social reckoning they face, and their reintegration—if permitted—into communities of those who have not shared that experience. Public understandings of torture affect activism as well as any future for survivors' medical, moral, emotional, or legal claims. Public distinctions within the United States between police brutality and torture also affect witnesses, survivors, and participants in violence, including women and men in corrections, at home, or at war. Determinations like these also affect funding decisions concerning torture treatment.[3] Does the public share a common understanding of torture? What are the implications of such a claim?

Writing in the context of a consuming media debate on torture, Marcy Strauss, a Loyola Law School professor, ultimately relies on just such a conclusion to derive her working definition in "Torture," a 2004 article in the *New York Law School Law Review*.[4] She notes that the media rarely define "torture," and what is more, no decision in U.S. case law offers an "all-encompassing definition": "at best the courts make passing reference to police behavior *as* 'torture' or *like* a 'rack and screw.'" Strauss says, "It's as though we all have the same working definition or conception of torture in mind. Do we?"

The answer, of course, might depend on the meaning of "we." It is unlikely that bystanders, perpetrators, and subjects of such treatment hold the same "working definition" of torture in mind. This chapter outlines the archetypal representation of torture circulating widely in speculative news and legal argument with attention to "the quintessential picture of torture" that emerges, to use Strauss's terms.[5] That representation is pervasive. Examples are drawn from the speculative press from 2001 to 2005, as well as from earlier activist campaigns and much later academic arguments on torture.[6] Chapter 2 located the contemporary roots of that archetype in the mid-twentieth century and the effort of counterinsurgent propagandists to popularize a rationale for torture that narrowed the conception of its violence to serve their own ends. The features of that archetype that persist have implications not only for policy and debate but also for the kind of community torture describes and divides.

The first section of this chapter looks at writing both for and against the use of torture. Lines of argument, anecdotes, and imagery return to the scene of a high-stakes opposition between two opponents: interrogator and subject. They have made that scene iconic, archetypal. The archetype pervades public conversation and, as we will see, even complex arguments condemning torture.

The chapter's second section contrasts that archetype to the practice of violence described at scenes of torture in military, detainee, and human rights reports of the same period, investigative reporting from the U.S. wars in Iraq and Afghanistan, and the homeland torture experienced by Ehab Elmaghraby—and many, many more. The contrast will draw attention to three key arguments.

First, the one-on-one symmetry, existential stakes, and setting in the archetypal view of torture serve to undermine recognition and identification of torture, past and present. For instance, Elmaghraby's torture, although it meets the U.N. definition, falls outside the circle defined by this archetypal instance. This iconic depiction of torture is also far afield from, say, the violence photographed at Abu Ghraib prison in Iraq and published in 2004, or the circumstances alleged in the cases of the ninety-eight men known to have died while in U.S. custody between 2002 and 2006 in Iraq or Afghanistan. At least forty-five of these died in U.S. custody as a result of suspected or confirmed criminal homicides. Yet the iconic scenario continues to be mobilized routinely in news and other writing.[7]

Second, the prevalence of the archetype works to anchor our conception of torture, and therefore our debate, to interrogation, and hence to a national security rationale and to the premises that cohere around that rationale. The odd mirroring that occurs in arguments against torture is a piece of this. Even to reject torture, these arguments confirm the dualistic archetype, address the national security rationale of interrogation, and often simply repeat and reverse its premises, leaving those premises intact. The rationale sticks even when details show security hardly seemed to be at stake, as was the case with just one example: the anecdotal telling and retelling of the torture of Abdul Hakim Murad from 2001 to 2005, described in chapter 1. This fixation on interrogation comes with political and cultural consequences for torture prevention. As will be taken up in chapter 4, it also distorts our perception of intelligence gathering and its real challenges.

The third and final argument of this section holds that repeated resort to the dualistic archetype removes people from the scene who are necessary for a proper reckoning with the practice. Repopulating the scene with a layered hive of players can enable us to reconnect the public imagination with the historical continuities in U.S. torture and the specifics of its powerful everyday role in liberal states. Their plural presence highlights two dimensions of torture that otherwise escape the scene and inquiry: organizational setting and social function.

In all these ways, the archetype not only cuts off discussion of the social and communal functions of torture; it not only binds our conception and debate to interrogation; but it also works to disconnect torture from its role in community formation and misogynist racial terror. As argued in the introduction, U.S. torture emerges from at least three mutually supporting branches: its use as terror in massacre, lynching, and internal racial repression; its use in colonial and neocolonial expansion, cold war client states, and counterinsurgency; and its use in raids, policing contexts, and prisons.

The third and final section of the chapter considers unseating an archetype that so captivates the public imagination. Press speculation embracing the archetype launched only six days after September 11. No new doctrine, or legal memos, executive orders, or Defense Department protocols were necessary to suggest the archetype, and no orders were required to initiate torture that utterly departed from that mold. Elmaghraby and others who suffered from "widespread abuse of noncitizen detainees" were among the first to understand that however the public chose to imagine it, torture would build on old routines of racialized domination, detention, deportation, and suppression. Restoring historical and institutional context to the scene of torture is not enough. Instead, we need to alter what we see and what we ask when torture is our subject.

A Quintessential Picture of Torture

The prologue to this volume identified the wave of speculative news and media commentary debating torture's desirability and practicality that came immediately after terror strikes in September 2001. What received the most attention there was the Hypothetical group of speculations—those features and stories that used imagined scenarios to pose the "should we or shouldn't we?" question to members of the public or to so-called specialists. Such stories elicited comment on a ticking time bomb scenario, or they discussed results of opinion surveys or student quizzes on torture.[8] But the speculative writing then began to appear in additional types worth discussing: Historical and Heart of Darkness narratives. The Historical group ponders torture through two primary models, both of which reference campaigns against Muslim populations: France's use of torture against Algerians and Israel's use of torture against Palestinians.[9]

The third group of news speculation, Heart of Darkness, draws core elements from both Hypothetical and Historical stories, fusing them into a larger colonialist narrative. Here, a lone journalist sets forth to explore the practice and practitioners of torture. He exudes a calculated moral ambivalence and exhibits a powerful fascination with the torturer and his "dark arts," "hard questions," and "unthinkable choices."[10] In tone, and often in first-person ruminations, these stories borrow from late nineteenth-century colonial travel writing, a form exploited brilliantly in Joseph Conrad's 1901 classic by the same name.[11] In journalism, the Heart of Darkness form and its approach to torture is descended more directly from writers like war correspondent and novelist Jean Lartéguy, whose novels made melodrama of the security rationale to justify the mass torture wielded by French paratroopers in Algeria. Chapter 2 discussed the mark Lartéguy has left on War Is Hell–style reporting from Vietnam, Afghanistan, and Iraq.

Whether Hypothetical, Historical, or Heart of Darkness, these speculative news features and commentaries on torture have several common features, and they influenced and reflected qualities found in the legal and ethical scholarship appearing in the same period and after. For instance, all do the cultural and political work of imagining and projecting a unified community that dutifully considers its moral stake in torture. The Historical and Heart of Darkness forms also promote certain views of history—for instance, weighing the utility of torture by conflating quite distinct land-based occupations and anticolonial struggles, typically in Palestine and Algeria, with al-Qaeda and its twenty-first-century strain of Islamist terrorist franchise. Like the media speculation, the academic arguments refer to the U.S. history on torture selectively, if at all. They also strike narrative postures that promote the reader's identification with the would-be torturers or with the protected citizenry, but not with those subjected to torture.

The critical focus here is the reliance on a simple and pernicious staging of torture they all share. The explicit features of this scene will be immediately familiar, as if they were representational prerequisites that in themselves define torture. The setting is an interrogation, a one-on-one encounter between the subject of questioning and a skilled, goal-oriented professional who inflicts calculated amounts of pain. The pain inflicted is managed by a technique that has a definite beginning and a specific duration, and the pain is produced in a controlled and incremental fashion (that is, one neither murders the subject outright nor begins with the most extreme pain). At times this archetypal staging leads the writer to pursue the techniques in detail: which were authorized, which were out of bounds, which are torture, which are so-called torture lite, and so on. This preoccupation will be discussed further in the next chapter (chapter 4). But it is the one-on-one encounter at close quarters in detention, this symmetrical pairing and opposition, that bears the most significance here. That pairing will seem an obvious inheritance from the counterinsurgency proponents Trinquier and Larteguy we just discussed in chapter 2, whose imaginative rendering depicted torture as a limited, modern, and specialist mode of interrogation, and therefore uncontaminated by race.

Once this one-on-one scene has been invoked, torture has been named, even looked in the face, and we know what it's made of, as in Jonathan Alter's 2001 piece "Time to Think about Torture" or Peter Maass's 2003 "Torture Tough or Lite: If a Terror Suspect Won't Talk, Should He Be Made To?"[12] The scene is so common, so iconic, that one element can imply another: the subject in "the fetid basement cell" and the technique or injury—"the teeth extracted," "limbs broken"—can together invoke the torturer and his demands. In a Historical piece such as Bruce Hoffman's "A Nasty Business" or a Heart of Darkness feature such as Mark Bowden's "The Dark Art of Interrogation," the struggle between potential torturer and subject is Manichean in tone and drives the structure of the report.[13] The language lyricizes the torturer's dire world of urgency and ethical quandary or the subject's world of pain and isolation, or both.

The dual agonists of the iconic scenario obviously are underscored by the graphics that accompany these articles. The articles by Hoffman and Bowden, for instance, and most of the longer features carry sidebar illustrations that suggest a single perpetrator—a long shadow leaning in through a cell door—or a single subject dangling from shackled wrists, or a man blindfolded and strapped to a chair beneath a bare light bulb, and the like. At times, the news writing may use the example of a single subject who is being implicitly worked over by many perpetrators, whom the story renders as a larger entity: "the Philippine police" or "Jordan." Not only is a team personified as a single entity, but the group nature of the event may be underplayed or erased through passive voice construction that accents the technique, not the technicians: "teeth pulled," "limbs broken," and so on.

The Archetype in Antitorture Scholarship

Many of the legal arguments as well as the speculative news debating torture in the wake of 9/11 defined torture implicitly through this archetypal interplay between interrogator and subject, torturer and victim. Indeed, the ticking time bomb scenario, so prevalent in torture debate articles responding to legal commentary or arguments by Alan Dershowitz, Sanford Levinson, Richard Posner, and the like, simply recombines features of the archetype, making artful enhancements to the motives of the key figures and the circumstances in which they meet.[14] The archetype and the time bomb, however, are not identical. While the time bomb scenario recasts the archetype in order to justify torture, even those who reject torture and do so absolutely often portray torture in the iconic mold, imagining the same duo locked in the same elemental battle. The key difference is they cast their lot with the subject.

Early examples of this in the modern campaign to end torture are instructive. For instance, Amnesty International's groundbreaking 1973 campaign to abolish torture opened its appeal to the public with selections from a Turkish survivor's testimony, which closely followed this formula: an isolated subject, a torturer, an array of graphic techniques. Amnesty International reassessed its representational strategy a decade later, incorporating an empowered spectator acting to prevent torture, but the point here is the power and recurrence of the archetypal representation of torture.[15]

Scholar Elaine Scarry produced a widely read treatise on the practice of torture and the symbolic language of pain in 1985.[16] *The Body in Pain* looked beyond the rhetoric of Amnesty International's opening appeals to draw on the full complexity of their documentation from 1975 to 1980 of torture in Greece, South Vietnam, Brazil, and the Philippines. Scarry's work is a literary and philosophical meditation on pain and injury that is based on these reports and other sources. On the one hand, her profound contribution was to expose interrogation as alibi and performance. On the other hand, Scarry argues "the basic structure of torture" is the iconic scenario described above. Her analysis keeps torture structurally bound to the charade of interrogation and to the archetypal depiction. Torture is "essentially a two-person event . . . premised on one-directional injuring."[17] To better delineate its features, she lifts the players out of historical and cultural space and time: "Torture has a structure that is as narrow and consistent as its geographical incidence is widespread." She explains that structure and event transmute the infliction of physical pain into "the insignia of the regime," a display of state power.[18] For Scarry, questioning with violence is a ritualized drama meant not to elicit answers but to reduce the subject's voice to silence or to an echo of the interrogator's own. Defining torture, therefore, through this archetypal exchange between torturer and subject, Scarry concludes that torture is an extreme limit, the "condensed case," the "absolute model" of destruction, more exemplary of total destruction than war. By eliminating the subject's ability to speak at will, torture destroys language, the self, and the social world. Torture reverses the process of creative labor. It is civilization deliberately unmade.

She had her critics at the time, but Scarry has been widely influential, and she was cited in one of the most provocative and thorough legal rebuttals to the post-9/11, 2001–5 time bomb debate.[19] In an essay published in the *Virginia Law Review* in December 2005, David Luban persuasively unravels the time bomb scenario as a "jejune" cheat, an "intellectual fraud."[20] His piece offers historical range on attitudes toward cruelty in liberal democracy; he urges us to look away from the mesmerizing ticking time bomb and toward the "torture lawyers of Washington" and the legal apparatus they have attempted to establish for state torture. His essay points to torture as a practice that would require social networks to sustain it, but ironically, his understanding of torture keeps pulling him back to the narrow archetypal dyad. Why is torture more repugnant than killing or war? Luban's response: "The answer lies in the relationship between torturer and victim." He explains with a stress on the twoness of torture:

> Torture aims, in other words, to strip away from its victim all the qualities of human dignity that liberalism prizes. It does this by the deliberate actions of a torturer, who inflicts pain one-on-one, up close and personal, in order to break the spirit of the victim—in other words, to tyrannize and dominate the victim. The relationship between them becomes a perverse parody of friendship and intimacy: intimacy transformed into its inverse image, where the torturer focuses on the victim's body with the intensity of a lover, except that every bit of that focus is bent to causing pain and tyrannizing the victim's spirit. At bottom all torture is rape, and all rape is tyranny.[21]

Luban says, "Torture is a microcosm (raised to the highest level of intensity) of the tyrannical political relationships that liberalism hates the most."[22] In 2014, Luban repeats this claim for torture, "the greatest human evil."[23]

Philosopher David Sussman, too, defines torture in its elemental duality and diabolical intimacy in a 2005 issue of the *Case Western Journal of International Law*. "For torture to occur," the antagonists must be "standing in a particular kind of relationship with one another and understand that the other understands this as well."[24] In a 2018 essay, Sussman grounds this claim further, pinpointing what is "morally special" about torture: "torture is a paradigm instance of" the fundamentally personal, I–thou relation that "Thomas Nagel called 'dirty fighting.'" Among torture's "special features" is the aim it takes at the enemy's "vulnerabilities and concerns . . . as a human being," the very humanity he shares with the torturer.[25] This perverse relationship, Sussman writes, is a "living death," a kind of "anti-life," a "natural slavery."[26] For Sussman, torture inverts, again and at the highest level of intensity, the very principle of human dignity in social relations.

For Scarry, then, torture is the inverse of civilization, human labor, and creation, and for Sussman and Luban, torture is the inverse of human dignity or the liberal democratic social bond. For New York University law professor Jeremy Waldron, torture is the inverse of law itself. In a *Columbia Law Review* article printed in October 2005, in the midst of the speculative debate, Waldron argues that torture and its prohibition play an "archetypal function" within law—what he also describes as a "background function." Torture is an image and exemplum, persistently embodying and communicating a vital standard. It is a form of brutal violation so fundamental that its prohibition is the basis of all legal prohibitions; it "expresses and epitomizes the spirit of the entire legal enterprise." The prohibition is "vividly emblematic of our determination to sever the link between law and brutality, between law and terror, and the enterprise of breaking a person's will."[27] As do Scarry and Luban, Waldron chooses examples that stress an interrogational setting as the place of torture, and his language emphasizes the visual character and power of this legal archetype: the prohibition on torture "sums up or makes vivid to us" the point or purpose of law.

Scarry, Luban, Sussman, and Waldron animate the quintessential picture, the iconic instance, so visible in the speculative press debate, pro and con. Their work reduces torture to this "basic structure," paradigm, or model, the better to enlarge it as a theory of pain and civilization, liberal democracy, or law. Although they know better, to warn against it and to bring the warning home, they lift the practice out of its historical, social, and institutional complexity and continuities. What is more, these essays and the speculative news across 2001 to 2005 installed an image of torture as a threshold the United States had yet to cross, for there is a before and an after to torture—what Jeremy Waldron terms the "gateway by which the demonic and depraved enter into public life."[28] For liberal democracy, permission to torture is a fall from moral coherence; it is a plunge into the unknown.

For his part, historian of human rights Samuel Moyn knows there is something wrong here. In a 2007 review, he blasted Lynn Hunt's *Inventing Human Rights* and its audience "for whom torture—and other visible state action—is the most grievous affront to morality." The "exclusive concern with spectacular wrongs like torture," he writes, "will seem less praiseworthy for anyone who suspects that the focus on visible forms of cruelty obscures structural wrongs that are less easy to see—even when they sometimes also cause the body to suffer, as with the pangs of hunger or the exhaustion of work."[29] The contrast he draws between "spectacular" and structural wrongs is curious. He echoes this concern some time later, reviewing a handful of works on torture appearing between 2007 and 2013 alongside five varied works by Scarry. Moyn reaches back to Scarry to fault her apolitical yet influential treatment of torture, and to set her work in a larger cold war, 1970s era that oversaw "the emergence of the attitude that torture is a singular abomination and banning it our highest task." Behind this "shift in our contemporary moral consciousness," he writes, must lurk "a deeper reason why torture has become a signature evil like no other."

> It may seem cynical to imply that it was this retreat from the violence of imperial rule that suddenly made torture beyond the pale for Westerners, especially if others were perpetrating it. But there is no other way to make sense of the timing of the norm's global emergence . . . The truth seems to be that torture acquired its insidious glamour as the worst thing *they* can do—once Western violence was done, and the places it had shaped for so long now looked like scenes of indigenous misrule.

He betrays annoyance, as he will again in an exchange in *Dissent* in 2015: "We have read about torture, and Guantánamo, and torture again, glowing with outrage at every turn." The left's outrage at torture, he suggests, is a sign of the general fatigue with chronic problems such as inequality or endless war, which they seem to have accepted as intractable. Civil libertarians can busy themselves cleaning "wars of their outrageous excesses—as if those excesses were the main problem."[30]

"Stopping torture should be our first step, not our only hope," he writes. "At the very least, no one has figured out how to broaden the prohibition against the suffering caused by torture to include the suffering caused by a global inequality of wealth and power," the argument he will make at length in 2018 with *Not Enough*. "Indeed, in some respects," he writes, "we have achieved consensus denouncing the one only by averting our gaze from the other."[31]

Moyn may be put out specifically by the representation of torture here, although he does not quite say as much. He understandably regrets that Scarry extracted it from political systems, but he does not unpack torture as the ongoing, daily Western process it is—in solitary confinement, policing, security alliances, or immigrant detention. Nor does he see it as an anchor of racial capitalism and neoliberal imperialism, and therefore a motor of the very economic inequalities he contrasts with torture and calls on activists to address. Although Moyn chides the likes of Scarry, Hunt, and Richard Rorty for elevating torture as especially egregious, he too remains trapped by the archetype, juxtaposing torture as he does to sweeping deprivations engineered against large populations. That we can conceive of state torture as spectacular rather than mundane is a problem. That we repeatedly cast it as a duel between individuals, which Moyn does not, or as an ultimate, threshold violation demonstrates the spell cast by the archetype and the national security imagination we have inherited. When we elevate torture as a primary instance of something . . . say, of what liberalism gets right (Luban, Sussman, Waldron) or of what liberalism has gotten decidedly wrong (Moyn), perhaps the problem is with the way we see torture—or rather, the way the archetype keeps blocking our view. We fail to see torture as essential to today's racial-colonial tool kit and as a chronic structural issue. What is perhaps worse, when we do see it as endemic, we see it as an excess that can be defined or regulated away.

Challenging the Archetype

All of these authors—journalists, academics, and jurists—mobilize an image of torture that is already a stylized image of interrogation, a one-on-one encounter, an archetype that was presented repeatedly to the public in speculative news commentary since 2001. It was a depiction popularized long before. What is fascinating is how far afield this iconic depiction is from actual interrogation, let alone torture. Even noncoercive questioning is not a one-on-one encounter. Nor is torture itself secluded, a single identifiable incident, or a one-on-one practice. These environments are densely populated.

The Plurals of Torture

Military investigations, military memoirs, detainee statements, and reporting details in the first years after 9/11 emerged more rapidly after the scandal provoked by torture photos at Abu Ghraib in 2004. These routinely indicate multiple persons at the scene of physical and psychological violence in custody. This is the case when group violence closely approximates recreation: the High Five Paintball Club of Camp Nama, in Baghdad, used prisoners for target practice.[32] Soldiers at Forward Operating Base Mercury in Iraq lined up to strike prisoners' knees and shins with a baseball bat and also assembled human pyramids as at Abu Ghraib.[33] Groups of guards at the detention center in Bagram Airbase in Afghanistan used severely painful and eventually fatal kneeing in the thigh because they were amused to hear the prisoner's cries of "Allah!" with each strike.[34]

These are straightforwardly group undertakings, as is sexual assault. Masquerading as a security measure, sexualized violence and harassment are persistent features of detention. Such was the case with Elmaghraby's flashlight torture, which opened this chapter.[35] This form of rape follows a pattern of anal "searches" reported by detainees freed from Guantánamo and confirmed by military personnel. They are described as unnecessary because they are performed on men who had been under guard, hands shackled far from the anus between searches.[36] Interrogator Chris Mackey writes that at Kandahar, Afghanistan, new detainees were brought through what they called the "abbatoir," a pin-down area that "was like a theater in miniature" where off-duty military police (MPs) gathered for nightly "diversion." Onlookers, he says, "couldn't help but sing or hum" the theme from the television reality show *COPS*, "Bad boys, bad boys, / Watcha gonna do?" Three men managed each captive, and to the shout of "Ass inspection!" in Arabic, bent them over and pinned them with a knee in the neck and another in the back. Anal searches were a group production that was meant to threaten rape, elicit screams, humiliate the individual, and intimidate the other group.[37]

Much of the other daily work at Kandahar and Bagram was conducted by MPs who functioned in pairs and teams while escorting, "controlling," caging, feeding, attending, and supervising prisoners' bathing and bathroom trips or depriving them of same. The daily attentions of MPs can be unpredictable, violent, and humiliating. Released detainees detail weeks and days of interminable "softening-up" activities or the violent and degrading contact surrounding daily needs.[38] Some detainees released from Guantánamo have described actual questioning as a period of respite from the mental and physical violence of "care" in detention.[39]

When torture poses as interrogation, it too is a group event. At Baghdad airport, several U.S. Navy SEALs and CIA officers were said to have interrogated homicide victim Manadel al-Jamadi in the so-called Romper Room "in a rough manner." When transferred to Abu Ghraib, two MPs, CIA officer Mark Swanner, and a translator worked together to lift and steady the battered prisoner into a "Palestinian hanging" position, in which he died.[40] Indeed, the shackling, overhead or otherwise, as well as forced standing and sleep deprivation, not to mention waterboarding or beatings, all require teamwork: to restrain, lift, position, or return the prisoner to consciousness.

These reports challenge the common archetype for torture in powerful ways. Isolating a technique, a moment, or a basic structure that constitutes torture is difficult here; neither captives nor captors are isolated. These accounts exist because spectators are present. In the face of these unmistakably plural settings, it can only seem strange that so many speculative news features as well as legal and philosophical arguments for and against torture, when reaching for what is elemental in this violence, scrub from the scene all onlookers, fellow participants, and other captives, leaving in place only the dyad of torturer and tortured.

Consequences

Taking all this together, there are important ramifications to the persistence of the archetype, its twoness, its interrogational setting, and its seeming position at the threshold of something exceptional, ultimate, or new. First, the sheer prevalence of that archetype animates and enlivens a "quintessential picture of torture," as Marcy Strauss saw it—a picture that binds torture to interrogation and encodes the security rationale for torture with that very gesture. As a result, violence well within the bounds of the U.N. definition that occurs in other settings and varieties can escape recognition, further study, or reflection. As Erik Saar writes of Guantánamo: "I didn't personally see anything that I would label torture as most people understand the word."[41]

Second, despite all evidence to the contrary, the dyad and the presumptive interrogation that frames it join the archetype to the national security rationale. That rationale travels with premises that set the terms of debate. Too often opposing claims simply mirror each other, confirm aspects of the archetype, and go no further. For instance, the repetition of the archetype promotes a dubious understanding of a purported end that torture serves, one to which it either is or is not an effective means.

Third, state torture cannot be rightly assessed or addressed until we repopulate that quintessential picture—that is, until we understand torture differently and thereby reflect less on the dimensions of torture we often foreground (the techniques of injuring, the rationale) and more on the dimensions we do not: the organizational setting and the social functions. Simply reintroducing other players opens torture to both these different paths of analysis and political action by posing alternative problems and questions.

Peopling the scene. The people present who carry the heaviest emotional, political, and material burdens are the subjects targeted for torture, and these are many. Subjects are not simply or only "isolated in their pain," as Scarry and Luban put it, although isolation may be a psychic or physical technique for provoking pain.[42] Over 150 persons have been identified as subjects of torture by the Chicago police department over two decades; Afghanistan's Kandahar and Bagram processed hundreds, as did Guantánamo; dozens were raped and injured at New York's Metropolitan Detention Center alongside Ehab Elmaghraby, and such assaults are systemic in U.S. prisons; injury at Abu Ghraib extended well beyond what was photographed and beyond a single cellblock; and over two thousand photographic records of abuse taken at over two dozen U.S.-run facilities in Afghanistan, Iraq, and Guantánamo have been the subject of ACLU freedom of information requests since early 2004.[43] If it is hard to imagine that torture happens by the hundreds rather than the handful, surely our imagination is to blame.

Moreover, the people subjected to torture in the accounts noted here were assaulted together or forced to hear or witness the terror and humiliation of others. To reorient our thinking toward torture as a communal assault on hundreds and thousands, groups and aggregates, obviously lays bare a broader range of social functions and insists we attend to the enduring relation among torture and racism, misogyny, religious persecution, and other subjugations. This is social function in a macro sense, yet these predations are also always local. In each context and setting, those who torture make their language and abuses resonate with local lives and meanings, targeting and degrading precisely those aspects of socialization that give subjects value, faith, connection, status, and identity among their kin. These are attacks on the "social body" of persons—enacting or marking out ethnic, linguistic, class-based, sexualized, gendered degradation and domination. Such attacks project terror that erodes allegiances and attacks "the entire social network that has given rise to trust and solidarity among people," writes psychiatrist and survivor Carlos Alberto Arestivo.[44] Humans target groups and types for torture. Torture broadcasts terror, discredits individuals, and divides families. It can stratify and organize the social order, spatially, economically, and legally.

Organizational setting. Once we consider the subjects of torture, we must consider the organizational setting in which they are held and how it reveals additional layers of human activity. It may be clear that a dyadic view of torture does not make a chain of command basic to that structure, although torture certainly is embedded in bureaucratic and professional hierarchies, as well as organizational dynamics, procedures, incentives, and routines. These certainly include formal and informal social arrangements designed to train and condition violence workers, such as those described in the study of Brazilian torturers by Martha Huggins et al., or first-person accounts of torture in Fallujah or Baghdad or Mosul.[45] Details of supervision and requirements for liability establish routines to monitor, time, and record daily life and work. Former army chaplain James Yee remarks that soldiers at Guantánamo talked circumspectly about the semiclandestine total surveillance environment, referring to the "secret squirrels" who could be watching and listening to a soldier's every move.[46]

Interagency, interpersonal relationships. More intimate than electronic surveillance is the host of peers, colleagues, and supervisors involved at close range. As soldiers and intelligence officers observe prisoners, they also observe each other. Interrogator Mackey, writing later about his time at Bagram, describes the populated detention camp as a setting organized by rank, clear division of labor, peer rivalries, and complex sets of mixed agendas. Accounts by interrogators and military reports on abuse at Abu Ghraib by Major General Antonio M. Taguba, Major General George R. Fay, and Lieutenant General Anthony R. Jones all point to the mystique, envy, and admiration with which the workers at U.S. bases watched the CIA or Special Operations personnel who moved among them. At Camp Nama, Special Ops personnel took care to watch their watchers, monitoring the email and phone communications of their CIA or FBI colleagues.[47] Workers are hyperaware of their own specialized task—scheduling, questioning, translating, writing reports, editing, and transmitting—but they also are acutely aware of negotiating roles among a hierarchy of players, including military or civilian police and multiple contractors, service branches, and intelligence services. There is much more at play than chain of command. Exceptional work by Danielle Celermajer on security organizations in Sri Lanka and Nepal argues that torture prevention must account for layered interagency contexts where even the expectations and routines of seemingly external organizations (e.g., provincial or national governance, or funding organizations) play a role in the worlds that produce torture.[48]

Material infrastructure. Collaborative environments of any sort are also structured by a material and procedural infrastructure—rooms, floor plans, reports, time sheets, duty assignments, shift changes, and a variety of written and unwritten policies, prohibitions, expectations, and loopholes, along with requirements and customs that mediate interactions, consume time, and frame choices. Orlando Tizon, Laurence Ralph, John Conroy, and Flint Taylor illuminate the role of material and procedural circumstances in the persistence of torture.[49]

Community building. What remains to be said here, and that which the archetypal instance also holds from view, is that not only do humans torture humans in the presence of others, but also such violence produces a powerful communal dynamic in a context marked by complicated interpersonal dynamics.[50] What is clear from the studies by Huggins et al., Conroy, participant memoirs, investigative accounts, and survivor testimony is that captors are attuned to their impact on detainees and each other. Consider the close physical presence of coworkers, the camaraderie and energy of people together, responding to, performing for, and competing with one another, the real physical intimacy, eroticism, and ambivalence forged among spectators and perpetrators of sexual, psychological, and physical violence. The symmetrical battle of wills and "perverse parody of friendship and intimacy" described in the antitorture scholarship must be revised in this light. Mackey's memoir and others show violence is a social and multilevel process. For perpetrators and spectators, it is a means to facilitate bonds, alleviate boredom, assert status, and construct professional identities and sexual personae; align with the aura of Special Forces; and demonstrate things like professional skill, stamina, and patriotism. Chaplain James Yee describes the group rituals of the Initial Reaction Force (IRF) at Guantánamo: initial huddles, chanting, and "pumping up" before an attack on a "resistant" detainee and the adrenalized high fives and chest-to-chest body slams afterward. One company swapped attack counts at shift changes.[51] What is more, the process of coordinating violence and suffering conscripts those subjected to torture and those who watch into multiple roles: debased beings, accomplices in terror, targets for retaliation. Ervin Staub has argued that violence evolves and escalates precisely through group processes of this kind.[52] As we look beyond the immediate setting and participants and follow the compartmentalized professional networks that support torture, these relations of social posturing, mutual influence, impact, animosity, risk, and even dependency form around the violence of torture even for those at a remove, such as different cohorts of coworkers: lawyers penning permissive definitions in their memos, psychologists crafting codes of ethics, and so on. (See chapter 4 and the Epilogue.)

Networks. The groups and aggregates subjected to torture—the organizational, interagency, and interpersonal setting; the bureaucratic, procedural, and material infrastructure; the communal and community-building work of torture—comprise social features that challenge our understanding of torture in ways that require new metaphors and a shift in imagination. I use the word "networks" to characterize these interlocking communities and chains of collaboration and material conditions that, wittingly or not, come together to coordinate and sustain torture in such a multisystem, populated, professional, and procedural environment. Salaries, paperwork, goods, and people, not to mention meaning, connect and flow along these networks and comprise them. State torture occurs within organizations that are also workplaces, or places where people do their work.

Repopulating the scene, enlarging the situational context, presents torture in a way that challenges the archetype and its exceptional status. Just as state torture destroys a social network of trust and solidarity among its target populations, it forms communities and networks among others. The fact that the Abu Ghraib torture photos were taken to enhance the experience of the perpetrators—that cameras implied spectators and anticipated reminiscence; that torture became an occasion for heightening performative interaction with each other and with the subjects—was as profoundly disturbing to some viewers as the brutalities depicted. For many viewers, this did not resemble the iconic scene of torture. While many recognized it and named it torture, neither the scandal over the photographs nor the discussion revealed the archetype for what it was or wrested us away from its repetition. It is telling that when the crowded cell block of Abu Ghraib or other scenes of torture have been memorialized visually to signify torture on book jackets and elsewhere, it has been through the silhouette of a single hooded man, not the group silhouette of human backs, buttocks, and genitals exposed in a human pyramid or a masturbation circle of captives and captors. That the Abu Ghraib tortures were community building and dividing events—enacting, drawing, or securing lines of racial, gender, and religious division through interpersonal bonds and forms of sexual and religious violence—was captured in some of the writing in 2004.[53] However, this insight was fleeting; it made little dent in the "emblematic" case, as Waldron might say. The skill with which torture targets particular marginalized groups for ethnic, racial, sexual, and/or religious terror goes unspoken, lost in the author's effort to find in torture something universally human, universally ugly. The dyadic view of torture as a trespass on law and individual dignity was not remade in order to accommodate an understanding of torture as a community-building rite of domination in the local or aggregate case—one endemic to prisons, or one that, like prisons themselves, has a critical place in securing racial hierarchy and colonial dominance.[54]

Fearful Symmetry

Many physicians and researchers have already worked diligently to highlight the institutional ties and situational context in which torture occurs.[55] So why has the archetypal scene found such a consistent and ready place in our imagining of torture? Why does it recur in a field so broad as to include journalism, memoir, academic essay, legal writing, and punditry? Certainly in part it is because it builds on older meanings. A dyadic view of existence or conflict is a habit of mind with many debts, some ancient and not all Western. But the dualism rooted in Western philosophy and elevated by way of Hegel, Marx, colonial rhetoric, and even important anticolonial rhetoric expressed by writers like Fanon saturated the Anglo-European sphere of the nineteenth and twentieth centuries in powerful ways. It attached to the nature of human consciousness itself, to economic and national development, to political power, slavery, and suffering.[56] What leads even those who know better back to the archetype may be, in part, disciplinary training: academic course readers on torture routinely base themselves in disciplines—law, philosophy, psychology—committed to a paradigm of relational, contractual, and individual exchange. These collections by and large continue to be caught up in the one-on-one interrogation fantasy.[57]

However, this symmetry of force was certainly not the way torture as a public sentence or in racial domination or rampant colonial warfare was conducted or understood. Soldier-propagandists like Trinquier knew that intimately. His powerful depiction of torture as one-on-one interrogation leveraged these older dyadic traditions of thought and artfully fused them to a justification. He encoded the subject as a dishonorable, premodern, racial type.

Perhaps Trinquier understood that ultimately the attraction to the torture archetype derives not only from habit but its utility as misdirection. Consider two examples. First, in the archetypal depiction, the entire power of the state is scaled down into the form of one person matched against one subject. In reality, though, whether torture occurs in the context of detention or a police stop, the matchup between captives and captors is so desperately one-sided and the power imbalance so patent as to be ridiculous. The archetype, as a resting feature in a shared imagination, allows people to adjust that gross imbalance rhetorically and psychologically. That type of manipulation is engraved in strange but common imagery in the daily speech of contemporary policy makers and practitioners. For example, constitutional protections are depicted as forms of bondage, captivity, or even torture for the captor. To stand by the conventional rules of war is to fight with one hand tied behind the back. In contemplating coercive interrogation, former attorney general Dick Thornburgh told the *Washington Post*: "We put an emphasis on due process and sometimes it strangles us."[58] Military interrogator in Iraq Tony Lagouranis writes that subjects who did not acknowledge his power made him feel "naked and unarmed standing before these prisoners."[59] Yet in Lagouranis's case, the prisoners were hooded, shackled, and squatting; they were bombarded with sound and threatened at close range by dogs. These disturbing turns of phrase offer graphic (and outrageous) role reversals. They invert the symmetry of the archetype to falsely position the speaker as a victim and invest the prisoner with power.

The commitment to an exaggerated intelligence threat is a commonplace of the security imaginary, and a second misdirection native to the archetype. The posture of urgent protection and exaggerated threat draws attention to interrogation and away from other considerations, casting a shadow over the many forms, functions, and settings for torture that do not conform to the archetype. Torture obviously violates captives, but it is typically said to signal the converse: the prisoner's latent violence—the shiv or weapon or secret contained in her anus, her mind, or her being. The flashlight used in Elmaghraby's torture is an instructive example. It enacts a pretense of security. Because it bears a commonsense association with the act of searching, when a flashlight is used to rape, it is simultaneously a tool of torture and a powerful tool of misdirection. This kind of prop is an aid to ordinary people who have already been conditioned to misconstrue torture and rename it as some kind of excess. Indeed, the *New York Times'* description of the flashlight rape as an "unnecessary body cavity search" goes a long way toward demonstrating this point.

Like the flashlight, ritual questioning too becomes merely a performative prop reinforcing pretense and personal humiliation. As argued by practitioners themselves, while questioning might devolve into physical and mental assault, it ceases to be effective questioning at precisely that point. It becomes merely assault. Questioning prisoners requires different skills.[60] "Questioning" and abusive remarks while beating or freezing or hanging or drowning a prisoner are no more related to intelligence gathering than a flashlight in the anus is related to a search.

Social imaginaries are a cultural force in their own right. They are repertoires of meanings and associations that are interactive and mediating, and therefore shape human understandings, values, and beliefs. In turn, human actions and interactions revive and circulate those same understandings. The circulation of the archetypal scene offers insight into the larger national security imagination in which these associations with torture reside. The archetype is a sense of what torture is, and beyond that, what security is, what constitutes threat, and how these come together in society. The need to constantly assert the perceived threat and attribute it to racial and caste difference is deeply lodged in that shared imagination.

• • •

How might we imagine and discuss torture differently?

Idelber Avelar suggests we think of torture as ubiquitous instead of an accident or excess.[61] To analyze and organize effectively, we cannot afford a distinction between civilization and torture, and we need to quit company with a vision of torture as individual suffering that is therefore somehow distinct from structural wrongs used to regulate populations. It is surely the latter. Those of us who have not yet been subject to torture need to see it all around us and think carefully when and why we think "brutality" or "excessive force," but not "torture." We are said to be beneficiaries of daily violence that keeps us safer, that keeps public order. This is on us.

Political scientist Jinee Lokaneeta and John Parry both argue that a continuum of violence is a feature of liberal states and that those states will always work to accommodate excesses of force into law. In this sense, as Parry notes, "torture sits in a continuum of violent state practices where the use of these forms of violence by modern states as a way of regulating populations is far more significant than whether 'torture' is the particular form of violence used."[62] There is something to this, but as we have seen, we require something more. On the one hand, we dare not elevate torture practice as unique, exceptional, archetypal, or elemental in its form or its power. Nor, on the other hand, can we risk submerging torture into a spectrum of state violence if the result means we emphasize its excess on that spectrum. To do so is to continue to mistake the social functions and the damage particular to its work. Chapter 4 will address this problem.

We can return to Marnia Lazreg's keen observation that when terror is the game plan, torture may travel with an ensemble of violations, but torture is essential as a terror multiplier and analytically distinct. The distinctions matter, but they do not make torture any more or less heinous. The distinctions lie not in the extremity of the violence or suffering caused by torture (in comparison to other violations) but in its social functions and therefore its use.[63] This reframes the questions we must ask. If torture is one among many forms of violence used by the modern state as a way of regulating populations, then why this form, here? What social work does torture do at this specific place, at this specific time? How does the organizational setting and situational context condition or assist the violence? What historical and cultural meanings and relationships does the torture practice support or weaponize? In this organizational and neighborhood setting, who benefits, and how? What terror does it generate, and for whom? Whom does it control, keep in line? What local communities come together around that work? What other cohorts, units, allegiances, or communities does it lift up, stratify, or divide? How many and whom does it destroy? What roles are being enacted, what identities challenged or assigned?

This chapter has argued that the dualism of the archetype and its other features hamper analysis and recognition of torture. Torture is the action and interaction, intense and mundane, of a variety of intersecting groups. So too the archetypal view of torture tightly binds the concept to interrogation, a move that is rife with political and cultural consequences of its own. Better we craft and broadcast representations that bring into view the multiple forms of torture humans choose and the populated environments in which torture takes place, its complex institutional and communal conditions of possibility, its multiple social functions and effects for groups and for liberal states, its terror, its breadth of impact historically, and its function as a mode of domestic control and domestic order in the present. Without seeing the multiples and plurals involved and at stake in the process of torture, we close off avenues of thought that lead to theories of complicity and back to ourselves—as consumers of news and popular culture, spectators, students, families, and participants in conversations on torture. Chapter 4, to which we turn next, investigates these lines of public complicity and the communities formed around the depiction of the waterboard in 2007.

4

Technique

The Waterboard Spectacle

> To a spectator it would look like torture. And torture is wrong.
> —John C. Gannon, former CIA deputy director, on the destruction of ninety-two video records of waterboarding

> "Torture" is never a word we'd say—but [it is] sort of a very tough television show. . . . You want to get the tailwind of the whole cultural Zeitgeist.
> —Producers of *Solitary* for Fox Reality Television

> Torture me on television.
> —Jacobo Timerman, Argentine torture survivor, to *CBS Reports*

By late 2007, speculative, dramatic, and political interest all seized on "the waterboard" as a technique of torture. Although the press surged out of the gate in September 2001, eager to pose questions on the utility of torture in the war on terror, that speculation failed to connect to torture as a feature of daily domestic terror in precincts and prisons. Concerted investigative reporting on U.S. torture failed to follow until 2004. As both speculation and investigative reporting unfolded from 2004 to 2007, a rapid rise in the number of portrayals of torture in dramatic television and film fueled concern for the impact on the civilian public and on the military interrogators themselves. By 2007, journalists had pointed to torture cases across a range of locations and indicated the executive branch, specifically the departments of Justice and Defense, and the National Security Agency had approved techniques of violence that had been recognized and prosecuted as torture historically.[1] This was the landscape when, in early October, news broke of secret torture memos. Authored by the Office of Legal Counsel (OLC) years before and addressed to the CIA, these memos approved the combined use of "head-slapping, simulated drowning, and frigid temperatures" on detainees.[2] Their existence became public just as the president nominated a new boss for the OLC and the rest of the Department of Justice, Michael Mukasey. This meant that senators reviewing his nomination to the post of attorney general would quiz him publicly on torture. A new wave of media coverage, Senate hearings, activist political theater, and live reenactments would highlight one technique in particular: the waterboard.

This chapter will foreground events in the year 2007 to argue that torture, as it resides in the U.S. national security imagination, energetically spotlights the isolated technique, implement, or tool of torture in ways that cast extended torture networks in doubt. The political spectacle peaked just as one survivor of a kidnap and rendition network anticipated his hearing before the U.S. Second Circuit Court of Appeals. The torture of Canadian Maher Arar and the fate of *Arar v. Ashcroft* points up the professional network fundamental to producing his ordeal. He was snatched in 2002 during a layover at JFK airport in New York, where he was awaiting a connection home to Toronto. Relying on information from Canadian authorities, the U.S. activated an international network of state and private actors, moving Arar out of the United States and across Jordan to Syria. He was beaten along the way and finally held for over ten months in a dark isolation cell called "the grave." There he was beaten with electric cables and subjected to other torture. Secretive abductions like these were known in the Bush years as "extraordinary rendition" and had been reported since early 2002.[3] They caught up dozens of hapless noncombatants and involved up to fifty-four different governments, twenty-five of them in Europe.[4] Over a year later, Arar was returned to his family. Canada granted him an apology and financial restitution.

Two feature films inspired by Arar's ordeal—*Rendition* and *Extraordinary Rendition*—made note of the soaring public interest in the waterboard. Although Arar himself had never been subjected to this technique, both films, one a U.S. effort and the other British, inserted extended portrayals of the waterboard as dramatic turning points. These films opened in late 2007, just weeks before Arar's appeal. The appeal would be denied. The higher court sided with the executive branch, finding that his case could not be heard without risk to national security. This juxtaposition between the public contention over the waterboard and the lesser attention paid Arar and his case neatly illustrates the relation of the torture Tool to the torture network in the national security imagination.

When speaking of the peculiar quality of focus on an isolated act, in this chapter, I will capitalize references to that instrument, method, or "enhanced technique" like the Tool, denoting its popular obsession and symbolic weight. More than political happenstance or legal maneuvering ensured the waterboard was met with fanfare while Arar's rendition network was wrapped in silence. Even when key elements of the human torture network are legible, operating in plain sight, and, as it happened, affirmed by the Canadian government, it is the isolated technique of torture that diverts public and legal attention from the compartmentalized, collaborative, and bureaucratic means by which torture is implemented. The single technique steals the spotlight while the network escapes reckoning.

This chapter's first section, therefore, takes up the Tool's role in generating certainty and doubt. Examples from early twenty-first-century U.S. public and press conversation consider ways the national security imagination relies on and proliferates unstable evidence. First, Tools of torture, isolated and held up for public contemplation in debate, prose, performance, or pictures, summon shared understandings about violence that already circulate in a society. Those understandings routinely provoke reaction and debate on the Tool's place in a civilized society—its fitness or its features—but less often on these shared understandings or their colonial roots. Second, public complicity is necessary to the manufacture of certainty and doubt. Humans coordinate the violence and suffering of torture. It takes imaginative work and public participation to construct, deny, and disregard certain aspects of that process and outcomes of that violence. The public and legal preoccupation with the Tool plays an important role in cultivating the selective attention required to disregard torture networks.

The second section of this chapter tracks the display of the Tool in 2007, and especially the waterboard, across prime-time television and film, in the Bush legal memos on enhanced techniques, and in all manner of political theater including Senate hearings, waterboard art, protests, and reenactments. To read Bush Justice Department memos alongside narratives drawn from popular or political culture and antitorture activism is not to equate them in significance for those who were tortured. Rather, it is to note that across this varied lot, whether the waterboard is denounced or defended, arguments stage a drama of community formation. The display of the Tool gathers people around it, engaging people in a loud but shallow civilizational debate about state torture and encouraging them to locate themselves in a community that shares similar views. This is community-building work, in this way forging identities and assembling or severing new or old social connections. As passions are stirred by that work, the

Tool ushers in a quieter story about values, hierarchy, and obligations: who belongs, who does not; what people owe each other and the state; what the state owes them. That is, when the debate over the fitness or the features of the Tool is enjoined, then the subtext of debate is not the many forms, settings, social functions, and consequences of torture. Nor is it the specific claims of the survivors or the dead. Instead, the narrative subtext is the powerful assertion of the place of the self or citizen in the (civilized) community, the proper roles within that community, and the power of the state. Found alike in depictions of torture proponents and detractors, anxiety over social order, stratification, and exclusion are central to this story.

In the end, the failure of Arar's legal case stands as a reminder of how and why hairsplitting over the Tool or visualizing the violence can never in themselves illuminate the practice of torture or facilitate a robust account of public and cultural complicity.

Certainty and Doubt

Fascination greets Tools of torture whether they are displayed in prose, performance, or picture. The preoccupation with isolatable, visualizable, disembodied torture instruments and techniques is a wide-reaching habit of both discourse and imagination in Western culture and history. Museums and visual representations of torture showcase the instruments of pain, not the paperwork and those who craft and sign it. However, as we will see, the paperwork and its scribes are just as obsessed with isolating and foregrounding the technique.

The Colonial Tool Kit

In 1902, the water cure and sand cure—used in either the U.S.–Philippine war or the Carolinas—drew Senate interest and public furor, as discussed in chapter 2.[5] One century later, the Tool still activates a submerged racial-colonial logic. When arguing against particular methods, they are described as uncivilized: barbaric, brutal, inhuman. For this reason, counterinsurgents battling anticolonial forces in the mid-twentieth century promoted torture in the opposite terms: as the modern tool best able to combat a new kind of nonracialized foe, but one without honor and implicitly primitive. They argued that "interrogators must always strive not to injure" but also "must not trifle" over these matters or put faith in moderation. After all, as noted in chapter 2, "science" can easily assist. When arguing that such-and-such a Tool is appropriate, it becomes the embodiment of civilization itself: restrained, calibrated, scientific, efficient, controlled by technical expertise.[6] Tools and all manner of technology hold a sacred place in the construction of the self-congratulatory mythos of Western superiority.

In these earlier imperial moments and now, however, the Tool attaches other meanings to this colonial script. It activates the common notion that interpersonal violence can be organized and understood along a spectrum or continuum, one that we presume to escalate (from least bad to worst, civilized to barbaric, liberal to illiberal, psychological to physical, etc.). Implicit in the spectrum stands the belief that acts, incidents, or implements of violence can be isolated, and once isolated, their impact ranked—a project that seemingly can be undertaken objectively. These are reassuring notions that allow those who use violence to gauge it "proportionately" and in advance.[7] But the implementation, impact, and aftermath of violence are embodied, plural, and subjective; it is never so neat and predictable. A spectrum or continuum of violence discounts the survivors' experience, the entire process of torture, and the many subjective landscapes of pain, as discussed in the Introduction.

If the certainty that allows us to appraise the tools and techniques of torture is one colonial legacy we see carried forward in the national security imagination, so too is the tendency to amass unstable evidence. The two of course are linked. Interrogator Chris Mackey offers a national security success story that illustrates this well. His memoir of Afghanistan culminates by describing an innovation on sleep deprivation his team called monstering. Its use over many days on one subject led to a dramatic break for interrogators. In this case, both the lead interrogator and the prisoner became physically and mentally unstable, even delusional; Mackey writes both at one point believed they were seeing lobsters climbing the walls. Pushed to the brink, Mackey recalls, the detainee revealed the location of the deadly nerve agent ricin. Yet Mackey casts immediate doubt on his own story, saying no member of his team remembered the outcome or the importance of the interrogation in the same way. Even the lead interrogator—who obtained the information, spoke of seeing lobsters, and sent the formal report up the chain of command—categorically denied ricin or any toxin was ever at stake. The outcome of Mackey's torture example is unstable and unknowable. "Distortion is unavoidable," says Mackey, "and sometimes irreconcilable."[8] Mackey's certainty and ease in the face of the irreconcilable is startling, especially in this particular moment, the episode meant to demonstrate his central claim: torture is bad, but the features of this technique befit a civilized nation (so they therefore are not torture), and it was an effective means to obtain lifesaving intelligence. Other elements of the story are prone to distortion, but his confidence in the technique remains unshaken.

Scholars of colonial torture and terror offer insight into Mackey's example and its space of ambiguous certainty. They indicate that both ambiguity and certainty are strategic, the product of work. Sociologist Michael Taussig describes the distorting effect of the colonizing imagination as a crisis of knowing. Writing about colonial terror and torture used against the nineteenth-century Putamayo in the rubber plantations of colonial Brazil, Taussig notes that in the stories that surrounded torture, murder, and insurrection, any sense of "what really happened" was inevitably steeped in a miasma of doubt and distortion. So it is with Mackey's sleep deprivation. What was real, what was rumor, and what was achieved—lobsters? Ricin? Preventive intelligence? Taussig argues that a fog of the plausible–implausible, a haze of knowing–not knowing, surrounds stories of torture and converts accounts or rumors of threat, atrocity, torture, and terror into vehicles of terror themselves. Taussig calls this phenomenon "epistemic murk." That murk—the doubt and uncertainty that rise to meet torture and project its terror—is a kind of "phantasmic social force."[9]

Scholar Ann Stoler suggests that both certainty and doubt in such a culture of terror require substantial mental labor. Reading the records kept by Dutch colonial administrators during the insurgencies in Aceh of 1873–1903, she seeks to explain how and why the morally sensitive colonial agents she studies objected righteously to some incidents of violence against indigenous subjects yet seemed indifferent to the evidence of other pain all around them. They experienced violence as simultaneously "ordinary and outrageous." Stoler's colonial managers and stewards, in effect, became skilled wielders of unstable evidence, Taussig's epistemic murk. Riddled with anxiety over rebellion, they relied on rumors of violence for news, but "facts were constituted out of rumor as frequently as the other way around."[10] Power enabled her subjects to choose. They could manipulate doubt to their advantage, amplifying rumor in order to generate facts or in order to defeat them.

Their writing, she finds, documents a form of selective attention deliberately cultivated, what Stoler terms an "imperial disposition of disregard." She notes that when it came to violence, these colonial era women and men "tended" this capacity daily, and she refers to this habit of trained awareness evocatively as active not-knowing or "skittish seeing, averted gaze, acts of ignoring rather than ignorance . . . that from which those with privilege and standing could excuse themselves . . . [a] refusal to witness."[11] How did they choose what to believe and what to report? They channeled the violence and terror through social "hierarchies of credibility": what those to whom they were socially or professionally obliged were likely to find possible, then plausible, then relevant. All else could be subject to doubt, irrelevance, disregard.[12] In other words, violence was ranked on a spectrum and scale. Ordinary was sorted from outrageous according to one's alignment with a social set—and, of course, power.

In torture, racialized and gendered social hierarchies assign certainty and doubt in one other critical dimension. Political scientist Darius Rejali argues that state torture in liberal democracies wraps those subjected to it in what he calls civic doubt. Torture targets persons already marginalized socially, and the violence discredits them further. The claims of these subjects are always uncertain simply because the state says they are. To borrow Stoler's terms, we have inherited and cultivated a habit, a disposition of disregard. The community at large aligns the tortured with the suspect, treacherous, guilty, and in-credible. By generating terror and doubt, torture functions to sever its subjects from community, shut them from common political space, and then flood that space with murk.[13]

To the extent the national security imagination immerses us in a culture of terror, a murky, violent, fear-based world, it is no wonder we invest psychic energy in isolating Tools, the seemingly discrete techniques of violence. That focus forecloses the subjects' experience. Tools, we believe, can be paced and measured and weighed on a fantastical civilizational scale. When we train our attention on the Tool, we can identify its features, determine its fitness, and ban it. Or not.

Seeing Is Believing

The Tool yields up its evidence best when on display. In discussion of torture, what is invisible is in doubt, and seeing may seem like certainty. Perhaps for these reasons, an eyewitness account can be pivotal in public discussion. Listeners find a graphic account useful to judge for themselves, to feel sure. What is visible in a particular moment—the archetypal encounter, the technique at work—is believed to be unmistakable. Soldier Kayla Williams captures this hope, reprising the old legal formula on obscenity: "I don't know what torture is, but I know it when I see it."[14]

Although Private Williams may trust the evidence of her eyes, the certainty of "I know it when I see it" is the twin of doubt: "I'll believe it when I see it." Those companion phrases capture the instability of visual evidence. Mackey, for instance, contrasts the monstering he approved with the images he denounces from Iraq's Abu Ghraib prison. There U.S. soldiers and contractors tortured captive subjects with beatings, anal and vaginal rape, sleep deprivation, stress positions, group masturbation scenarios, water, and mock executions.[15] Mackey repudiates it as torture. He and his team may have bent the rules, he concludes, but nothing he saw while stationed in Kandahar or Bagram amounted to torture.

Mackey's eyewitness appraisal of the Tool recurs in many military memoirs. Military linguist Erik Saar recounts experiences at Guantánamo Bay that are harrowing and shaming for captors as well as captives. He records abundant evidence of severe pain and suffering, both mental and physical: stress positions, sexual violence, frigid temperatures, sleep deprivation, and coordinated beatings known as IRFings after the Initial Reaction Force, a five- to six-person team called to take down and control prisoners.[16] But Saar looks at the bottom line: "I didn't personally see anything that I would label torture as most people understand the word."[17] He speaks of two things: what he sees, and what other people imagine. Put another way: I know this looks bad, but we can all imagine worse.

Some thirty years earlier, in 1973, military advisor Richard Welcome helped others visualize his work on the lethal CORDS and Phoenix programs during the Vietnam War.

> Prisoners were abused. Were they tortured? It depends on what you call torture. Electricity was used by the Vietnamese, water was used, occasionally some of the prisoners got beat up. Were any of them put on the rack, eyes gouged out, bones broken? No. I never saw any evidence of that at all.[18]

Mackey's defense of extreme sleep deprivation echoes Welcome's low-key acknowledgment of "electricity" and "water."[19] Generations apart, these military men deny torture with the authority of their own eyewitness observation, but then reach for something more. They weigh what they saw against a larger collective understanding of torture as defined by specific Tools stored in the historical imagination: the rack, dismemberment, Abu Ghraib photos, more. Put another way, the eyewitness tells us, "This looks bad, but we all can imagine worse." Mackey, Saar, and Welcome gesture toward a spectrum of barbarism in order to dismiss the violence all around them as more civilized, ordinary, relative.[20]

The eyewitness's reach to a communal imagination has its counterpart in most of the rest of us, consumers of torture news and entertainment. It is the desire of witnesses to align themselves with a wider public. When others can see what we see, there is a shared moment of insight. Proof is helpful. Images are coveted in this respect; they approach certainty best when they capture an act, a weapon, or a method. That image may confirm first the Tool's action (the equipment, the technique) or second its residue (the Wound and wounded), or, third, the presence of one who wielded the tool or delivered the blow (whether in the frame or not). Best are images that capture all three: Tool, Wound, and Perpetrator.

The battle to see such images can be fierce. Over two thousand photographic records, many expected to capture precisely these details and taken at over two dozen U.S.-run facilities in Afghanistan, Iraq, and Guantánamo, have been the subject of an ACLU freedom of information request since early 2004, a couple months before the photos from Abu Ghraib prison in Iraq leaked to the public.[21] The Obama administration refused a judge's order to release them in 2009. Congress nailed down that refusal with legislation that criminalized release of any video, photo, or recorded material of the sort for the time spanning September 2001 to 2009. The sweeping Detainee Photographic Record Protection Act passed in 2009.[22] Five years later, under order from the same judge, the government finally released 198 of the thousands of records to the ACLU. This handful did not prove the powerful evidentiary cache anticipated; instead, it showed only wounds and close-ups of body parts, and it omitted detainee identities and contextual information.[23]

It is this sharing, the imaginative energy expended viewing and interpreting, that generates either certainty or doubt and aligns us with community—those who see torture or those who do not, or those who have experienced torture and those who have not. One powerful social function of torture is just this: to build, divide, and stratify community. That is, in part, why we need to see for ourselves and to reaffirm our own place in the group. As soldier Williams and these other examples illustrate, images of torture seem most convincingly to be so when they mirror our cultural investment in what we have imagined torture to be. They require less mental labor to accept or deny.

The collective mental activity through which we wield power to make certainty and doubt is more obvious with widely circulated photos. When still images of prisoner treatment leaked from Abu Ghraib prison in Iraq in 2004, an overwhelming amount of the mainstream and scholarly discussion centered on exactly what an image can and cannot be said to reveal.[24] For many viewers in the United States, in order to be understood, the group photos of Abu Ghraib needed to be aligned against something familiar. Some doubt focused on putative elements of ruse, pretend, or play seemingly visible in the techniques of the photos—mock electricity, mock executions, the forced pantomime (it was claimed) of masturbation, fellatio, and sexual domination. Absent Tools that inspire awe, torture may look more like farce. The familiar (and also egregious) nature of "prankish" group-based sexual assault and subjugation in domestic U.S. culture drew comparisons between the Abu Ghraib images and homoerotic and homosocial fraternity parties or pledging rituals. It was in that sense that investigator Schlesinger's description, "'Animal House' on the night shift," became a readily repeated reference.[25]

Caught up by the clamor as this contest over fact multiplies murk, it is easy to miss how images train our attention to moments, not durations, and to Tools, not entire processes. The careful coordination over time that generates torture is hard to represent visually, let alone capture in a snapshot. However, the collaborative elements of torture are often quite legible in other ways, as are causes and consequences. Again, Erik Saar at Guantánamo offers an example, re-creating one episode for the reader in terms that defy a snapshot and isolate no single actor or technique. Saar and an interrogator join on a captive man who had been forced to suffer extended sleep deprivation and hypothermia in the days and hours before their encounter. The interrogator gave Saar the plan: "I want to try something. . . . to make him feel so dirty he can no longer talk to his god." With Saar interpreting, the man was subjected to forced sexual touching, derogatory abuse, religious humiliation, and finally to red fluid smeared on his face. Because the interrogator pulled the fluid from inside her pants, the subject was made to believe it was menstrual blood and was told he would not be able to wash or pray that evening. The subject's resistance to the whole was strong; he wrenched an ankle trying to jerk free of the shackle that pinned it to the floor. Even Saar, who was in no way the target of the abuse, broke down afterward, crouching and sobbing in his shower. Depicting it in prose, Saar cannot put a name to the whole of the social, emotional, and physical situation he created—a situation in which the man remained, but from which Saar walked away.[26]

Pain and suffering are cumulative and the collaborative achievement of a network. A portion of that network is legible here but cannot be captured in a photograph. If Saar's team had set out to snap this subject's ankle, the aspect of torture here would not be questioned. Rather, the injury and technique would be palpable, with the extreme conduct of a Perpetrator implied by the Wound; the moment of the mental snapshot would be simple if one chose to see torture. In contrast, the entwined emotional, psychic, and physical injuries, every bit as substantive, are harder to isolate and visualize. Over hours and days, the team set out to ensure the man's powerlessness, to maximize stress, and to induce fragile mental and physical health via hypothermia and sleep deprivation. Then they forced themselves on the captive physically, combining coercive sexual touching with a verbal, religious, and emotional assault so repellant the subject hurt himself trying to escape. This treatment has long constituted torture under historical definitions, in U.S. courts, and under international law. A deliberately sexualized assault was specifically intended, as was acute psychic pain: "so dirty he can no longer talk to his god." Forceful resistance had been foreseeable, even if the sum total of exact injuries was not. Although collaboratively constructed and extended situations such as those Saar describes are inherent in torture, they do not fit the national security archetype; they do not capture a discrete act or Tool. Therefore, they verge on the unrecognizable.

Legal Murk

The Tool, displayed in image or prose, merely purports to offer an oasis of certainty in a realm of unavoidable distortion, to use Mackey's term. In contrast, key elements of networked violence—duration, coordination, and compartmentalized tasks—seem to cloud the events and diffuse responsibility. So does the language of the law. While the precise definitions and regulations are essential for prosecution, they also routinely generate murk. The law roots the standard for "torture" in the invisible: the level of the subjects' pain, the alleged perpetrators' "extreme and outrageous" conduct, their "specific intention" and "knowledge of the outcome."[27] Legal scholar David Luban argues all of this is "a fundamental trick" when techniques are appraised (on the civilizational spectrum) and declared "not severe" in advance. "Interrogators could truthfully say they lacked guilty intention because they had been told by the lawyers the pain and suffering"—even when perfectly visible before their eyes—"did not cross the legal threshold."[28]

Yet violence, like collaboration, always initiates the uncontrollable. Phrases like "specific intention" and "knowledge of outcome" freight collaboration with doubt. In Saar's case, which outcome, and at which point, is at stake? Given the interaction of the team—setting the temperature, refusing the subject sleep, transporting him, interpreting the interrogator's verbal abuse, witnessing the subject's reactions—could any participant control or predict all the outcomes and their severity?

Likewise improvisation. It is the nature of military protocols and rules of engagement to rely on interpretation and improvisation. "I want to try something," Saar's partner had said. Contract interrogator Eric Fair, stationed in Abu Ghraib and Fallujah, Iraq, admitted to torture and recalled a sergeant's demand: "Think outside of the fucking manual."[29] One headline faulted "brutal improvisation by GIs" for a detainee homicide and "sleeping-bag death."[30] Improvisation relies on projected outcomes that are ultimately unpredictable. All improvisation thereby comes with a margin of deniability—the term used when the construction of doubt requires obvious, collaborative labor. With uncertainty generated by what we see and what we cannot, we cling to shared ideas about the observability, instrumentality, and proportionality of violence.

When news broke in 2007 that slapping, freezing, and waterboarding had been approved in combination, journalists, politicians, and activists seized on an identifiable Tool, one that was also lodged in the historical imagination.[31] What remained was only to hold it up and forge relationships around it, so we could take our places within a set of national values and community roles.

Seeing the Waterboard and Reading Its Narrative

Malcolm Nance, a prominent military voice against torture and a onetime Navy Survival, Evasion, Resistance, and Escape (SERE) instructor who had supervised hundreds of men subjected to the waterboard, described the technique in his testimony before Congress in late 2007, at the height of the waterboarding contention. He detailed the procedure in what remains one of the most read blog posts to *Small Wars Journal*. Nance firmly answered the "is it or isn't it" question with graphic description:

> Waterboarding is not a simulation. Unless you have been strapped down to the board, have endured the agonizing feeling of the water overpowering your gag reflex, and then feel your throat open and allow pint after pint of water to involuntarily fill your lungs, you will not know the meaning of the word.
>
> Waterboarding is a controlled drowning.... It does not simulate drowning, as the lungs are actually filling with water. There is no way to simulate that.... A team doctor watches ... for the physiological signs which show when the drowning effect goes from painful psychological experience, to horrific suffocating punishment to the final death spiral.
>
> Waterboarding is slow motion suffocation with enough time to contemplate the inevitability of black out and expiration—usually the person goes into hysterics on the board.... When done right it is controlled death. Its lack of physical scarring allows the victim to recover and be threatened with its use again and again.[32]

Now its impact on a spectator. Nance locates torture in technique:

> I know these [enhanced interrogation] techniques.... Performed with even moderate intensity over an extended period of time on an unsuspecting prisoner—*it is torture,* without a doubt. Couple that with waterboarding and the entire medley will not only "shock the conscience" as the statute forbids—it would terrify you. *Most people cannot stand to watch....* One has to overcome basic human decency *to endure watching or causing* the effects. The brutality would force you into a personal moral dilemma between humanity and hatred. It would leave you to question the meaning of what it is to be an American.[33]

Nance is unusual in his effort to mention the longer process of torture, the "extended period of time," the "medley" of combined violations, the unsuspecting, unconvicted suspects. But his purpose is to present specific features of the Tool. Above all, he insists the sight would trigger unnerving doubts about self and nation.

I have argued that the national security imagination shared by most in the United States in the twenty-first century tends to recognize torture only in a specific guise. In that security imagination, and within its Archetype of interrogation, the display of the Tool locates torture within the object itself and the one who wields it. Brutish or civilized, the isolated technique or implement seems to bear evidentiary value even as it proliferates murk. The Tool is depicted time and again to rivet our attention and to cultivate disregard for all else. Much escapes attention: the process by which targets are identified and held, the responsibility borne by a long chain of participants who design tools and permissions, the spectators and social functions that accrue around the violence, the impact on the subjects, and the consequences for society at large.

Whether pro or con, the depictions of the waterboard routinely underwrite the foundational narrative that Nance laid out. That narrative is not about the Tool per se but about the relationship of the viewer to a civilized community ("humanity vs. hate") and the relationship of the viewer to the power of the state. In the midst of the decolonial and counterinsurgency era, Guy Debord argued that in a society of the spectacle, the power of spectacle lies not in the image but rather in a series of social relations mediated by images—that is, by the exchange of looks.[34] So it is with the Tool, imagined and presented in order to convene and clarify human relationships around it. In these narratives, the Tool is displayed to provoke precisely those questions: what do I see? Those who matter to me, to whom I am socially and professionally obliged, what do they see? Who is among the civilized community? What values bind this community, this nation? How are those values served, ensured, or undermined by the power of the state? Who corrects the state? What does state power owe that community, and what do members of that community owe the state?

In arguments for or against a Tool, the stories that answer these questions vary only a little. Whether depictions arrived in prime-time television, dramatic film, the executive branch's torture memos, or art and activist performance, the narrative that accompanied the Tool sprang from the same national security vision. That narrative consistently eclipsed survivors from the civilized community even as it called for a just state. In doing so, it posited anemic democratic norms and strange justice, and it pulled public attention from the networked apparatus of torture operating at home or abroad. Rather than fixate on the debate over the Tool and its barbarism, we would do better to question the values and roles it quietly ushers in.

Torture Tools in TV and Film

In the run-up to 2007, as news media speculated furiously over the practicality of torture in the newly declared war on terror, dramatic film and television joined the trend, increasing images of torture and holding fast to the Archetype. A content analysis by the Parents Television Council counted 110 prime-time TV portrayals of torture in the five years from 1997 to 2001. The number jumped to 625 over the next four years, 2002–5, with a peak number in 2003, before the Abu Ghraib photos broke.[35] In the aftermath of the Abu Ghraib scandal, and with growing public attention to Guantánamo Bay, many creators now also incorporated torture along with topical references as they fictionalized the national security apparatus or took up terrorism from different angles; for example, the films *Syriana* and *V for Vendetta,* as well as the Bourne trilogy, were all made during this period.

Torture worked its way into the era's newer genres. When producers Andrew Golder and Lincoln Hiatt pitched *Solitary* to Fox Reality Channel, they sought to capitalize on the public interest: "'Torture' is never a word we'd say—but [it is] sort of a very tough television show. . . . You want to get the tailwind of the whole cultural Zeitgeist."[36] Premiering in 2006, the show placed nine contestants in small isolation pods for up to twelve days with no human contact or interaction except the voice of their electronic taskmaster, Val. Referred to by number, subjected to hunger, sleep deprivation, extreme temperatures, audio distress—including amplified baby screams—and a variety of tasks both grueling and humiliating (walking on gravel, eating disgusting food to the point of vomiting), the contestant to hold out the longest would win $50,000. Torture motifs are well suited to a television genre that combines total surveillance, degradation, and suffering for the promise of recognition and reward. *Solitary* increased its audience each of three seasons.

True to form, where the U.S. public saw the archetype at work, these shows triggered what we settle for as debate: Does torture work? Is it or isn't it torture? Owing in part to tracking by organizations like Parents Television Council, critiques of Fox television drama *24* were widespread by 2007. The show had debuted just two months after the attacks of September 11, 2001, and in its first four seasons, *24* was responsible for sixty-seven instances of torture—more than any other prime-time drama—with most conducted by the hero, Jack Bauer.[37] Each season followed a fictionalized Counter Terrorism Unit hour by hour through a single day, enacting the ticking time bomb scenario every week. It kept the beloved security rationale for torture at center stage.

The show became a cultural touchstone in political debates on torture and an influential reference point in the shaping of actual policy. In terms of the "is it or isn't it debate" over Tools, Philippe Sands writes that Diane Beaver, the Department of Defense staff judge advocate general who approved eighteen "harsh" interrogation techniques that included waterboarding, sexual humiliation, and dogs, said *24* "gave people lots of ideas" in policy brainstorming sessions.[38] The show was the subject of a 2006 Heritage Foundation policy conference, where the Homeland Security chief, Michael Chertoff, noted that *24* "reflects real life." It was referenced prominently in the Republican presidential primary debates in 2007 and rapidly fueled two collections of essays as well as interviews and myriad print and internet commentaries.[39]

The national Intelligence Science Board warned of what audiences might be learning from such shows, arguing that raising public expectations for quick, foolproof interrogation results was in itself an obstacle to effective intelligence gathering.[40] Retired U.S. Army colonel Stuart Herrington called the tactics on view "illegal, immoral and stupid," yet said a show like *24* is nonetheless influential for the young recruits he talks to at Fort Bliss. In February 2007, U.S. Army Brigadier General Patrick Finnegan, dean of West Point, accompanied by FBI and military interrogators, visited the set of *24* to tell producers that the show's misrepresentation of the effectiveness of torture had a damaging effect on troops. Parents Television Council launched a campaign against *24* in 2007. Perhaps because of the level of criticism, *24* resisted a depiction of waterboarding even at the height of the procedure's national attention in 2007. While it had illustrated other forms of smothering, strangling, and water torture, the face-up form of water torture only appeared in the final season in 2010.

Monitoring organization Human Rights First gamely tried to draw attention away from *24* with its Prime Time Torture Project, an initiative meant to encourage and reward "responsible, nuanced and realistic portrayals of torture," whatever that might mean. Big shows of that season were nominated: *Lost, The Shield, The Closer,* and *Boston Legal.* An episode of *Criminal Minds* got the award.[41] All contenders offered dissenting views on the utility of torture in interrogation. But as with the critiques launched in the speculative news debates, the antitorture TV episodes repeated false premises and reinforced the Archetype.[42]

Well before 2001, stylized torture sequences in film and television drama often functioned as didactic moments or plot points that precipitated revelation, decision, or action on the part of a particular character, be it the suffering subject, the perpetrators, or the bystanders.[43] Torture confers wisdom, power, status, emotional depth, and special skills. Audiences may pity Jason Bourne as each film of the Bourne trilogy reveals more about his subjection to the experimental government tortures that lurk behind his suppressed memory. Yet at the same time, it is this very history of torture that makes him the super death-dealing antiagency agent the viewer so admires. Even representations that argued torture does not work, too often retained, insidiously, torture as a rite of passage for the hero—specifically, a rite of manhood.[44]

Dramatic worlds. As always, though, it is important to take a look beyond the Archetype and the noisy debate it triggers. Of greater importance in *24* was the narrative accompanying its array of Tools—that is, the weekly illustrations of the power of the state, the personal transformations wrought by torture, and the communities so forged. The show presented a fantastically efficient, flawlessly networked total digital information and surveillance environment. With few exceptions, in *24*, the police, FBI, and counterterror agents coordinate effortlessly on complex tactical missions. Information databases and control systems are comprehensive and networked seamlessly across agencies and institutions; they respond to complex searches and commands in nanoseconds. A single tap of a key repositions satellites, accesses public and private surveillance camera feeds, deciphers encryption, builds complex profiles of individuals, locates building schematics complete with readings of biological and radiological signatures, and much more. Much of each episode of *24* was spent watching this array of technological wonders in "real time." In the aftermath of real terrorist strikes, *24* reveled in a particular fantasy of state power and protection. The state's control of knowledge was absolute.

In a way ironic but not coincidental, this kind of dramatic showcase for the national security imagination typically portrays U.S. strength in the realm of its greatest actual vulnerability. Back in the real world of U.S. security agencies, across the same ten years of *24*'s ascendance, the first twelve years of Google's rise, and well after, the FBI was unable to implement a software platform capable of searching case files by keyword. The attempt to improve this technology generated embarrassing failure after failure, first as the $170 million Virtual Case File project, then as the $451 million Sentinel project launched in 2012.[45] The failings of U.S. national security before September 11 and for decades after were pointedly failures of information technology, as well as bureaucratic competence, turf wars, and insufficient capacity devoted to (and low priority placed on) the analytical steps that convert data collection into usable intelligence—skilled translation, cultural knowledge, theories tested through adversarial internal dialogue, and synthesis over time. These are the human and technological realms where the United States struggled and lagged for decades after the September 11 wake-up call. The nation is still seeking adequate tools to cope with geopolitical challenges posed by cybersecurity attacks or social media disinformation campaigns.

However, on screen, we would never know. The only chink in the state's total information armor, it seems, is the terrorist's ability to keep secrets. Tools of torture hold the solution and embody the clean superiority of the state's power. Agencies in *24* have at the ready technologically assured interrogation packages. These incrementally administer the pain of torture hands-free. Serum injection is automated. Ear-shattering sound is administered by headphones as counterterror heroes work their computers in silence nearby. When scientific tools are far from reach, however, Agent Bauer is able to improvise expertly with his hands. On *24,* the tools of torture offered speed, sophistication, immediate effect, and improvisational range—the same features *24* prizes in its surveillance state. As with Bauer, so with the state; power is absolute and capacity complete, but, for reasons of their own, they may choose restraint.

Human bonds. As *24* depicts near-total state power over information, it also structures the roles and relationships necessary to its version of democracy. This is the heart of the Tool's narrative. Threats are embodied in ethnic outsiders—and, worse, in weak, double-crossing government insiders. Righteous patriots must root out both unprincipled conservatives and erring liberals who wittingly or unwittingly attach themselves to terrorists. Often the weakness of the U.S. citizen is the largest potential threat.

In a world where people are routinely manipulated into improper allegiances, Tools of torture clarify then purify these relationships. In *24,* torture tests the mettle of friends, foes, and family, and transforms them, producing accurate preventive intelligence but also alliances. The president tortures his cabinet members, the secretary of Defense tortures his son, Agent Jack Bauer tortures, then suffocates, his brother. In a weird domestic triangle, Jack tortures his girlfriend's ex, using electricity to convert his rival in love into a brother in arms who fights by Jack's side. Torture even establishes erotic bonds: one FBI agent finds in Jack and his tactics an irresistible allure.

The social benefits of torture go far, offering proof of loyalty, patriotism, and professional and personal commitment. The message is simply that torture tests, consummates allegiances, and binds intimacies. National security torture secures one's place among others in the democratic state. Innocents understand that testing is necessary. Public protection is based on the premise that personal safety—of one's body and psyche, and those of loved ones—may be sacrificed at any time to state needs. Citizens owe the state this debt because the reverse is also true; without state torture, there would be no certainty or safety in which to form emotional bonds. Torture and its tools provide certainty in a murky world, and certainty means safety from both terror and the treacheries of the human heart.

Citizens, then, need play no part in the life of the state, aside from loyalty. Not so strangely, in *24* and other dramatic worlds that prize information control in this way, the relationship between state power, media, and citizen fits a pattern. On the one hand, when torture works to obtain information in these depictions, the state or its vigilante protectors know best how to manage and use information. Media impede the state. This is a long tradition in spy thrillers: one conspiracy is best fought by another conspiracy, not by public exposure and comment, political organizing, or civic action. On the other hand, seemingly liberal critiques of torture use the Tool to assemble the same deep connections between state power, media, and community. Media can assist the state, but the citizen is just as extraneous. In these, the media exposé of torture evokes a thrilling democratic sensation, standing as a victory in itself. This is an old formula in political cinema about torture and other atrocities.[46] Antitorture narratives tend to end in a blizzard of headlines and news broadcasts, where symbolic logic suggests that "to expose it is to end it." Democracy is an act of public bonding with elite protectors in government or media, not a function of informed judgment, critical consciousness, or community effort.

The 2007 U.S. film *Rendition* illustrates the relation between state and civic action well. The powerful, civilized state is on some level self-correcting, and as in *24,* citizen action has nothing to do with it. This star-packed Gavin Hood film aimed for box-office returns in October.[47] At the same time Maher Arar awaited court, the waterboard was under contention in the Senate, and the Human Rights First Prime Time Torture Awards were announced. The film's action turns on the waterboard, which, predictability, figures as a Tool of transformation and a rite of passage.

As *Rendition* opens, an unfortunate Egyptian U.S. resident, innocent husband, father, and engineer is intercepted by U.S. agents on a flight home and taken to a North African prison. As do the setting and tools of *24*, Anwar's gritty foreign cell, the leering local accomplices, and the rudimentary tools of torture illustrate the crudeness of power wielded by this tyrannical state. U.S. power is sophisticated enough to disappear a man efficiently, but waterboard torture rests in the hands of civilizational inferiors—brutal, backward men. The film viewer watches the subject tipped back and struggling against the water poured over his airway, and then the camera switches to CIA analyst and observer Doug Freeman, who experiences the full visual power of the torture. Freeman, played by Jake Gyllenhaal, is racked by the same national and moral dilemma that SERE instructor Malcolm Nance described as integral to confrontation with the technique earlier in this chapter. The waterboarding breaks the *spectator*. To see the Tool up close, as Freeman does, to really see it, teaches him, and perhaps the viewer, that torture is horrible, unreliable, and untenable. The sight shifts personal and professional allegiances. Freeman stops Anwar's torture, sets him free, arranges safe passage, and—importantly, inevitably—alerts the press. *Rendition* ends as Anwar's rescue makes front-page news and villain Meryl Streep is beset at breakfast by ringing phones. It is as if the best one can do is embarrass and annoy torture perpetrators. Publicity will tow justice in its wake.

Here the antitorture film beautifully demonstrates a common social logic that swaps media attention for political action. Civic action has been a dead end. Anwar's pregnant wife has a single government contact who makes a futile inquiry.[48] Only the CIA operative can clean up the CIA's mess—exactly the same story told by *24*. The film returns the survivor to his home, but neither his moral and legal claims nor his psychological and physical needs are articulated.

Extraordinary Rendition, a thematically similar British film released at the same time, offers just as dim a view on civic action. Informed once again by the Arar story, when the tortured protagonist is finally able to channel shame and rage into human interaction at the end, it is a protest by British Muslims he encounters on the street. The film casts community mobilization as an ominous problem of Arab radicalization. Organized, peaceful, but impassioned citizen action is democracy's problem, not its most powerful mechanism.[49]

The facts of family and community organizing in rendition struggles could not be more different. Siblings, wives, mothers, and fathers in Western nations have been singularly effective in mobilizing others to bring the pressure of their governments to bear on the United States, to secure the release of their loved ones, and to push for redress. Monia Mazigh achieved the release of her husband Arar by speaking to the Canadian press, acquiring legal representation, and organizing an effective and broad coalition consisting of a Muslim women's association, her local members of parliament, the U.S. and Canadian consular offices, Amnesty International, and others.[50] It is no coincidence that both these rendition films made graphic depictions of the Tool pivotal and at the same time obscured the role of civic organizing in asserting the survivors' claims.

Torture Memos Parse the Tools

Although less compact, accessible, or thrilling than the exhibition of torture on prime-time TV, the now declassified Bush legal memoranda on enhanced techniques also deserve scrutiny with attention to the narrative hooks in the security imagination. Legal memos and popular culture emerged in the same moment and worked by the same mechanism; discrete Tools of torture illustrate the precise characteristics and quality of state power. These depictions dabble in the same intimacy; they project and align civilized community, a protected public of the imagination and a human network of violence professionals protected by the memos themselves. In a real way that popular narratives are unable to do, the memos attempt to limit the role of civic action in relation to justice and the state.

Within the legal field, the memos on enhanced techniques have been amply excoriated as flawed by their manipulated reasoning and a result-oriented approach.[51] While legal limits are necessary to deter and prosecute torture, legal permissions have never been necessary to its practice. Yet by 2001, Bush administration lawyers were attempting, for the first time in U.S. history, to grapple with the legal instruments spawned by the human rights activism of recent decades. Despite the nation's vaunted rhetoric, the United States had long delayed, hedged, and only belatedly signed the U.N. Convention Against Torture in 1988, failing to ratify it until 1994. The instrument was partly implemented by federal statute in the Torture Victim Protections Act of 1991, which provided civil damages. Not until the addition of Title 18 U.S.C. 2340A did torture outside of the United States allow for a criminal penalty. If the United States wanted to protect its players from prosecution and wield torture abroad not by proxy but directly, as a fact and threat in the terror war, it would help to have a legal counterinterpretation handy.

Just as counterinsurgency theorists did four decades earlier, the first 2002 memo laid claim to imperial power by redefining torture.[52] A revision followed in 2004, replacing the overt assertion with the equivalent of a careful "no comment."[53] It states there is no need to talk about the president's power to torture because he has directed against it; therefore, the techniques approved here are clearly not torture.[54] This is a standard retrenchment strategy in both colonial management and torture discourse.[55] The claim to (imperial) power is coupled with (benevolent) restraint. Not incidentally, this retraction was written by the acting head of the OLC, Daniel Levin.[56] Levin will reappear among the waterboard reenactors in the section to follow.

Specific Tools of torture are discussed in the 2002 memo "Interrogation of al Qaeda Operative" and the 2005 memo "Certain Techniques," where Tools illustrate the benevolence, competence, and even the care of a state that exercises restraint despite its expansive powers. Excerpts from discussions of sleep deprivation, cramped confinement, and the waterboard will illustrate. Grave violence is soberly eliminated by a plodding series of calibrations and numbing prose that would render anything mundane. The memos exhibit the Tools with a finer and finer grain, making the features of each as concretely, quantifiably tangible, even as visible as possible. In each case, an ensemble of props appears, singly and slowly.

The result is something of an inverse striptease, examining each accessory but erasing reference to a whole body. Sleep deprivation requires subjects to be "fed by hand" a "reduced-calorie diet" during "long periods of standing."[57] Because standing can induce swelling followed by circulatory failure, it will be monitored by a "medical professional." The detainee "would be shackled and prevented from moving freely." Then there is a final surprise regarding "we believe that the use of a diaper cannot be . . ."[58] The detainee is hungry, standing, monitored by a medical professional, and shackled—and, we now understand, naked and wearing a diaper.

More on shackling. It "is used only as a passive means of keeping the detainee awake and, in both the tightness of the shackles and the positioning of the hands, is not intended to cause pain." Each element is examined likewise, demonstrating the pain it does *not* cause: "When the sitting position is used the detainee is seated on a small stool to which he is shackled; the stool supports his weight but is too small to let the detainee balance himself and fall asleep."[59] Quite the opposite of pain, enhanced techniques achieve a state approaching care:

> In the rare instances when horizontal sleep deprivation may be used, a thick towel or blanket is placed under the detainee to protect against reduction of body temperature from contact with the floor, and the manacles and shackles are anchored so as not to cause pain or create tension on any joint. If the detainee is nude and is using an adult diaper, the diaper is checked regularly to prevent skin irritation.[60]

The memos reason that a captive denied sleep in this way for an exact 7.5 days and no more would feel neither severe pain nor suffering, physical or mental.[61]

The memo pointedly contrasts this care and restraint to vivid examples of conduct ruled "extreme and outrageous" in U.S. courts, such as "severe beatings to the genitals, head and other parts of the body with metal pipes and various other items; removal of teeth with pliers; kicking in the face and ribs; breaking of bones and ribs and dislocation of fingers; cutting a figure into the victim's forehead; hanging the victim and beating him; extreme limitations of food and water; and subjection to games of 'Russian roulette.'"[62] The clear suggestion: a week of being hand-fed on a comfy towel is a far cry from pliers, and it is no kick in the face. That is, sleep deprivation may look bad, but we all can imagine worse.

In these memos, the technical descriptions often invite the nonsensical. So it is with "Cramped Confinement," which is to say "placing a detainee in a dark cramped space": "Although . . . physically uncomfortable . . . [the boxes] are not so small as to require the individual to contort his body to sit (small box) or stand (large box)." Brilliantly, even cramped confinement will not cause a cramp. More: "The introduction of an insect does not alter this assessment."[63]

In a 2002 memo, approval for the waterboard depicted the procedure as follows:

Finally, you would like to use a technique called the "waterboard." In this procedure, the individual is bound securely to an inclined bench, which is approximately four feet by seven feet. The individual's feet are generally elevated. A cloth is placed over the forehead and eyes. Water is then applied to the cloth in a controlled manner. As this is done, the cloth is lowered until it covers both the nose and mouth. Once the cloth is saturated and completely covers the mouth and nose, air flow is slightly restricted for 20 to 40 seconds due to the presence of the cloth. This causes an increase in carbon dioxide level in the individual's blood. This increase in the carbon dioxide level stimulates increased effort to breathe. This effort plus the cloth produces the perception of "suffocation and incipient panic," i.e., the perception of drowning. The individual does not breath any water into his lungs. During those 20 to 40 seconds, water is continuously applied from a height of twelve to twenty-four inches. After this period, the cloth is lifted, and the individual is allowed to breathe unimpeded for three or four full breaths. The sensation of drowning is immediately relieved by the removal of the cloth. The procedure may then be repeated. The water is usually applied from a canteen cup or small watering can with a spout. . . . You have also orally informed us that it is likely that this procedure would not last more than 20 minutes in any one application.[64]

Passages such as this reply directly to a highly critical but classified report issued by the CIA inspector general (IG) in 2004. That report found the waterboard was being used "with far greater frequency than initially indicated . . . and . . . in a different manner."[65] The responding memos quote directly from the IG's report—an astonishing move because the IG indicates departure from the guidelines was intentional, if improvisational.

The *IG Report* noted . . . "By contrast, the Agency interrogator . . . applied large volumes of water to a cloth that covered the detainee's mouth and nose. One of the psychologists/interrogators acknowledged this is different . . . *because it is 'for real' and is more poignant and convincing.* . . . There is no *a priori* reason to believe that . . . the frequency and intensity . . . was either efficacious or medically safe." [This has] resulted in a number of changes . . . including limits on the frequency and cumulative use.[66]

To reply to the damning IG report, the memos simply add additional layers of procedure, then again approve the waterboard.

These technical parameters are regulatory fantasy; the mirage of control and limitation quickly disappears when agents decide to apply the techniques "for real" in a manner "poignant and convincing," as the IG report states. As with the language of corporate deniability and colonial governance, parameters exist on the books to be enforced only at will—say, to cast blame on a wayward perpetrator when things go south. The fate of a survivors' lawsuit against the psychologist-interrogators is discussed in the Epilogue.

The gravity of the waterboard in relation to other techniques is noted several times: "We understand that in the escalating regimen of interrogation techniques, the waterboard is considered to be the most serious."[67] It "is by far the most traumatic of the enhanced interrogation techniques" and "presents the most substantial question under the statute."[68] It "could cause choking or similar physical—as opposed to mental—sensations . . . [at] an intensity approaching the degree contemplated by the statute."[69] Further, "the physiological sensation of drowning associated . . . may constitute a 'threat of imminent death' within the meaning of sections 2340–2340A."[70] But simple authorization can allay any fears on the part of interrogators or subjects: "We conclude that its authorized use by adequately trained interrogators could not reasonably be considered specifically intended to cause 'severe physical suffering.'"[71]

At points, the Tool itself starts to disappear beneath the weight of specifications.

> To be sure, in SERE training, the technique is confined to at most two applications (and usually only one). . . . Here, there may be two sessions of up to two hours each, during a 24-hour period, and each session may include multiple applications, of which six may last 10 seconds or longer (but no more than 40 seconds), for a total time of application of as much as 12 minutes in a 24-hour period. Furthermore, the waterboard may be used on up to five days during the 30-day period for which it is approved.[72]

Were one interested to work the math here, the new, tighter limitations indicate that a prisoner can be drowned thirty-two times a day across a four-hour period. This can continue for five days.[73]

As for the community convened by the Tool, survivors disappear entirely. The technique can only appear sanitized and benign if the actual experience of survivors can be kept off the page. The single reference to survivor testimony is fourth hand, and it occurs in a misnumbered footnote on the waterboard. "We are aware," it begins, that Mr. Johnson "testified that some U.S. military personnel who have undergone waterboard training have apparently stated 'that it's taken them 15 years to get over it.' You have informed us that, in 2002 the CIA made inquiries to . . . personnel involved in SERE training and that the DOD was not aware of any information that would substantiate such statements nor is the CIA."[74] Already excerpted, scarcely sourced, and cast in doubt, the footnote goes on to dismiss his testimony on the basis of what the memo authors *heard* the CIA *heard* of what the Defense personnel "were aware."[75] The observation refers to a torture treatment director's summary of what some military SERE trainees "have apparently stated."

Just as the memos unceremoniously banish survivors from their imagined nation, they also incarnate two other vague group identities: "enemy combatants" and their spectral opposite, the citizen-subjects of empire, "the U.S. population." "Both [Khalid Sheikh Mohammed] and Abu Zubaydah had 'expressed their belief that the general U.S. population was "weak," lacked resilience, and would be unable to "do what was necessary" to prevent terrorists from succeeding in their goals.'"[76] Incredibly, this secondhand ridicule stands alone in support of the CIA belief that it would have been unable to obtain critical information without harshest coercion.

Outside medical experts are but a flickering presence, an occlusion that points directly to the tight circle of relationships being forged and the network constructed. The refrains "we have learned" and "we understand" continuously indicate that it is the CIA that both requests legal guidance and supplies the only data. The result is an epistolary, almost intimate mode of address between the author-lawyers and the CIA: "You have asked us," "We understand," "We believe" alongside evidence no better than rumor or gossip—"your opinion" and "our belief." The actual practice of torture, and certainly those subjected to it, are irrelevant.

In this, the memos illustrate the insights by Michael Taussig and Ann Stoler discussed earlier. They are the essence of neocolonial disregard and the labor required to construct it. Forging a self-interested and tight in-house community, a series of partial understandings and anecdotal impressions are converted into facts and thereby into stunningly, grossly ineffective policy.[77] As a result, policy is based on fascinating leaps of faith, deference to intimate assurances, conditional conditions, and triple negatives. As with depictions in prime time or Hollywood, the government is self-sufficient and self-correcting. The memos' laborious demonstration suggests bureaucratic networks can regulate themselves and do so through a process of in-house consultation that stands in for the democratic process itself. Despite the intimate threads that structure memos and bind the professional network, each memo also sets the terms of distrust, self-preservation, and blame. If error is to be found, it will be with what "you have told us." The bargain struck here is a professional commonplace, but one that is far from neutral or amoral. It underwrites a partnership in violence and impunity.

Given the mixed agendas and distrust that join this community, real faith is invested in the legal profession and its codes of practice as well as the state. Indeed, it has proven difficult from within the codes of the profession to point to authorization of torture as misconduct. A five-year ethics review by the Office of Professional Responsibility discovered as much when their boss reversed their findings.[78]

In this sense, the memos live completely within the Archetype's illusory world, as every Tool must, where violence takes an incremental, creeping approach to an exact number of minutes and seconds, when it suddenly crosses the line to torture. The memos imagine a world in which civilizational threats can be contained by carefully performed rituals of state power, a world in which mere functionaries, interrogators, or others apply the technique without improvisation, without charged emotional or professional investment, and without bravado inspired by spectators or urgency inspired by a supervisor.

The memos contributed to the practical task of creating and expanding the network of violence workers—men and women who will never read them but are assured continuously that they exist. The network extended to key leaders in the American Psychological Association, who altered their code of ethics to support the work of the psychologist-interrogators and the OLC, as I discuss in the Epilogue. Word of such assurances circulated across real communities of practice in environments where many borrowed and picked up tactics from others. Because the memos offer seeming protections, they strengthen collaboration and pull in the more risk-averse players.

These memos are the Tool at its most sweeping and lethal because they tap the power of the state to bind a community in violence. In this social function, they mirror the compelling plot on *24* that was convening a broad television audience, elite and nonelite, around the Tool.

The Waterboard in Political Coverage

All the events of October 2007—the press releases by the Parents Television Council, Human Rights First's Prime Time Torture Awards, and the celebrity-laden *Rendition*—were certainly timed and intended to generate debate, provoke larger discussion, and reach expanding audiences. Breaking news of secret memos actually did.

Members of the Senate reacted strongly to the *New York Times* report of secret memos, and they made clear these revelations would be a point of contention in the attorney general nomination hearings just weeks away.[79] This was a test of nominee Mukasey as well as Senate oversight itself. If approved, Mukasey would head the Justice Department. It was the Department's Office of Legal Counsel (OLC) under Alberto Gonzalez that first engineered immunity for perpetrators. Would the Senate correct course and hold the nominee to a higher standard?

When Mukasey met with the Senate over the next weeks, he was quizzed about his legal opinion on waterboarding (but not, however, on the combined techniques of freezing temperatures or head slapping, also reported by the *Times*). In his view, was this torture, or was it not? Many media outlets were soon reporting the technicalities; most described it as simulated drowning. When Mukasey said he did not know what the technique actually involved, Rhode Island senator Sheldon Whitehouse described it in some detail. Although Mukasey called the procedure "repugnant," he refused to classify it legally. Despite consternation, the two critical votes that ultimately confirmed him came from the Democratic senators who had led the initial charge against him, Diane Feinstein and Charles Schumer.[80]

Four aspects of the news coverage deserve emphasis. First, the community of experts convened for the Mukasey hearings and quizzed on the waterboard included interrogators and Malcolm Nance, the retired Navy instructor for SERE. No torture survivors were invited to testify in this capacity; nor were persons expert in the treatment of survivors. News coverage followed suit. Torture survivors in the United States are numerous. Their perspectives and experience could have informed speculative news, the ongoing debate, the depictions in drama, the writing of memos, investigative reporting, or these Senate hearings at any point.[81] In this moment, among the many dozens of U.S. articles published relevant to Mukasey, torture, and waterboarding, only one story in the *Washington Post*, three in the *New York Times*, and one editorial even mentioned torture survivors.[82] Physicians for Human Rights tried to correct this and hosted a press event featuring two survivors, Henri Alleg, author of *The Question*, a testimonial account of his own torture by the French in Algeria, and Vann Nath, a survivor of the Khmer Rouge torture camp Tuol Sleng. As a result, a piece on Alleg ran in the British *Independent* in November 2007.[83]

Second, instead of survivor perspectives, the Mukasey coverage repeated CIA claims, for instance, that waterboarding had been approved for use only three times, was used by the CIA only, and was last used in 2003.[84] To parrot the CIA's claims demonstrated a grossly trusting or incurious stance toward a technique that had been initiated as part of a secret program. These secretive approvals were more shocking than torture elsewhere. Even though members of the U.S. Special Forces, military interrogators, and military police had reported varieties of water treatment and abuse since 2004 across Iraq and Afghanistan, news did not pursue the variety or reach of dunking or drowning tortures.[85] Even Malcolm Nance, who insisted the waterboard was torture, suggested the CIA use was worse, because "these things will happen on the battlefield."[86]

Third, the waterboard was described in the *New York Times* and the OLC memos alike as the "ultimate" on the civilizational scale, or "by far the most traumatic of the enhanced interrogation techniques," regardless of subjective experience.[87] If the waterboard received attention as the ultimate, it did so because its presentation conformed so perfectly to the audience's archetypal view of torture and the Tool. By this time, sleep deprivation, hypothermia along with cramped confinement, audio assault, lengthy stress positions, and prolonged isolation had been reported from all corners of Iraq, Afghanistan, and Guantánamo. Yet supervisors in the CIA had moved quickly and secretly to destroy ninety-two video recordings of interrogators waterboarding prisoners. As former CIA deputy director John Gannon explained: "To a spectator it would look like torture. And torture is wrong."[88]

The fourth and final aspect of the coverage to stress is that the mythos of the ultimate technique seemed to correspond with the claim the waterboard was the most efficient tool at an interrogator's disposal. Former CIA officer John Kiriakou stepped into the limelight with a torture anecdote that confirmed these assumptions on ABC News in December 2007. Kiriakou claimed waterboarding had worked to obtain lifesaving information from captive Abu Zubaydah in a mere thirty or thirty-five seconds: "From that day on he answered every question just as I'm talking to you now."[89] Kiriakou was dubbed "the man of the hour" by a CNN anchor, and his tale was repeated across a number of outlets. Media embraced him as credible and virtually ignored survivor expertise. The lack of skeptical reporting was especially tragic in light of the revelation in spring 2009 that in the cases of just two men, the drowning technique had been used a total of 266 times.[90] These flabbergasting numbers gave lie to claims for efficiency of the Tool or its judicious use. Even this total of 266 uses on two men should have been received skeptically. In January 2010, Kiriakou recanted to hype a book tour. He admitted he was not present when Zubaydah was interrogated; as one should expect from a torture anecdote, he had relied on CIA gossip when peddling the original tale.[91]

Waterboard Reenactors

Perhaps as striking as the exclusion of survivors from the hearings and news was the attention garnered by waterboard reenactors. In circular fashion, proof of one's position on its fitness and features relies on further display of the Tool. While fueling the circular debate, these reenactments efficiently delivered the Tool's foundational narrative. Current TV, for example, capitalized on the interest with "Kaj Larsen Goes Waterboarding," a feature in which a correspondent, himself a former Navy SEAL who experienced waterboarding in training, paid two professionals $800 to subject him to the technique on camera. In the broadcast, the tone is sensational, part extreme sport and part deadly experiment. The participants had agreed to a safe signal that could end the procedure immediately. On camera, one sees Larsen on his back, mouth and nose covered with cloth, as two men pour water over his face and torso. They use their bodies to increase pressure to his chest in response to Larsen's reflexive struggle. When the producer finally halts the torture, Larsen sits up coughing, trying to recover his breathing. A meek question from his producer can be heard off-camera: "Are you okay?" Larsen simultaneously laughs and gasps: "That was truly horrible. . . . I thought I was going to die. . . . [Although] you know it is controlled, it's not by you. It doesn't feel controlled."[92]

Larsen's voluntary torture repeated a similar waterboard demonstration by Fox News's Steve Harrigan in 2006. Harrigan's feature showed him undergoing three variations of waterboarding at the side of a pristine blue pool. Interviewed afterward, he was clear that what he underwent was torture: "I don't know what else you could call it." One year later, in the context of the Mukasey hearings, Fox Reports recalled that experiment. Brit Hume reinterpreted it, qualifying Harrigan's own account in a familiar way: "We even had our own correspondent Steve Harrigan subject himself to waterboarding. He was placed on his back, upside-down, water poured over him and up his nose, his feet above his head. It scared the daylights out of him, but he is still with us, and we have not asked him, but I don't think he feels that he has been subjected to the prisons of tyrant regimes and Saddam Hussein's torture chambers, or any dark and descending stairways."[93] In a word: it looked bad, but we all can imagine worse.

Reenactment on this order soon became a media phenomenon and a mode of activism in its own right. Showmanship increased. Conservative radio talk host Erik Mancow Mueller volunteered for the treatment on camera in May 2009.[94] Christopher Hitchens underwent waterboarding for an August 2008 piece in *Vanity Fair*.[95] Both declared it torture as soon as they could collect themselves enough to speak. Ex–professional wrestler, onetime Navy SEAL, and former governor of Minnesota Jesse "The Body" Ventura filled airwaves by challenging right-wing Fox News pundit and waterboard supporter Sean Hannity.[96] With braggadocio that echoed World Wrestling Entertainment promotionals, Ventura claimed he could change Hannity's mind about torture and make him sing praise to Obama within a few heart-pounding seconds. Numerous homemade waterboard videos cropped up on YouTube. They attempted political seriousness, political humor, or *Jackass*-style feats of daring. In 2007, some activists and human rights organizations also took up live waterboard performance. For instance, Code Pink and the ACLU held waterboard protest demonstrations on Capitol Hill during the Mukasey hearings.

In the same vein, Amnesty International released two short films in 2007, hoping to run them in movie theaters and thereby direct viewers to its Unsubscribe-Me campaign against torture. One, called *Waiting for the Guards*, offers a "real demonstration" of the pain induced by stress positions. Viewers are told that the actor, "a performance artist" who had done "endurance work in the past," agreed with the directors that the only way to show the suffering of torture was to endure it himself. He subjected himself to forced standing on unstable boxes in a garage-like warehouse and did this for six hours. Website information about the film says, "The sounds you hear are real, the pain is real, this is not acting." The opening shots feature the man bent and struggling to balance on the box, accompanied by sounds of labored breathing and anguished groans. The second of these Amnesty shorts, called *The Stuff of Life,* films the same man enduring a drowning technique. Up-tempo music plays as a slow-motion strand of clear water flows horizontally across a black screen and then turns downward into the man's nose and throat. He is strapped to a tilted board.[97]

In short order, artistic endeavors staged the waterboard. In "Waterboard Thrill Ride," an installation by Steve Powers that debuted in 2008 in a small space along the Coney Island boardwalk, passers-by could pay a dollar to watch from behind a barred window as two animatronic figures, one dressed as a hooded captor and the other as an orange-jumpsuited captive, enact a waterboarding. Says Powers, "What's more obscene, the official position that waterboarding is not torture, or *our* official position that it's a thrill ride?"[98] *Waterboard,* a 2009 multimedia performance by Massachusetts playwright Stephanie Skier, offered a campy mix of song and dance, historical news reports, redacted government documents, video interviews, and children's water games to explore the history of U.S. citizens involved with the tactic as both perpetrators or subjects (in the Philippines, World War II–era Japan, and Texas). Advertised as an event "featuring live waterboarding," the two-person show did not disappoint. The actors alternately waterboard each other on stage. Water pours and complete silence reigns until the first finally sits up, soaking and gasping, to sing what becomes a duet ("I am waterboarding you / are waterboarding me . . .") in front of a stunned audience.

All these examples hold to the same faith that seeing is believing. In pundit exhibitions, human rights messaging, or activist demonstrations, the subject on the waterboard is expected to endure it, then promptly sit up and offer a verdict for the viewers. These bizarre intersections of political theater and film, or reality TV and "news," do capture the "cultural Zeitgeist" surrounding torture, as the *Solitary* TV producers had put it. But if the involuntary and uncontrollable are central to torture, what exactly do voluntary enactments demonstrate or reveal?

Such visual and physical confrontation with the Tool confirms the authority of firsthand experience to locate certainty and displace doubt. The rational, open-minded subject goes to the brink in order to bring back an unbiased and definitive account. Fortuitously, the waterboard offers a moral education and epiphany for both the subject and the watching public. Each venture enacts a small drama ready-made for media; it mimes investigative reporting and evokes a sensation like democracy. In this it precisely parallels the Heart of Darkness form of speculative news that appeared across 2001 and 2004, discussed in chapter 3. A seemingly objective citizen-reporter journeys into the terrain of so-called dark arts to explore the torturer and his tools, then returns to us with tragic knowledge and an ambivalent lament. But in contrast to long-form journalism, where the Heart of Darkness template has its home, the live enactment is made to be viewed as well as copied, sampled, and circulated. Clips are shared, interpreted, and mimicked in different contexts to different ends, be it a YouTube prank or Brit Hume's unsolicited pronouncement "we all can imagine worse" on his colleague's experience. These are torture events, but they are thoroughly mediatized from their inception and carefully produced as spectacle.

The limits of technique. Graphic depictions of the waterboard, or any Tool, teach nothing about torture. Like depictions on film and television, these displays engineer looking and an exchange of looks; they animate emotional, political, and social alignments as they escort in fundamental cultural plots. No matter the reenactor's stance on the Tool or whether the reenactment persuades the viewer it is barbaric or sophisticated; the focus on technique enacts a pantomime of community formation and national identity. As it brings state power center stage, it describes the citizens' relation to that power and asserts the role of media and civic action in the democratic state. Like the classified depictions of the Tool in legal discourse, the mass-mediated epiphany purports to perform a service to democracy. As it enacts a small notional paradigm of torture, it activates a small and equally notional paradigm of democratic debate. What is more, like Kiriakou and his concocted anecdote, the reenactor earns status and attention for insider knowledge, strength, and daring.

However, core aspects of that worldview were engineered decades ago. The reenactments raise questions that lead us directly to the national security imagination and what it tries to push off stage: And what is missing? Actual torture survivors are cast from the debate; in fact, as with the executive memos, the performance itself depends on their absence. The third party who travels into the realm of experience is more interesting, credible, and informative than the survivor who has already been there.

The necessary eclipse of the survivor from community is illustrated well when considering two unexpected participants. First, consider survivor Jacobo Timerman's jarring request to relive his torture for a U.S. TV audience. In 1981, the Argentine survivor had just released his powerful and now classic testimonial of mass violence under the military junta, *Prisoner without a Name, Cell without a Number*. He told *CBS Reports* to forget the TV interview and to torture him instead; electricity and water would replace question and answer: "They want me in twenty minutes to explain what I've already written in hundreds of pages. How do you explain to the American people what torture is in twenty minutes. . . . Torture me on television."[99] He continued, "A doctor would make sure I don't die. . . . There are excellent torture doctors in abundance—in Argentina, El Salvador, Iran, Cuba, Brazil, the Soviet Union."

Hearing Timerman, the CBS producer was "struck silent," finally telling him: "If you volunteer to be tortured, you will trivialize the evil of torture. People will call it a publicity stunt." Recalling the offer in 2005, the *Columbia Journalism Review* noted Timerman's "point [was] profoundly serious. How, given the media glut, do you break through and communicate the *terrible truth?*" The question haunts. One might think the answer depends on which truth one hopes to convey. But as I argue in these chapters, the very question is wrong. The truths of torture do not and cannot lurk within the Anecdote, Archetype, or Tool—elements that purport to end the dithering on torture but actually drive it in circles. To believe in the revelatory power of seeing any of these is to enter a familiar trap. It is a distraction that cultivates disregard.

Torture is a complex social undertaking. Consider what Timerman—in place of, say, the supposedly objective freelance correspondent—could make visible about such a process. In order to engage a survivor in such theater or even to interview that person, would coverage be forced to frame the event with historical, political, and personal background, as well as to provide context on the ideology, allegiances, and funding fueling Argentina's dirty war? Might coverage discuss the process by which Argentina and its people constructed and debased particular groups as national security threats and targets for torture, and how Jewish journalist Timerman was cast among them? Might coverage explore the consequences for the survivors and dead, the postregime immunity legislation erected in Argentina with the complicity of civil institutions and decades later undone by community action? For that matter, might the conversation also weigh the

U.S. record of complicity in repressive Central and South American counterinsurgency and security alliances? Placing a survivor at the center of the spectacle might begin to direct attention toward the networks and public complicity, and toward the social mechanisms that feed, define, sustain, and excuse torture. But likely even that would not.

No less disturbing than the reenactments proposed by Timerman and Amnesty International was the news of a second unexpected volunteer: memo author Daniel Levin, who served as acting assistant attorney general in the OLC from 2004 to 2005. After he penned the cosmetic revision to the president's torture power, he decided that he too ought to experience the waterboard if he was to determine its legality. At Levin's request, "a Washington area military installation" administered his lesson in torture.[100] What Levin learned was that waterboarding is tolerable. He returned to his office not to outlaw it but to add his calibrations to a set of guidelines for its use, setting additional limits concerning procedures, duration, and the medical personnel on site (whom Timerman bluntly termed "torture doctors"). Before Levin could finish that approval, he was replaced with a more aggressively prowaterboard Stephen Bradbury. Bradbury became the author of the secret memos on techniques.

Now, the lesson Amnesty International might want to draw from Daniel Levin's self-study in torture could be that a Washington lawyer would be treated more carefully than a rendition detainee. The more appropriate caution would be that detailing, visualizing, or reenacting a technique brings us no closer to torture. The evidence is unstable. The lesson, like the visual record, is up for grabs. The Tool can fuel a range of different political stances while peddling very consistent cultural narratives.

The fascination with the Tool is neither natural nor neutral. Unspoken assumptions underpin the spectacle. The waterboard display reinforces the national security fantasy of torture in which pain and suffering emanate from the techniques and can therefore be regulated just short of the point at which torture begins. In that fantasy, torture can be separated from gendered racial and colonial suppression and from the network of psychologists, lawyers, other torturecrats, rendition operatives, linguists, guards, witnesses, or the supply chain for torture equipment, transport, or profit. It ignores the constructed detention environment of total powerlessness and the collaborative process of pain. The performance enacts the limits of moral exploration and democratic debate, but nothing more. As viewers, we come no closer to torture, but we do assemble around the debate to participate in its social functions. We forge identities, align and position ourselves against others, and reanimate shared assumptions about violence.

The Triumph of Technique, the Failure of Justice: Maher Arar

Arar v. Ashcroft was taken up on November 9, the same day Michael Mukasey was confirmed by the Senate. Contrast the media scrum convened around waterboarding with the small attention devoted to Maher Arar's court proceedings. The ritual obsession with the Tool outplayed the man.

From the perspective of 2007, one may not have considered *Arar v. Ashcroft* a long shot on its merits. Many rendition cases had come to light since Arar filed suit in 2004. The body of evidence supporting his case included the official Canadian Commission of Inquiry findings on Arar and Canada's formal apology clearing his name and granting financial compensation for torture. Yet the United States continued to list Arar as a terrorist suspect and barred him from the country. Despite this, Arar and his team secured a video conference before subcommittees of the U.S. House of Representatives on October 18, 2007. This was two weeks before his case was to be heard, and it was meant to draw public attention. Several lawmakers took the opportunity to apologize to him for his treatment; others pointedly did not. In a statement, Secretary of State Condoleeza Rice, who had organized Arar's rendition to Syria when she was head of the National Security Agency, called it a "deportation" case that had been "mishandled."[101] The covert, collaborative multistate arrangement that intercepted and abducted him and delivered him to "the grave" is no less an apparatus for torture than the other Tools considered in this chapter. In rendition, this practice was repeated for a large set of captives far from any battlefield using different corporate and geographical partners and switch points.

However, the court found the act of laying out Arar's claims might divulge state secrets threatening national security. The confidential agreements linking private and state actors could indeed be considered state secrets. Law professor David Luban explains the breadth of this government defense, and it is staggering: "The 'states secrets defense' declares that a case . . . must be dismissed—even if the plaintiff offers to prove his case without using government sources."[102] "In real world terms," he writes, "that would be indistinguishable from covering for torture."[103] Arar's case was dismissed in 2007, a decision that was later reheard before the entire twelve-judge panel of the same court and dismissed once again. In June 2010, the U.S. Supreme Court denied his petition, ending his case in U.S. courts.

Many other innocent boys and men seized for torture had cases quashed by the Bush and then the Obama Justice Department in exactly this way. British citizen Binyam Mohamed had his penis cut repeatedly with a razor in Morocco; German citizen Khalid El-Masri was subjected to months of positional torture in Afghanistan and Macedonia; the torture of Mauritanian Mohamedou Slahi and German Murat Kurnaz began in rendition and continued in Guantánamo.[104] The Obama administration also pressured other governments to keep details of survivor treatment classified.[105] Although the Obama team repudiated torture on entering office, they examined the rendition program and asserted those networks must remain available but be more closely monitored.[106] The Obama finding deftly kept past activity along these confidential circuits secret and out of open court. Cases attempting to sue private aircraft and other corporate partners for participating in U.S. rendition networks have also failed.[107]

But it is no good to blame lawyers, the OLC, or the president if, after much sound and fury, the Senate confirmed an attorney general despite his punt on torture. Public attention surrounded the waterboard as the claims of a survivor were thrown out. This chapter has argued that like legal discourse, popular culture, and media, political discourse and activism too easily narrow our attention to the Tools. Each form testifies with the same faith in the image, with the same conviction that we will know it when we see it. We stay locked within an interrogational stereotype, reinforcing a so-called science of calibrated torture and a scale that does not exist, debating a false opposition between civilization and torture. We need a larger reckoning with the social imaginary on torture. The next chapter considers media preoccupation with perpetrators and the way the active presence of survivors can disrupt that spell.

5

Perpetrators

Sabrina Harman, Tony Lagouranis, and Crafted Confession

>   LAGOURANIS: Well, it's funny, because at that time [the Abu Ghraib] scandal broke and the pictures came out, I was using the harshest tactics that I used all year in Mosul. I was using dogs, I was using stress positions. And I look at those pictures and I was horrified. And I thought . . . you know, these were bad apples. Because . . .
>   MATTHEWS: But you were doing the same thing.
>   LAGOURANIS: Well not exactly.
>   MATTHEWS: Were you doing that, putting dogs within a couple feet of a guy's face?
>   LAGOURANIS: Yes, we were doing that.
>   MATTHEWS: Well what were they doing differently than you?
>   LAGOURANIS: Well that particular picture could have been a picture of me.
>
>   —*Hardball with Chris Matthews,* MSNBC, January 16, 2006
>
>   Perhaps, I've thought for a long time, I also deserve to be prosecuted.
>
>   —Tony Lagouranis, "Tortured Logic," *New York Times,* February 28, 2006

Specialist Tony Lagouranis does not shy away from complexity. A Chicagoan, Great Books enthusiast, student of ancient Greek, Hebrew, and Arabic, and military interrogator, Lagouranis was thirty-one at the time he entered Iraq, where he served from 2004 to 2005. There he read literary classics, including Hemingway, Tom Wolfe, Twain, Orwell, and Tolstoy's *War and Peace,* twice. Like other soldiers he watched and rewatched Reagan-era war-and-glory standbys—*Top Gun, Red Dawn, Rambo*—and antiwar classics like *Full Metal Jacket, Platoon, Apocalypse Now,* and *Three Kings.*

Lagouranis also watched CNN's coverage of Senate hearings on the torture of Iraqis at Abu Ghraib prison where he was stationed, and he listened in anger and confusion to the bafflement expressed by top military and civilian commanders, including Secretary of Defense Donald Rumsfeld. When

General Antonio Taguba's investigation leaked to the media in April 2004, he read the report, which detailed numerous specific assaults not visible in the widely circulated photographs, including rape, sodomy, and twelve corpses.[1]

Tony Lagouranis also tortured prisoners in Iraq. He planned and perpetrated torture in Mosul and Al-Asad airfield. He was witness to severe injuries and heard testimony from those who suffered brutality at Forward Operating Base Kalsu in North Babel and at Abu Ghraib, where he was stationed. His book records evidence of severe beating at Abu Ghraib well after the prison had been "sanitized" in the wake of the scandal. Lagouranis himself conducted torture by hypothermia, isolation, sleep deprivation, extended stress positions (kneeling, standing, and ninety-degree wall squats), hooding, high-decibel sound, hunger, strobe lights, and staged attacks with dogs. At one point he grappled with a deep desire to cut off a subject's fingers.

When Lagouranis stepped forward, voluntarily offering interviews on torture after an honorable discharge in July 2005, media outlets were ready to run his story, and human rights monitoring organizations turned to him for evidence and a form of expertise.

The fascination with perpetrators is as central to torture in the national security imagination as is the Anecdote and the Rationale it supports; it is as powerful as the Archetype with its twin agonists, perpetrator and subject; it is as compelling as the Tool, the instrument or technique applied professionally or barbarically. His interviews sparked angry exchanges with ex-military and right-wing bloggers on sites like Blackfive.net or HaloScan.com, who vehemently rejected Lagouranis's testimony and called him a hypocrite, "buddy fucker," and worse. In part owing to this response, Lagouranis published his own book-length testimonial with the assistance of Allen Mikaelian in 2007.

In *Fear Up Harsh: An Army Interrogator's Dark Journey through Iraq*, Lagouranis claims responsibility and tells his story: how within five months of his arrival in Iraq he had not only become a torturer but also had begun to recognize himself as such, and how he spent the rest of his deployment trying to reckon with that knowledge emotionally, morally, and procedurally. As a firsthand account, Lagouranis's story is important for the way it documents patterns of torture well beyond Abu Ghraib prison. Cast as a developmental narrative, the book attempts to trace several strands of causation and shows them converge at Mosul where, by Lagouranis's account, he undertook the worst tortures and faced the worst in himself.

Yet just as Lagouranis's press interviews seem to mix acknowledgment, denial, and responsibility for torture, the book-length narrative is no straightforward journey from moral blindness and failure onward to recognition, responsibility, and remorse. Even as his behavior escalates, his responses are simultaneously remorseful, sadistic, and perfunctory. Many times Lagouranis allows himself to recognize and explore some of these inconsistencies; often they go unremarked. Worse, his media interviewers did no better.

In this chapter, I use Lagouranis's account of torture in Iraq to explore the quality of attention granted perpetrator voices in U.S. media. The first section looks to early documentary efforts that enlisted perpetrators in responding to torture in the war on terror. Given the performative dimensions of perpetrator confessions, it explores how formal choices on the part of producers and directors pressure (or fail to pressure) that performance in pursuit of their own tale.

The second section uses Lagouranis's analysis to highlight the role of the civilian world and media in generating and sustaining a fantasy that supports torture. Excerpts from press interviews are positioned against discussion of the memoir to point up the extent to which his expectations, and others' expectations of him, were propelled by the fantasy of the expert interrogator whose dark arts—that is, secret, illicit knowledge and skill—unlock the mysteries in men. In disrupting this fantasy, the memoir makes a strong case that torture was ineffective and counterproductive from an intelligence-gathering point of view.

The section that follows speaks to two dimensions of torture's work made clear in this book: the details of organizational setting, and the many social functions of torture it describes. Lagouranis demonstrates torture was systematically encouraged and protected by the intent and incompetence of the command; by organizational, material and procedural infrastructure; and by a culture of communal influence, competition, and individuals' own psychological needs.

The fourth and final section identifies key contradictions and omissions in Lagouranis's performance. Lagouranis expresses remorse and owns up to terrible acts capable of producing severe pain and lifelong physical, emotional, and psychological damage in the survivors, as documented by Physicians for Human Rights.[2] His account demonstrates torture was systematic and pervasive in many regions inside Iraq. By speaking out, Lagouranis counters official denials and identifies the ideology, infrastructure, and social functions supporting criminal acts. Even so, the book is careful not to give up names. Nor does it land him in jail. It does not advance criminal proceedings, call out perpetrators, identify victims, or locate survivors. Instead, numerous contradictions and silences in the memoir and his press interviews demand we confront the dangerous political implications of a persona easily embraced by media yet carefully crafted to claim responsibility and diffuse it at the same time.

This chapter concludes with examples from Argentina, Brazil, Chile, and South Africa that show the pressure survivors can exert to challenge comfortable media formats and assumptions in the face of perpetrator confessions and denials.

Perpetrator Performance

At a midpoint in his memoir, Tony Lagouranis pauses to assess himself for the reader: "I'd been skeptical of all the things we were doing—the whole torture lite package—and I'd been following orders, and I tried to make sure we didn't go too far."[3] As Lagouranis does here, torturers have been telling their stories for a long time, whether in the context of truth commissions or tabloid TV, from within the postdictatorial transitions in countries like Argentina or Chile, or within long-standing democracies such as France. What have we learned?

Documentary films that emerged during the early twenty-first-century torture debate, such as *Ghosts of Abu Ghraib* (2007) and *Standard Operating Procedure* or *SOP* (2008), showcase perpetrator testimony from the military police and interrogators (MPs, MIs) of Abu Ghraib, who were sentenced on charges ranging from assault to dereliction of duty. Their statements on video are by and large flat but fascinating; they show little remorse for torture, violence, or humiliation, although sometimes a speaker will agree the acts captured in photos were "uncomfortable" or "bizarre." They blame the interrogators who tasked them and they blame the system and each other, in effect justifying themselves. In this sense, their testimony, as one might expect, supports the narrative thrust of the films, which attempt to look through the eyes of these low-ranking perpetrators upward to establish responsibility for torture up the chain of command.

The Abu Ghraib photos triggered many other testimonial and confessional acts. Several MPs, linguists, and interrogators in Afghanistan and Guantánamo as well as Abu Ghraib published first-person, mass-market accounts in this period. These participant-observers—such as Chris Mackey, Erik Saar, James Yee, Janis Karpinski, Lynndie England, and Sabrina Harman—earnestly excuse themselves from responsibility as they bear witness to a range of other abuses and indict the system. Their personal denials notwithstanding, these narratives point to torture as systematic and system-wide. As author of the first sustained narrative to attempt personal responsibility for acts of torture, Tony Lagouranis is exceptional among this group. He too appears in at least one of the documentary films; I will return to discuss his case later.

In contrast to a common focus on perpetrator confession and command environment, it is hard not to notice how few documentaries appearing at the time of Lagouranis's memoir follow the story of those who survived torture or died (*Taxi to the Dark Side,* 2007; *GITMO: New Rules of War,* 2006; *The Road to Guantánamo,* 2006). Fewer still carry the survivor's own testimony at length (*The Prisoner, or How I Planned to Kill Tony Blair,* 2006).

Extraordinary as this confessional phenomenon may seem in the United States, it exists within a larger field. Political scientist Leigh Payne has studied torturer confessions in the wake of deadly regimes in Brazil, South Africa, Argentina, and Chile. She foregrounds perpetrator testimonial as public performance. Each disclosure has a specific set of incentives and circumstances that bring it into being. According to Payne, confessions are not truths: "They are merely accounts, explanations, and justifications . . . or personal versions of the past." Most never apologize, they do not recognize their actions as wrong, and they use common strategies to diffuse and minimize responsibility. As selective "salvage operations," they reinvent the past in moral terms.[4] To do so, they borrow the language of the interviewer and whatever "culturally available vocabulary . . . [will] make past deviance more compatible with current norms."[5] As performance, perpetrator accounts are not static; they change form with changing political contexts and opportunities. Further, each manipulates a particular setting, timing, staging, script, audience, and gestural and tonal language.

Payne found that perpetrators resort to recurring modes of confessional performance, including (most rarely) Remorse, and more frequently Heroism, Denial, Betrayal, Sadism, and Amnesia. Note that each is a narrative device and a device with specific social functions. Betrayal, denial, or remorse may be most dramatically satisfying to audiences (to all but the survivors) because they can bring dialogue and investigation to an end. Interviews with MP Sabrina Harman, who served at Abu Ghraib before Lagouranis, present a good example of how perpetrators wield these modes and craft their own accounts to meet the moment and opportunity. Filmed for two different documentaries, her scenes also capture the formal dimensions of perpetrator performance Payne stresses. The army found Harman guilty of six of seven counts against her for participation in the Abu Ghraib tortures. She was then an Army Reserve specialist in the 372nd MP Company. She received a sentence of six months. In one scene from Rory Kennedy's *Ghosts of Abu Ghraib*, Harman offers an account of her relationship to the Abu Ghraib torture photographs and to photography itself. Harman holds up to the camera an enlarged photo of herself posing next to the corpse of Manadel al-Jamadi. She describes the scene.

> We came to the prison, we were told a prisoner just died and died of a heart attack. He was in the shower . . . in a body bag. . . . We went in and I believe Corporal Graner took a photo of me. It was just the dead guy, it was supposed to be just the dead guy, and we didn't realize until after this photo that he was bleeding in places that you wouldn't bleed from, me getting a heart attack. The thumbs up: I got that from little kids; the smile. . . . I smile for cameras; it's the natural thing you do in front of a camera. It wasn't anything negative toward this guy. I didn't know he was just murdered. It's war, it's a dead guy, no big deal.

Harman's interview in *Ghosts* offers a posture of denial: a corpse was not unusual; flashing smiles and thumbs-up for a camera were natural things; someone else initiated the photo.

The explanation for Harman's photographs differs in *SOP*, a 2008 film that foregrounds the evidentiary nature and chronology of the photographs.[6] There, true to the narrative of the larger film, she explains her involvement with photography as evidentiary. Harman's interview suggests her photos were meant to record "proof" or evidence of the unbelievable "shit that goes down." To convey this, *SOP* features letters from Harman to her wife. Images of the text with Harman's voice-over offer a more intimate and in-the-moment confessional performance, which is positioned as authentic. In a letter dated days after her photographs with the corpse, she notes she may be under investigation. She writes that she will be "forced to" continue to "fake a smile" in every photograph if she wants "to keep taking pictures of these events."[7] The statement explains her thumbs-up smile for another photographer as a means to justify her own use of the camera. Yet Harman's claim to false gestures of enjoyment seems at odds with a fact that is cut from the film but reported in the book *SOP* that was issued at the same time. She notoriously necropsied a cat and mummified its head in Iraq. She then positioned the head in different locations and situations to feature it in an obsessive sequence of ninety photos and two short videos. The dead clearly hold other attractions and pleasures for Harman. Photography does as well—perhaps as amusement for herself or an anticipated audience, as a form of creativity, or as a way to engage in trophy keeping. These the film obscures. The *New York Times* reported at the time that Harman had "forensic interests"; her father, a homicide policeman, brought home photographs of crime scenes and autopsies to analyze with the family.

Harman's performances in these two films, *Ghosts* and *SOP,* show the fluidity of confessional acts, but also, importantly, the formal choices interviewers and filmmakers exert to craft a larger narrative. They control the interview and editing process and establish the context at hand. For example, *Ghosts of Abu Ghraib* establishes its own narrative at the start with footage from Stanley Milgram's 1961 studies on obedience to authority. The director then offers two additional explanatory contexts for the torture: first, the trauma of September 11, and second, the ghostly and dangerous prison setting. In Abu Ghraib, terrorized soldiers transform into "monsters" and "robots," in MP Javal Davis's words.

The director of *Ghosts* uses soldier interviews to describe this ominous prison setting, narrate events, and detail their actions while framed as talking heads. Their stories are intercut with titles, newsreel footage, or headshots of other informants who offer fact or chronology, but not critique, lending credibility to the soldiers' statements. Military interrogator Tony Lagouranis is featured twice in *Ghosts*. Lagouranis's own admission to torture came slowly. After leaving the military, he struggled with medication and therapy. He objected to a therapist who, like the film director, framed his acts of torture within the context of Milgram's studies. In his memoir, Lagouranis deemed the resort to Milgram "the worst kind of moral relativism."[8] His rejection of the explanatory frame that *Ghosts* took pains to establish offers a valuable caution as to why the narrative of command responsibility is both absolutely critical and insufficient. That narrative inadvertently frames accountability as a choice between soldiers and commanders. State torture is collaborative; many contribute, many are responsible, and many are implicated, including those who will view and remark on *Ghosts*. But when assigning responsibility, the framework forces a choice pointing to two sets of perpetrators. It implicitly lets everyone else—the supporting players and networks, the morbidly curious—off the hook.

Ghosts of Abu Ghraib comes down strongly indicting the command side of this equation, of course. But there is more at stake than rank or military culture or culpability of the commander in chief. Perpetrators fascinate. To exit this false choice, one needs to attune narratives of accountability to survivor perspectives—a framework so rare that in documentaries on Abu Ghraib it has scarcely been tried. As participants in the mid-1990s South African truth and reconciliation process noted, perpetrators receive a different intensity and quality of public attention than do their survivors.[9] This has been the case with Tony Lagouranis. Notably, U.S. media reports did not investigate from the perspective of those Lagouranis harmed. It took a Danish filmmaker to ask him directly why he should not be tried for war crimes.[10] Strikingly, *Ghosts* does include six survivors and former inmates of Abu Ghraib among more standard informants: a journalist, historian, and lawyers. But the focus remains on the perpetrators.

A director's formal choices surrounding perpetrators matter. Consider the solemnity and etiquette of the string-of-interviews documentary style for perpetrator subjects in both *SOP* and *Ghosts of Abu Ghraib.* Its eye-to-eye intimacy underscores the assumption behind the method; an approach to the face is an approach to the truth, and lies, perhaps, are read in the wince, the tic, the pause or misspoken and revised word. In *Ghosts,* no questions are overheard; viewers are not distracted by thoughts of how the interviewer is prompting, pushing, softballing, or leading the interviewee. Juxtaposition signifies. Interestingly, while former Justice Department lawyer John Yoo's interview is challenged and countered by the civilian and military respondents that follow him, in contrast, the low-ranking specialists, sergeants, MPs, and MIs go unchallenged.

The Sabrina Harman sequence in this film asks her to pose with her own image taken alongside the dead General al-Jamadi and offers an unusual departure from this pattern. Her scene is juxtaposed with two others. One features an Abu Ghraib inmate and the other a humanitarian law expert, Scott Horton. In an unusual move, all three reflect on precisely the same event: the murder of al-Jamadi. The filmmaker asks all three to interact with the enlarged reproductions of the Abu Ghraib torture photos. Throughout the film, these artifacts become gestural props for the speaker as much as subjects of discussion. For instance, one survivor filmed in a different sequence kisses the image of his older brother, who suffers in a hood and stress position. In the conversations on al-Jamadi's homicide, the lawyer Scott Horton, like other lawyers and journalists in the film, holds the photos down and to the side, tracing the features they describe while the camera follows their arm. In Harman's scenes, she holds the photo up at shoulder height, near her head, and facing the camera, both owning it and displaying it as—what, the trophy it is? A formal presentation of her work? It is unclear, but the gesture significantly identifies her with the action in the photo rather than distancing her from it. Her broad grin and the corpse in the photo serve as silent counterpoint to her odd confessional tone. The result is a rare combination of formal features that puts pressure on her story. The photograph itself and the manner in which she holds it double and discount her flattened, detached account that attempts to deny the extremity of the scene. This is juxtaposed with the gestural language of survivor Abbas and the weight of his testimony as well as lawyer Horton describing murder by torture. *Ghosts of Abu Ghraib* is unusual in its attention to six such survivors of torture at the prison. However, their faces are shot at partial angles, supposedly to protect anonymity, and their stories are cropped as well.

The filmmaker's moment of formal pressure placed on Harman's account is fleeting. In the next interview, Sergeant Ken Davis points to a high-level cover-up for the murder; in other words, the editing quickly tucks contradictions raised about Harman, the corpse, and the survivor back into the narrative of command responsibility. Davis's presence on screen, in fact, is another point of contradiction and a story left untold. Even as Davis argues that Abu Ghraib's MPs were responding to commands, Davis has been clear that he refused to participate without repercussion, as did others. Just as importantly, some who were not under the command at that cell block found their way there to participate—Lynndie England, for one.

The problems with presenting perpetrator confession are compounded when films present no insight from survivors. While the credibility of the string-of-interview documentary form is typically critiqued for its selective interview style, in *Ghosts*, the formal treatment of slippery and predictable self-justifications is especially dicey (or infuriating). Like the mummified cat or Ken Davis's refusal to torture, disconcerting background has been left out of this and other similar films. *SOP*, for example, situates CACI contractor and seasoned interrogator Tim Dugan as an authority. He claims the first and last word in the film and argues forcefully that extreme techniques are useless and wrong. But Dugan has been named in a lawsuit against CACI alleging heinous acts against detainees. In *Taxi to the Dark Side,* Alex Gibney's documentary on Bagram, Private First Class Damien Corsetti is hugely sympathetic, speaking with concern for prisoners' safety. But in Bagram, he was known as the King of Torture and walked around with "Monster" written across his stomach. Interviewing Gibney, Melissa Block of National Public Radio raised a rare challenge to the narrative at work here: "[Is] there . . . a danger in sanitizing what lower level soldiers did in order to make a broader point about the chain of command?"[11]

It is worth noting that there are examples from the larger international field that approach perpetrator performance differently and destabilize the familiar interview format. I conclude the chapter with examples that deliberately contest confessional performance, involve the public and survivors, and provoke new questions about the conventions and cultural logic that support media appearances by torturers who mask the consequences of their work. What is lost when perpetrators are used to condemn the chain of command rather than to explore their individual choices, rewards, incentives, and responsibility? How did they come to participate when others refused? What of the benefits gained by participation in communal rituals, the individual and group identities and erotic energies forged through violence? More importantly, how does the quality of attention to MPs/MIs involved in the violence differ from the quality of attention given to survivors and their claims? How does this very omission from the conversation further impunity?

With this understanding, a return to Tony Lagouranis's press appearances and his remorseful testimony in *Fear Up Harsh* can point us to command culpability, yes. However, a reader can also find a different story, one detailing a dense collaborative world of influence but also of individual choice and personal, social benefits. His story invites attention to a civilian world and its milieu of fantasy and expectation—the media, viewers, and readers who solicit different aspects of that confession, and to those elements that undermine his story but present answers to the questions posed above.

The Civilian World and Media Culture

Tony Lagouranis was developing his 2007 account within the context of multiple media interviews and exchanges. Across 2005 to 2007, National Public Radio, *Frontline, Hardball,* Democracy Now!, the *Washington Post,* the *Chicago Reader,* and others got interviews. Lagouranis turned down many more requests than he accepted. He was driven not by a desire for celebrity, he says, but by a compulsion: "I went to the media fully admitting that I'd done terrible things. . . . I hoped that if I made a few appearances, it could reframe the public debate, spur a more serious investigation, and let people know about some of the things that were being done in their names."[12]

Human rights monitoring organizations also responded to Lagouranis's testimony. John Sifton of Human Rights Watch found corroboration for Lagouranis's account in 2006.[13] Human Rights First involved Lagouranis in an antitorture training video for West Point cadets. Lagouranis was invited onto the set of Fox Television's *24* in 2006, and Human Rights First invited him to judge television depictions of torture for their complexity and accuracy in their first Prime Time Torture Award competition in 2007 (taken up in chapter 4).

Although Lagouranis turned down discussions with reporters and producers who "had that same creepy tone I got from people who asked if I'd killed anyone," he found even the well-informed interviews "generally wanted to hear about the worst abuses." "The problem was that the worst abuses I knew about always came to me secondhand. I saw the injuries, and I heard the stories, but I was not witness to those actual events . . . leaving behind the facts of what I actually did myself."[14] Almost exclusively, media attention in the United States was interested in the extent to which Lagouranis's exposed inefficiency in the larger military effort and pointed toward command responsibility for torture and abusive detention practice. Interviews did not pose questions concerning his legal culpability. U.S. interviewers were more likely to ask him for personal reflection on his role as whistleblower, his posttraumatic suffering, or the meaning of "moral courage"—a question that, to his credit, he said he was the wrong man to answer.

Mass-mediated culture plays a role worth observing throughout *Fear Up Harsh.* From the beginning, the author tethers moments of his own experience to insights from ancient and contemporary texts on war, ranging from the *Iliad* to *A Few Good Men.* The memoir itself features headnotes from such sources as the book of Hebrews, Dostoevsky, and military historians of Algeria or Vietnam. His cultural references include literature, comics, film, sociology, and history and reflect the multimedia-saturated, pop culture–laden milieu in and through which soldiers work, play, and understand their lives at war. In this way, his book is much like other "grunt lit" from Iraq and Afghanistan.[15] Yet Lagouranis also uses cultural references to craft a persona and bridge contradictions. High-minded connections to Hemingway or Orwell counter negative associations that might attach to his dissent—for example, unmanly weakness or unpatriotic buddy fucker—or to stereotypes that attach to torture: unthinking monstrosity. Instead, he is the dissenting warrior or the humane perpetrator.

More importantly, cultural references alert the reader to ways literary culture, cinematic images, and the ongoing media debate on torture preceded his involvement and actually propelled him toward what he describes as the dark corners. Lagouranis's book points again and again to these, as well as to informal circuits of conversation—primary pathways of learning, as Darius Rejali has noted, in the apprenticeship of torturers.[16] For instance, while awaiting deployment with other newly trained interrogators at Fort Gordon, Georgia, he tells us they eagerly read and discussed Mark Bowden's 2003 speculative feature, titled "The Dark Art of Interrogation": "The most effective way to gather intelligence and thwart terrorism can also be a direct route into morally repugnant terrain." Bowden, like many who adopt the formulaic Heart of Darkness conceit when writing on torture, situates himself as a narrator who exudes a calculated moral ambivalence as he seeks out the torturer, not the survivors, and examines his tools. The feature's fascination with torture and its title—all signal a foregone conclusion. According to Lagouranis, Bowden's piece was read as a type of underground guidebook, one that offered the term "torture lite" and justification for stealth torture techniques that leave no mark.[17]

Those stealth techniques—sleep deprivation, hooding, stress positions, noise, hunger, and temperature—had been ruled out by his formal Fort Huachuca training.[18] Contemplating this array, he says: "Only the sexual humiliation seemed distasteful to me. . . . Aside from that, I was ready to try this stuff myself."[19] This is significant because, although Lagouranis will follow with a narrative explaining the military climate and group dynamics that authorized and rewarded torture, he is clear that even before he left for Iraq, he held "a coiled mass of contradictory beliefs and urges inside. . . . Torturing helpless prisoners was morally reprehensible . . . [yet] the 'enhancements' I just learned about were fair and legal. I saw lines and boundaries, however vague . . . and I desperately wanted to push against them as hard as I could."[20]

As Lagouranis carefully examines the roots of his own "moral failing," he blames the military, and he blames himself. But he does not let the civilian world off the hook. For instance, on leave in the second half of 2004, Lagouranis "heard more debate over *American Idol* than over the presidential election and the war combined," and, he adds, nothing on the "still-fresh" Abu Ghraib scandal. Worse, "the casual and even enthusiastic way people expressed their morbid curiosity was a horrible, unbearable contrast to my despair over the tragic violence and suffering I'd witnessed, and in some measure caused."[21] An explosive fight with his cousin is representative. He asked if Lagouranis had tortured anyone "because he wanted those terrorists either in severe pain or dead. Our family separated us once he learned my views on the subject and called me a traitor."[22]

If the mixture of morbid curiosity and fascination he finds in the civilian world of journalists, family, and friends is maddening for Lagouranis, it is also familiar. The speculative media features on torture he had read so avidly before deployment played on this combination of desire and dread. In retrospect, he writes, he had shared these same feelings well into his first year in Iraq.

Seeking the Phantom Expert

Lagouranis frames his story as a quest, and his subtitle, "an interrogator's dark journey," implies as much. That quest is for extreme experience and the true knowledge of interrogation. As in the Heart of Darkness speculative news features, "true knowledge" for Lagouranis is embodied by the perpetrator. From early on Lagouranis seeks a professional who had mastered the putative dark arts of interrogation and therefore had license to use them. He identifies himself as an independent thinker and actor, not simply a mindless cog in a machine. As a professional and an independent moral being able to perceive and set limits, he also portrays his inner struggle against those limits, "to push those boundaries." The result is a consistent anxiety over his own professionalism provoked by conflicting desires: his desire to be seen as a productive team member, yet to rise above the team in independent judgment and to move beyond protocols in search of extremes. No wonder, then, that he falls prey to the appeal of the phantom professional—an ideal type, someone with the license and skill to cross those lines. Lagouranis clung to this belief long past the point he suspected it an empty quest.

For good reasons, he found his lessons in interrogation at Fort Huachuca unsatisfactory. The trainers had little or no experience in the field, and the lessons were based on old, outdated cold war scenarios when "most, 90%, of prisoners cooperate under direct questioning." Any lessons interrogators learned from Vietnam were forgotten or not passed on.[23] He recalls clear and ample discussion of the Geneva Conventions, and short histories of torture derived from Soviet Union examples. Approaches to build rapport or psychologically disarm the subject were given scant attention. The instruction seemed too basic and cleanly practical, with protocols and limits that seemed too absolute.

Instructors drew a clear line: No good information comes of it. Don't ever do it. "We heard that, but never really believed it." He held instead to moments when his instructors made joking asides about torture: clipping generators to genitals, hanging people by their hands, throwing them out of helicopters. These moments students discussed "with relish," debating what "the British and Israelis do." Awaiting deployment, he also received "highly informal trainings and briefings from interrogators who'd just returned from Afghanistan and Iraq." These informal gatherings offered the lore and seeming know-how he had been hoping for—stories of sleep "adjustment," music, lights, diet manipulation, sexual humiliation, and more.[24]

The training he received was patently misogynist and racist. Lagouranis describes "hate-filled rants and bombast" targeting the Koran and Arabs in general from his Arabic language instructors at the Defense Language Institute. He says these racist asides topped even the transparently racist briefing he received on arrival at Abu Ghraib in early 2004. At that time, episodes of torture at the prison were under investigation and under a tight lid. A colonel opened the briefing: "Something very bad happened here. . . . Don't ask anyone about it. Don't talk about it with anyone here. . . . We're not doing anything wrong." Then an army psychiatrist offered a PowerPoint presentation on "Arab culture," based on Raphael Patai's 1973 nonfiction book *The Arab Mind*, a book that draws on Orientalist fictions, among other things, for its observations of the Arab world and was denounced among scholars decades ago.[25] A 2002 edition of Patai circulated in military circles, no doubt issued to coincide with the U.S. war on terror. Lagouranis felt absurd claims concerning Arab sexuality and phobias should be apparent, but it seemed "very few of us recognized this as racist bullshit."[26]

Lagouranis learned by watching others. Because he had heard informal stories of such treatment before he arrived, what he saw—exposure and cold, exhaustion by exercise, isolation, diet manipulation—"seemed totally reasonable," although it may have "flatly contradicted what we had learned in school." He found his immediate supervisors know less about interrogation than he did, and he began to notice they believed "that there was some magic to interrogation, that we interrogators 'have ways to make you talk.'" Among these, he discusses the officer in charge at Mosul. Captain "Lamb" shared his ideas for designing a new interrogation facility on the base that would allow mock executions and rig up audio channels in the booth that permitted subjects to listen to screaming from the chamber next door. Yet like these superiors, Lagouranis himself bought into the "aura of mystery around it," and his lack of results left him frustrated: "If there was a high art to the dark art of interrogation, I was missing it."[27]

Others presumed him to be an expert. Satisfying their expectations required showmanship more than magic or expertise. He was rushed out of bed to interrogate men at the Abu Ghraib prison gate in front of expectant infantry. "I did my best to put on a show," he writes. "Lots of yelling, lots of intimidation. The rest of my team ate it up."[28] Freeing one man, jailing two others with signs of appreciation and admiration from his audience, he was pleased with his intimidating and hostile "fear up harsh" performance. Yet once the adrenaline faded, he realized that he made poor judgments based on illogical inferences. As new techniques for fear and pain were added to his repertoire, there was a constant tension between the thrill of performance, immediate feedback from his team, and the lack of results.

> These techniques were propagated throughout the Cold War, picked up again after 9/11, used by CIA, filtered down to army interrogators at Guantánamo, filtered again through Abu Ghraib, and used apparently around the country by special forces. Probably someone in this chain was a real professional, and if torture works—which is debatable—maybe they had the training to make sure it worked. But at our end we had no idea what we were doing . . . we were just trying shit out to see if it worked, venting our frustration and acting like bad asses when, in the dark art of torture, we were really just a bunch of rank amateurs.[29]

As Lagouranis learns, the "real professional" is a phantom, like the other relics of the national security imagination he has encountered throughout civilian life. Belatedly and far too quietly, the national Intelligence Science Board conceded the same: no professionals get good intelligence by relying on "dark arts," torture, or coercion.[30] Lagouranis's experience showed as much. At most, one in ten captives he processed had any information to offer at all, and what they had merely confirmed things the soldiers already knew.

Torture as Community Building
Social and Organizational Setting

Lagouranis's work carefully highlights the social functions and organizational factors that laid the groundwork for the torture he watched escalate and committed himself. His account confirms much of what was being reported from military and journalistic investigations into detention practices, the research of human rights monitoring organizations, and the testimony of other soldiers who have spoken out in other forums.

Although he was based at Abu Ghraib prison in early 2004, he was quickly mustered into a mobile intelligence unit that would serve elsewhere for weeks at a time, including Al-Asad airfield, Mosul, and North Babel. Manadel al-Jamadi was murdered at Abu Ghraib before Lagouranis got there, and once again, a detainee had been murdered before his arrival at Al-Asad.[31] Likewise, Mosul had seen a homicide in custody just before his arrival, and another man was to die while Lagouranis was on site.[32]

Among the organizational elements supporting torture and homicide, Lagouranis points to incompetence. This existed in multiple dimensions: the absence of basic cultural knowledge, a pervasive presumption of guilt when dealing with Iraqis that reflected and reinforced racist assumptions, and gross procedural inefficiency and malaise. These factors worked together to ensure increasing numbers of unnecessary arrests, lengthy detentions, and mounting numbers of detainees. The number of prolonged unproductive interrogations rose accordingly, as did frustration among commanders and interrogators who escalated their methods to get results. Results never came because the families, farmers, and professors taken and held by the dozens had no intelligence to share.

Alongside incompetence, Lagouranis points to command intention as a key feature of the institutional climate for torture. Carefully designed protocols—authorizing prolonged use of stress positions, sleep deprivation, and dogs, among other things—were signed by Secretary of Defense Donald Rumsfeld in late 2002 (circulated and later rescinded), and reauthorized by the commander of coalition forces in Iraq, Lieutenant General Ricardo S. Sanchez, on September 14, 2003. Although dogs had been strictly forbidden at Abu Ghraib by early 2004 (as quiet investigations into photographs began), when Lagouranis arrived in Mosul, the chief warrant officer and officer in charge pointed to documentation authorizing dogs. These commanders initiated twenty-four-hour interrogation operations that liberally interpreted guidelines on sleep for detainees, among other things.

Pressure from commanders was coupled with an interagency, interpersonal culture of creative interpretation necessitated by the shifting patchwork of Interrogation Rules of Engagement. Rules were everywhere, but they differed in every location and changed frequently in any single site. In addition, elite forces and different branches of the military were sharing the same location and interrogating the same prisoners, yet each served under different rules. Moreover, improvisation was expected. These Interrogation Rules of Engagement were "broad, self-contradictory, malleable," with one central purpose: "to permit us to push the limits of what we learned in school . . . the army interrogation manual, and . . . Geneva Conventions."[33] Scholars have said the same. Doctrine presents a broad, ideal response and anticipates that specific contexts will require departures and adaptation of the rules of engagement by those on the ground.[34] Marnia Lazreg's work on French torture in Algeria demonstrates the strategy of terror and insurgent suppression depended on precisely this sort of improvisation.

The effects of improvisation and a patchwork of rules were exemplified when Iraqi cousins became the first two subjects of the new twenty-four-hour routine initiated by Mosul commanders. Their ordeal lasted four weeks. The chief routinely called for more intensity without suggesting specifics. The interrogators complied with a host of creative variations on sleep deprivation, positional torture, exercise exhaustion, and hypothermia (e.g., kneeling in forty-degree temperatures and rain for hours). In the third week, the subjects' severe weight loss, physical deterioration, and mental debilitation were clear. Strikingly, a team meeting at this point revealed that questioning had not only tapered off but stopped altogether, yet the torture still continued. Material and procedural requirements drove it forward: "By now, it was torment done for its own sake, and so I could put down on my report that I did this all night."[35] Despite the complete lack of results, the combined assault represented by a twenty-four-hour process, sleep deprivation, and other pain and fear tactics including attack dogs quickly extended to many other prisoners throughout Mosul.[36]

Even as these shifting and generalized authorizations and vague inducements came down a chain of command, Lagouranis's book illustrates a horizontal culture of community and mutual influence. As returning soldiers had done in informal chats during his training, new arrivals among the guards and interrogators swapped tactics in an atmosphere that mixed bragging, gossip, and professional advice. His examples document the migration of personnel, lore, and tactics from Guantánamo and Afghanistan to Iraq, and how new innovations in suffering quickly spread to all prisoners and interrogation units. Prisoners themselves passed along descriptions of techniques as they moved through the system. For instance, while it was Lagouranis's commander who authorized the use of a shipping container as a space for long nights of audio torture combining hoods, stress positions, death metal music, strobe lights, and attack dogs, the tactics were inspired, he says, by a series of prisoners who reported what the Navy SEALs had done to them on the same base. Lagouranis will later describe SEAL tactics to the *Chicago Reader* in order to minimize his own violence.[37] In the context of his memoir, this competitive and comparative torture environment is devoid of intelligence gains or even rumors of results; each new practice proves its own value by simply existing. According to the strained circular logic pervasive in these communal exchanges, and even in debates among jurists and senators on Capitol Hill, torture tactics must be working for intelligence or must be legal or they would not be common. Torture was permitted by a command environment that encouraged pain and improvisation, but it thrived also on these informal, interpersonal, and self-confirming pathways of observation, envy, and encouragement.

Social Benefits: Pleasure and Danger

As Lagouranis evaluates his organizational environment including the impact of command structures, folklore, and incompetence, he also identifies the psychological needs and social rewards that draw him forward. He describes himself as a boundary crosser, someone who had always been attracted to the kind of extreme experience that pushed past limits. These desires drew him to the army, as did the chance to learn Arabic and to get a good deal on student loan repayment. Beyond limits, he imagined realms where he could give up control and experience chaos. Ironically, he says, interrogation demands strict control because one holds absolute power over other human beings: "I did these things, basically, for my own amusement. Just to see how far I would go, just to seek out an extreme experience. Here I was in a god-awful war zone . . . and I was acting like a tourist."[38]

He quickly found that power to be deeply addicting. Detainees who understood they could defy him must be punished for that defiance. The deepest dread was of symbolic loss, to lose face or lose the power to increase the detainee's fear. Those who did not acknowledge his power or who exhibited a calm dignity even in the midst of their terror drove him to distraction—a point where he hated himself and the subject.[39]

His inverted justification, dependence, and need become clear as Lagouranis describes dogs entering the routine in the "little discotheque"— the shipping container where sleep-deprived captives faced painful positional torture, strobe lights, and excruciating audio bombardment. He depicts the power this setting has over *him:* "The music and lights were making me increasingly more aggressive. The prisoner, still not cooperating, was making me increasingly angry." When he and his partner escalated with an attack dog, "a darker, less rational part of me liked seeing the man who had defied us for so long try to cover his balls in fear." One prisoner, given the alias Jafar, urinated in fright. When a second man, "Khalid," endured even the dog with resignation, Lagouranis's anger triggered a serious desire to "chop his fucking fingers off." It is significant that in both cases, Lagouranis describes this point of seething, volatile frustration suddenly interrupted by roaming soldiers who "heard the music . . . and decided to join the party." They hit the sides of the container, jump on top, with "wrath and chaos in their screams." In Khalid's case, just as Lagouranis realized he would like to mutilate the man, four sergeants arrived, entering the container with guns—yelling at, encircling, and shoving the prisoner, who was shackled and on his knees.[40]

By establishing his own control in these dicey situations, Lagouranis tells us he prevented a differently organized and potentially worse attack. The reader notes, however, that he also restored his own dominance over something—here, a group of four peers. Lagouranis uses the moment to contrast his forms of assault with the seemingly more sadistic pleasure of group violence as recreation. While later he saw his own "cruelty reflected in the cruelty of the four men I had just restrained from beating Khalid," he nonetheless maintained he rescued the prisoner.[41] In fact, he had created the setting that made Khalid more vulnerable to this kind of group energy and assault.

Many times, in this way, Lagouranis contrasts his behavior with the violence of others so as to forge an identity more professional, rational, and controlled—even humane or compassionate—by comparison. Yet his compassion and violence prove less distinct and more complementary and mutually reinforcing than he suspects.

For example, Lagouranis began apologizing to prisoners at their cages, seeking out "prisoners I'd just tormented, trying to connect on a more human level." Prisoners found this behavior strange or outrageous; some glared with resentment even while seeming to submit politely. However, as he writes, he was still "behaving badly back in the booth," not backing down on harsh tactics but the opposite. "Still psyched" on interrogation, "I wanted to take it as far as I could."[42] This is to say, these seeming demonstrations of remorse are a mixed bag. They indicate the extent to which both his emotional equilibrium and professional identity were then dependent on getting something—a great variety of things—from the detainees.

"Serious torture requires steady escalation" says Lagouranis. "If they figured out where the limit was . . . they'd won. I felt naked and unarmed standing before these prisoners."[43] The fully sadistic dimensions of this behavior remain unclear to him. He used his power to force others to fill a range of emotional needs—not only pleasure, but also absolution, comfort, and entertainment. Consider his discussion of a prisoner assigned to "another interrogator." The man was made to kneel in the cold for hours while his (unprofessional) interrogator "slept or watched a stupid movie." Afraid of being called "weak or sympathetic," Lagouranis waited until his superior was asleep and then pulled the man into the heated interrogation booth: "He wanted to go to bed and so I made a deal. Sing me a song, and you can sleep. . . . Night after night, he'd sing, and then I'd take him back to his cage to sleep."[44] Lagouranis portrays this as an act of conscience and compassion. Yet when one imagines a prisoner at the farthest brink of pain and exhaustion asked to sing as a condition of sleep, it seems perversely sadistic, not merciful. How would the prisoner describe this scenario? However earnest or self-congratulatory, these displays of compassion—as with the displays of remorse—demonstrate Lagouranis's power to manipulate the captives emotionally in ways that humanize the perpetrator and confirm his view of himself.

Lagouranis marks the urge to chop off fingers as a frightening moment and the first of two turning points, after which his own escalation soon stopped. The second comes when photos from the Abu Ghraib site were leaked to the news. Suddenly Abu Ghraib's "something bad" was all over television and the internet. His first response was indeed to believe these soldiers were exceptions, "bad apples" as the government declared; he did not in any way connect the MPs' behavior to himself or Mosul, but for the Senate hearings on CNN: "The only difference they would have noticed between our prison and Abu Ghraib was that our prisoners had their clothes on."[45] Top commanders who signed off on his own extraordinary tactics were condemning them. The doublespeak was jarring.[46]

When Lagouranis finally tells his superiors he will not work the disco anymore, the entire program ends abruptly. Many weeks later, back at Abu Ghraib, halfway into his year in Iraq, the Criminal Investigation Division (CID) called him in. Lagouranis sent word to a friend and a lawyer back home. When he realized CID was not, in fact, investigating him, he still went ahead and made a full report on his actions at Mosul. He decided not to participate again in "enhanced" interrogations, but he did not escape scenes of torture. Other interrogators returning from different mobile assignments shared their stories of terrorizing prisoners. At North Babel, he found that soldiers broke prisoners' feet with axe handles, burned their legs with exhaust pipes, waterboarded them, and performed mock executions.

Tony Lagouranis was honorably discharged a few months after his return from Iraq in 2005. He suffered from insomnia, panic, hallucinations, and other severe psychological disturbances. He rejected a therapist's attempts to help him by blaming the phenomenon of obedience to authority, Stanley Milgram's thesis. As noted, this was the explanatory framework embraced by *Ghosts of Abu Ghraib*. Lagouranis's rejection of such an excuse is in keeping with the level of critical thought and individual responsibility his book brings to his involvement in torture. It remains unique among perpetrator writing from the war on terror.[47] Dramatic and voluntary, his perpetrator confession is nonetheless strategic.

Contradictions and Silence
Violence Workers and Moral Positioning

When Lagouranis finally told his superiors at Mosul that he would no longer work the disco, his objection ended the entire program: "The steady escalation was over. . . . It was so easy it made me wonder why I didn't kill this project long ago. . . . If I had stood up at any point in this process and said, 'This is wrong,' it would have lurched to a halt. Why didn't I do this?"[48] Lagouranis's book, of course, is an attempt to answer this question. Certainly, elements of his organizational setting present a textbook case in the formation of a "violence worker."[49] Without question, attention to this environment is critical. The ways such an approach is insufficient will be taken up momentarily.

His case features important communal aspects of his organizational environment. First, escalation to harsher and harsher techniques was carefully and openly discussed. The benchmarks considered along the way were those of legality, he says, not morality. He thought in terms of legal authorization, not "what is right."[50] Second, the epiphany forced by the Abu Ghraib scandal, creating sudden awareness of his moral isolation in the "military cocoon," highlights the kind of organizational and psychological insulation known to be common in the production of violence workers. A moral universe removed from influence of wider legal and ethical standards is carefully devised and helps normalize and perpetuate violence. Lagouranis described this setting on *Frontline* as one of collective "psychosis": "you really do feel like you are outside normal society, you know? Your family, your friends, they're not there to see what's going on. And everybody is participating in this, I don't know what psychosis . . . this delusion about what you're doing there."[51] Finally, the compartmentalization produced by division of labor ensures a fragmentary awareness, or cultivated disregard, of his actions and their consequences. This is the kind of purposeful ignoring—not ignorance—that characterizes what Ann Stoler calls the "imperial disposition" and affect.[52] He and the Navy SEALs might be interrogating and abusing the same prisoners in shifts within the same twenty-four hours, but he allows himself to think of the abusive efforts of each group as distinct and unrelated, not working hand in hand. The prisoners, however, are feeling the accumulated effects of both.

The notion of command pressure, communal energy, and moral blinders that all trigger a spiraling descent into darkness makes a good tale. His narrative of increasing addiction to power, remorse, and confession make a dramatically satisfying story. Yet many single moments disrupt these narrative threads and hint at stories left untold. Consider that although Lagouranis identifies command pressures, it is clear that others around him simply refuse to participate. They bow out, without repercussion.[53] So does he, eventually. Like the presence of Sergeant Ken Davis who refused to torture in the film *Ghosts of Abu Ghraib,* this fact draws a deep wrinkle across the narrative.

Lagouranis had always made a habit of underscoring command authority by listing specific tactics for psychological and physical suffering in each interrogation report, including stress positions and dogs. He continued even after a commander directed him not to.[54] He knew the pressure to conceal indicated the controversial nature of the techniques and internal divisions up the chain of command. On the one hand, he refused to hide what he was doing on paper, yet on the other hand, he went to the trouble of hiding injured prisoners from Iraqi councilmen and a U.S. colonel when they visited the facility.

He made a small handful of formal abuse reports in Iraq, some in his first months and some in his last. His book discusses significantly more cases that he did not report on—men who suffered burning, crushed feet, severe beatings, debilitating isolation, and various other torture techniques. He was confused by his randomness. Ultimately, he is unsatisfied with his own rationalizations, saying only that "at the time, it seemed to make sense." In retrospect, Lagouranis suspects his reporting was related to how much sympathy he felt for any given detainee, or that he was proceeding on a case-by-case basis, without formulating clear lines to "resolve the hazy morality of this war zone."[55] The reader notes, of course, that he reported abuses by assailants who were unknown to him, and he does nothing about highly damaging assaults by soldiers he knew.[56] No reports on interrogational abuse are sent in from Mosul, although he claims this is where the most damaging daily violence occurred, and he took full part.

He considered some behaviors abusive and others not. He says he was appalled by the bragging tales of another interrogator, "Dan," who described kneeling on top of restrained prisoners the better to manipulate painful pressure points. Dan clearly enjoyed relaying the story and hearing the howls of pain. Lagouranis admittedly closed his eyes and reported this to no one. However, he also returned to Dan for advice on how to break a particular prisoner, and he took that advice—leading the prisoner, a man who had survived torture under Saddam, into a pitch-black empty hangar, chaining him to a bed frame that had been nailed to the wall for that purpose, and leaving him there to induce a panic attack.[57]

Ultimately, his reports were few: two early reports on abuse at Abu Ghraib, three reports late in his deployment in North Babel, and of course a report on himself when he returned to Abu Ghraib at the midpoint of his year. The inconsistencies appear to him to be plateaus or even backward steps in his moral journey (and therefore the developmental narrative that structures his book). However, as argued, his story of moral descent then understanding, his self-portrayal as an independent professional and a compassionate exception—these are often contradictory in their own right, and at odds with that larger storyline. The contradictions serve a purpose. The shifting allows Lagouranis to craft a persona that is simultaneously tough, patriotic, and contrite. This makes narrative positioning and timing critical to consider as well.

Dominance Personae

Fear Up Harsh is an effort to address multiple contending audiences. In 2007, the public was divided on the war in Iraq, and perhaps more so on the question of torture. Low-ranking military police were serving sentences relating to Abu Ghraib, while military and contract interrogators like Lagouranis were being insulated. Media and public attention came to focus on the waterboard, the Department of Justice, and permission granted the CIA by high-level attorneys. Meanwhile, reporting on detention deaths and abuses continued, and U.S. journalism was reporting the torture, execution, and public display of bodies in the thousands across Iraq as war news and Iraqi-on-Iraqi violence, the subject of chapter 6.

In this atmosphere, Tony Lagouranis's feelings of guilt and confusion, as well as the traumatic repercussions of his involvement in torture, were no doubt real and heartfelt. The quality of introspection his book offers is rare. His confessional testimony is voluntary. It does not emerge after he has been formally disciplined or charged. A careful reading of his account should pose questions, though, about his audiences and their set of interlocking moral and imaginative universes that make it difficult for Lagouranis and his media interviewers to really look squarely at the extent of his crimes or to see the role they play in the broader pattern, first of torture discourse, and second of the quite different pattern of torture and terror being practiced at the time. How should one view Lagouranis's total confession and the media attention it drew?

To present himself as a torturer, Lagouranis designs a persona meant to counter accusations of monstrosity. Central to the dignity and humanity of that speaking subject is an alternate dominance persona—a persona intriguing for its contradictions, distinctions, and silences.[58] For instance, in framing his masculinity, race, and sexuality, the book crafts a warrior identity, yet it refuses a heroic narrative. He says torture is inexcusable, but he carefully depicts his worst violence as a response to personal dishonor, disrespect, or failure to acknowledge his dominance. He distances himself from violence used for pleasure, stress, recreation, competition, or racial, cultural, or other bonding. He bemoans the folly of empire but enacts its dominance, trying to distance his depictions from racist, misogynist, or sexualized verbal (or physical) abuse. In fact, he tells us little of what he yelled at detainees during hours of torture. Although the set of Navy SEAL techniques that spread quickly throughout Mosul also included nudity, he offers little discussion. Sexual abuse, he repeats, was an absolute limit. He avoids the subject even though sexualized violence appears in many reports from detention centers in Iraq. He disassociates himself entirely from sexual circuits of pleasure, aggression, intimidation, or anxiety that unite or divide groups of soldiers, elite forces, and commanders, or that play out in their captives' subjugation.

Martha Huggins, Mika Haritos-Fatouros, and Philip Zimbardo found three distinctly different "masculine performances" in testimony of Brazilian police torturers and death-squad workers: personal, bureaucratic, and blended. Lagouranis's persona somewhat approximates blended masculinity in their terms, combining bureaucratic rationales and personal honor in his defense. The insight by Huggins, Haritos-Fatouros, and Zimbardo that perpetrator masculinities are multiple is welcome, although they seem aware their terminology (and their discussion) might fuse masculinity with violence in deceptive ways. I would argue that "masculinity performance" is better analyzed as a multifaceted dominance persona—a performance that also incorporates differently racialized and sexualized and gendered positions; queer, straight, or class-based performances; imperial and nationalist projections; and more. Torturers all enact dominance as well as intergroup identity-making and bonding through violence that is misogynist, racializing, and nationally instrumental. They later recraft and recombine multiple modes of masculinity and femininity and other markers to choreograph confessional performances for other communal groups: the loved ones and friends they message from the war zone, the military and civilian audiences they confront when they return. In presenting themselves for criminal investigation or to media audiences, they mobilize and combine these and other aspects yet again, differently.

Lagouranis's own complex persona works in tandem with a shifting strategy of narrative positioning that allows the speaker to reflect on, deflect, or own responsibility at different moments. Sometimes Lagouranis's anecdotes and commentary reinforce the storyline of organizational, social, and psychological forces against which he struggles and yields. At other times, he undercuts that narrative, claiming full personal responsibility for torture.

Each claim to responsibility elevates the speaker, identifying him in the same instant as perpetrator, victim of larger forces, and man of moral courage, as Democracy Now! implied.[59] But this is calculated courage. He comes clean without naming names, inviting retribution from the system, or triggering prosecution for his crimes.

Unfortunately, such a persona is well received. Civilian and military culture are mutually sustaining, driven as they are by insular fixations, short-range solutions, common levels of cultural ignorance, a booming security economy, and shared fantasies of what constitutes power and protection. His experience in front of interviewers' cameras and the recurring patterns in the media response traced by this chapter further condemn the media and the viewer in our shared acceptance of a narrow range of questions and enormous omissions.

Counternarratives

Fear Up Harsh is a multifaceted performance, but as a confession to torture, this book is much more; it is a record of assaults against human beings in custody.

We learn late in the book that Lagouranis was named in a criminal complaint by at least one man, an individual he refers to as Jafar Ali Abdul Naser. He is the man described as urinating when Lagouranis orders the attack dog to lunge. Jafar's complaint to the Criminal Investigative Division concerned the Mosul disco under Lagouranis and naked ice water treatment in the SEAL compound. That compound was where one man, twenty-seven-year-old civilian Fashad Mohammad, was subjected to hooding, beating, water, and hypothermia; he died during Lagouranis's term.[60] Lagouranis mentions the military investigation into Jafar's complaint against him at two points and says he disputed some details. Then ostensibly he hears no more about it, and the question of criminal liability together with the survivor claims—Jafar's or any of the survivors' claims—simply disappear from the book.[61]

Where these same men are now—and the long-term economic, physical, and psychological consequences of their suffering—we are not to know. But they live with these consequences as well as with unanswered moral and legal claims. How, one wonders, might they or the survivors included in *Ghosts of Abu Ghraib* react—or their parents, children, spouses, and families of the dead—to learn that Lagouranis, once back in the United States, was situated as something of an expert, not only an outspoken opponent of torture but also a spokesman at human rights conferences and a judge for television depictions of torture?

There is an outrageous, gaping silence concerning survivors here and in other accounts that feature perpetrators that mutes all practical exploration of responsibility and leaves the deeper problem of justice unsounded. More outrageous, interviewers and filmmakers who elicit and package torturers' tales scarcely seem to note this silence, let alone protest it (using explicit verbal or formal interventions in their creation). Little poses a significant challenge to perpetrator elisions and euphemisms.

Argentina, South Africa, and others have led the United States in this regard, offering a few interview formats that approach perpetrator performance in order to destabilize it. These formats presented different modes of public challenge to both the confessions and the confessors, captured wide attention, and at times spurred broad democratic debate that included voices and experience of survivors.

Notorious Argentine torturer Julio Simón, a man accused of disappearing two hundred people and found guilty of fifty-eight crimes during the dirty war, used the cover of amnesty legislation that followed the dictatorship to offer heroic public accounts of his role. He denied use of torture save in "very few instances," where it "proved counterproductive" because it left the victim "too destroyed."[62] Leigh Payne described his early television interview on *Telenoche* as self-righteous and bored. Yet a second television program challenged that image by putting at center stage a rowdy debate concerning Simón as he looked on from above, back to the camera, offering commentary on the heated exchange below. The format pitted "older upper-class Argentines who considered Simón a war hero" against "the young students and children of the disappeared." She notes, "At one moment, a young woman who had lost family members . . . climbed the stairs to Simón's [seat], and hit him from behind with her purse. His face was revealed to the camera and once exposed, he left his refuge and joined the fray on the main studio stage."[63] The opening this woman took to interrupt the format unexpectedly is evocative in the same way the original decision to allow survivor participation, confrontation, counterpoint, and even vengeful aggression is suggestive of all that has not been done in the United States. The path by which a free-for-all might lead to political action or justice may not be apparent in the Argentine example, but neither is it shut down.

As did this experiment, the proceedings of the South African Truth and Reconciliation Commission also allowed perpetrators and survivors to face each other before journalists. When police torturer and security officer Captain Jeffrey Benzien attempted to confess in exchange for amnesty, he was the only member of his unit to have done so. He described his mastery of certain so-called interrogation techniques in benign, bland, and bureaucratic terms. His sanitized description of the "wet bag" smothering technique was directly challenged by a man Benzien had subjected to it, Tony Yengeni, an ANC member of parliament who demanded Benzien demonstrate the technique. Yengeni produced a volunteer and a pillowcase on the spot. Photographers captured the Benzien reenactment and a shocked audience. Benzien sat on the back of the stand-in and suffocated him with a bag. The reenactment encircled by survivors audibly and visibly contradicted Benzien's expressionless verbal statements of moments before. Antjie Krog, who regularly covered the proceedings, called the result "one of the most loaded, disturbing images in the life of the Truth Commission."[64]

Less sensational but as daring and politically charged is the challenge posed by journalist Horacio Verbitsky to Adolfo Scilongo, an officer stationed at Argentina's infamous Navy Mechanics School torture camp. Scilongo had carried out death flights, among other things, dropping some thirty bound captives to their deaths in the ocean. Scilongo was the first to break silence on acts that had been firmly denied by the military. He took his confession to Verbitsky, a man who had built his career exposing military atrocities. Instead of running with the scoop, Verbitsky interrogated the story and the teller and set ground rules. Verbitsky would use antagonism to refuse evasions and digressions, and Scilongo would be forced to name atrocities directly. Euphemisms were forbidden. The interview triggered confessional performances for the press by six other military men directly involved in kidnapping, torture, and murder. Scholar Marguerite Feitlowitz called the broader media impact of this proportionately small series of torturers "the Scilongo Effect."[65]

As Lagouranis's case and the films and commentary on Abu Ghraib demonstrate, perpetrator confessions can evoke fascination and sympathy, just as they can retraumatize survivors or trigger renewed defenses or denials from regime supporters. Payne maintains that they can also advance fact-gathering and legal action—but, she adds, only if others force the confessions to these ends. In each case offered here—the staged debate, the reenactment, and the antagonistic interview—formal arrangements center survivors, expose contradictions, and impose formal pressure as well as direct refutation on the perpetrator's self-presentation. The formats invite audience participation, dialogue, and judgment, not the enforced intimacy of perpetrator faces and performances filling the screen or the page. Survivors, citizens, and human rights groups must work to challenge such performances in the press, film, and television in order to put them to political use.

The fantasy of the dark arts expert that drove Lagouranis is the twin of our fascination and repugnance with the perpetrator. Both emanate from a national security imaginary. In the U.S. case, unlike Brazil, South Africa, Argentina, and Chile, most of those who suffered or died by torture in war on terror detention centers and secret prisons are not and were not part of the U.S. body politic. U.S. detainees have been deported and silenced by the terms of their release and stripped of standing in court.[66] However, many additional U.S. torture survivors are residents and citizens; they are representatives of the surveillance, terror, and torture common in expansive policing, incarceration, or immigrant detention regimes. But we have yet to fully recognize the modes of systematic, violent suppression they face in the same conversation as torture.

We do not move out of the shadow of that national imaginary without survivors. Without political participation and policy making by survivors and full attention to their experience and demands, there can be no transformation or justice. The increased presence, pressure, and perspectives of survivors—in political movements and legislation as well as in investigative, historical, and documentary accounts—will be critical in the U.S. context.[67] That pressure can help us reconfigure our understanding of complicity and better attend to the networks and professional habits that support it, a subject to which we next turn in chapter 6.

6

Networks

Deploying the Salvador Option

> The system itself was the torture.
>
> —Stephen Grey, *Ghost Plane*

> Then 20 minutes later we got a call from the Iraqi Ministry of Interior telling us the same thing, that General Petraeus didn't want the torture victims shown on TV.
>
> —General Muntadher al-Samari, on forced confessions running nightly on Iraqi television

Many people assemble around the work of torture and interact throughout the process. Bush-era renditions, which organized the capture of noncombatants and their delivery to allied nations for torture, illustrate this well. In the case of Maher Arar, discussed in chapter 4, logistics were coordinated across four intelligence services, multiple security forces, and international air and ground crews. The networks necessary to state torture are composed precisely of such interpersonal and interorganizational relationships, routines, and resources.[1]

In this chapter, I use an operational chain of personnel and funding extending from Washington to Baghdad in 2003–7 to illustrate that key elements of a torture network are legible despite the layers of uncertainty we construct around them. Their outcomes are often, as was the case here, not only undeniable but even predictable and consistent. The trouble apprehending networks illustrates a larger problem of the U.S. security imagination. The understanding of torture within that imaginary recognizes torture through an archetypal scene via a focus on tools or individual perpetrators. Like survivor testimony, evidence that does not fit that mold is less definitive—evidence like formal and informal relationships, historical and structural patterns, written statements, funding streams, and body counts. The same operational mechanics necessary to torture practice support its denial and diffuse responsibility.

During the same period Maher Arar was captured and held, a collaborative network was crafted that produced torture and death squads in Iraq. The network operated with the knowledge of key civilian and military leadership in Washington and Baghdad; some planners in the United States referred to its work as the Salvador Option. The network tapped personnel who brought experience from cold war engagements in El Salvador and from U.S. Drug Enforcement Agency (DEA) activity in Latin America. Because this Washington–Baghdad collaboration was open to public view in a way that rendition networks and CIA interrogation programs were not, it could rely on established structures and public routines to optimize denial and disregard from its outset.

Sociologist Stanley Cohen has argued that denial of atrocity is a social phenomenon that takes place on a personal, official, and cultural level. He notes official interpretations are constructed from those rationales or obsessions already present in the culture—justifications that have worked before.[2] Previous chapters in this volume have argued that an ample and ready reservoir of such rationales, obsessions, and beliefs regarding torture exist within a shared social imaginary, one that arose in the anticolonial and cold war era when torture—an effective tool of oppression, war, public order, and domestic control—required new rationales. I have termed that larger reservoir the U.S. national security imagination, the shared quality of which cultivates broad public participation in the misrecognition of torture and therefore facilitates its daily social work all around us.

Christina Nadler has extended Cohen's work, contending that not only is denial organized through social patterns, but that denial is also manifest spatially in our built environments: "Space is used and produced to facilitate denial."[3] She complements work by Loïc Wacquant, Ruth Gilmore, and Andrea Smith that holds that deep-seated changes in the U.S. economy since the 1960s have a functional linkage to the spatial containment, exclusion, and elimination of minoritized populations through the construction of ghettos, prisons, and "public" land. Nadler adds to this the element of denial; the constructions of space used to regulate race and capital simultaneously construct denial in material form.[4] They enable the sociospatial distancing that dominant populations use to actively know and not-know these violations continue. This is not denial, precisely. It is cultivated disregard, diminished attention, and "skittish seeing," as Ann Stoler has said, and as I discuss in chapter 4. People outside of prisons understand prisons exist, and public parks are colonized spaces hotly contested into the present by Native populations. But out of sight, out of mind.

I am making a parallel suggestion here. The walls, spaces, and relations that construct one group's violation, containment, and elimination construct another group's disregard. The social arrangements and networks through which humans torture not only proactively build rhetorical justifications and denials, as Cohen notes, but also build structures of denial into their organizational design. The compartmentalization we use as a metaphor of mind is enacted in the professional and procedural world of networked assignments, reports, and locations. Those forms and arrangements legitimate or mandate disregard as an expectation of the work. They diffuse culpability. Torture is the outcome of a coordinated, compartmentalized, networked process. Structural distance or detachment does not preclude or offset complicity. It may institutionalize it.

The chapter begins the examination of torture by network with a step outside the U.S. national security imagination to see how one Iraqi created an incisive analysis of the U.S.–Baghdad torture network by critiquing a popular television broadcast aired nightly on Iraqi media.

The second section lays out the U.S.–Iraqi torture arrangement. The section focuses on identifiable features particular to this violence network to suggest that a range of collaborative features, although perhaps not these precisely, will be identifiable in other torture networks. The U.S.–Iraq network models several. First, it evolved and transferred a shared understanding of concept and purpose. Second, it carefully arranged key personnel in a structure of relationships. Third, those relationships coordinated funding and other incentives, while fourth, the structure also protected the agencies and individuals that supported its work. Finally, specific formal arrangements coordinated denial and disregard. Although these network elements were clear in U.S. reporting in 2005, it was not until 2013 that the British press brought to this torture network new questions and new eyes.[5] This meant that over that eight-year span, news consumers could both substantively see and disregard U.S.–Iraqi collaboration in torture.

The chapter's third section will use the U.S.–Iraq network to illustrate three organized forms of denial or disregard: those coordinated at the official level, others at the organizational level that required broad participation, and still others at the public level that were organized with the participation of journalists and their readers. The final discussion centers the work of a seasoned investigative journalist able to view the whole story at close proximity—the network and its outcomes—in 2005. Conventions of his trade and a security imaginary came easily to hand for him, naturalizing the compartmentalized collaboration in terror as if fogged in war.

I am not here producing a typology of torture networks, nor an exhaustive list of features. The end is to alter and expand what we look for when we look for torture, to make it more difficult for legible features and networks themselves to be met successfully with standard forms of denial or disregard, thereby opening new possibilities for recognition, intervention, prevention, deterrence, and prosecution. My hope is that a network lens on torture practice can move us away from the figments of the national security imagination.

Terror TV: An Iraqi View

In May 2005, an unnamed videographer posted his analysis of this international violence network and its impact in a fifteen-minute YouTube video. I will continue to call this anonymous critic the videographer or video maker. What that critic reveals will be familiar from the analysis of the waterboard in chapter 4: a national media spectacle that is a pantomime of justice, obsessed with the effort to project state power and define the new (Iraqi) nation. The videographer argues that the programming he sees on Iraqi television amounts to torture, but he does not fixate on intelligence needs or locate techniques on a spectrum of instrumental violence. He rejects the circular questions that obsessed the United States in this period: Is it torture, or isn't it? Or should we or shouldn't we use torture? Instead, his video identifies an organized campaign of terror and torture for what it was. He points to important links between U.S. funding, the Iraqi Interior Ministry, and special police commandos. These paramilitary units produced a nightly broadcast that advertised torture and disappearances on U.S.-sponsored, ministry-run television in Iraq. That nightly production was called *Terrorism in the Hands of Justice*. His YouTube analysis of it was titled *Terror TV*.

The maker of *Terror TV* suggests that it is possible to confront state torture unencumbered by U.S. forms of calculated uncertainty or epistemic murk, to recall Michael Taussig's phrase. What is more, he concludes media exposure cannot, must not, be allowed to substitute for democracy, civic institutions, or justice. The video takes the viewer inside an Iraqi school turned detention center. There, ministry interrogators told captives a state camera would record their confessions for the ministry's records only, but in fact, their words and faces would play as the central content of a popular program. The show was designed to humiliate captives and demonstrate commando success against the insurgency. "It's all about power and fear," says the YouTube narrator. "It's a psychological weapon. Video has become the favorite weapon of abuse in Iraq."[6] The broadcasts come at prime time, six nights a week, from al-Iraqiya, a station in Mosul. The videographer is careful to tell the viewer that U.S. money set up the station, and it "is supposed to be independent. But it's run by the Interior Ministry." He points to the show's enormous and eager audience of Iraqis who discuss it everywhere in the shops and streets of Iraq, along with "football and the new Iraqi government."

Terrorism in the Hands of Justice began in January 2005, and it received some attention in the U.S. press, mostly ironic and quipping.[7] It was compared to a reality show with reluctant stars. Alongside these dark notes of amusement, U.S. writing also indicated that many appeared on camera with injuries—bruises and blackened eyes, visible pain while breathing.[8] As does the Iraqi documentarian, U.S. news accounts concluded the program was a "powerful psychological tool in the counterinsurgency." But the Iraqi videographer offers clearer connections and more serious analysis. He tells the viewer that the confessions have been forced and are recorded without consent. He records his parents watching the show together at home. Both insist the confessions must be true; all are criminals. "I really like it," says his mother. "It's like a detective program or cartoon." He protests in disbelief—what of determining guilt, lawyers, evidence, a trial? He tells us that most subjected to capture and torture are Sunni, and many who appear on the show disappear or later turn up dead—a phenomenon reported in the U.S. stories on the show as well.

The forced confessions have recurrent themes. They reveal those captured to be deviant thugs who take small amounts of money to commit heinous beheadings, explosions, and thefts; some confess drunken behavior or sex—sodomy—in mosques and other public places. Torture is integral to the undertaking. Whoever these men are, they are captured, beaten, and debased, and they and their communities and relations are humiliated in prime time. In this way, the torture and the show play a fundamental social function: both send a message that defines the acceptable new nation and publicly casts people from it. The viewers are constituted as a protected "we, the people," and the price of that protection is commando-style violence enacting the new social order. For many thousands, most but not all Sunni men, torture for TV in this school turned detention center began the process of their final elimination.

The videographer interviews the al-Iraqiya station head, Basr Mufti. Mufti was tortured in the 1990s, and Saddam's regime videotaped the amputation of his hand. Mufti sees no comparison between the Saddam-era tortures and brandings and the televised terror now. The narrator asks why Iraq televises a program that would be illegal in the United States or the United Kingdom; Mufti's rationale borrows from the repertoire of exception and colonial management: "Iraq in this time is different than any country," meaning terror is the price of public order or victory in this place, among these people. Americans respond well to this genre of explanation. It has a familiar place in the U.S. national security imagination, invoked repeatedly to support long terror wars in Vietnam, El Salvador, and more. But the critic who made *Terror TV* sharply counters its (colonialist) presumption that Iraq is exceptional or that terror is inevitable for a backward people. Instead, the video insists Iraqis understand the difference between procedural justice and government disappearances, between torture, executions, and criminal law: "What happened to all those promises of human rights and ideas of international law?" His YouTube video does not single out some savage breed of commando perpetrator for blame; nor does he characterize commandos as U.S. puppets. Instead, he connects U.S. funding to Interior Ministry terror and disappearances, and he connects both to the complicity of a large viewing audience. He announces he will choose exile for this reason; he cannot raise his three-year-old in Iraq.

The videographer could not have been alone in this analysis. By 2005, torture in Iraq was on brash display. Handcuffed, executed, and mutilated bodies were dumped on the streets, faces sometimes burned. Sunni men were found "dead in ditches and fields, with bullet holes in their temples, acid burns on their skin, and holes in their bodies apparently made by electric drills."[9] The number of bodies in June 2006 topped three thousand.[10] Monthly counts of discarded corpses reached or numbered above that level through early 2007. Entrepreneurial "body contractors" earned $300 to $500 per person from families who wanted to trace the whereabouts or identify the bodies of loved ones.[11] By 2007, the International Committee of the Red Cross and the U.S. State Department reported that the single year between August 2005 and August 2006 had left ten thousand unidentified bodies still in the morgue.[12]

The Iraqi videographer's clarity and condemnation of the engines behind the violence—and the show that exalted it—stand in contrast to much U.S. journalism that was surveying the same Iraqi terrain at that moment and well after. In 2005, the United States was still reeling from scandal provoked by U.S. torture of Iraqi detainees at Abu Ghraib exposed a year earlier, but the torture debate had largely moved away from Abu Ghraib questions.[13] Instead, across 2005 to 2007, as we have seen, that U.S. debate turned increasingly to concern over media representations of torture in dramatic television, to Guantánamo as a place of legal exception, and eventually to CIA and White House approval for a specific technique: the waterboard. However, considerable public information implicated the United States in the broader map of Iraqi torture where the conflict between various militias and the U.S.-led forces was killing and detaining tens of thousands of civilians.

The U.S. press was aware of the commandos and their show from its outset in 2005 and could see evidence of torture. That year the press also became aware that death squads were at work in Iraq, that the Pentagon had obtained funding to recruit covert militias, and that the U.S. military and civilian leaders had entertained the possibility of what they called the Salvador Option as a strategic possibility. Why did these connections get no traction in that torture debate?

What follows will speak briefly to networks for violence in Chicago to lay out basic features. From there, I use the news record of the time to trace key features in U.S.–Iraqi relationships and torture practice: a shared understanding of the Salvador Option, a set of key personnel, and a structure of relations that channeled streams of funding, equipment, and incentives. The same structure outfitted the network with a set of official, organizational, and public modes of denial.

Networking a Salvador Option

To perceive U.S. responsibility and participation in torture conducted by Iraqi hands requires an altered analysis of torture as a collaborative practice perpetrated by a network; it therefore benefits from a network approach. Sociologist Andrew Papachristos has argued for the value of qualitative and statistical mapping of social networks in the field of criminology, and he uses a form of network analysis to contend that gang homicides in Chicago were in fact "murder by social structure."[14] This understanding of violence networks is worth comment. For those who study them, network phenomena open attention outward from individuals to their relationship ties: What is the quality, kind, and frequency of the interactions between participants? What are the patterns of interdependence that bind individuals into these cliques, teams, and organizations? What seemingly ancillary conditions of setting, routine, procedure, and surveillance shape and affect those interactions? The answers can produce different actions, effects, and outcomes.[15] When construed as networks, unexpected dynamics appear (e.g., third or fourth parties), or even conditions whose interaction may turn out to drive behavior or may illuminate what we often render in the abstract. Network analysis, Papachristos writes, can "unpack the black box often associated with ideas such as 'peer influence,' 'group processes,' or 'facilitation effects.'"[16] The complicities of "peer influence," "facilitation effects," procedural requirements, and material conditions saturate the examples examined in this book—precisely the elements of torture networks that are decentered in our activism and evade legal accountability.

Papachristos found that in groups predicated on the interdependence of their members, patterns of interaction persist in organizational memory. New members inherit this networked memory and method and use it as a schematic for their actions. Among individual gangs, the combination of organizational design and historical memory produced a patterned understanding, or schematic, that guided their daily interactions and their dominance struggles with rival gangs. This shared schematic linked actors through an organizational sensibility that directed and interpreted their acts of territorial dominance or reprisal. Individuals remained responsible for their actions, but the schematic mapped out the range of individual action that might come as a result of violence: "While an individual member pulls the trigger it is the structure that determines who kills whom."[17] Individual participants in a violence network cannot then be the sole focus of investigation or blame. It is the organizational design and the sense of purpose as well as the quality of relationships that inform, direct, and constrain individual action and outcomes.[18] The schematic and structure endure even as individuals are replaced. Similar features enable the networks that drive and sustain state torture.

I will use the term "schematic" to capture this group-level worldview: a group's particular sense of memory, motivation, and method, or a map of how they and all the puzzle pieces are supposed to fit together to diagnose a problem or realize the vision that motivates them. Continual interaction and recourse to this motivational map forge a sense of common purpose and incentive; that shared worldview maintains the structure of interpersonal relationships and practices that tend a network, manage internal dissent, and deflect media scrutiny. Motivating schematics orient players to their work and each other. A schematic establishes an understanding of design, memory, and purpose as one. It also lays the groundwork for denial, as the Salvador Option in Iraq illustrates.

Shared Schematic

Death-squad activity in Iraq was foreshadowed as much as coordinated via a shared concept of El Salvador (meaning the years of U.S. funding and military and political engagement with El Salvador's rightist government and its war in the 1980s). The U.S. engaged heavily in El Salvador as a security trainer, advisor, and accomplice in counterinsurgency. All were aspects of the wider cold war counterinsurgency strategy in Latin America. The strategy was written into organizational memory for the U.S. military, the State Department, and others. In 2001, the Bush administration gathered into top posts personnel who had significant connections to U.S. work in Central America in the 1980s: Iran–contra/Nicaragua, El Salvador, and the DEA.[19] In the Iraq of 2003, insurgent retaliation grew quickly, fueled by U.S. occupation and incompetence and aggravated by local conflicts.[20] A concept dubbed the Salvador Option was circulated among the U.S. administration's war planners, and by 2005, some were speaking off the record to reporters.

The informal, almost casual Salvador Option implied common ideas that would be transferrable to Iraq—and, for that matter, to a set of "as many as ten nations in the Middle East and South Asia," according to reporting by Seymour Hersh in January 2005.

"Do you remember the right-wing execution squads in El Salvador?" the former high-level intelligence official asked me, referring to the military-led gangs that committed atrocities in the early nineteen-eighties. "We founded them and we financed them," he said. "The objective now is to recruit locals in any area we want. And we aren't going to tell Congress about it."[21]

In 2003, in fact, Secretary of Defense Rumsfeld called a Salvador expert to Iraq: retired colonel James Steele. Steele had been the head U.S. military advisor to battalions of El Salvadoran fighters in the 1980s. Although Steele's official designation in Iraq was energy contractor, his recruitment pointed toward an advisory role for the U.S. and work with Iraqi commando units on intimate terms. The structure is a legacy of compartmentalized terror units Lansdale and others had pioneered in 1950s counterinsurgency: U.S. advisors, local commandos, a "humane" military.

It is no coincidence, then, that across 2003 to 2004, the Bush administration was working publicly to burnish the "Salvador" of the 1980s as a foreign policy success. This, however, was a tall order, given the U.N. Commission on the Truth for El Salvador report of 1993, the track record of the Office of Public Safety, and the wave of historical work since on U.S. cold war interventions throughout Latin America, which I touch on in chapter 2.[22]

The U.N. Commission found the twelve-year conflict had killed 75,000, mostly civilians, in a country of only eight million. The U.S. had spent $1 billion to assist El Salvador's military, and an additional $5 million to support the 1982 and 1984 election campaigns of authoritarian president José Napoleón Duarte. With another $90,000 annually, the CIA had salaried one of the death-squad organizers. Although the war had been packaged for U.S. audiences as a civil war and antidote to the spread of leftist terror, 85 percent of the 75,000 dead were killed by government death squads. These squads included the Salvadoran military forces advised by fifty-five U.S. officers, with James Steele at their head. Over the years of U.S. financial and operational support, the Salvadoran military grew from 10,000 to 50,000, and its officers and men were trained at U.S. war schools and provided top-flight battle gear.[23]

To recharacterize that past engagement, the Bush administration relied on largely symbolic actions. For instance, in a vice presidential debate during the 2004 U.S. election cycle, incumbent Dick Cheney defended the U.S. mission in El Salvador as a great success.[24] Days after the administration's reelection in November of that year, Secretary of Defense Donald Rumsfeld flew in to preside over a Veterans Day celebration at the embassy in San

Salvador. Commemorating the 20 U.S. personnel who had died in El Salvador's civil war and honoring the thousands then deployed in Iraq, Rumsfeld thanked them for their commitment of 360 troops to the "global war on terror."[25] The publicity served both administrations. El Salvador was holding its own presidential election in 2004, pitting a former leftist guerilla and candidate of the Farabundo Martí National Liberation Front (Frente Farabundo Martí para la Liberación Nacional, or FMLN) against celebrity sportscaster and media mogul Elias Antonio Saca on the right.[26] In 2007, President Bush welcomed Saca to the White House, and a body named the International Republican Institute honored him with a special 2007 Freedom Award.[27] Little press attention was paid to these symbolic gestures, but key Iraq planners were at work tending the schematic, asserting that the techniques used in El Salvador could achieve a laudable end in Iraq, and in both cases could cement a lasting geopolitical partnership.

In 2005, Bush administration sources explained to *Newsweek* reporters that the "Salvador" concept meant "offensive operations" that would "create a *fear of aiding* the insurgency." A second Pentagon source repeated this veiled language for funding a terror campaign, the use of Iraqi security and militias to take a toll on the larger population: "'The Sunni *population is paying no price* for the support it is giving to the terrorists,' he said. 'From their point of view, it is cost-free. We have to change that equation.'"[28] These sources spoke in 2005, but important players like James Steele had arrived in Iraq two years before. They shared a motivating belief that a terrorized population could lead to success because terror could be managed effectively by superior combatants—a belief showcased in Roger Trinquier's handbook for counterinsurgents four decades before.

Personnel and Structure

The Washington–Iraq network connected a handful of players who had shared personal or organizational histories around a common understanding of Salvador strategy: heavy U.S. funding and a light U.S. footprint to galvanize suppressive terror. James Steele was tasked with building special forces–style security units. He would work closely with another formidable paramilitary man, Iraqi Adnan Thabit. Thabit, instigator of the commandos' TV show, was also head of the special police commando units that were integrated with ministry security forces under U.S. advisors, and he captained his own force, known as the Wolf Brigade. The U.S. State Department had full warning what partnership with him would deliver. A cable summarized one meeting with Thabit, saying he "expressed the view that it is necessary to fight terror with terror, and it is critical that their forces be respected and feared as this was what was required in Iraqi society to command authority."[29] Thabit's language echoed the voices in Washington, and Steele referred to Thabit with a term familiar from El Salvador: Thabit was "a real caudillo," a true strong man.[30]

The work promoted by the network is legible in its deployment of personnel and the links among them. The leadership circle was tight and familiar. On the Iraq side, Steele worked closely with commando leader Thabit. Thabit's nephew was the Interior minister, Falah al-Naqib, the man responsible for Iraqi conduct of security personnel, policing, and prisons.[31] Steele partnered with American Steve Casteel, who served as Interior Minister Naqib's closest U.S. advisor. Casteel brought experience from DEA drug wars in Latin America. James Steele, however, did not answer to the Interior Ministry or to U.S. military commanders in Iraq. He reported directly to Secretary of Defense Donald Rumsfeld in Washington. The joint mission of these men was to build teams of commandos from remnants of the Iraqi republican guard and others wanting a paycheck.

Their work was assisted by two major structural changes engineered by Rumsfeld in 2004. First, the U.S. legislature authorized funding that permitted the Defense Department to recruit and pay militias, formerly the sole preserve of the CIA. According to *Newsweek,* the change meant that "counterterrorist strike squads, even operating covertly could be deemed to fall within the Defense department's orbit."[32] Second, the Defense Department brought the civilian police training effort in Iraq under a military command and assigned it to the newly promoted Lieutenant General David Petraeus. Before this structural shift, the police and security forces were trained by consulting U.S. police personnel. That effort was underfunded, understaffed, and consequently failing, and focused attacks on U.S. and Iraqi forces were increasing.[33] Under his new command in 2004, Petraeus was to train, equip, and mentor the Iraqi police and security forces as well as the Iraqi army. He was to develop security institutions and infrastructure such as police stations, training bases, and border fortifications.[34]

A trusted assistant to Petraeus, Colonel James Coffman had led a U.S. unit in Mosul in 2003 and would now work with James Steele; *Stars and Stripes* referred to Coffman as Petraeus's "eyes and ears on the ground."[35]

Coffman and Steele worked together closely to coordinate U.S. military teams to escort Iraqi commandos on patrol. One reported directly to Petraeus, the other directly to Rumsfeld. An Iraqi general who worked with both Coffman and Steele told reporters for the *Guardian* and the BBC that the special police commandos developed thirteen or fourteen secret detention bunkers in Baghdad run by the Interior Ministry, and these two had access to them all.[36]

David Petraeus, like James Steele, had cut his teeth in El Salvador. In fact, their paths had crossed there in 1986, while Petraeus was conducting doctoral research. Petraeus was studying the war in Vietnam when his mentor, General Jack Galvin, head of SOUTHCOM, invited him to travel for a summer of research comparing the counterinsurgency in Vietnam with ongoing U.S. military activities in Central America. They traveled widely in Panama, Honduras, and finally El Salvador, where Petraeus stayed in Steele's home. In El Salvador, Petraeus talked with the fighters and observed Steele's work. Paula Broadwell's biography of Petraeus records the significance of this tour for the future general—an indicator that, in retrospect, he saw it as an important precursor to Iraq. As a young man, Petraeus described El Salvador to a friend, saying, "This has been a tremendous experience," and after returning to West Point in 1986, he sent a note to Galvan suggesting his mentor create "a new version of a field circular on low-intensity conflict." He wrote, "To really make an impact on Army thinking ... you need to institutionalize your ideas. That requires, of course that you get your ideas/concepts into doctrinal manuals."[37] Petraeus would author this counterinsurgency manual himself twenty years later.

In sum, the shared Salvador schematic helped assemble key personnel around a classic counterinsurgency directive. As the Washington insider described it to Hersh, "the population would pay a price for the support it is giving to the terrorists." The U.S. civilian and military leadership recruited old hands from El Salvador and worked to revise the U.S. role in that war in modern memory. The organizational structure arranged social ties and relationships into formal and informal structures. Interior Ministry actors and commandos were separated from U.S. military personnel and patrols by distinct lines of command. Despite the compartmentalization, key leaders and players were all connected via "one degree of separation" and informal ties—relatives, old friends, and assistants who served as hubs connecting otherwise discrete realms of funding and activity.[38] When the guiding concept of such a network made space for torture of the populace as a terror multiplier, this structure protected top Defense players (Rumsfeld, Petraeus) from direct involvement in Iraqi conduct or ministries. Their assistants (Steele, Casteel, Coffman) crossed these lines of command to access detention sites, deliver information, and coordinate action or inaction. So too did reconstruction and defense dollars flow freely to support informants, paramilitary salaries, training, and equipment. That formal structure supported an illusion of separation among players at work in a common enterprise.

Funding and Incentives

Before U.S. military command of the policing effort, Iraq's police had been trained by U.S. civilians and issued baseball caps and pistols. In June 2004, Petraeus was determined, in his words, to cultivate an "Iraqi solution to an Iraqi problem."[39] The phrase taps a lexicon familiar from Vietnam and El Salvador and invokes a mirage common to counterinsurgencies. By June 28, the institutions and people of U.S.-occupied Iraq would become simultaneously sovereign and dependent—a neocolonial paradox useful for both the United States and the new Iraqi government. Parties could invoke one side of the coin or the other to explain a range of (in)action.

Petraeus militarized the security forces.[40] He inserted combat training into the curriculum, brought in AK-47s, and opened the gates for enormous military spending—more than $11.8 billion in weapons, body armor, Dodge Ram pickup trucks and Humvees, video cameras, and detention equipment. Subject to notoriously mismanaged accounting, the enormous procurement and distribution effort Petraeus began saw weaponry flood government ministries, and the runoff also fed Sunni insurgents, their foreign allies, and groups like the Badr Organization, one of the Shi'ite militias that was quickly incorporated into commando units.[41] Meanwhile, U.S. funds marked for civilian and political support buoyed the Iraqi government and the Interior Ministry, including the television network that broadcast the commando's nightly terror program.

Petraeus and the Interior Ministry worked together to increase the numbers of police and military, endorsing Steele as advisor to the Iraqi commandos. According to one report, Petraeus assisted with their recruitment, working to weed out untenable Iraqi applicants. These special forces–style teams departed from conventional uniforms, wearing instead berets and emblems to match ferocious new brigade names, like Scorpion and Wolf.

They organized joint U.S.–Iraqi patrols.[42] Teams of a dozen or more U.S. Special Forces, National Guard, and military infantry partnered with Iraqi commandos on raids and swapped target information.

Coordinating Denial and Disregard

By June's end in 2004, about to hand over power to a sovereign Iraqi interim government, U.S. knowledge of torture in Interior Ministry detention centers was undeniable. Meanwhile, the joint U.S.–Iraq undertaking demonstrably incubated and supplied terror and torture and scaled up its delivery. However, it is important to stress that the professional network that evolved around the Salvador Option took an utterly common bureaucratic and professional shape. One might argue that mass torture and exemplary executions might not have resulted or were not intended, instead being unpredictable and tragic by-products of a difficult war. Indeed, as is the case with all counterinsurgencies, this network was built to accomplish multiple broad missions beyond instilling fear in the population. However, terror used to orchestrate fear was in the mind of top U.S. planners who spoke early to the press, and it was a part of the experience of key actors on the ground in Washington and Baghdad. The possibility of terror was neither foreclosed nor carefully, actively prevented.

Abetting denial were the forms of professional inattention built into the organizational design. But these would not be enough. In the face of mounting numbers of the disappeared, mounds of corpses, and nightly broadcasts on Iraq's commando TV, the Washington–Baghdad network actively coordinated denial and disregard in three overlapping spheres: first, official denials; second, organizational disregard in which official use of forms and procedures optimized group participation; and finally, public disregard in which media routines and a common reportorial lens would enlist broad public participation.

Official Denial and Organizational Disregard

An incident covered in the Oregon press in June 2004 illustrates well the official coordination of silence. When a unit of Oregon National Guardsmen witnessed torture in the open yard of an Interior Ministry prison outside of Baghdad, they notified U.S. command. They called it in twice, waited for orders, and then announced they were going to intervene. Hearing them, battalion commander Dan Hendrickson rushed with a detachment to back them up. On site, they found over a hundred prisoners who showed signs of torture and malnutrition being guarded by the Shi'ite Badr Brigade. The soldiers offered what they could in emergency aid, food, and water on the spot, but they soon received an order "from high up" to stand down: Leave the prisoners to their keepers and return to base. A U.S. commander back at base ordered them not to acknowledge or speak of the event.[43]

Distraught soldiers spoke with the press anyway, and Oregon senator Ron Wyden asked top brass for clarification. Only weeks after the international impact of images of U.S. soldiers torturing captives at Abu Ghraib, these soldiers learned that superiors who publicly denounced torture would tolerate it when it was committed by the Iraqi teams they were to train and assist. In fact, military leadership had issued an Iraq-wide policy that clearly anticipated more such incidents. These were "fragmentary orders" (in military parlance, FRAGOs) 242 and 039. They required U.S. military personnel witnessing torture by Iraqis to submit a written report but not to intervene or investigate. That would be left to the new Iraqi government. The military and State Department documents printed as the Wiki War Logs capture a first mention of this nonintervention mandate, FRAGO 242, in June 2004. It was supplemented in April 2005 with FRAGO 039, which required U.S. soldiers to file a written report but not investigate.[44]

It is clear that Donald Rumsfeld, as secretary of Defense, understood the requirement. In a November 2005 press conference, when asked directly, Rumsfeld told reporters he had seen no information on death squads operating in Iraq. But his statement was false. The secretary had in fact received a memo from Steele verifying such activity six weeks earlier.[45] Rumsfeld did, however, state the plan should U.S. troops witness such activity: they were not to intervene. General Peter Pace, who had recently succeeded Richard Meyers as chairman of the Joint Chiefs of Staff, was present and spoke to correct him.

> PACE: It is absolutely the responsibility of every U.S. service member, if they see inhumane treatment being conducted, to intervene, to stop it.
> RUMSFELD: But I don't think you mean they have an obligation to physically stop it, it's to report it.
> PACE: If they are physically present when inhumane treatment is taking place, sir, they have an obligation to try to stop it.[46]

This stark division in front of a U.S. audience suggests that Pace was either unaware of the order not to intervene in torture or he disagreed with it. Yet the soldiers on the ground were clear. Many complied with FRAGO 242 and 039, sending a minimum of 1,365 formal reports on torture up the U.S. chain of command from 2005 to 2009.[47] Soldiers reported eyewitness accounts of broken and dislocated limbs, men and women hung upside down from their wrists, whipping, fingernails pulled out, anal rape, vaginal rape, and rapes by proxy in which captors force one prisoner to rape another. The reports verified what human rights organizations had been finding all along as they investigated survivors' and families' claims.

The very existence of the orders was confirmation of and preparation for widespread eyewitness evidence of torture. These orders were extraordinarily powerful forms of disregard, and they enlisted organization-wide participation, mandating both inaction (nonintervention) and symbolic action (filing a written report to be dealt with by the Interior Ministry). This material and procedural mechanism managed dissent. It empowered upset witnesses to object to torture, and it distanced the U.S. military from the outcomes as it enabled ongoing U.S. complicity. By substituting documentation for intervention, the orders gave denial and disregard an active, material form that would not slow, prevent, or discourage torture.

There is a strong partnership here. Forms of official public disapproval and denunciation rest easily alongside active facilitation of torture and of the conditions and personnel that sustain it. They reinforce an illusion of distance that media seem to accept. For instance, these nonintervention orders were in effect as the commandos launched their nightly hit, *Terrorism in the Hands of Justice*. As stated flatly by the Iraqi videographer's critique, the U.S.-sponsored, ministry, and commando TV show was tangible evidence, making apparent an organized system of torture, terror, and disappearance. U.S. funding and its popularity suggested that the results of torture were tolerable so long as neither the Wound nor the Tool was too visible, nor the Perpetrator tied too closely to the United States, as I discuss in chapter 4. Media merely noted the gruesome implications with distance and dark humor.

A similar message of public denunciation and active facilitation came from the U.S. command in Iraq. An investigation years later by the Guardian/BBC World would confirm that Lieutenant General David Petraeus telephoned Thabit at home in 2005 to demand he stop showing tortured men on TV.[48] Petraeus's special translator, Sadi Othman, confirmed bearing the message but forcefully insisted that "General Petraeus does not support torture. . . . To suggest he does support torture is horseshit."[49] Nor does commando strongman Thabit support torture. As he told a U.S. reporter in 2005: "Torture is not humane, I don't approve of it, but there are some procedures which you need to understand you have to follow in order to make criminals confess."[50] These rejections are obligatory. Early counterinsurgents stressed the need to be humane as well, all while dramatizing the necessity of torture in modern warfare.

Petraeus cycled back from Iraq to a U.S. administrative post in September 2005; shortly after, the Jadriyah torture bunker was identified and exposed by the United States' new man placed in charge of security in and around Baghdad: Brigadier General Karl Horst. Horst had been persistent in his search for a fifteen-year-old boy, went himself to the detention center, and spoke to the press about what he found. Jadriyah held 169 men; of these, three were Shia, and the rest were Sunni. General Horst said 25 percent of them appeared to be recently tortured.[51] The new Interior minister, Bayan Jabr, told the press, "I reject torture and I will punish those who perform torture. . . . No one was beheaded, no one was killed."[52]

When Petraeus was asked about torture bunkers like those discovered in and around Baghdad for a 2010 biographical profile, he said atrocities were widely rumored, but it was tough to get hard evidence, although he did remove one commando leader. He did not mention over a thousand reports filed by witnesses who were ordered not to intervene. U.S. teams "couldn't keep eyes on the Iraqis twenty-four hours a day. 'You had such limited means to put hands on [the commandos] and the need was so urgent to get them out there,' Petraeus recalled."[53]

A leader's flat and public denial of support for torture may be sincere, but it is also a requisite of leadership and advancement. Petraeus issued a clear statement rejecting torture in 2007, before he returned to Iraq as head of a U.S. troop surge meant to tamp down a roaring insurgency.[54] However, he reopened the torture issue with a ticking time bomb question for Congress in his confirmation hearings for a 2011 post as Obama's director of the CIA.[55] It matters little whether Petraeus and Thabit reject torture as a public matter of principle when their actions supported it as a fact on the ground. They knew where to find detention sites and each other. Both supported the commando TV broadcast used to illustrate the power and success of the U.S.–Iraqi mission. Disapproval of torture coexists neatly with torture. Indeed, the disapproval enables some to continue its work and others to disregard it.

Given the gruesome spectacle and high body count, the U.S. press began to question the rash of raids and kidnappings using official vehicles that were targeting predominantly Sunni civilians. The torture network met this with a united media strategy. In comments to the press, the Interior Ministry and the U.S. military speculated that daylight kidnappings were carried out by "men in police uniforms," imposters in commando gear, or others "masquerading" as official security. The U.S. press largely followed this odd premise and misleading language.[56]

As Petraeus knew, official disapproval creates doubt in the press. It is important to see, however, that the press also has tools at its disposal, templates capable of enlisting reader participation in denial and disregard. The work of a seasoned investigative journalist Peter Maass demonstrates this effectively.

Organizing Public Disregard: Reporting through the Colonial Lens

Although his reporting allowed him to view key features of the Washington–Baghdad network and evidence of torture at close proximity, the formal conventions of journalism enabled Maass to present that network as a murky uncertainty in the midst of a chaotic war. He published "The Way of the Commandos" in the *New York Times Magazine* in May 2005, and the piece makes apt comparison to the work of the Iraqi videographer with which I opened this chapter. As the streets of Iraq came to look a lot like those in El Salvador decades earlier, those who survived and families of the disappeared were not confused about the systemic nature of torture and disappearances. They understood the U.S. role in precipitating, funding, and tolerating indiscriminate kidnapping, torture, and death squads as a demonstration of power and as a means to terrorize the public, thereby suppressing resistance.

War Is Hell: A narrative template. Across 2005 to 2007, there existed ample criticism of the war in Iraq. Yet when it came to a media debate on torture per se, the U.S. Salvador Option was considered war news and Iraq an ordeal, not a window on U.S. torture. When Peter Maass published "The Way of the Commandos," it was an important, detailed piece of reporting that discussed terror, including the Salvador Option and its roots. But Maass bends his analysis through a colonial lens—one the Iraqi videographer rejected. That lens is an enduring imperial narrative form familiar to war reporting in the national security imagination. The form bears debts to journalist-novelist warriors like Lartéguy, whom Petraeus recommended to young soldiers.[57] Like the Heart of Darkness profiles on torturers discussed in chapter 3, the form sends a lone reporter or witness, never a survivor, to collect grim wisdom from Kurtz-like aficionados, and the witness brings back the truth of torture to the general public. The War Is Hell template in journalism converts the quest to a vehicle for event-based reporting on war abroad, specifically counterinsurgencies, and Maass echoes the careful postures struck in William Tuohy's 1965 report on "fighting terror with terror" in Vietnam (discussed in chapter 2). The result clouds evidence of structured torture networks in colonial mists, specious distinctions, and epistemic murk. It was readily borrowed and updated by even the best U.S. reporters in Iraq.

The effect of this War Is Hell form, whether reporting from Vietnam or Iraq, is first to record torture within the larger landscape of violence, executions, and disappearances, and second to cite multiple participants who explain the violence as a tragic but inescapable circumstance when war is among those people in that place—a land where modern beings, be they U.S. contractors, soldiers, or journalists, are thrown back in civilizational time. Third, the form embodies colonial ambivalence in its narrative strategy and tone. As reporters and narrators, Tuohy and Maass both lament indications of U.S. soldiers' and advisors' involvement, and they nod to the national security rationale for torture, invoking the realities of a war for intelligence.

On the record. In Iraq, Maass met with important players in the network, including Thabit, Steele, Casteel, and Petraeus. Maass bore witness to the system that was funding, arming, and training paramilitary units, and he knew that in Washington, the conceptual approach was being likened to El Salvador. He went on joint raids with Iraqi commandos and U.S. troops. He witnessed violence, visited a commando detention center, and watched their work in *Terror in the Hands of Justice*. However, the analysis of the U.S. journalist and the Iraqi videographer of *Terror TV* could not be more at odds.

In his reporting on commando teams, Maass lends context: prior U.S. efforts to defeat the Iraqi insurgency failed "thanks to questionable American methods." The story implies that the Interior Ministry formed the commando teams in 2004 because the U.S. military would not. He cites a report from the Center for Strategic International Studies that blames senior U.S. officials for the public disorder. The "grossly inadequate" training and equipment provided the civilian police meant "unprepared Iraqis were sent out to die." That neglect "was the equivalent of bureaucratic murder."[58] He suggests that Iraq presented commandos to the United States as a fait accompli. He does not note that Rumsfeld brought in El Salvador expert Steele on this assignment in 2003.

Where the civilian approach to training police had been incompetent, underfunded, and passive, it had failed. The commandos offer a more aggressive path. Therefore, "U.S. soldiers and officers are increasingly moving to a Salvador-style advisory role." Maass offers longer context on the twelve-year war in El Salvador and the phenomenally high Salvadoran body count, mostly civilian:

> Most of the killing and torturing was done by army and the right-wing death squads. . . . Whole villages were targeted by the armed forces and inhabitants massacred. . . . As part of President Reagan's policy of supporting anti-Communist forces, hundreds of millions of dollars in United States aid was funneled to the Army, and a team of 55 Special Forces advisors, led for several years by Jim Steele, trained front-line battalions that were accused of significant human rights abuses.

Historical photos published alongside his report and their captions highlight El Salvadoran bodies piled for display. Of the strategy applied to Iraq, he writes, "it is no coincidence that this new strategy is most visible in a paramilitary unit that has Steele as its main adviser." Once prized out from the rest, this is already a damning account. But it is still early in the piece.

Colonial contrasts. Like Tuohy in Vietnam, Maass concentrates his interviews on U.S. operatives, advisors, and military men. In 2005, however, he has a vantage point on history that Tuohy does not. Still, he follows the template, indulging colonial contrasts that artificially distance the United States from Iraqi (or Vietnamese) methods even as their teams patrol side by side, equipped, trained, and funded by the same source.

While on patrol with U.S. troops, commandos deliver a sustained beatdown to one subject using fists and boots. Maass is blunt: "It was a dockyard mugging." Again, out on a raid, a commando captain aimed an AK-47 at a boy and demanded to know where his father was. Maass's military escort intervened. One soldier present, Lieutenant Colonel Andrew Johansen, leader of a Wisconsin National Guard unit, offered his thinking on the incident: "I'm about 99 percent sure it was intimidation to put fear into the guy.... I didn't expect them to raise a weapon at a detainee. I don't think they know the value of human life Americans have. If they shoot somebody, I don't think they would have remorse, even if they killed someone who was innocent." Maass reinforces the soldiers' colonial contrasts with his own, describing the American way of war (planned, "honed skills and high-tech") with the Iraqi way ("improvisational . . . gut instinct . . . bare knuckles"). Although distasteful, he says, a pact with commando knuckles spares the U.S. something worse: "integration of commandos [with U.S. troops] . . . stanches one flow of experienced fighters into the insurgency."

Steele invites Maass to a library turned detention center, where he encounters evidence of torture without naming it as such. This includes extended screaming, the sight of a hundred men squatting in shackles, and fresh bloodstains on a desk in a room used for interrogating detainees. He overhears a U.S. soldier describe seeing a captive "hanging from the ceiling by his arms and legs like an animal being hauled back from a hunt"—something the soldier would not discuss directly. Maass watches with the commandos as they enjoy the nightly TV program of forced confessions. Lieutenant Colonel Mark Wald, "a graduate of the University of California at Berkeley," offers his own take on leader Thabit's menacing tactics: "This is what I consider an Iraqi solution. . . . The beauty of an Iraqi solution is that they know how justice has been dealt with in the past years. They know what they are subject to. We are bound by laws. I think they are, too, but that doesn't mean a guy like Sheik Taha doesn't go in [to meet Thabit] fearing it's an eye for an eye, tooth for a tooth."

Later, Maass allows Thabit's partners James Steele and his DEA colleague Steve Casteel to distance themselves; both men "stressed that torture and death-squad activity are counterproductive." Even after a tour of their facility, he receives their claim with a tepid tragic acceptance: "Yet excesses of that sort were endemic in Latin America and in virtually every modern counterinsurgency. American abuses at Abu Ghraib and other detention centers in Iraq and Afghanistan show that first-world armies are not immune to the seductions of torture." Although it seems thoroughly operationalized, violence against captives is "excess." What is native or endemic for some people and places can be a seduction for first world others who linger on colonial frontiers. His acknowledgment again separates the work of locals (whether in Latin America or Iraq) from their U.S. funders, trainers, and patrol partners. No wonder he points without irony to paperwork that offers the same distinction: "At the bottom of printed briefings that American soldiers receive at the bases in Samarra, a quotation from T. E. Lawrence is appended: 'Better the Arabs do it tolerably than that you do it perfectly. It is their war, and you are to help them, not to win it for them.'" The empire is cast as a self-effacing helpmate and observer. The quote is the colonial-era version of Petraeus's Iraqi solution to an Iraqi problem, of course, and a motto echoed by the Berkeley graduate above. Given a war that kicked off with a U.S. invasion and an insurgent response inflamed by ongoing U.S. choices and funding, one might wonder in what sense the conflict is "their" problem or war. But platitudes stamped onto briefing reports like this are meant to resonate in minds, reinforcing a national imaginary, a shared schematic transmitted successfully across decades of U.S. counterinsurgency in Vietnam, El Salvador, and elsewhere. The solution in each case—counterinsurgency—requires terror and torture. The reportorial form shares key premises of that schematic.

The platitudes and contrasts point up the absence of anticolonial analysis. Maass interviews no one who can offer an alternate assessment—no one like the Iraqi whose video *Terror TV* called for international law and human rights. Nor does Maass visit the morgue. He fails to interview the families of the disappeared, talks to no one who was held in commando detention or can present that perspective, speaks with no one who can knock the colonialist dust off the War Is Hell conventions or critique the worn assumptions about fighting terror with terror, or torture with torture. Such dissent existed in other parts of the Iraqi government, including its Office for Human Rights.[59] Other Iraqi human rights monitoring organizations were busy counting bodies and trying to identify them throughout this period. Many Sunni, Kurdish, and Turkman populations saw this carnage as a U.S.–Shi'ite power grab through indiscriminate terror.

Manufacturing epistemic murk. When reporting from his experience on patrol or in conversation, Maass leans away from that U.S.–Iraq connection, using stark colonial contrasts that purport to distinguish and distance methods, daily work, and relations—political, economic, and social—that are fundamentally complex, interrelated, and mutually supporting. This is also the case when he cites historical material and human rights documentation, where he makes structural choices that muddy mutual relationships, framing third-party reports with murk.

He cites external reports toward the end, after details of his visit to the detention center. He prefaces them with this remarkable statement: "It was impossible to determine what was happening at the detention center, but there was certainly cause to worry." He then cites reports issued in 2005 by the U.S. State Department and Human Rights Watch, respectively. Iraqi authorities have been accused of "arbitrary deprivation of life, torture, impunity, poor prison conditions—particularly in pretrial detention . . . and arbitrary arrest and detention," and in addition, "unlawful arrest, long-term incommunicado detention, torture and other ill treatment of detainees (including children) by Iraqi authorities have become routine and commonplace." He bookends this with the Interior Ministry's emailed denial: "The Ministry . . . does not allow any human rights abuses against prisoners."

In the context he creates, these reports merely highlight "cause to worry" and the culpability of the Interior Ministry alone, despite his engagement on site with U.S. advisors, administrators, troops, and commandos who work side by side. Throughout, Maass's tone is lyrical and foreboding, and in drawing conclusions, he again offers the unknowable and uncontrollable: "In the country's unstable military and political landscape, it is impossible to know where [the commandos] are heading." Maass turns again toward tragic inevitability in his last line: "In El Salvador, Honduras, Peru, Turkey, Algeria and other crucibles of insurgency and counterinsurgency, the battles went on and on. They were, without exception, dirty wars." War is chaos, even when networks deliberately plan, recruit, and implement the methods that have produced exactly such terror in the past.

On the ground in Iraq, Maass documents every link in a deliberate chain—the network's shared concept, legacy players, careful structure, bloody detention spaces, and deadly outcomes. The U.S. men who provide him access to it all offer official denials at the same time. Yet Maass refuses to credit that network as a technique of torture at work before his eyes.[60] He records damning details, but he pours them into a classic mold. His explanatory quotations are rich in colonial contrasts and distance; his tone, structure, and conclusion turn away from investigatory interest toward resignation and remorse. Every historical link to El Salvador in the piece— the weight of the documentation he cites, and of what he himself has witnessed—is belied by a narrative conclusion that amounts to a halt and shrug on the threshold of an unknowable future. This final equivocation is a staple of the War Is Hell form, a means to exit the article without drawing conclusions. Such tools of colonialist thinking are stock elements in features on war abroad. The torture network—although planned, coordinated, compartmentalized, funded, and officially denied—seems inscrutable and beyond control. Ultimately, Maass calls the commandos "a conundrum," not an orchestrated blight on human life, as does the Iraqi who made *Terror TV*—a man with less evidence before him, but far more at stake.

· · ·

In November 2005, once Maass is gone and, as noted, Petraeus is on assignment in the United States, General Karl Horst takes charge of Baghdad security and enters a detention site he is accustomed to let alone.[61] Seeking a woman's kidnapped son, he does not find the boy, but he finds a torture bunker, as he knew he might. For the moment, he eschews the imperial paradox of sovereign dependency; he steps over the threshold and into a space of interdependence, mutual responsibility, and blame. He calls in three quick reaction teams to take control of the center, reports it to the Interior Ministry and to multinational forces, and goes to the press. In contrast to Maass, Horst handles the message with clarity, and so does the press. This was not the first time U.S. soldiers had visited the bunker.[62] Nor did Horst's interview stop torture under the same Iraqi intelligence head and militia commander.[63] But it did alter the future of those being harmed there, and it delegitimated, at least somewhat, a few military and media conventions of disregard. It also forced wider acknowledgment of torture as an institutionalized feature of the U.S.–Iraq partnership, a thriving symbiosis of U.S. military, corporate contractors, Iraqi militias, ministries, and politicians that has continued across all the years since.[64]

Eight years after Horst's intervention, Ben Emmerson, the U.N. special rapporteur on terrorism and human rights, called for a Pentagon investigation into links between torture, death squads, Petraeus, Steele, Coffman, and the Interior Ministry. He was responding to a fifteen-month investigation published by BBC Arabic/The Guardian. This team approached the project with a different narrative template. Interviewed in this context, Peter Maass recounts his 2005 experience with the detention center, Steele the U.S. patrols, and on. Years later, the same details that Maass once cast in a fog corroborate torture and a network.[65] Whether the intervening eight years brought him insight is unclear. They surely brought more torture and more dead. In response to the 2013 investigative report, the Pentagon announced it would pursue an inquiry, but that it "would take time."[66]

These circuits producing torture were legible, inscribed in the public record, in plain sight as they developed and over many years. As Maass's work demonstrates, many of the common cultural and professional templates we use for interpretation are of a piece with the larger security imagination. They support torture and assist denial.

Torture and terror of the scale and duration experienced by Iraqis in this period would not have happened without the direct material, operational, financial, and advisory support of the Department of Defense, international partners, private companies, and the U.S. military. The United States was not all-controlling; nor was it on the sidelines. To be sure, the United States initiated Iraqis and numerous militias into what became the full economic and political partnership of counterinsurgency: mutual manipulation, competing advantage, and ugly interdependencies. The Salvador Option outcome—torture that all parties sought to manage to their advantage—was not incidental. It was integral to terror. The nightmare in Iraq demonstrated what histories of torture and terror by proxy ought to have taught: that the United States can incubate, support, and facilitate terror and torture via such networks and proxy arrangements, but these cannot ensure control. They should not ensure impunity either.

The Epilogue, to which we turn next, uses the case of the American Psychological Association's collaboration in torture to discuss the ways torture networks and the national security imagination should alter understandings of public complicity.

Epilogue

Complicity

Torture networks function in the practical time and space of a rational process, of professional approval and advancement, not timelines of civilizational decay or cycles of the culturally repressed. Neither sophisticated conspiracy nor barbaric impulse are useful explanations for torture in this regard. It is along the breadth of professional networks—whether those of commerce, the military, journalism, scholarship, or the judiciary—that important decisions about torture are made and putative benefits are reaped.

This book has argued that we cannot regard torture in the war on terror as a problem separate from the torture integral to the U.S. local and federal punishment systems, or from the policing violence meant to send a message of caste stratification or to supposedly secure certain neighborhoods or borders. Nor do these phenomena stand apart from the alliances and markets in security by terror that we feed and sponsor. While these may be organized as distinct systems, they are culturally connected and propelled by a shared and often submerged understanding of what constitutes a threat to the U.S. racialized economic order, misogynist hierarchies, and geopolitical dominance. The national security imaginary functions, at least in part, to direct our attention away from these connections. Failure to readily see how the work of torture supports all these systems can only serve the national security imaginary, sustain the entire mosaic of state violence uncritically, and make waste of human lives and energies.

The national security imaginary is a medium in which we all swim together. Violence networks tap that imaginary to enlist supporters; those most injured are best positioned to see national security and the place of torture within it—the presumptions, beliefs, and professional networks— for the total system of social organization that it is.

Just as the security imaginary involves us all, so do torture networks. Far from being inscrutable or uncivilized, collaborations in violence are carefully coordinated and compartmentalized. As was the case with the U.S.–Iraqi network, the constitutive parts may be composed of witting, interdependent transnational relationships, including advisory roles that come with funding, communications assistance, target lists, logistics, transportation, nonintervention orders, and official rationales. However, the actions of many players and components may appear unwitting because their behavior is supported and mediated by a set of beliefs and practices that are shared more widely. Their involvement seems a matter of customary procedures, specific material conditions, and cultivated mind-sets. Interpretation is inextricable from human action. It is done through the shared cultural frameworks and professional templates that we inhabit.

In torture networks, the parts sustain the whole even as the compartmentalization thwarts recognition of shared professional and cultural complicity in torture. Every person placed along a torture network need not know, have known, or intended everything in order to be complicit in the result. Like the U.S. war reporter described in chapter 6, participants need only be careful of what they see and how they interpret it. Those who are aware need not always approve to be complicit. All of us are entangled in violence networks. To sustain the mass violence of torture, we need only bow to professional relationships or a national security imaginary and racial order that mediates what counts as evidence, who counts as credible, what deserves attention, and what merits disregard.

However, the points of our entanglement and complicity with torture can become points of intervention. People lend support to torture in ways that are both material and imaginative. Put differently, complicity is built, on the one hand, from elements we can identify with some ease—institutional, relational routines as well as social incentives and needs. On the other hand, these material elements are inseparable from internalized, value-laden models, our accepted ways of interacting with others and making sense of the world. Both material and imaginative support for violence can be interrupted and withdrawn.

This analysis suggests at least four levels for the work of unwinding these entanglements, withdrawing support, and building a different social order. The amount of collaborative energy and labor these undertakings require is staggering, essential, and, importantly, already underway.

First, those of us who want to confront and end torture need to broaden our notions of complicity and culpability. This requires us to confront and take responsibility for our own complicity in violence.

Second, we need to make violence networks and the imaginary supporting them salient, with the understanding that this insight will reveal multiple new points for intervention.

Third, we will need to interrupt and intervene in current violence networks while simultaneously building collaborations bent on different social goals. This is transformational, long-term work that will learn from current experiments that successfully center health, stability, and equity as they reduce and redress harm—not with "securitization" but with systems of acknowledgment, accountability, education, and healing.[1]

Fourth, a shift in the security imaginary is obviously central to this enterprise. An altered imaginary will necessarily be assembled through this transformational work to support it. However, to expand these efforts, that social imaginary must be widely shared.

In order to point to collaborations that are interrupting violence networks as they build something better, I use a final example drawn from the involvement of psychologists and the American Psychological Association (APA) in torture. The example helps us rethink complicity and illustrates harmful entanglements we all share. In 2015, war on terror torture survivors filed a case against two U.S. psychologists. James E. Mitchell and Bruce Jessen were contracted by the CIA to design a program that put the supposed stamp of innovation and science on torture techniques that were well known and studied by psychologists, the CIA, and the Pentagon since the 1950s. The case against them was the first in which the U.S. government did not use a "state secrets" claim to shield the defendants from criminal prosecution. Other motions to dismiss the case were denied. This made *Salim v. Mitchell* the first case to prosecute U.S. actors in a U.S. court for the torture of captives taken in the post-9/11 raids and wars.

In August 2017, a settlement was reached. The undisclosed monetary payout was a notable if insufficient victory for two men, Suleiman Abdullah Salim and Mohamed Ahmed Ben Soud, who survived Mitchell and Jessen's brand of torture, and for the family of the third, Gul Rahman, who was tortured to death.[2] The financial details, however, are disquieting: the CIA had signed a multimillion-dollar, multiyear indemnification contract with Mitchell, Jessen, and the firm Mitchell, Jessen & Associates years earlier. By contract, Mitchell and Jessen lost nothing; U.S. taxpayers would foot their legal bills and pay this settlement.[3] This hefty indemnity came on top of the $180 million the CIA paid to their company and the $81 million they earned as individuals.[4]

Both men are torture perpetrators. They seem easily identifiable as such because they were in the room where torture occurred. However, they would not have been there if it were not for others who comprised the network of relationships and agreements linking several organizations. The actions of those not in the room are always integral to the damage done. To be clear, beginning in December 2001, the head of the American Psychological Association ethics office and four past and present APA presidents—two of whom served on a CIA advisory group at this time—held frequent conversations with Mitchell, Jessen, and top officials from Defense, the CIA, and the RAND Corporation. A different APA task force and a CIA director of operations, himself a psychologist, produced a 2005 revision of the APA code of ethics. It was coordinated carefully with the military and White House to ensure precise alignment with the language of still-secret torture memos issued by the Office of Legal Counsel, which I cover in chapter 4. That new APA ethics code did not go unnoticed. The World Medical Association and other critics referred to it flatly as the Nuremberg defense.[5] It indeed stipulated that a professional psychologist engaged in unethical practice can claim to be just following orders.[6] Several facilitators of this code received contracts, grants, and appointments supplied by the Pentagon and the torture contractor, Mitchell, Jessen & Associates. Other lucrative contracts and positions went to former APA presidents, their director of ethics, and their White House–CIA liaison.[7]

Beyond the monetary gain, the intent of this elaborate activity was to protect the profession, not just Mitchell and Jessen. The new code loosened ethical restrictions that could damage professional reputations, licensure, or livelihoods and thereby preserved a long-standing pipeline of jobs and funding flowing from the security state to the psychology profession. The CIA was not the only collaborator. The Department of Defense had also enlisted psychologists at Guantánamo Bay to assist in interrogation, forming special behavioral science consulting teams. That tactic spread to other U.S. detention sites.

As is the case with many violence networks, much of these psychologists' involvement in torture activity appeared in mainstream publications and circulated widely in human rights reports beginning in 2004.[8] Throughout this period, member associations denounced the APA for torture, terror, trauma, and death that fell disproportionately on communities marginalized by race, ethnicity, or religion. The U.N. Human Rights Council, four special rapporteurs, the World Medical Organization, the American Psychiatry Association, the American Medical Association, and human rights investigators, along with a large proportion of the APA's membership, condemned the APA's participation in and defense of torture.

The personal and community-building benefits of this interagency, interorganizational collaboration in torture were outlined in a shadow report issued by dissident APA members in 2015 entitled *All the President's Psychologists*. An independent review of APA involvement in torture took place that same year and assigned culpability to five top APA officials who colluded with both the Department of Defense and the CIA. These figures actively insulated Mitchell, Jessen, and others from torture complaints and the APA from reform.[9]

In this example so far, a court case and an independently administered organizational review investigated complicity. Each assigned culpability to different players. The step from the two perpetrators in the court case to identifying an interorganizational network connecting the APA, CIA, and Department of Defense widened the circle of culpability.[10] We further widen the scope of networked complicity and culpability when we consider the place of torture in the national security imagination. That lens extends complicity to an interorganizational history, generations of professionals, and the public.

Across the twentieth century, specific networks of scholars and schools of psychology left a clear trail of mutual benefit and social harm as torture generated what are now decades-old professional and financial entanglements among universities, private think tanks, the CIA, and the Pentagon. The bundle of assumptions and orientations that emerged as "national security" was bound together with behavioral science immediately in 1948, when the term "cybernetics" was coined to mean the study of "command and control in the machine and the animal."[11] The Pentagon and CIA quickly engaged psychologists, psychiatrists, and neurologists at major research institutions, boosting them to prominence by funding experimentation on humans aimed at "modifying individual behavior by covert means."[12] Psywar, psyops, and counterinsurgency become intimate partners in this period as networks for security by terror expanded.

No reliable means to control behavior and no science of torture emerged from this experimentation, but it did have lasting results.[13] One is the widespread and enduring fascination with CIA "science" and its seemingly all-encompassing capabilities—an atmospheric investment found everywhere in popular culture. Among those who over decades lent imaginative as well as material support to this collaboration are certainly U.S. taxpayers and the makers and consumers of popular culture, including speculative news that mystifies or celebrates the technology or expertise surrounding torture or mind control. Like any social imaginary, the national security imagination is animated by public participation, repetition, and improvisation.

A second durable outcome of this collaboration in experimentation has been the funding relationships, university influence, professional ties, and organizations developed over this time. Given the history of close interaction and professional incentives on all sides, the outreach to psychologists was a natural step in 2001 for the CIA and Pentagon. In 2006, APA Division 19 (Military Psychologists) announced that the U.S. Department of Defense was the largest employer of psychologists worldwide, a claim repeated in a 2012 publication. Psychologists design expensive assessment tools, develop recruitment and training programs, decide who is fit for redeployment, and manage disability claims. Psychiatry, psychology, and neurology are used to enhance a military's own troops—and, as we have seen, to destroy enemies.[14]

The imaginative and material outcomes of this security collaboration have been realized over generations and have had direct impact on many lives and regions, El Salvador among them. We have seen that war on terror planners found inspiration in the 1980s U.S.-sponsored counterinsurgency, a Salvador Option that they applied to devastating effect in Iraq. Those who are dismantling the security state can also find in El Salvador a lesson in resistance, critique, and the creation of something new.

Indigenous communities suffered the largest share of mass violations during the war in the 1980s. In the midst of that violence, El Salvadoran survivors modeled the path to transformation that I described earlier. They began identifying points of complicity in violence networks and disrupting the imaginary behind them. As they did, they built new systems and understandings. These survivors pushed a Jesuit scholar and Spanish social psychologist who worked among them to new theory and practice. Ignacio Martín-Baró came to understand that trauma and suffering are shared social phenomena. He realized that problems in mental health signaled the "crystallization within individuals of aberrant and dehumanizing social relations," and that psychosocial problems required collaborative solutions.[15] The community knew achieving health in the wake of deep trauma required collective, participatory techniques and that these methods must foreground their right to understand and fight the causes of their situation, including the political and economic processes behind militarization. Martín-Baró learned that healing, not to mention psychology itself, required a thorough, lived critique of individualism. Faced with this challenge, he understood his professional imaginary to be complicit, and he came to demand that psychologists overturn the models of health promoted by Western medicine and psychology, and that they align with the oppressed, not the state. Martín-Baró was killed by the El Salvadoran military in 1989.

As they did in the case of Martín-Baró, survivors have urged psychologists as well as social service and development workers to confront the complicity of their own professions in torture. In a scathing critique of the APA's support for torture in 2007, psychologists Mark Burton and Carolyn Kagan turn to the impact of El Salvadoran survivors on Martín-Baró: "the security apparatus in North American psychology is the hegemonic force in world psychology, one that touches us all." Moreover, "the imperialist state has for years harnessed psychology for social control through antidemocratic, pro-system propaganda in core countries of the West or those who resist the West."[16]

Today, the work of survivors and Martín-Baró's liberation psychology have grounded transnational, interdisciplinary, and community-based innovations.[17] Examples of U.S.-based movements include the Fireweed Collective, the Audre Lorde Project, and BEAM (Black Emotional and Mental Health Collective). All these efforts displace the biomedical model of mental illness to redefine what medicine is and increase who has access to it. The Fireweed Collective describes its framework as "healing justice," a model "rooted in racial justice, disability justice, and economic justice."[18] As do these other collaboratives, the organization centers the persons most affected by oppressive social systems, embracing collective organizing as one important source of healing.[19] It is no surprise that El Salvador's liberation psychology, as well as coalition-building efforts like the Audre Lorde Project, have aligned healing with the call to invent alternatives that can rethink safety and replace U.S. security systems. As are these efforts, "transformative justice" is made up of "creative and dynamic experiments happening across the world."[20] All are identifying their own points of complicity in violence networks and disrupting the imaginary behind them. As they divest from the old, they build new systems and understandings.

State torture is not a closed chapter for the APA, any more than it is for the United States.[21] U.S. torture is supported by a fabric of public associations and unspoken beliefs and is driven by social benefits. Torture's place in the national security imaginary makes it easy to focus debate and denunciation of torture on matters of interrogation and imperial warfare while expecting that criminalization on the books will be enough to address torture's active presence and social, racializing work in mass migrant detentions, SWAT raids, police chokeholds, beatdowns, or prison discipline.[22] This volume has held that the post-1947 phase of racial capitalism that developed this vision of security torture strategically distinguished it from the violence that still grounds the U.S. racial-economic order. That same phase of racial capitalism implemented what we now call national security, counterinsurgency, and law-and-order policing as a package deal. Over decades from the 1970s onward, as transnational antitorture campaigns found their footing and grew, a bipartisan U.S. consensus on prison building and incarceration gained momentum and generated massive profits.

To grapple with torture, we have to look away from the compelling national security vision of torture and to ask different questions about the work that torture does for us and for our society. Ending torture means rethinking safety and changing institutions, workplaces, and our commonplaces about security. Ending torture, therefore, means aligning with the call to replace prisons and policing with new collaborations, organizations, and visions. People who flinch at the term "abolition" when used by antipolice or prison activists may understand the word's resonance with the historical movement to abolish the slave trade and slavery. However, they fail to understand contemporary abolition as the collaborative process of replacement—steady disentanglement and replacement, not a headlong fall into a vacuum.

In June 2020, in the aftermath of a viral video that captured the slow suffocation and agony of George Floyd under the knee of Minneapolis police officer Derek Chauvin, abolitionist Mariame Kaba writes: "The first thing to point out is that police officers don't do what you think they do."[23] Significant studies, not to mention the officers themselves, note that "crime-related tasks are a tiny portion of a police officer's daily labor."[24] They spend time instead handling noise complaints, traffic and parking violations, and disputes among drivers, customers, or neighbors. Asking "what work does policing do?" invites the practical effort of replacement: the process of having this work done by nonviolent bodies, like "social workers, EMTs, fire fighters, traffic directors, garbage collectors, counselors, neighborhood associations, friends and so on."[25]

But at that moment in 2020, Kaba also insisted that this process alone, though powerful, is insufficient. She pressed her readers to redefine safety, a task critical to unseating the security imaginary and its racial imperative: "A safe world is not one in which police keep Black and other marginalized people in check through threats of arrest, incarceration, violence and death."[26] Police and prisons do not reduce harm; they do not do what we think they do. Rather, "the criminal punishment system promises accountability for violence but we know that in actuality it is a form of targeted violence against poor people, disabled, people of color and does not reduce violence."[27] Torture is integral to that system. We cannot separate torture from this mix with the intention to oppose it alone and not the modes of state violence it serves and supports.

A change in the national security imagination will rely on the insight and activism of torture survivors and abolition activists. A just society must be built from new modes of safety, accountability, health, and equity, not surveillance, terror, and torture. Participation in that work reduces harm and saves lives now. It will have to continue generations into the future. The case of the APA's participation in torture urges all industries and disciplines, public and private, to inspect our own networks, benefactors, and complicity with the courage modeled by torture survivors, dissident psychologists, and prison abolitionists. Like them, we have to engage in everyday disentanglement from torture networks and the security imaginary. Like them, we need to accept the challenge of radical, constructive imagination and collaboration, building something new as we dismantle the old.

Notes

Prologue

1. Speculative news writing began September 17: Amy Argetsinger discussed U.S. torture through the lens of a philosophy class quiz in "At Colleges, Students Are Facing a Big Test," *Washington Post,* September 17, 2001, https://www.washingtonpost.com/. One day before, Vice President Dick Cheney had a wide-ranging television interview about military force in Afghanistan and the events of September 11. When asked by Tim Russert on NBC's *Meet the Press,* Cheney indicated suggestively that in this new era, "We're going to have to work on the dark side." The meaning in context is not torture; rather, the United States will have "unsavory characters" and "bad guys on the payroll" to infiltrate terrorist networks and inform on them. *Meet the Press,* NBC, September 16, 2001, https://youtu.be/KLwXGEOvTWQ. On September 17, the president signed a secret memorandum of understanding outlining the new reach of a variety of executive powers, but it was silent on interrogation and the application of the Geneva Conventions. Jane Mayer, *The Dark Side: The Inside Story of How the War on Terror Turned into a War on American Ideals* (New York: Doubleday, 2008), 39–42. On January 25, 2002, the head of the Office of Legal Counsel, Alberto R. Gonzalez, issued a "Memorandum for the President, Decision RE: Application of the Geneva Convention on Prisoners of War to the Conflict with Al Qaeda and the Taliban." Mark Danner, *Torture and Truth: America, Abu Ghraib, and the War on Terror* (New York: NYRB, 2004), 83. "Humane Treatment of al Qaeda and Taliban Detainees," memo from the president, *Washington Post,* February 7, 2002, https://www.washingtonpost.com/wp-srv/nation/documents/020702bush.pdf. Standards of conduct for interrogation under Sections 2340–2340A of Title 18 of the United States Code, memorandum for Alberto R. Gonzales, counsel to the president, August 1, 2002, U.S. Department of Justice, www.washingtonpost.com/wp-srv/nation/documents/dojinterrogationmemo20020801.pdf.

2. For quizzes and surveys, see Amy Argetsinger, "At Colleges, Students Are Facing a Big Test," *Washington Post,* September 17, 2001, https://www.washingtonpost.com/; and Abraham McLaughlin, "How Far Americans Would Go to Fight Terror," *Christian Science Monitor,* November 14, 2001, https://www.csmonitor.com/. Other speculative pieces in the Hypothetical vein are John Blake, "Seeking

a Moral Compass while Chasing Terrorists: How to React to Enemies Raises Tough Issues for People of Faith," *Atlanta Journal Constitution,* September 22, 2001; Jay Winik, "Security Comes before Liberty," *Wall Street Journal,* October 23, 2001, https://www.wsj.com/; Jonathan Alter, "Time to Think about Torture," *Newsweek,* November 5, 2001, https://www.newsweek.com/; Jim Rutenberg, "Torture Seeps into Discussion by News Media," *New York Times,* November 5, 2001, https://www.nytimes.com/; Sandi Dolbee, "Agonizing over Torture: Can Deliberate Hurt Be Justified in Times of Terror?," *San Diego Union-Tribune,* November 23, 2001; Jess Bravin, "Interrogation School Tells Army Recruits How Grilling Works—30 Techniques in 16 Weeks, Just Short of Torture; Do They Yield Much?," *Wall Street Journal,* April 26, 2002, https://www.wsj.com/; E. V. Kantorovich, "Make Them Talk," *Wall Street Journal,* June 18, 2002, https://www.wsj.com/; Peter Maass, "Torture, Tough or Lite: If a Terror Suspect Won't Talk, Should He Be Made To?," *New York Times,* March 9, 2003, https://www.nytimes.com/; Steve Chapman, "No Tortured Dilemma," *Washington Times,* November 5, 2001; Bruce Hoffman, "A Nasty Business," *Atlantic,* January 2002, 49–52, https://www.theatlantic.com/magazine/archive/2002/01/a-nasty-business/302379/; Michael T. Kaufman, "The World: Film Studies: What Does the Pentagon See in 'Battle of Algiers'?," *New York Times,* September 7, 2003, https://www.nytimes.com/; Drake Bennett: "The War in the Mind," *Boston Globe,* November 27, 2005, https://www.bostonglobe.com/; Mark Bowden, "The Dark Art of Interrogation," *Atlantic,* October 2003, 51–70. See also "Psychology and Sometimes a Slap: The Man Who Made Prisoners Talk," *New York Times,* December 12, 2004, https://www.nytimes.com/; Joseph Lelyveld, "Interrogating Ourselves," *New York Times Magazine,* June 12, 2005, https://www.nytimes.com/; William Schulz, "The Torturer's Apprentice," *Nation,* April 25, 2002, https://www.thenation.com/.

3. Tony Lagouranis with Allen Mikaelian, *Fear Up Harsh: An Army Interrogator's Dark Journey through Iraq* (New York: New American Library, 2007).

4. Jodi Wilgoren, "Swept Up in a Dragnet, Hundreds Sit in Custody and Ask, 'Why?,'" *New York Times,* November 25, 2001, https://www.nytimes.com/. Documents released under the Freedom of Information Act show that at the time of arrest, 300 of the first 725 bore no relationship to terror. Of the 1,200, only one was charged with a terror-related crime, and 600 were charged with immigration violations. Several others were said to be "material witnesses." Quoted in Kristian Williams, *American Methods: Torture and the Logic of Domination* (Boston: South End, 2006), 169. A large share was kept incommunicado and denied family contact and legal representatives. Ostensibly arrested for civil immigration violations, like overstaying a visa or working unlawfully, the 9/11 detainees at Metropolitan Detention Center were placed in an ultrarestrictive solitary confinement unit called ADMAX SHU. They were in cells twenty-three hours a day, with the lights on all day and night. Detention center guards beat and harassed them, denied them soap

and toilet paper, and refused to let them pray or sleep. Many were eventually released only when they complied with a charge of credit card fraud, forfeited citizenship, and were deported. See Center for Constitutional Rights, "The State of Civil Liberties One Year Later: Erosion of Civil Liberties in the Post 9/11 Era," http://www.ccr-ny.org/v2/reports/docs/Civil_Liberities.pdf. Tram Nguyen, *We Are All Suspects Now: Untold Stories from Immigrant Communities after 9/11* (Boston: Beacon, 2005), xvii. Nguyen provides a useful timeline of major events and policies from 2001 to 2004 affecting immigrants and civil liberties (159–77).

5. Officer Burge brought torture tactics back from his tour in Vietnam and, supported by many others, applied them extensively to force confessions from African Americans throughout the 1980s and 1990s, sending many innocent citizens of Illinois to death row. Of the numbers tortured, subjects were overwhelmingly African American. John Conroy, *Unspeakable Acts, Ordinary People: Dynamics of Torture* (New York: Knopf, 2000); John Conroy, "Annals of Police Torture: What Price Is Freedom?," *Chicago Reader,* March 2, 2001, https://chicagoreader.com/; John Conroy, "Tools of Torture," *Chicago Reader,* February 4, 2005, https://chicagoreader.com/. The extensive use of torture among Chicago police undermined justice proceedings so thoroughly that it eventually forced the Illinois governor to convert all death row sentences to life in prison, noting, "The category of horrors was hard to believe. If I hadn't reviewed the cases myself, I wouldn't believe it." Even this sweeping commutation was a mere half measure for Chicago's innocent whose cases lacked DNA evidence that might result in their release. Flint Taylor, "Police Torture and the Death Penalty in Illinois: Ten Years Later," *Nation,* January 11, 2013, https://www.thenation.com/. Chicago and other U.S. cities continue to struggle with allegations of police torture; see Kristine Phillips, "Dozens Claim a Chicago Detective Beat Them into Confessions. A Pattern of Abuse or a Pattern of Lies?," *Washington Post,* June 9, 2018, https://www.washingtonpost.com/.

6. See Sherry Ricchiardi, "Missed Signals," *American Journalism Review* 26, no. 4 (2004): 22–29. See also Eric Umansky, "Failures of Imagination," *Columbia Journalism Review* 45, no. 3 (2006): 16–31. Ricchiardi counted six investigative pieces from September 2001 to April 2004.

7. Rajiv Chandrasekaran and Peter Finn, "U.S. Behind Secret Transfer of Terror Suspects," *Washington Post,* March 11, 2002, https://www.washingtonpost.com/.

8. Dana Priest and Barton Gellman, "U.S. Decries Abuse but Defends Interrogations; 'Stress and Duress' Tactics Used on Terrorism Suspects Held in Secret Overseas Facilities," *Washington Post,* December 26, 2002, https://www.washingtonpost.com/.

9. A more honest assessment of this activity as torture was published a year later in the British press, but as its title indicates, even that piece allowed for different shades of torture—useful or abusive: Dana Priest and Barton Gellman, "Ends, Means and Brutality: The Use and Abuse of Torture," *Economist,* January 11, 2003.

10. Ricchiardi, "Missed Signals."

11. Important investigative work was pursued by Dana Priest, Jane Mayer, Seymour Hersh, Mark Danner, Michael Hersh, and more.

12. Brigette L. Nacos, *Mass-Mediated Terrorism: The Central Role of the Media in Terrorism and Counterterrorism* (Lanham, Md.: Rowman & Littlefield, 2002), 61. Nacos cites a *Los Angeles Times* telephone poll on September 13–14, 2001. She reports similar findings from Gallup Organization, conducted September 14–15, 2001.

13. Nacos, *Mass-Mediated Terrorism,* cites results from a poll by Pew Center for People and the Press, October 17–21, 2001: "78% of the respondents said that they watched terrorism news very closely, 16% watched closely, 4% not closely. 1% gave no answer. This result was nearly the same level of interest as in mid-September (13–17) when 74% of survey respondents revealed that they watched terrorism news very closely, 22% closely" (61).

14. Robert J. Samuelson, "Unwitting Accomplices?," editorial, *Washington Post,* November 7, 2001, https://www.washingtonpost.com/: "The perverse result is that we may become the terrorists' silent allies." No studies of the media response to 9/11 have analyzed the role of sheer speculation in spreading legal distortions and false notions of torture. In contrast, studies of violence in the quantity and quality of event "coverage" and visual representation emerged quickly. Nacos, *Mass-Mediated Terrorism;* Valerie Scatamburlo-D'Annibale, "In 'Sync': Bush's War Propaganda Machine and the American Mainstream Media," in *Filtering the News: Essays on Herman and Chomsky's Propaganda Model,* ed. Jeffrey Klaehn (Montreal: Black Rose, 2005), 21–62; Lila Rajiva, *The Language of Empire: Abu Ghraib and the American Media* (New York: Monthly Review Press, 2005).

15. Nacos, *Mass-Mediated Terrorism,* 57. Nacos counts 288 stories on anthrax and biological and chemical terror from September 11 to October 4. In the month after the first case's report, these reached a count of 2,940 on biological/chemical terror, with 631 of these specifically about anthrax. She counts 222 reports on biological/chemical terror and 66 on anthrax from September 11 to the appearance of the first case of anthrax. She reviewed ABC News, CBS News, NBC News, CNN, Fox News, National Public Radio, the *New York Times,* and the *Washington Post.*

16. Walter Pincus, "Silence of 4 Terror Suspects Poses Dilemma for FBI," *Washington Post,* October 21, 2001, https://www.washingtonpost.com/.

17. Damian Whitworth, "Stymied FBI Looks to Torture," *Australian Times,* October 23, 2001; John E. Collingwood, "The FBI: Protector of Individual Rights," letter to the editor, *Washington Post,* October 26, 2001, https://www.washingtonpost.com/; Douglas E. Johnson, "Torture Isn't the Way to Make Them Talk," letter to the editor, *Washington Post,* October 30, 2001, https://www.washingtonpost.com/.

18. "The four key suspects, held in New York's Metropolitan Correctional Center, are Zacarias Moussaoui, a French Moroccan detained in August initially in Minnesota after he sought lessons on how to fly commercial jetliners but not how to take off or land them; Mohammed Jaweed Azmath and Ayub Ali Khan, Indians traveling with false passports who were detained the day after the World Trade Center and Pentagon attacks with box cutters, hair dye and $5000 in cash, and Nabil Almarabh, a former Boston cabdriver with alleged links to al Qaeda." Pincus, "Silence." See also "A Novel Approach to Thinking about Two Jailed after Attack," *St. Louis Post Dispatch*, October 24, 2001. Note that Aybu Ali Khan is also known as Gul Mohammed Shah.

19. Steve Fainaru, "Sept. 11 Detainee Is Ordered Deported," *Washington Post*, September 4, 2002, http://www.newsmine.org/; Steve Fainaru, "Deportation Expected for 9/11 Detainee, Former Suspect Guilty on Immigration Charge," *Washington Post*, July 18, 2002, https://www.washingtonpost.com/. "Unterrorist Unwelcome," *Detroit Metro Times*, September 17, 2003.

20. Daniel Pipes, "To Profile or Not to Profile?," *New York Sun*, September 21, 2004, available at https://danielpipes.org (accessed July 5, 2023). "Ayub Ali Khan and Jaweed Azmath . . . were detained for a year on suspicion of being part of the 9/11 operation. Eventually exonerated and freed, they claimed to have been profiled. This is self-evidently correct; had the two not been Muslim, the police would have had little interest."

21. In 2016, Cole became legal director of the American Civil Liberties Union.

22. It was not unusual for speculators to use legal commentators to bolster authority and suggest ambiguity in the law at the same time, as Pincus does here. Moreover, telling metaphors, like Thornburgh's "strangulation," appear often, inverting the actual power dynamics of the state over its captives. They portray the rule of law as a physical threat and suggest that torture of unarmed persons is necessary self-defense.

23. Alter, "Time to Think about Torture," 45. The *Newsweek* issue featured America's most appealing targets: "airports, chemical plants, dams, food supplies, the Internet, malls, mass transit, nuclear power plants, post offices, seaports, skyscrapers, stadiums, water supplies." Nacos, *Mass-Mediated Terrorism*, 58.

24. Alter's example, for instance, requires us to ignore the obvious fact that high-decibel sound impacts and pains the body and compromises the nervous system. This is the case with all tortures deemed psychological and is discussed further in chapter 1.

25. Jim Rutenberg, "Torture Seeps into Discussion by News Media," *New York Times*, November 5, 2001, https://www.nytimes.com/. The story notes as well the CBS News decision to steer clear of "speculation about torture and discussion of its merits." A choice example of the trend in regional papers is Dolbee, "Agonizing over Torture."

26. Senate Select Committee on Intelligence, *The Senate Intelligence Committee Report on Torture: Committee Study of the Central Intelligence Agency's Detention and Interrogation Program* (Brooklyn: Melville House, 2014).

Introduction

1. Danielle Knight, "Trade in the Tools of Torture: The U.S. Government OKs the Export of Shackles and Stun Guns," *U.S. News and World Report*, November 24, 2003.
2. The U.S. Commerce Control List is published annually by the Department of Commerce Bureau of Industry and Security and is available at https://www.bis.doc.gov/. Year by year, these devices may be sorted into different control numbers—one year as "implements of torture," another year not. In 2001, for instance, Commerce had thumb cuffs grouped with body-worn shock devices and restraints such as shock belts, shock sleeves, straitjackets, stun cuffs, tilting multipoint restraint chairs, and leg irons. These were approved for sale to otherwise "restricted" nations, such as Cambodia and Estonia; in 2013, they went to Georgia, Iraq, Moldova, Russia, and Tajikistan. Thumb cuffs, shock restraint exports, and the like totaled 11.6 percent of the $1.7 million in exports documented in all Commerce Control List categories. Department of Commerce Bureau of Industry and Security, "2013 Annual Report to Congress," https://www.commerce.gov/doc/bureau-industry-and-security#4/34.64/-96.48 (accessed July 2015). While the year 2014 culminated in a narrow Senate Select Committee report condemning CIA enhanced interrogation, torture in commerce steamed on. By 2015, thumb cuffs had rejoined thumbscrews under "specially designed for torture" and were approved for Colombia and Syria; shock restraints, moved to a different category number, went to Russia and Mongolia. It is necessary to look at three different data sets for 2015 to obtain this information. Syria only appears under the "2015_BIS_license" spreadsheet. Colombia's $155,321 purchase only appears in the "2015 U.S. Exports" spreadsheet. Neither buyer for implements of torture (now 0A983) appears in the "2015 Annual Report to Congress." The annual report does, however, list the sale of restricted restraints (now 0A982) to Mongolia and the Russian Federation. These last do not appear on the Export or Licensing spreadsheets. See Department of Commerce Bureau of Industry and Security, "2015 BIS Licensing" data set, https://www.bis.doc.gov/index.php/all-articles/28-technology-evaluation/1108-2015-bis-licensing, and "2015 U.S. Exports," https://www.bis.doc.gov/index.php/all-articles/28-technology-evaluation/1107-2015-u-s-exports. Department of Commerce Bureau of Industry and Security, "2015 Annual Report to Congress," October 30, 2015, https://www.bis.doc.gov/index.php/forms-documents/policy-guidance/1389-bis-annual-report-2015 (the fiscal year 2015 runs from October 1, 2014, to September 30, 2015). Export Administration Commerce Control List category definitions can

be found in Department of Commerce Bureau of Industry and Security, "2015 Export Administration Regulations, CCL Supplement No. 1 to Part 774," December 31, 2016. Category 0A983 includes "'specially designed' implements of torture, including thumbscrews, thumbcuffs, fingercuffs, spiked batons, and 'specially designed' 'parts,' 'accessories' n.e.s. Control applies to entire entry for ALL destinations, except Canada, regardless of end-use. List Based License Exceptions (See Part 740 for a description of all license exceptions)" (11–12). Note the proximity of torture implements and the restraints listed in category 0A982: "Law enforcement restraint devices, including leg irons, shackles, and handcuffs; straitjackets; stun cuffs; shock belts; shock sleeves; multipoint restraint devices such as restraint chairs; and 'specially designed' 'parts,' 'components' and 'accessories'" (11). Also important is category 0A978: "Law enforcement striking weapons, including saps, police batons, side handle batons, tonfas, sjamboks, and whips" (9).

3. The operations of gender and race oppression are different but interlocking, compounding, and inextricable.

4. COINTELPRO operated from 1956 to 1971, but the report to the United Nations reached back to 1918, detailing collaborations among the Bureau of Investigation (now known as the FBI), the immigration bureau, local police, and business interests targeting organizing in U.S. immigrant, labor, Black, and Indigenous communities. See Paul Wolf et al., *COINTELPRO—The Unknown Story,* presented September 1, 2001, https://cldc.org/wp-content/uploads/2011/12/COINTELPRO.pdf. On the torture of Taylor, Bowman, and Scott, see transcript, "Former Black Panther Details Brutal Police Torture to Extract Confession in 1971 Murder Case," Democracy Now!, November 30, 2007, https://www.democracynow.org/.

5. John Conroy, "Annals of Police Torture: What Price Is Freedom?," *Chicago Reader,* March 2, 2001, https://chicagoreader.com/. Darrell Cannon was expected to testify against Detective Peter Dignan, Detective Grunhard, and Sergeant John Byrne about beating, electroshock, and torture. Instead, Devine offered to drop murder charges in exchange for pleading guilty to two lesser charges. The deal meant the officers would not have to testify as part of the trial. "Cannon achieved the promise of freedom in about two and a half years, and the state kept Dignan and Byrne off the witness stand," Conroy writes. "It's hard to say who got the better deal." About the deal for men on death row, see "September 26, 2001: Death Row Inmates Offered Deal to Drop Torture Claims," on Timeline: Jon Burge and Chicago's Legacy of Torture, *Chicago Tribune,* September 19, 2018, https://www.chicagotribune.com/news/ct-jon-burge-chicago-police-torture-timeline-20180919-htmlstory.html. The prologue to this book speaks to the impact of Chicago torture on the justice system years later. One of the most notorious officers on the torture team, Jon Burge, was hired in 1970, one year after Fred Hampton and Mark Clark were killed in their sleep in a COINTELPRO raid with cooperation from the Cook County state's attorney tactical unit and the Chicago police department.

6. A host of abuses emerged under investigation after fourteen-year-old Gina Score died in 1999 after collapsing from heat exhaustion during a forced run. She was left on the ground for three hours. Associated Press, "Boot-Camp Death of Girl Goes to Court in S.D.," *Deseret News,* December 11, 2000, https://www.deseret.com/2000/12/11/19543601/boot-camp-death-of-girl-goes-to-court-in-s-d.

7. Terry L. Cross, "Native Americans and Juvenile Justice: A Hidden Tragedy," *Poverty and Race* 17, no. 6 (2008): 19–22, http://www.prrac.org/newsletters/novdec 2008.pdf. For U.S. history and other resources, see the National Native American Boarding School Healing Coalition at https://boardingschoolhealing.org/education/us-indian-boarding-school-history.

8. "Native Lives Matter," a report of Lakota People's Law Project, February 2015, https://lakotalaw.org/resources/native-lives-matter. Op-ed by Vincent Schiraldi and Mark Soler, "Locked Up Too Tight," *Washington Post,* September 19, 2004, https://www.washingtonpost.com/: "Guards moved young inmates around the prison on a leash. To control youths who disobeyed orders, guards would sometimes don riot gear and use 'pepper spray'—tear gas mixed with cayenne pepper. At other times, groups of guards surrounded young inmates and handcuffed them by their wrists and ankles to the four corners of their beds. Young prisoners were held in isolation cells for weeks at a time. This mistreatment went on for more than a year, occurred regularly in the lockdown area of the prison, and involved more than 100 young people."

9. Senate Select Committee on Intelligence, *The Senate Intelligence Committee Report on Torture: Committee Study of the Central Intelligence Agency's Detention and Interrogation Program* (Brooklyn: Melville House, 2014).

10. I call this "torture lore" after Rejali's observation that much "torture talk" and so-called fact is folklore. Darius Rejali, *Torture and Democracy* (Princeton, N.J.: Princeton University Press, 2007), 7.

11. See chapter 2 on the large numbers targeted for torture in the U.S. war on terror and earlier counterinsurgencies.

12. United Nations Convention Against Torture and Other Cruel, Inhuman or Degrading Treatment or Punishment, 1984. See Ann Marie Clark, *Diplomacy of Conscience: Amnesty International and Changing Human Rights Norms* (Princeton, N.J.: Princeton University Press, 2001). Loopholes for extreme circumstances should be hard to find because the instruments that condemn torture arose against a background of extremes: acknowledged genocide, terrorism, national emergency, warfare, and authoritarian atrocity. However, states work through signing reservations and national statutes to incorporate a variety of objections, interpretations, and exceptions as they adopt the convention.

13. United Nations Convention Against Torture.

14. Celermajer offers an exemplary contribution that combines empirical, site-specific prevention work, a review of behavioral science studies on organizational

change, and new theoretical labor. She demonstrates the need for this new vision of prevention. See Danielle Celermajer, *The Prevention of Torture: An Ecological Approach* (Cambridge: Cambridge University Press, 2018), 44. See also John T. Parry, *Understanding Torture, Law, Violence, and Political Identity* (Ann Arbor: University of Michigan Press, 2010), 5.

15. In the United States, there are continuing efforts to move one form of state violence out of the "legitimate" or "incidental to" category in the 1984 convention and across the line into what is considered state torture: the death penalty, solitary confinement, forced feeding, and so-called consensual sex between police and persons in custody.

16. Celermajer nicely synthesizes resistance and tensions that inform the definitional work on torture and speaks to the ongoing conversations about rape as torture, violence against women, and the attribution of torture to nonstate actors; see Celermajer, *Prevention of Torture*, 3, 35–44. Treatment language is evolving to specify forms of torture with effects that encompass attacks on "survivors' embodied identities, roles and statuses and away from disembodied coital, genital, and sexual sites"—for instance, forms that "impact one's vulnerability and capacity to act in gendered ways; in the meaning of a person's identity in relation to culturally patterned gender roles; genderized consequences in relation to gender identity and gendered hierarchies of power." Pau Pérez-Sales and Maggie Zraly, "From Sexualized Torture and Gender-Based Torture to Genderized Torture: The Urgent Need for a Conceptual Evolution," *Torture Journal* 28, no. 3 (2018): 9, https://doi.org/10.7146/torture.v28i3.111179. They cite Molara Ogundipe-Leslie, *Re-creating Ourselves: African Women and Critical Transformations* (Trenton, N.J.: Africa World Press, 1994); and Victoria Canning, "Unsilencing Sexual Torture: Responses to Refugees and Asylum Seekers in Denmark," *British Journal of Criminology* 56, no. 3 (2016): 438–55, https://doi.org/10.1093/bjc/azv079.

17. "Legal No. 1," fact sheet collection, Dignity: Danish Institute against Torture, https://www.dignity.dk/.

18. Parry, *Understanding Torture*, 12–13, 163.

19. In 2017, Nils Melzer, special rapporteur on torture, announced that "arbitrary police violence can amount to torture even in public spaces." United Nations, "Governments Must Regulate Extra-custodial Use of Force to Prevent Torture within National Jurisdictions, Special Rapporteur Tells Third Committee," press release, October 13, 2017, https://press.un.org/en/2017/gashc4204.doc.htm.

20. Adriana Caravero, *Horrorism: Naming Contemporary Violence,* trans. William McCuaig (New York: Columbia University Press, 2009), 41.

21. Carlos Alberto Arestivo, "Torture: The Catastrophe of a Bond," trans. Laurie Ball Cooper, in *Witnessing Torture: Perspectives of Torture Survivors and Human Rights Workers,* ed. Alexandra S. Moore and Elizabeth Swanson (Cham, Switzerland: Palgrave Macmillan, 2018), 13, 9. Arestivo's work is based on direct testimony from

survivors he treats; comparative studies of Greece, Argentina, Uruguay, and Chile; and his own experience in Paraguay, where he was tortured by security forces for three months. "Torture implies a scientifically prepared process; it requires trained, suitable, and efficient human resources" (11).

22. Arestivo, "Torture," 8. "The climax of fear and terror expands like waves, maintaining the population in a state of permanent tension and collective fear, generating distrust as well as isolating families and social groups." The Istanbul Protocol—which provides guidelines on how to conduct effective legal and medical investigations into allegations of torture and ill-treatment—emphasizes the same; torturers attempt to destroy a "sense of being grounded in a family and society as a human being with dreams, hopes and aspirations." In this way, these attacks "profoundly damage" relationships between subjects, family, and community. United Nations Office of the High Commissioner for Human Rights, *Manual on the Effective Investigation and Documentation of Torture and Other Cruel, Inhuman, or Degrading Treatment or Punishment,* aka the Istanbul Protocol, updated June 29, 2022, https://www.ohchr.org/sites/default/files/documents/publications/2022-06-29/Istanbul-Protocol_Rev2_EN.pdf.

23. Kristian Williams, *American Methods: Torture and the Logic of Domination* (Boston: South End, 2006), 246.

24. Marnia Lazreg, *Torture and the Twilight of Empire: From Algiers to Baghdad* (Princeton, N.J.: Princeton University Press, 2007), 7.

25. Lazreg, *Torture,* 7.

26. John H. Langbein, *Torture and the Law of Proof* (Chicago: University of Chicago Press, 1977); Edward Peters, *Torture: Expanded Edition* (Philadelphia: University of Pennsylvania Press, 1999).

27. See Saidiya Hartman, *Scenes of Subjection: Terror, Slavery, and Self-Making in Nineteenth-Century America* (Oxford: Oxford University Press, 1997). Friedrich Nietzsche, *The Will to Power* (New York: Vintage, 1968). Adam Smith, *The Theory of Moral Sentiments* (1759), part 1.2.24 (on suffering) and part 5.1.18–21 (on torture), https://www.econlib.org/library/Smith/smMS.html. John Stuart Mill, "Civilization" (1836), in *Essays on Politics and Culture,* ed. Gertrude Himmelfarb (Gloucester, Mass.: Peter Smith, 1962).

28. See chapter 3. Elaine Scarry, *The Body in Pain: The Making and Unmaking of the World* (Oxford: Oxford University Press, 1987).

29. Page DuBois, *Torture and Truth* (New York: Routledge, 1991); Colin Dayan, *The Story of Cruel and Unusual* (Boston: MIT Press, 2007).

30. Parry's legal analysis concludes that although not welcome, "torture is consistent with liberal government." Parry, *Understanding Torture,* 13.

31. Rejali, *Torture and Democracy,* 15–16.

32. Roxanne Dunbar-Ortiz, *An Indigenous People's History of the United States* (Boston: Beacon, 2014); Dayan, *Story of Cruel and Unusual;* W. Fitzhugh Brundage,

Civilizing Torture: An American Tradition (Cambridge, Mass.: Belknap, 2018). On electroshock in policing, see Laurence Ralph's discussion of Dominque Franklin's death by Taser and the subsequent Chicago youth action, Laurence Ralph, "We Charge Torture. We Charge Genocide," presented before the 2014 U.N. Committee on Torture, in *The Torture Letters: Reckoning with Police Violence* (Chicago: University of Chicago Press, 2020), 114–41. See also Human Rights Clinic, *In the Shadows of the War on Terror: Persistent Police Brutality and Abuse in the United States. A Report Prepared for the U.N. Human Rights Committee, Columbia Law School,* May 2006, https://www2.ohchr.org/english/bodies/cerd/docs/ngos/usa/USHRN15.pdf.

33. Nelson makes a powerful argument that any dollar calculation in the struggle for African American reparations must tally up the value of Black women's reproductive lives and work over generations. Tauren Nelson, "Getting Free: Towards Anti-colonial and Black Feminist Praxis in Public Policy," African Diaspora Day keynote address with support of Dr. Charlotte Frazier, Lasell University, Auburndale, Mass., December 8, 2020. On racial capitalism, Kendi concludes that anti-Black racism emerged historically to justify a trade in slaves as it began to narrow its focus to exclusively sub-Saharan labor and to globalize. Ibram X. Kendi, *Stamped from the Beginning: The Definitive History of Racist Ideas in America* (New York: Nation, 2016), 20, 23–27. Singh's useful work on racial capitalism acknowledges the literature on the subject has grown enormously. Nikil Pal Singh, *Race and America's Long War* (Berkeley: University of California Press, 2017). Most use the term "racial capitalism" to indicate that capitalism evolved as a racializing force. The making of race and capitalism are inextricable. See also Destin Jenkins and Justin Leroy, eds., *Histories of Racial Capitalism* (New York: Columbia University Press, 2021).

34. John Grenier, *The First Way of War: American War Making on the Frontier, 1607–1814* (Cambridge: Cambridge University Press, 2010), 27–28.

35. Grenier, *First Way of War,* 12.

36. Assistant Secretary for Indian Affairs Bryan Newland, *Federal Indian Boarding School Initiative Investigative Report,* vol. 1, May 2022, https://www.bia.gov. This report shows for the first time that between 1819 and 1969, the United States operated or supported 408 boarding schools across 37 states (or what were then territories), including 21 schools in Alaska and 7 schools in Hawaii.

37. Brundage's history aptly calls that struggle the most sustained debate on torture in U.S. history. Brundage, *Civilizing Torture,* 90.

38. Julietta Hua and Katsari Ray, "The Lives of Things: Native Objects, Human Rights and NDN–Indian Relationality," in "Revaluing the Human: The Moral Economy of Human Rights," special issue, *Prose Studies* 38, no. 1 (2016): 12–33, https://doi.org/10.1080/01440357.2016.1144464. Dunbar-Ortiz, *Indigenous People's History,* 8.

39. Sexton and Lee write that mass incarceration and Abu Ghraib show torture to be "gratuitous and instrumental" as well as racialized in its essence. Jared Sexton and Elizabeth Lee, "Figuring the Prison: Prerequisites of Torture at Abu Ghraib," *Antipode* 38, no. 5 (2006): 1005–22, https://doi.org/10.1111/j.1467-8330.2006.00490.x.

40. Patrick Wolfe, *Traces of History: Elementary Structures of Race* (London: Verso, 2016), 12–13.

41. Mark Neocleous, "Theoretical Foundations of the 'New Police Science,'" in *The New Police Science*, ed. Markus Dirk Dubber and Mariana Valverde (Redwood City, Calif.: Stanford University Press, 2006), 22. See also Mark Neocleous, *Fabrication of the Social Order: A Critical Theory of Police Power* (London: Pluto, 2000).

42. This includes the public lynching of eighteen Chinese people in 1871. See "The Chinese Massacre: One of Los Angeles' Worst Atrocities," PBS video, broadcast October 17, 2017, https://www.pbs.org/video/the-chinese-massacre-one-of-los-angeles-worst-atrocities/.

43. Neocleous, *Fabrication,* 100.

44. Laleh Khalili, *Time in the Shadows: Confinement in Counterinsurgencies* (Redwood City, Calif.: Stanford University Press, 2012); Patricia Owens, *The Economy of Force: Counterinsurgency and the Historical Rise of the Social* (Cambridge: Cambridge University Press, 2015). Owens describes counterinsurgency as one of many styles of despotic, patriarchal "household" governance. Like the feudal or plantation household, the despotic household model has been basic to governance in the modern era. It pairs social regulation with violent repression. Owens describes households as relations of reproduction that extend beyond the immediate family and incorporate all the varieties of servitude and enslaved labor that support it. The model she refers to as counterinsurgency does not distinguish between colonial and neocolonial forms. I attach significance to the later period and the act of renaming as people took pains to invent, define, and promote the term "counterinsurgency" as distinct from the colonial.

45. Micol Seigel, *Violence Work: State Power and the Limits of Police* (Durham, N.C.: Duke University Press, 2018); Stuart Schrader, *Badges without Borders: How Global Counterinsurgency Transformed American Policing* (Berkeley: University of California Press, 2019). On law and order as a spending and policy premise entwined with counterinsurgency theory, see Seigel, *Violence Work,* 21–34.

46. Alfred W. McCoy, *Torture and Impunity: The U.S. Doctrine of Coercive Interrogation* (Madison: University of Wisconsin Press, 2012); A. J. Langguth, *Hidden Terrors: The Truth about U.S. Police Operations in Latin America* (New York: Pantheon, 1979).

47. Loïc Wacquant, "From Slavery to Mass Incarceration," *New Left Review* 13 (2002): 41–60. Michelle Alexander, *The New Jim Crow: Mass Incarceration in the Age of Colorblindness*, 10th anniversary ed. (New York: New Press, 2020). Ruth Wilson

Gilmore, *Golden Gulag: Prisons, Surplus, Crisis, and Opposition in Globalizing California* (Berkeley: University of California Press, 2007). Angela Y. Davis, *Are Prisons Obsolete?* (New York: Seven Stories, 2003); Angela Y. Davis, *Abolition Democracy: Beyond Empire, Prisons, and Torture* (New York: Seven Stories, 2005); Mariame Kaba, *We Do This 'til We Free Us: Abolitionist Organizing and Transforming Justice* (Chicago: Haymarket, 2021). Many writers do document torture in prison; see, e.g., Rejali, *Torture and Democracy,* 242–43; Center for Constitutional Rights and Allard K. Lowenstein International Human Rights Clinic, Yale Law School, "The Darkest Corner: Special Administrative Measures and Extreme Isolation in the Federal Bureau of Prisons," September 2017, https://ccrjustice.org/sites/default/files/attach/2017/09/SAMs%20Report.Final_.pdf; Tom Kutsch, "Inmates Strike in Prisons Nationwide over 'Slave Labor' Working Conditions," *Guardian,* September 9, 2016, https://www.theguardian.com/. On torture inside the United States, see Center for Constitutional Rights, *Shadow Report Submission to the United Nations Committee on the Convention Against Torture and Other Cruel, Inhuman or Degrading Treatment or Punishment (CAT),* March 1, 2016, http://www.ushrnetwork.org/sites/ushrnetwork.org/files/committee_against_torture_ccr_response_to_us_follow_up_1_march_2016.pdf.

48. See Kaba, *We Do This 'til We Free Us,* 83–85; LeRon Barton, "Stop Sharing Black Pain," Good Men Project, August 26, 2020, https://goodmenproject.com/featured-content/stop-sharing-black-pain-wcz/; Hartman, *Scenes of Subjection;* Karen Sanchez-Eppler, *Touching Liberty: Abolition, Feminism, and the Politics of the Body* (Berkeley: University of California Press, 1993).

49. Ralph, *Torture Letters,* xvii–xviii. Ralph agrees, yet notes that for many survivors, the specificity of detail has been crucial to revealing the extent of the violence, helping survivors find each other, and challenging those who would downplay the harm.

50. Ralph, *Torture Letters,* 162, 160–70.

51. See Ralph, *Torture Letters,* 134, 177.

52. See Ralph, *Torture Letters,* 64, 70–76, 82, 153.

53. Interview with Mariame Kaba, "Prison and Police Abolition—Finding True Safety," conducted by Ibram X. Khendi for the *Be Anti-racist* podcast, season 1, July 28, 2021, https://www.pushkin.fm/podcasts/be-antiracist-with-ibram-x-kendi/prison-police-abolition-finding-true-safety. See also Kaba, *We Do This 'til We Free Us.*

54. Adam Liptak, "Supreme Court Sides with Border Agent in Excessive Use of Force Claim," *New York Times,* June 8, 2022, https://www.nytimes.com/. Citing "national security interest in border security," the 6–3 decision in *Egbert v. Boule* shielded border agents from claims of physical assault extending within a hundred-mile zone from any U.S. border, land or sea.

55. Parry, *Understanding Torture*, 160, 163. Parry notes that "immigration provides the primary area of U.S. law that considers and decides torture claims on a regular basis." This was the template for immigration control from the start. Parry cites Bill Ong Hing on the Angel Island facility between 1910 and 1940; there, "50,000 Chinese were confined—often for months and years at a time . . . where inspectors would conduct grueling interrogations"; further, Ellis Island's final twenty-five years was as a site of detention (161). Fabio Perocco, "Torture against Migrants: A Structural and Global Phenomenon and Its Social Roots," *Welfare e Erogonomia* 2 (2021): 50–64, http://dx.doi.org/10.3280/WE2020-002005. Perocco notes that "torture has become a structural element of the migratory experience," 50. Torture is not only a cause for departure and a frequent experience along the migratory path, but also a reality of confinement in receiving countries. Pitter describes the growing use of incommunicado detentions on U.S. Coast Guard ships and other vessels since 2012 as a means around *Miranda* warnings or time limits for bringing suspects to a judge. Laura Pitter, "National Security and Court Deference: Ramifications and Worrying Trends," in *Reimagining the National Security State: Liberalism on the Brink,* ed. Karen J. Greenberg (Cambridge: Cambridge University Press, 2020), 94–99.

56. McNeill details the harms of mass supervision through various arms of the court. Fergus McNeill, *Pervasive Punishment: Making Sense of Mass Supervision* (Bingley, England, U.K.: Emerald, 2018).

57. Sexton and Lee, "Figuring the Prison," 1007.

58. Dorothy Roberts, "Torture and the Biopolitics of Race," *University of Miami Law Review* 62 (2008): 244.

59. Dorothy Roberts, "Foreword—Abolition Constitutionalism," *Harvard Law Review* 133, no. 1 (2019): 18–19, https://harvardlawreview.org/. See also Dylan Rodríguez, "Abolition as Praxis of Human Being: A Foreword," *Harvard Law Review* 132 (2019): 1575, 1578, https://harvardlawreview.org/.

60. Roberts, "Foreword," 12–13.

61. On U.S. criminal procedure codes for "waywardness" and the incarceration of girls and women, see Hugh Ryan, *The Women's House of Detention: A Queer History of a Forgotten Prison* (New York: Bold Type, 2022); and Saidiya Hartman, *Wayward Lives, Beautiful Experiments: Intimate Histories of Riotous Black Girls, Troublesome Women, and Queer Radicals* (New York: Norton, 2019), 221–25.

62. Roberts cites Dan Berger, "Rise in White Prisoners Doesn't Change Innate Racism of Prisons," Truthout, April 28, 2019, https://truthout.org/.

63. Davis, *Are Prisons Obsolete?,* 20.

64. Celermajer, *Prevention of Torture,* 314. This exceptional contribution details the organizational and interagency ecology of security forces at particular sites in Sri Lanka and Nepal. Looking at the paucity of prevention work and its failures, she argues that only with more robust conceptual tools can one conduct a

situational mapping of torture and its functions, then identify points of intervention. Her work offers theoretical approaches to human responsibility within a layered situational ecology that creates the specific worlds of feeling, perception, and institutional routine. She fuses this with careful attention to the social science on organizational and behavioral change. The result is an excellent resource for antitorture theory and work.

65. Celermajer, *Prevention of Torture,* 197.

66. Torture and terror are not driven by a historical track record of success in interrogation. Studies reaffirming this over the time frame studied here include one authored by the Interrogation Science Board and another by the CIA inspector general investigators appointed by the George W. Bush administration. Exhaustive reviews followed in the Obama years; see Senate Select Committee on Intelligence, *The Senate Intelligence Committee Report on Torture: Committee Study of the Central Intelligence Agency's Detention and Interrogation Program* (Brooklyn: Melville House, 2014), 4–5, 17–18. All confirmed the same. Rejali's expert tome, *Torture and Democracy,* is, among other things, a thoroughgoing response to this question; see especially 446–66.

67. Rejali notes that "does it work" omits the key to answering the question at all: "does it work to do what," precisely? Rejali, *Torture and Democracy,* 23–24.

68. Latour wishes to redirect the term "social" toward the action in its meaning, "a peculiar movement" of assembling, aligning, bringing into relation, redesigning one type of eclectic assembly and producing another—persons, agencies, commerce—extending well beyond the human or interpersonal. Bruno Latour, *Reassembling the Social: An Introduction to Actor–Network–Theory* (Oxford: Oxford University Press, 2005), 6–7.

69. See Marguerite Feitlowitz, *A Lexicon of Terror* (Oxford: Oxford University Press, 1998); Martha K. Huggins, Mika Haritos-Fatouros, and Philip G. Zimbardo, *Violence Workers: Police Torturers and Murderers Reconstruct Brazilian Atrocities* (Berkeley: University of California Press, 2002); Munú Actis et al., *That Inferno: Conversations of Five Women Survivors of an Argentine Torture Camp* (Nashville, Tenn.: Vanderbilt University Press, 2006); E. K. Mpinga et al., "Estimating the Costs of Torture: Challenges and Opportunities," *Applied Health Economics and Health Policy* 13, no. 6 (2015): 567–81, https://doi.org/10.1007/s40258-015-0196-z.

70. Rejali, *Torture and Democracy,* 21, 332, 426, 573–74.

71. Cited in Malcolm Nance, "Waterboarding Is Torture ... Period," *Small Wars Journal* (blog), December 9, 2016, https://smallwarsjournal.com/jrnl/art/waterboarding-is-torture-period.

72. "Memorandum for Alberto R. Gonzales, 'Standards of Conduct for Interrogation under 18 U.S.C. 2340–2340A, August 1, 2002,'" in *The Torture Memos: Rationalizing the Unthinkable,* ed. David Cole (New York: New Press, 2009), 80. A politically motivated revision of Yoo's lines followed in 2004; this replaced the

overt assertion with the equivalent of a careful "no comment." Yoo notes the revision was cosmetic: "Yeah, so when they rewrote the memo, they made the lines less clear. They deleted that sentence. But it's not all that different in what it actually says and what it actually allows." John Yoo, "Exclusive: Torture Memo Author John Yoo Responds to This Week's Revelations," *Esquire,* April 3, 2008, https://www.esquire.com/.

73. One enthusiast was Michael Forrestal, who was sent to Vietnam as eyes on the ground to inform both the Kennedy and Johnson administrations. He thought Trinquier should be required reading for the National Security Council. John Gans, *White House Warriors: How the National Security Council Transformed the American Way of War* (New York: Liveright, 2019), 26.

74. Douglas T. Stuart, *Creating the National Security State: A History of the Law that Transformed America* (Princeton, N.J.: Princeton University Press, 2008), 2.

75. Stuart, *Creating the National Security State,* 284–86.

76. Michael J. Glennon, *National Security and Double Government* (Oxford: Oxford University Press, 2015), 13.

77. Cited by Glennon, *National Security,* 16.

78. About this history, see Gans, *White House Warriors;* and John Gray, "The Deep State and the Failed State: Illusions and Realities in the Pursuit of Security," in Greenberg, *Reimagining the National Security State,* 15.

79. Douglass Cassel, "A Tale of Two Countries: Fundamental Rights in the 'War on Terror,'" in Greenberg, *Reimagining the National Security State,* 28.

80. Charles Taylor, *Modern Social Imaginaries* (Durham, N.C.: Duke University Press, 2003), 23. Psychologist Charlotte Frazier devised a software app analogy for understanding race and racial identity development.

81. Meili Steele, "The Social Imaginary as a Problematic for Human Rights," in *Theoretical Perspectives on Human Rights and Literature,* ed. Elizabeth Swanson Goldberg and Alexandra S. Moore (New York: Routledge, 2012), 93. Taylor, *Modern Social Imaginaries.*

82. Interesting and somewhat different analyses of this phenomenon can be found in Seigel, *Violence Work,* 27, 58; and Schrader, *Badges without Borders,* 41. Both demonstrate that policy makers were writing and talking openly about the need to change the narrative on U.S. racism lest it jeopardize U.S. foreign policy.

83. For roots of U.S. surveillance and policing tactics in the institution of slavery, see Seigel, *Violence Work;* and Simone Browne, *Dark Matters: On the Surveillance of Blackness* (Durham, N.C.: Duke University Press, 2015). McCoy's work is essential in locating the origins of the surveillance state in the excrescence of policing methods designed in the colonial Philippines and imported back home. See also Alfred W. McCoy, *Policing America's Empire: The United States, the Philippines, and the Rise of the Surveillance State* (Madison: University of Wisconsin Press, 2009).

Across the war and postwar periods, racist violence and suppression intersected with gendered surveillance and anti-Semitic campaigns, with eugenic control asserted over the disabled, so-called degenerate, and the growing immigrant populations from southeastern Europe, the internment of Asian Americans, anticommunist political purges, assimilationist and termination policies engineered for Indigenous nations, and "law and order" solutions to urban unrest that equated foreign and domestic conflict requiring a heavy police response. Ryan, *Women's House;* Scott Zesch, *The Chinatown War: Chinese Los Angeles and the Massacre of 1871* (Oxford: Oxford University Press, 2012).

84. Werner Binder, "Social Imaginaries and the Limits of Differential Meaning: A Cultural Sociological Critique of Symbolic Meaning Structures," *Österreich Gesellschaft für Soziologie* 44, suppl. 2 (2019): 28. See also Werner Binder, "Shifting Imaginaries in the War on Terror: The Rise and Fall of the Ticking Bomb Torturer," *Social Imaginaries* 2, no. 1 (2016): 119–50. Cornelius Castoriadis, *The Imaginary Institution of Society* (1975), trans. Kathleen Blamey (Cambridge: Polity, 1998). Charles Taylor, *A Secular Age* (Cambridge, Mass.: Harvard University Press, 2007).

85. Michael J. Glennon, "Who's Checking Whom?," in Greenberg, *Reimagining the National Security State,* 11; and Gray, "Deep State," 15.

86. Singh, *Race and America's Long War,* 27.

87. For this orientation in private enforcement historically, see Adam Hochschild, "All-American Vigilantism," *New York Review of Books,* July 22, 2021, 35–36. For a spate of 2022 legislation empowering citizens to enforce bans on abortion access, LGBTQ information, or critical race theory in classrooms, see Jon D. Michaels and David L. Noll, "Vigilante Federalism," *Cornell Law Review* 108, no.5 (September 2023): 1187–264.

88. See Khalili, *Time in the Shadows;* Elana Zilberg, *Space of Detention: The Making of a Transnational Gang Crisis between Los Angeles and San Salvador* (Durham, N.C.: Duke University Press, 2011); Gans, *White House Warriors,* 208.

89. McCoy, *Policing;* Browne, *Dark Matters;* and Seigel, *Violence Work.*

90. See Scott Selisker, *Human Programming: Brainwashing, Automatons and American Unfreedom* (Minneapolis: University of Minnesota Press, 2016); Timothy Melley, *The Covert Sphere: Secrecy, Fiction, and the National Security State* (Ithaca, N.Y.: Cornell University Press, 2012); McCoy, *Policing;* Khalili, *Time in the Shadows.*

91. Several works explore the literary, scientific, and cinematic landscape of the cold war relative to the operations of national security. Useful here are Melley, who names a "covert sphere" of culture and policy making, and Selisker, who studies the cold war fascination with automatons and human programmability. Jagoda focuses on cultural depictions of surveillance and communication technology in what he calls an "imaginary" and a "network aesthetic." Finally, Masco's "national security affect" considers the constant emotional recruitment and generation of

fear that makes for "a special kind of collective experience" that "constitutes a zone of interaction between the citizen and state." My use draws instead on the literature on social imaginaries and challenges the cold war periodization in order to point to colonial and racial origins before the security state. I emphasize official legal, political, technocratic, journalistic, activist, and scientific discourse in that imagination as well as popular culture; these others do not. Melley, *Covert Sphere*; Selisker, *Human Programming*; Patrick Jagoda, *Network Aesthetics* (Chicago: University of Chicago Press, 2016); Joseph Masco, *Theater of Operation: National Security Affect from Cold War to the War on Terror* (Durham, N.C.: Duke University Press, 2014).

92. Cassel, "Tale of Two Countries," 33.

93. Celermajer, *Prevention of Torture*, 190–91, 200–201.

94. Celermajer argues that most work against torture has attended to factors at the legal level (criminalization, prosecution, and admissibility of evidence, with some attention paid to conditions of detention). Her book is an astute articulation of why criminalization is an insufficient strategy for the normative and institutional change required to end torture. Celermajer, *Prevention of Torture*, 188–98.

1. Anecdote

1. The first epigraph is from Intelligence Science Board (created and tasked by the director of National Intelligence under George W. Bush), "Educing Information: Interrogation: Science and Art. Phase 1 Report" (Washington, D.C.: National Defense Intelligence College Press, 2006), https://fas.org/irp/dni/educing.pdf. Scott A. Allen et al., "Deaths of Detainees in Custody of U.S. Forces in Iraq and Afghanistan from 2002 to 2005," *Medscape General Medicine* 8, no. 4 (2006): 46, https://www.ncbi.nlm.nih.gov/pmc/articles/PMC1868355/ (available at https://pubmed.ncbi.nlm.nih.gov/). The second epigraph reflects figures known in the same year as the Intelligence Science Board issued its report. These grew as the war on terror continued. The 2006 numbers represent a review of all known war on terror detainee deaths between 2002 and early 2005 based on Department of Defense documents obtained through a Freedom of Information Act request, combined with published press accounts. During a longer six-year, three-month period, October 2003 and the end of 2009, there were 107 deaths in Immigration and Customs Enforcement detention. See Jon Feere, "Detention Deaths, Now with Context," Center for Immigration Studies, January 31, 2010, https://cis.org/Feere/Detention-Deaths-Now-Context. CIS is a conservative "low-immigration, pro-immigrant" organization. Feere includes fifteen ICE detainee suicides and finds approximately 2,062,500 people passed though the ICE detention system during the period represented. He notes that the Bureau of Justice Statistics puts the suicide rate among inmates in the U.S. state prison system at 14 per 100,000. The number is higher in local jails: 47 per 100,000.

2. See the introduction for discussion concerning Arestivo and torture, terror, and a systematic attack on social bodies. Carlos Alberto Arestivo, "Torture: The Catastrophe of a Bond," trans. Laurie Ball Cooper, in *Witnessing Torture: Perspectives of Torture Survivors and Human Rights Workers,* ed. Alexandra S. Moore and Elizabeth Swanson (Cham, Switzerland: Palgrave Macmillan, 2018).

3. Marites Vitug and Glenda M. Gloria, *Under the Crescent Moon: Rebellion in Mindanao* (Manila: Ateneo Center/Institute for Popular Democracy, 2000). In addition, "Pakistani Claims Torture at Hands of Filipino Men," *Hobart* (Australia) *Mercury,* May 11, 1996, reported that Murad testified to being raped and suffered treatment not printed in the United States, including electroshock to the genitals. One U.S. article says that Murad feared the "possibility of being raped to death," but adds he feared the Mossad more, so he confessed. Victorino Matus, "Making Terrorists Talk: America Doesn't Use Torture to Get Information Out of Terrorists. Perhaps We Just Need to Use the Magic Word: Mossad," *Daily Standard,* January 29, 2002.

4. For Judge Duffy's opinion on the motion to suppress: *U.S. v. Yousef, Murad and Shah,* 925 F. Supp. 1063, 1065 (S.D.N.Y. 1996). Two medical experts testified at trial that Murad's record and behavior were consistent with torture. Christopher Wren, "Experts Say Plot Suspect Showed Signs of Torture," *New York Times,* August 23, 1996, https://www.nytimes.com/. Murad said he would have been returned to the PNP if he recanted his confession under torture.

5. In 2001, Abdul Hakim Murad and coconspirators Walid Shah and the more notorious Ramzi Yousef were serving sentences in federal prisons.

6. Alan Dershowitz, *Why Terrorism Works* (New Haven, Conn.: Yale University Press, 2002), 137.

7. Interview with Alan Dershowitz, "Dershowitz: U.S. Needs Improved Torture Tactics," Newsmax, May 22, 2004, http://email.newsmax.com/archives/ic/2004/5/22/132018.html.

8. Slackman's story quotes an objection to Murad's case as a ticking time bomb scenario. Michael Slackman, "The World: A Dangerous Calculus; What's Wrong with Torturing a Qaeda Higher-Up?," *New York Times,* May 16, 2004, https://www.nytimes.com/. Luban notes conflicted wording in one description of Murad's torture. His 2005 *Virginia Law Review* essay was reprinted as David Luban, "Liberalism, Torture, and the Ticking Bomb," in *The Torture Debate in America,* ed. Karen J. Greenberg (Cambridge: Cambridge University Press, 2006), 35–83.

9. The relevant question is reformulated and proposed by Rejali: does torture work *better than* something else—better than other modes of investigation? Darius Rejali, *Torture and Democracy* (Princeton, N.J.: Princeton University Press, 2007).

10. See Vitug and Gloria, *Under the Crescent Moon*; Rohan Gunaratna, *Inside Al Qaeda: Global Network of Terror* (New York: Berkley, 2003); Peter Lance, *1000 Years for Revenge: International Terrorism and the FBI* (New York: Regan, 2003); and Christopher Wren's *New York Times* coverage of the 1996 trial.

11. Jay Winik, "Security Comes before Liberty," *Wall Street Journal,* October 23, 2001, https://www.wsj.com/; Christopher Wren, "Terror Case Hinges on Laptop Computer," *New York Times,* July 18, 1996, https://www.nytimes.com/; Christopher Wren, "Terror Suspect Spoke Freely of Plot, Agent Says," *New York Times,* August 6, 1996, https://www.nytimes.com/; Luis H. Francia, "Local Is Global," *Village Voice,* September 25, 2001, https://www.villagevoice.com/; Matthew Brzezinski, "Bust and Boom," *Washington Post,* December 30, 2001, https://www.washingtonpost.com/; "Appendix I: FBI 302 Re: Interrogation of Abdul Hakim Murad, May 11, 1995," in Lance, *1000 Years for Revenge,* 509; Eleanor Hill, "[HPSCI-SSCI] Joint Inquiry Staff Statement. Part I," September 18, 2002, available at Federation of American Scientists Intelligence Resource Program, https://irp.fas.org/congress/2002_hr/091802hill.html (accessed September 11, 2006); *The 9/11 Commission Report* (New York: Norton, 2004), 491n33; Christopher Wren, "Computer Expert Testifies in Terror Trial," *New York Times,* July 24, 1996, https://www.nytimes.com/; Steve Fainaru, "Clues Pointed to Changed Terrorist Tactics," *Washington Post,* May 19, 2002, https://www.washingtonpost.com/; Julian Borger, "Unheeded Warnings," *Guardian,* December 19, 2003, https://www.theguardian.com/.

12. See Winik, "Security Comes before Liberty"; Fainaru, "Clues Pointed to Changed Terrorist Tactics."

13. Dershowitz, *Why Terrorism Works,* 137.

14. Michael Taussig's argument in *Shamanism, Colonialism, and the Wild Man* (Chicago: University of Chicago Press, 1987) concerning the rumors and doubts that circle torture is discussed in chapter 4. See Taussig, *Shamanism,* 121, 130–32.

15. Doug Struck et al., "Borderless Network of Terror, Bin Laden Followers Reach across the Globe," *Washington Post,* September 23, 2001, https://www.washingtonpost.com/.

16. Winik, "Security Comes before Liberty."

17. On electroshock in policing, see Ralph's discussion of Dominque Franklin's death by Taser and the subsequent Chicago youth action, "We Charge Torture. We Charge Genocide," presented before the 2014 U.N. Committee on Torture, in *The Torture Letters: Reckoning with Police Violence* (Chicago: University of Chicago Press, 2020), 114–41. Darius Rejali, "Modern Torture as a Civic Marker: Solving a Global Anxiety with a New Political Technology," *Journal of Human Rights* 2, no. 2 (2003): 153–71, https://doi.org/10.1080/1475483032000078152.

18. Peter Maass, "Torture, Tough or Lite: If a Terror Suspect Won't Talk, Should He Be Made To?," *New York Times,* March 9, 2003, https://www.nytimes.com/.

19. Jonathan Alter, "Time to Think about Torture," *Newsweek,* November 5, 2001, https://www.newsweek.com/.

20. The invocation of psychological torture is a problem in the courts and in the torture rehabilitation community. See Nimisha Patel, "Psychological Torture," letter to the editor, *Torture Journal* 29, no. 3 (2020): 79–81, https://doi.org/10.7146/torture.v29i3.117412; Ergun Cakal, "Debility, Dependency and Dread: On the Conceptual and Evidentiary Dimensions of Psychological Torture," *Torture Journal* 28, no. 2 (2018): 15–37, https://doi.org/10.7146/torture.v28i2.106908.

21. Peter Lance interviewed Colonel Rodolfo Mendoza in April 2002. Lance writes that Mendoza confronted Murad after being denied food for a long period. He is told the only thing left was to decide whether to turn Murad over to the "Americans or Mossad": "'You are a bomber. Tell me something now or I will call Tel Aviv.' Murad eyed him defiantly. Then Mendoza nodded to Major Ferro, who grabbed the burger and fries. Both of them started to leave the room when Murad blurted out, 'The Trade Center . . .' 'What?' said the colonel. . . . 'I'm involved in it,' said Murad." Lance, *1000 Years for Revenge,* 275–77.

22. Matus, "Making Terrorists Talk."

23. Dershowitz, *Why Terrorism Works,* 138.

24. Sanford Levinson, "The Debate on Torture: War against Virtual States," *Dissent* 50, no. 3 (2003): 79. See also Sanford Levinson, "Precommitment and Postcommitment: The Ban on Torture in the Wake of September 11," *Texas Law Review* 81 (2003); and Sanford Levinson, "Contemplating Torture," in *Torture: A Collection,* ed. Sanford Levinson (Oxford: Oxford University Press, 2004), 23–43. Richard Posner refers to Murad in "Torture, Terrorism, and Interrogation," in Levinson, *Torture: A Collection* (2004), 291–98.

25. Khalid Sheikh Mohammed was named a fellow conspirator on Murad's indictment years before he organized the devastating 2001 attack. Jane Mayer, "Zero Conscience in Zero Dark Thirty," *New Yorker,* December 14, 2012, https://www.newyorker.com/.

26. Vitug and Gloria, *Under the Crescent Moon,* 223.

27. Pope John Paul II's visit was January 12–16, 1995. Murad was captured on January 7.

28. Vitug and Gloria, *Under the Crescent Moon,* along with many post-2001 news reports, suggest that the police resorted to torture after two days of silence, but a tape entered into evidence suggests Murad's torture began the day of his capture. Even Judge Duffy noted that the tape's sounds were suspicious, noting, "The only objective evidence that remotely supports Murad's allegations of torture is a taped interrogation session dated January 7, 1995." "Certain portions of that tape were played during the hearing, which Murad claims reflect his condition immediately following an episode of the drowning procedure which he allegedly suffered." Yousef, 925 F. Supp. Lance adds, "Transcripts of Murad's interrogation

suggest that he was denied water and force-fed liquids." Lance, *1000 Years for Revenge,* 274.

29. Lance and Gunaratna draw substantive information from the January 7 and January 20 interrogation transcripts, and Vitug and Gloria, *Under the Crescent Moon,* cite February PNP intelligence debriefing reports. See Lance, *1000 Years for Revenge,* 311, 342; Gunaratna, *Inside Al Qaeda,* 240.

30. Shah was arrested January 12, 1995, in Manila. Lance, *1000 Years for Revenge,* 311. He later escaped PNP custody and was reapprehended in Malaysia on December 11. Yousef, 925 F. Supp.

31. Spokesman David Johnson said the State Department had received information on January 9 from the Philippines concerning bomb threats directed at U.S. airlines, and the FAA directed airlines flying into the region to increase their security measures. "World News Brief: U.S. Warns Airlines of Threat in East Asia," *New York Times,* January 16, 1995, https://www.nytimes.com/.

32. Only one 2005 story about Murad's "successful" torture also suggests the laptop evidence might have been of equal value: Joseph Lelyveld, "Interrogating Ourselves," *New York Times Magazine,* June 12, 2005, https://www.nytimes.com/. Rejali, in *Torture and Democracy,* argues that torture "deskills" the intelligence service that uses it, sapping energy and resources from actual modes of investigation. He reads Murad's case as reported by Brzezinski and Maass to underscore this point.

33. Jacobo Timerman, *Prisoner without a Name, Cell without a Number,* trans. Toby Talbot (New York: Vintage, 1981).

34. John Conroy, *Unspeakable Acts, Ordinary People: Dynamics of Torture* (New York: Knopf, 2000).

35. Wren, "Terror Case Hinges on Laptop Computer."

36. Brzezinski, "Bust and Boom." See also Yousef, 925 F. Supp.

37. The FBI said they did not receive the January 7 tape that lent some credence to the allegation of "drowning torture." Yousef, 925 F. Supp. On FBI visits, see Christopher Wren, "Case Accusing Three of Plotting to Bomb Jets Shows a Flaw," *New York Times,* August 8, 1996, https://www.nytimes.com/.

38. Jeff Stephens and Jay Boekelheide, *Interrogating // Torture* (Pushback Partners Productions, documentary in production).

39. Vitug and Gloria, *Under the Crescent Moon,* 2. Christopher Wren, "Computer Expert Testifies in Terror Trial," *New York Times,* July 24, 1996, https://www.nytimes.com/.

40. Amnesty International, "Philippines, 2017–2018," https://www.amnesty.org/.

41. See chapter 2; and see also Roland G. Simbulan, "Covert Operations and the CIA's Hidden History in the Philippines," lecture at the University of the Philippines, Manila, August 18, 2000.

42. See, e.g., Rejali's work in *Torture and Democracy* debunking torture anecdotes from the Algerian war for independence.

43. Rejali, *Torture and Democracy,* 60–61.

44. This synthesis occurs in her discussion of Tomas Martin's 2009 essay "Taking the Snake Out of the Basket." Danielle Celermajer, *The Prevention of Torture: An Ecological Approach* (Cambridge: Cambridge University Press, 2018), 153.

45. Celermajer, *Prevention of Torture,* 147. Celermajer's work makes an exceptional companion to Rejali's. She details the organizational and interagency ecology of security forces at particular sites in Sri Lanka and Nepal. She places this ecological map against social science studies of organizational behavior and behavioral change in order to offer a theoretical and strategic approach for planning torture prevention work. She explains how that work has been hampered and why prevention must use an ecological diagnosis to understand the local structures and systems that shape human behavior.

46. I differ in order to distinguish it from the instrumental use of the security rhetoric and imagination I hope to historicize. Rejali, *Torture and Democracy,* 46.

47. The Innocence Project, https://innocenceproject.org/exonerations-data/ (accessed July 4, 2022), is a national litigation and public policy organization dedicated to exonerating wrongfully convicted individuals. Kassin found that "20 to 25 percent of prisoners exonerated by DNA had confessed to police, that the percentage is far higher in capital murder cases and that these discovered instances represent the tip of an iceberg." Saul M. Kassin, "False Confessions: Causes, Consequences and Implications for Reform," *Current Directions in Psychological Science* 17, no. 4 (2008): 249–53 at 249. See also Guha Krishnamurthi, "The Case for the Abolition of Criminal Confessions," *Southern Methodist University Law Review* 75, no. 1 (2022), https://scholar.smu.edu/smulr/vol75/iss1/7. Saul Kassin and Holly Sukel, "Coerced Confession and the Jury," *Law and Human Behavior* 21 (1997): 27–46. LaPorte points out that the confessions were weighty factors, not sole causes of conviction. Gerald M. LaPorte, "Wrongful Convictions and DNA Exonerations: Understanding the Role of Forensic Science," National Institute of Justice, September 7, 2017, https://nij.ojp.gov.

48. Rejali, *Torture and Democracy,* 53–55.

49. Rejali, *Torture and Democracy,* 58.

50. Hope Lewis, "Global Intersections: Critical Race Feminist Human Rights and Inter/National Black Women," *Maine Law Review* 50, no. 2 (1998): 309–26, http://works.bepress.com/hlewis/17/. Pioneering legal writing by Mari Matsuda, Kimberlé Crenshaw, Richard Delgado, and Derrick Bell initiated scholarship under the heading of critical race theory. This term became a catchall buzzword used by conservative efforts to halt education on structural racism in the wake of the police murder of George Floyd in Minneapolis in 2020.

51. Studies in New York City, Baltimore, and Chicago offer examples. In August 2013, a court found in *Floyd v. City of New York* that the NYPD's stop-and-frisk practices were racially discriminatory and unconstitutional under the Fourth and Fourteenth amendments. See Center for Constitutional Rights, "Landmark Decision: Judge Rules NYPD Stop and Frisk Practices Unconstitutional, Racially Discriminatory," press release, updated August 21, 2014, https://ccrjustice.org/home/press-center/press-releases/landmark-decision-judge-rules-nypd-stop-and-frisk-practices. See also U.S. Department of Justice, Civil Rights Division, "Investigation of the Baltimore City Police Department," August 10, 2016, https://www.justice.gov/opa/file/883366/download. Richard A. Oppel Jr., Sheryl Gay Stolberg, and Matt Apuso, "Justice Department to Release Blistering Report of Racial Bias by Baltimore Police," *New York Times*, August 10, 2016, https://www.nytimes.com/, note that the city of Baltimore is 63 percent Black, but "91% of those arrested solely for 'failure to obey' or 'trespassing' were African-American." See also Timothy Williams and Joseph Goldstein, "In Baltimore Report Justice Department Revives Doubts about Zero-Tolerance Policing," *New York Times*, August 10, 2016, https://www.nytimes.com/; they cite a 2008–11 study that showed eight citations for riding bicycles on sidewalks in predominantly white Park Slope neighborhood of Brooklyn in those years but 2,050 citations in nearby Bedford-Stuyvesant, a predominantly African American and Latino neighborhood; other examples include "taking up too much space on a park bench in New York. Spitting in public in Minneapolis. Moving household goods at night in Atlanta." See also William Rhodes et al., "Federal Sentencing Disparity, 2005–2012," Bureau of Justice Statistics Working Paper Series 2015:01, October 22, 2015, https://www.bjs.gov/content/pub/pdf/fsd0512.pdf; American Civil Liberties Union of Illinois, "Chicago Police Department Racial Disparity in Traffic Stops and Resulting Searches, 2013," December 2014, https://www.aclu-il.org/sites/default/files/wp-content/uploads/2014/12/Report-re-CPD-traffic-stops-in-2013.pdf; Justin Nix et al., "A Bird's Eye View of Civilians Killed by Police in 2015: Further Evidence of Implicit Bias," *Criminology and Public Policy* 16, no. 1 (2017): 309–40; Michelle Alexander, *The New Jim Crow: Mass Incarceration in the Age of Colorblindness*, 10th anniversary ed. (New York: New Press, 2020); Wesley Lowry, *They Can't Kill Us All: Ferguson, Baltimore, and a New Era in America's Racial Justice Movement*. (Boston: Little, Brown, 2016).

52. Rejali, *Torture and Democracy*, 46–47.

53. U.S. Department of Justice, Office of the Inspector General, "Supplemental Report on September 11 Detainees' Allegations of Abuse at the Metropolitan Detention Center in Brooklyn, New York," December 2003, https://ccrjustice.org/sites/default/files/attach/2015/01/Supplemental%20Report.pdf.

54. The pattern in these cases bears investigation. Americans acknowledged control over interrogations of suspects in Kenya, where defendants alleged that the United States and Kenya worked in tag-team fashion to ensure defendants

relinquished rights to lawyers. Mohammed Saddiq Odeh said he was held by the Pakistanis for seven days, then transferred to Nairobi for twelve days. Pakistanis subjected him to "violence, threats of torture, psychological coercion, sleep deprivation and other inhumane conditions." Odeh alleged that the Kenyans threatened him with worse than Pakistan. See Benjamin Weiser, "Asserting Coercion, Embassy Bombing Suspect Tries to Suppress Statements," *New York Times,* July 13, 2000, https://www.nytimes.com/; Benjamin Weiser, "U.S. Faces Tough Challenge to Statements in Terrorism Case," *New York Times,* January 25, 2001, https://www.nytimes.com/. According to attorney Jack Sachs, who was initially assigned to Odeh's case, "Three days and three nights without food and without water, under bright lights, no sleep—what would anybody say?" Benjamin Weiser, "Bombing Defendant Said to Claim Coercion," *New York Times,* September 5, 1998, https://www.nytimes.com/. Judge Leonard Sands initially suppressed statements by Mohamed al-'Owhali, interrogated in Kenya. His defense "cited the presence of FBI agents and a senior prosecutor from New York during much of the interrogation and argued that the questioning was effectively controlled by the American government." Judge Sands allowed the prosecution to reargue the motion in closed court. Benjamin Weiser, "Terror Trial Judge to Again Weigh Suppression," *New York Times,* January 19, 2001, https://www.nytimes.com/. One year after the bombings, the *Washington Post* reported on a "new" structure for FBI work to better accommodate information "acquired by methods that might shock a U.S. court." Robert Suro, "FBI Clean Teams Follow Dirty Spywork," *Washington Post,* August 16, 1999, https://www.washingtonpost.com/.

55. Alfred McCoy has written an important book on the development of the CIA's "psychological paradigm" for torture. This terminology unwittingly reinforces the rhetoric I challenge here that disguises deliberate stress to the body as simply psychological. He makes no mention of torture allegations when he argues that the 1998 embassy bombing cases were models of "careful investigation and noncoercive interrogation" by the FBI, relying on Mayer's reporting in which FBI agent Daniel Coleman contrasts the bureau's work with CIA methods. Alfred McCoy, *A Question of Torture: CIA Interrogation from the Cold War to the War on Terror* (New York: Holt, 2006), 203. Jane Mayer, "Outsourcing Torture," *New Yorker,* February 14, 2005, 116–18.

2. Rationale

1. Epigraphs are from John T. Parry, *Understanding Torture, Law, Violence, and Political Identity* (Ann Arbor: University of Michigan Press, 2010), 152; Micol Seigel, *Violence Work: State Power and the Limits of Police* (Durham, N.C.: Duke University Press, 2018), 9.

2. Alfred W. McCoy, *Policing America's Empire: The United States, the Philippines, and the Rise of the Surveillance State* (Madison: University of Wisconsin Press, 2009), 19. See also Alexandre Rios-Bordes, "When Military Intelligence Reconsiders the Nature of War: Elements for an Archeology of 'National Security' (United States, 1919–1941)," *Politix* 104 (2013): 33–34.

3. "In the Philippines What Spanish Rule Means—The Torture of Prisoners," *Atlanta Constitution,* December 23, 1896.

4. Paul A. Kramer, *The Blood of Government: Race, Empire, the United States and the Philippines* (Chapel Hill: University of North Carolina Press, 2006); Amy Kaplan, *The Anarchy of Empire in the Making of U.S. Culture* (Cambridge, Mass.: Harvard University Press, 2005).

5. On surplus population: W. B. Gallagher, "Philippines and Negro Colonization," letter, *Chicago Daily Tribune,* December 11, 1898. On secondary rulers: "Conquest and Colonization: What Negro Troops Might Bring About in the Philippines," *Washington Post,* April 26, 1899, https://www.washingtonpost.com/.

6. Paul Kramer, "Annals of American History: The Water Cure," *New Yorker,* February 25, 2008. See also Kramer, *Blood of Government,* 230. Newspapers carried much of this vitriol; consider phrases like "especially such bloodthirsty and unruly Orientals as the conglomeration of races that infest rather than inhabit the Philippine Islands." Ex-Attaché, "Uncle Sam Sahib," letter to the editor, *Washington Post,* May 22, 1898, https://www.washingtonpost.com/.

7. Kramer, *Blood of Government,* 91. He cites General Young in 1901: "The keynote of the insurrection among the Filipinos past, present and future is not tyranny for we are not tyrants. It is race" (92).

8. Kramer, "Annals of American History." Kramer is citing Percy Hill, "The Anting-Anting," *American Old-Timer* 1, no. 12 (1934): 12.

9. Army Officer, Ret., Brooklyn, N.Y., "As We Treated Filipinos: The 'Water Cure' Was Necessary, Cruelty was Provoked," letter to the editor, *New York Times,* May 28, 1915, https://www.nytimes.com/.

10. Even as war officially wound down across 1902–4, the P.C. continued to "persuade or protect" and control the rural population through forceful removal and the "re-concentration" of many thousands into camps. A mass of 451,000 peasants was displaced this way in Luzon alone; in Samar, the P.C. removed 10 percent of the total population to camps. Once inside the camps, inhabitants were subjected to close surveillance and limited communication; they were also controlled by withholding food and other basic needs. McCoy, *Policing,* 125. Torture continued as well. Chief Henry T. Allen confirmed several events: military torture was used against natives in Tayabas province, including the so-called water cure and other methods; soldiers raped women in a Tayabas town; and troops worked two Catholic priests to death on a road crew (89). See also Jeremy Kuzmarov, "Modernizing Repression:

Police Training, Political Violence, and Nation-Building in the 'American Century,'" *Diplomatic History* 33, no. 2 (2009): 191–221.

11. Robert M. Cassidy, "The Long Small War: Indigenous Forces for Counterinsurgency," *Parameters* 36, no. 2 (2006): 47–62, https://dx.doi.org/10.55540/0031-1723.2302. Likewise, U.S. colonial administrators in the Philippines often returned to more prestigious political positions in the United States.

12. Darius Rejali, *Torture and Democracy* (Princeton, N.J.: Princeton University Press, 2007), 279. See also "Tells of 'Water Cure' Cases: Witness Gives Further Testimony Before the Senate Committee on the Philippines Regarding Filipino's Treatment," *New York Times,* June 13, 1902, https://www.nytimes.com/.

13. Christopher J. Einolf, *America in the Philippines, 1899–1902: The First Torture Scandal* (New York: Palgrave Macmillan, 2014), 97.

14. Einolf, *America in the Philippines,* 148.

15. In making this assessment, Einolf focuses primarily on the rhetorical strategies. Einolf, *America in the Philippines,* 192.

16. Einolf, *America in the Philippines,* 136. See Kramer, "Annals of American History." See also "One 'Water Cure' Victim: Witness Tells of the Case before Senate Committee," *New York Times,* May 11, 1902, https://www.nytimes.com/; and "Tells of 'Water Cure' Cases." Moreover, "In 1902 . . . U.S. soldiers put funnels in the mouths of Filipinos to force water into their organs. William Howard Taft, governor of the Philippines, carelessly conceded to the Senate that pumping was the policy in some cases. . . . President Theodore Roosevelt privately called pumping a mild torture." Darius Rejali, "Of Human Bondage," *Salon,* June 18, 2004, https://www.salon.com/. A soldier's testimony led to the court-martial of Captain Edwin Glenn for use of the water cure to torture a village president twice in 1900; see "More Courts-Martial in the Philippines," *New York Times,* April 16, 1902, https://www.nytimes.com/. Glenn was sentenced to a $50 fine and a one-month suspension. Glenn continued promotion up to the rank of brigadier general. One might gather that the penalty served only to encourage torture without condoning it directly (Einolf, *America in the Philippines,* 77). Kramer notes a 1902 marching song about torture depicts drowning and stomach pumping as forms of racist entertainment; see Paul Kramer, "The Water Cure: An American Debate on Torture and Counterinsurgency in the Philippines—A Century Ago," *Asia-Pacific Journal—Japan Focus* 6, no. 3 (2008), https://apjjf.org/-Paul-A.-Kramer/2685/article.html.

17. Major General John R. Brooke says that water cure is a means of getting information from "amigos" in the islands (Einolf, *America in the Philippines,* 128–29). Private Wm. J. Gibbs described the practice of obtaining saltwater mixed with sand "to make the punishment more severe"; see "One 'Water Cure' Victim." Judge Advocate General George B. Morris objected to Glenn's light sentence, arguing that Glenn's bland descriptors for water torture—"a method of conducting operations" and "the habitual method of obtaining information from individual insurgents"—

demonstrated that torture had been operationalized as warfare (Kramer, "Annals of American History"). Other details from the court-martial indicated torture was a basic element of a larger campaign of terror to achieve social and territorial ends. On torture as a reflex of the superior race, see Einolf, *America in the Philippines,* 128.

18. Captain Glenn in the Philippines had a "water detail," a five- or six-man team. The drowning of a village president was used to force compliance and establish cause to burn to the ground a town of four to five hundred houses. Einolf, *America in the Philippines,* 77.

19. "Blackens the Fame of His Own People in Excusing Smith: Pritchard Practically Asserts that North Carolinians Are as Barbarous as the General," *Atlanta Constitution,* May 3, 1902. Einolf references the sand cure; see Einolf, *America in the Philippines,* 127, 140.

20. Josh Ohl, "[Headline missing]: South Carolina Senator Baited by Republicans until He Explodes; Republicans Pleased but Democrats Angry: Many of Tillman's Colleagues Left the Senate while He was Speaking," publication source title illegible, likely date May [7], 1902.

21. Senator Pritchard (N.C.). Objections of Senator Simmons (N.C.) in "Blackens the Fame."

22. Prominent white citizens incited violence that killed sixty African American men, overthrew a state election, banished hundreds of terrified families, and removed Black city officials at gunpoint. David Zucchino, *Wilmington's Lie: The Murderous Coup of 1898 and the Rise of White Supremacy* (New York: Atlantic Monthly Press, 2020).

23. "Angry Tillman: He Makes Savage Attack on Philippine Policy," *Boston Daily Globe,* May 8, 1902.

24. Senator Joseph B. Foraker's description in Einolf, *America in the Philippines,* 141.

25. Einolf, *America in the Philippines,* 141.

26. "A Woman's Vain Plea: Miss Lopez's Story of Injustice Falls on Deaf Ears," *Washington Post,* May 24, 1902, https://www.washingtonpost.com/.

27. W. E. B. Du Bois famously spoke of a global color line and connected segregation in United States to "our ownership of P.R., Hawaii, Cuba and conquest of the Philippines." Laleh Khalili, *Time in the Shadows: Confinement in Counterinsurgencies* (Redwood City, Calif.: Stanford University Press, 2012), 284. Some in the Black press also noted white American soldiers in the Philippines treated the Filipinos even more brutally than African Americans because stateside, whites were at least somewhat shamed and constrained by Northern opinion; "The Philippine War Is No Race War," *Indianapolis Freeman,* October 7, 1899; "Ida Wells-Barnett against Expansion," *Cleveland Gazette,* January 7, 1899. *Colored American* and the *Washington Bee* are cited in Einolf, *America in the Philippines,* 127. For Wells-Barnett's talk, "Mob Violence and Anarchy, North and South," see "The Philippine

War—A Conflict of Conscience for African Americans," Presidio of San Francisco, National Park Service, updated February 9, 2022, https://www.nps.gov/prsf/learn/historyculture/the-philippine-insurrectiothe-philippine-war-a-conflict-of-consciencen-a-war-of-controversy.htm.

28. Kristin Hoganson, "'As Badly Off as the Filipinos': U.S. Women's Suffragists and the Imperial Issue at the Turn of the Twentieth Century," *Journal of Women's History* 13, no. 2 (2001): 9–33, https://doi.org/10.1353/jowh.2001.0050.

29. Scholars of colonial conquest and rule undertaken by European powers identify a common resort to racialized science, torture, coercion, and removals. This literature is expansive. Two relatively recent texts attempt overviews: Dierk Walter, *Colonial Violence: European Empires and the Use of Force* (Oxford: Oxford University Press, 2017); and Martin Thomas, *Violence and Colonial Order: Police, Workers, and Protest in the European Colonial Empires, 1918–1940* (reprint; Cambridge: Cambridge University Press, 2015).

30. Marnia Lazreg, *Torture and the Twilight of Empire: From Algiers to Baghdad* (Princeton, N.J.: Princeton University Press, 2007), 7.

31. The first P.C. chief, Henry Allen, began with 5,000 native troops working under a reduced force of 15,000 "white soldiers." The P.C. proper was formed with 68 white commanders in 1901; by 1903, it contained 212 white and 71 Filipino officers. The numbers of American officers declined slowly over time: 86 percent in 1902; 54 percent in 1916; and 2 percent in 1935. McCoy, *Policing*, 85–87, 90.

32. Kramer, "Annals of American History."

33. Other colonial powers used similar methods. Khalili, *Time in the Shadows*, 25.

34. Jeremy Kuzmarov, "American Police Training and Political Violence: From the Philippines Conquest to the Killing Fields of Afghanistan and Iraq," *Asia-Pacific Journal—Japan Focus* 8, no. 11 (2010), https://apjjf.org/-Jeremy-Kuzmarov/3319/article.html.

35. McCoy, *Policing*, 89.

36. For torture in U.S. police precincts, see the report of the Wickersham Commission: "Wickersham Report on Police," *American Journal of Police Science* 2, no. 4 (1931): 337–48, https://doi.org/10.2307/1147362. Wells's reporting and pamphlets of the 1890s detail state and private collaboration in lynching that was apparent at the time; she draws from the records of a white newspaper, the *Chicago Tribune*, to do so. Ida B. Wells, *Southern Horrors: Lynch Law in All Its Phases* (June 25, 1892; reprint, Delhi: Double 9 Books, 2023). Ida B. Wells-Barnett, *A Red Record, Tabulated Statistics, and Alleged Causes of Lynching in the United States* (1895; reprint, Madrid: Hard Press, 2006).

37. Kuzmarov, "American Police Training," 4. See also McCoy, *Policing*, 176.

38. Kuzmarov, "American Police Training," 4.

39. McCoy, *Policing*, 29; on Act 619 on torture, see 133.

40. McCoy, *Policing*, 127–42.
41. McCoy, *Policing*, 142.
42. McCoy, *Policing*, 138–40.
43. McCoy, *Policing*, 76–77.
44. McCoy, *Policing*, 28.
45. McCoy, *Policing*, 28, 29, 7. The P.C. was in step with modern methods in espionage that historian Alec Mellor traces to 1905 Russo-Japanese war; see Edward Peters, *Torture: Expanded Edition* (Philadelphia: University of Pennsylvania Press, 1999), 108.
46. McCoy, *Policing*, 127.
47. McCoy, *Policing*, 104.
48. Kramer, *Blood of Government*, 220, 230. Michael Salman, *The Embarrassment of Slavery: Controversies over Bondage and Nationalism in the American Colonial Philippines* (Berkeley: University of California Press, 2003), 151. Focused on authentically "Filipino" types, visibly mestizo Chinese or Spanish Filipinos were excluded. Planning for the exposition not only produced a photographic *Album of Philippine Types* and busts but also arranged for dissections to be performed live in the United States (upon the anticipated deaths of Filipinos brought for display). Michael Salman, "Nothing without Labor: Penology, Discipline and Independence in the Philippines under United States Colonial Rule, 1898–1914," in *Discrepant Histories: Translocal Essays on Filipino Cultures*, ed. Vincente L. Rafael (Philadelphia: Temple University Press, 1995), 119, 128.
49. As was the P.C., government labs were established during the war. These were consolidated as the Bureau of Science by 1905. Warwick Anderson, "'Where Every Prospect Pleases and Only Man Is Vile': Laboratory Medicine as Colonial Discourse," in Rafael, *Discrepant Histories*, 91.
50. Warwick Anderson, "Excremental Colonialism: Public Health and the Poetics of Pollution," *Critical Inquiry* 21, no. 3 (1995): 649, https://doi.org/10.1086/448767.
51. Anderson, "Excremental Colonialism," 656.
52. Anderson, "Excremental Colonialism," 668, 646. Scientific results of regional fecal studies were published in 1908 and 1910.
53. Anderson, "Where Every Prospect Pleases," 91.
54. Anderson, "Where Every Prospect Pleases," 100, citing Victor G. Heiser, *An American Doctor's Odyssey: Adventures in Forty-Five Countries* (New York, 1936).
55. Anderson, "Excremental Colonialism," 656.
56. Anderson, "Where Every Prospect Pleases," 100, citing Heiser, *American Doctor's Odyssey*.
57. Anderson, "Excremental Colonialism," 649.
58. McCoy, *Policing*, 125.
59. McCoy, *Policing*, 36, 139. Laws on vice were enforced after 1917.

60. McCoy's detailed work allows us to locate many roots of the national security paradigm for intelligence collection in the methodologies of colonial, political, economic, and racial control.

61. On a distinctly U.S. style of superficial acquisition and classification of knowledge, see McCoy, *Policing*, 44–45.

62. McCoy, *Policing*, 17, 454. As the Marcos presidency turned toward dictatorship, in 1969–73, OPS spent $5 million to install provincial communications networks, send 284 Filipino officers to the United States for advanced training, and build ten regional centers to train 23,902 police (60 percent of the nation's total police). "Between 1962–72, OPS trained an estimated 85 senior Filipino officers in interrogation techniques at the 'International Police Academy' in Washington, D.C., congressional investigations later found clear evidence of torture training in graduate theses. Elite Marcos era military units proved adept at the kinds of torture highlighted in OPS and CIA training materials, and in last years of the dictatorship tortured an estimated 35,000 political dissidents" (387–88). McCoy finds strong indications that top leaders such as Lieutenant Colonel Abadilla studied at Fort Leavenworth, and Lieutenant Colonel Rodolfo Aguinaldo trained with the CIA; Alfred McCoy, *A Question of Torture: CIA Interrogation from the Cold War to the War on Terror* (New York: Holt, 2006), 78.

63. Roland G. Simbulan, "Covert Operations and the CIA's Hidden History in the Philippines," lecture at the University of the Philippines, Manila, August 18, 2000.

64. Khalili, *Time in the Shadows*, 13–29.

65. Scholars have used the term "counterinsurgency" to describe guerilla engagements both before and after this point in time; they do so to acknowledge the real continuities of methods across eras. In discussing the national security rationale and the imaginary in which it came to exist, I distinguish early twentieth-century from mid-twentieth-century formations, when military thinkers began to speak of counterinsurgency as a conscious effort of self-naming, writing, and organizing around that label. Practitioners of counterinsurgency made a political choice to emphasize a break with the past, stressing the race neutrality and technical-theoretical superiority of their modern incarnation. On neutrality, see Lisa Stampnitzky, "Problematic Knowledge: How 'Terrorism' Resists Expertise," in *Security Expertise: Practice, Power, and Responsibility*, ed. Trine Villumsen Berling and Christian Bueger (New York: Routledge Press, 2015). In the genealogy and naming of "national security" scholars have made a similar case. See Andrew Preston, "Monsters Everywhere: A Genealogy of National Security," *Diplomatic History* 38, no. 3 (2014): 486.

66. General David H. Petraeus and James Nagl chose the name COIN in 2006 as they introduced a new field manual. It was said to be a return to classic counterinsurgency, and therefore it was a break with the disreputable mess of Vietnam and the failing methods in Iraq from 2003 to 2006. The manual and moniker gave

counterinsurgency new cachet among the military and civilian public, and it helped secure Petraeus's promotion at the head of a U.S. military troop surge in Iraq in 2007. On continual reinvention, see Thomas A. Bass, "Counterinsurgency and Torture," *American Quarterly* 60, no. 2 (2008): 233–40; and Colonel Gian Gentile, *Wrong Turn: America's Deadly Embrace of Counterinsurgency* (New York: New Press, 2013). The manual was published as a combined edition: General David H. Petraeus and Lieutenant Colonel John A. Nagel with a foreword by Lieutenant General James F. Amos, *The U.S. Army–Marine Corps Counterinsurgency Field Manual* (Chicago: University of Chicago Press, 2007); it was first issued as United States Army Field Manual No. 3-24 and Marine Corps Warfighting Publication No. 3-33-5, December 15, 2006.

67. Lazreg, *Torture,* 20. She distinguishes French theory and doctrine; theory attempted to "explain imperial power relationships," and doctrine "simplified the complexity of armed struggles and distorted their modalities." She notes this strange and monumental effort on the part of "hard-line officers to pause and theorize" at the very moment they fought to preserve the last of the French colonial empire (32–33).

68. Seigel, *Violence Work,* 27–28.

69. The Atlantic Charter of 1941 had embraced self-determination of peoples, but Winston Churchill worked to clarify that promise as one that applied to Hitler's empire, not empire itself. Samuel Moyn, *The Last Utopia: Human Rights in History* (Cambridge, Mass.: Belknap, 2010), 44–48, 115–19; Samuel Moyn, "Human Rights and History," *Nation,* August 11, 2010, https://www.thenation.com/. As Allies framed a Universal Declaration of Human Rights, a sense of global self-determination was not included, and the article against torture almost did not make the cut. Tobias Kelly, *This Side of Silence: Human Rights, Torture, and the Recognition of Cruelty* (Philadelphia: University of Pennsylvania Press, 2013).

70. Jason C. Parker, "Small Victory, Missed Chance: The Eisenhower Administration, the Bandung Conference, and the Turning of the Cold War," in *The Eisenhower Administration, The Third World, and the Globalization of the Cold War,* ed. Katryn C. Statler and Andrew L. Johns (Lanham, Md.: Rowman & Littlefield, 2006), 154. Five months later, Algeria was officially on the agenda of the U.N. General Assembly. Alistair Horne, *A Savage War for Peace: Algeria, 1954–1962* (New York: NYRB, 2006), 130–31.

71. A "powerful logical structure" emerged that cast the stakes of war to be "civilizational." Lazreg, *Torture,* 20. In contrast, Frantz Fanon offers an economic and structural analysis of the relation between colonizers and colonized based on his studies of Algerians.

72. For example, elaborate grids and barriers in urban areas or mass relocations in rural spaces paralleled the earlier Philippine "reconcentration camps." These "ideal" communities enhanced surveillance as well as control over food and

basic needs. Owens offers a sweeping study of counterinsurgency that grounds it in a far older model for patriarchal governance defined by violence and its restraint, or an "economy of force." The despot of the feudal estate or plantation household clearly dominates his subjects through force, but he can control people and economize on violence should he wish by withholding or granting their access to life needs. Modern military engagements have used the term "pacification" to refer to this kind of social control. Patricia Owens, *The Economy of Force: Counterinsurgency and the Historical Rise of the Social* (Cambridge: Cambridge University Press, 2015), 25. She demonstrates her points with excellent accounts of U.S. warfare in the Philippines, Vietnam, Afghanistan, and Iraq, as well as British campaigns.

73. David Kilcullen, *Counterinsurgency* (Oxford: Oxford University Press, 2010), 43, cited in Owens, *Economy of Force,* 10. See also Sebastian L.v. Gorka and David Kilcullen, "An Actor-centric Theory of War: Understanding the Difference between COIN and Counterinsurgency," *Joint Force Quarterly* 60, no. 1 (2011): 14–18, https://ndupress.ndu.edu/Portals/68/Documents/jfq/jfq-60/jfq-60_14-18_Gorka-Kilcullen.pdf. In contrast, retired U.S. Army colonel Andrew J. Bacevich critiqued the 2006 COIN manual, the enterprise of rebranding, and the 2007 surge in Iraq, noting, "For the U.S. military, [counterinsurgency became] not really war but something more akin to imperial policing combined with the systematic distribution of alms." Andrew J. Bacevich, *Washington Rules: America's Path to Permanent War* (New York: Metropolitan, 2010), 201.

74. Owens, *Economy of Force,* 61, 85.

75. In 1947, Truman conceptually and practically reorganized domestic intelligence, military, and security agencies, noting, "It must be the policy of the United States to support free peoples who are resisting attempted subjugation by armed minorities or by outside pressures." "Truman Doctrine (1947)," National Archives, https://www.archives.gov/milestone-documents/truman-doctrine. The National Security Act of 1947 created the CIA and the Department of Defense as a means to restructure and coordinate the branches of the armed forces, as well as the National Security Council. See Michael J. Hogan, *A Cross of Iron: Harry S. Truman and the Origins of the National Security State, 1945–1954* (Cambridge: Cambridge University Press, 1998).

76. The United States sent congressional and military delegations to Algeria to see French tactics in action; Robin writes that Massachusetts senator John F. Kennedy was among these visitors. In turn, U.S. war colleges at Fort Bragg and Fort Benning welcomed French torture generals and colonels, who were invited to teach on the "successes" of torture and counterinsurgency in Algeria. Some of these, like notorious generals Massu and Aussaresses, peddled this myth for decades. As president, Kennedy's interest was strong. He asked Defense Secretary John McNamara to confer with Pierre Mesmer, his French counterpart and an Algerian veteran. As a result, ten liaison officers who had served under Aussaresses

arrived in 1961 to train U.S. soldiers at Fort Bragg's Special Warfare Center; see Marie-Monique Robin, "Counterinsurgency and Torture: Exporting Torture Tactics from Indochina and Algeria to Latin America," in *Torture: Does It Make Us Safer, Is It Ever Okay?*, ed. Kenneth Roth and Minky Warden (New York: New Press, 2005), 44–68 at 51–52. The preface to Trinquier's English edition speaks directly to the U.S. engagement in Vietnam and the coming era of U.S. involvement in revolutionary wars.

77. Nick Turse, *Kill Anything That Moves: The Real American War in Vietnam* (New York: Metropolitan, 2013), 8.

78. Horne, *Savage War.*

79. Lazreg, *Torture*, 87, 88–107.

80. Lazreg, *Torture*, 20. Khalili, *Time in the Shadows*, 34–37.

81. Hanson W. Baldwin, "Terrorism in Vietnam: Violence against Civilians Complicates U.S. Efforts and May Force Policy Shift," *New York Times*, April 28, 1964, https://www.nytimes.com/.

82. Baldwin, "Terrorism in Vietnam."

83. Roger Trinquier, *Modern Warfare: A French View of Counterinsurgency*, trans. Daniel Lee (London: Pall Mall, 1964), 114.

84. In the United States and abroad, Black intellectuals and foreign policy teams saw white racist violence and Black and brown resistance as a national Achilles' heel; see Singh, *Race and America's Long War*, 4. Schrader's history traces policy disputes and shifts in how to address this at the federal and state level, especially through models for policing. He argues the rising "security" fetish solidifies a "new racialization." Analysis of these uprisings dispensed with racialized explanations such as inherent savagery, or "root causes" of poverty or crime, instead encoding race as an irrational resistance to law and order, "criminality." In this cost–benefit rational choice approach, behavior (disorder, crime) becomes the issue, not structural racism or racialized traits. Behavior control is achieved through a reward and punishment model. Broken-window policing models are one result; see Stuart Schrader, *Badges without Borders: How Global Counterinsurgency Transformed American Policing* (Berkeley: University of California Press, 2019), 38–51. For a slightly different analysis of the same period and shifting racial encoding, see Seigel, *Violence Work.*

85. Trinquier, *Modern Warfare*, 21–22.

86. Bernard Fall, "Counterinsurgency: The French Experience," lecture delivered at the Industrial College of the Armed Forces, Washington, D.C., January 18, 1963, 139. Fall was professor of government at Howard. He also paraphrases a 1961 story by Germaine Tillon, a French major: "Where is your moral standing as an officer? You know this fellow just placed two bombs in a department store. If those bombs go off, about 50 people will be killed on the spot and another hundred will be maimed in the ensuing trampling. Now, you have 50 minutes to get

information out of that guy as to where he placed those bombs." Major Germaine Tillon, *Algeria—The Realities* (New York: Knopf, 1959).
  87. Trinquier, *Modern Warfare,* 23.
  88. Trinquier, *Modern Warfare,* 115. "The army of the French King refused to use the bow and the arrow the English handled so effectively. For them, true combat, the only fair and permissible kind, remained man-to-man, body-to-body."
  89. Trinquier, *Modern Warfare,* 23.
  90. Trinquier, *Modern Warfare,* 22.
  91. Rejali's research dismisses the possibility methodically. Rejali, *Torture and Democracy,* 446–62.
  92. See the epilogue. Trinquier's popularity in the United States emerged just after a wave of anxiety over communist mind control, which was fed by propagandists like Ed Hunter and found popular expression in Richard Condon's 1959 novel *The Manchurian Candidate,* which became a film in 1962. Edward Hunter, *Brainwashing in Red China* (New York: Vanguard, 1951). The literature on CIA and Defense Department funding for such experimentation is extensive; see Annie Jacobsen, *Phenomena: The Secret History of the U.S. Government's Investigations into Extrasensory Perception and Psychokinesis* (Boston: Little, Brown, 2017); McCoy, *Question;* William Blum, *Killing Hope: U.S. Military and CIA Interventions since World War II,* updated ed. (Monroe, Maine: Common Courage, 2004); Timothy Melley, "Brain Warfare: The Covert Sphere, Terrorism, and the Legacy of the Cold War," *Grey Room* 45 (2011): 19–40; Susan Lisa Carruthers, *Cold War Captives: Imprisonment, Escape, and Brainwashing* (Berkeley: University of California Press, 2009); Scott Shane, "China Inspired Interrogations at Guantánamo," *New York Times,* July 2, 2008, https://www.nytimes.com/.
  93. Trinquier, *Modern Warfare,* 35.
  94. Trinquier, *Modern Warfare,* 29, 32, 33.
  95. Trinquier, *Modern Warfare,* 45.
  96. Trinquier, *Modern Warfare,* 48.
  97. Lazreg, *Torture,* 90–91, citing Antoine Argoud, *La décadence, l'imposture, et la tragédie* (Paris: Fayard, 1974).
  98. Galula's claims of success in Algeria have been disputed: Gregor Mathias, *Galula in Algeria: Counterinsurgency Practice versus Theory* (Westport, Conn.: Praeger, 2011), 92–103; Thomas Rid, "The Nineteenth Century Origins of Counterinsurgency Doctrine," *Journal of Strategic Studies* 33, no. 5 (2010): 727–58, https://doi.org/10.1080/01402390.2010.498259.
  99. David Galula, *Pacification in Algeria, 1956–1958* (1963; reprint, Santa Monica, Calif.: RAND Corporation, 2006), 183, https://www.rand.org/pubs/monographs/MG478-1.html.
  100. Galula, *Pacification in Algeria,* 152.
  101. Galula, *Pacification in Algeria,* 118–19.

102. Eighty percent of the men and 60 percent of the women were tortured. Although the rebel organization numbered approximately 1,400 in 1956, over 24,000 people were detained, amounting to a third of the population; the vast majority were tortured, and of course most were civilians. Rejali, *Torture and Democracy,* 482–83, 485.

103. Rejali, *Torture and Democracy,* 489.

104. In 1957, General Salan proposed a "shock method" of this type of "political re-education" meant to proceed zone to zone. Lazreg, *Torture,* 72–73.

105. Horne writes that veteran of Indochina and intelligence agent Captain Christian Léger was handpicked by Trinquier for work in Algiers. Goddard and Léger's torture produced double agents known as "Léger's blues," capable of leading the paras to FLN hideouts. The two men worked hand in hand with Trinquier's block-warden surveillance organization. Horne, *Savage War,* 212, 258–59; Rejali, *Torture and Democracy,* 483–84.

106. Jean Lartéguy, *The Centurions* (1960), foreword by Robert Kaplan, trans. Xan Fielding (New York: Penguin, 2015). The author was known everywhere by his pen name, and a series of similar novels earned him credibility as a war analyst. U.S. journalists and Paris newspapers cited Lartéguy's observations on Vietnam, as does Horne, *Savage War.* See Carl Sulzberger, "The Mirror of Vietnam," *New York Times,* October 22, 1967, https://www.nytimes.com/; "13 Bomb Blasts in Paris," *New York Times,* March 29, 1962, https://www.nytimes.com/.

107. Rejali, *Torture and Democracy,* 546–47.

108. Marks records an atomic bomb hypothetical from approximately 1951 in this context. John Marks, *The Search for the Manchurian Candidate: The CIA and Mind Control* (New York: Norton, 1979), 38. Jeremy Bentham (1748–1832), an English philosopher and early utilitarian, is often pointed to as the father of the ticking time bomb argument to defend torture in interrogation. The scenario devised and circulated in the 1950s differs substantially. In Bentham's scenario, authorities have caught an arsonist in the act, and they pursue his helper. There is no imminent threat, no lifesaving information, no large stakes, no time frame. Davies writes that as an argument for institutionalized torture, "the example is extremely weak." Bentham himself is not decided as to whether torture will work to compel speech, and he posits that the accomplice might be found through investigation or other means. Jeremy Davies, "The Fire-Raisers: Bentham and Torture," *Interdisciplinary Studies in the Long Nineteenth Century* 15 (2012), section 5, https://doi.org/10.16995/ntn.643.

109. "The Red Berets," review of *The Centurions,* by Jean Lartéguy, *Time,* January 19, 1962, https://time.com/.

110. McChrystal is cited on the back of the 2015 reprint edition of Lartéguy, *Centurions.*

111. Robert D. Kaplan, "Rereading Vietnam," *Atlantic,* August 24, 2007. See Rejali's discussion of race and masculinity in Lartéguy: Darius Rejali, "Torture

Makes the Man," in *On Torture,* ed. Thomas C. Hilde (Baltimore, Md.: Johns Hopkins University Press, 2008). On Petraeus and Bigeard, see Paula Broadwell, *All In: The Education of David Petraeus* (New York: Penguin, 2012), 64. Petraeus maintained a correspondence with Bigeard from the mid-1970s after his West Point graduation until 2010, when Bigeard died. See also Ehoward, "The Heroes of David Petraeus," review of Broadwell, *All In,* HistoryNet, February 10, 2012, https://www.historynet.com/mhq-reviews-the-heroes-of-david-petraeus/?f; Bigeard was France's most decorated serviceman. According to Rejali, he was "the first commander to use torture officially" in Algeria (Rejali, *Torture and Democracy,* 488). "Algiers Harbor became notorious for the bodies of torture victims that were dumped at night . . . which won his victims the derisive name *crevettes Bigeard,* shrimp Bigeard" (Lazreg, *Torture,* 53–54). See also Robin, "Counterinsurgency and Torture," 49; and Rejali, *Torture and Democracy,* 493.

112. Curtis Cate, "Adventures and Torments of Seven Modern Musketeers," *New York Times,* January 14, 1962, https://www.nytimes.com/.

113. Orville Prescott, "Books of the Times," *New York Times,* January 3, 1962, https://www.nytimes.com/.

114. Lartéguy, *Centurions,* 16.

115. Lartéguy, *Centurions,* 395, 444, 97.

116. Lartéguy, *Centurions,* 488.

117. Lartéguy, *Centurions,* 385.

118. Lartéguy, *Centurions,* 359.

119. Stanley McChrystal, introduction to Lartéguy, *Centurions,* xi.

120. Torture in this novel is alien to France and Asiatic in origin. Those able to apply it with detached facility are the most Asian: the son of a French diplomat raised in Hong Kong and his Chinese assistant. Lartéguy, *Centurions,* 372, 20; on capitalist warfare, see 96.

121. Lartéguy, *Centurions,* 342, 358. "The big Negro" Dia, with "a voice like Paul Robeson," who is a medic for France, embodies the life-force of Africa and celebrates the sexual passions born in war, where beautiful Arab terrorists and Vietnamese spies cannot resist rugged French warriors. See also, e.g., Lartéguy, *Centurions,* 182, 444, 270, 319.

122. Lartéguy, *Centurions,* 491.

123. Lartéguy, *Centurions,* 500, 501–2, 513. The rapist's romance imagined between Glatigny/Aicha purports to represent the interrogation of Djamilia Bouhired. Scholars have unfortunately continued to use the term "romance" for this relationship, with little critical reflection. Horne, *Savage War,* 212.

124. Lartéguy, *Centurions,* 504–12.

125. The context for counterinsurgency in the Philippines was quite different from that of French Indochina or French Algeria. The islands were a client state, formally independent and not at war with the United States.

126. Progressive framing is paradigmatic of counterinsurgency. Owens, *Economy of Force*, 30.

127. Max Boot, "'The Road Not Taken' in Vietnam," interview conducted by John Harwood, NPR, *On Point* (podcast), January 18, 2018, https://www.wbur.org/onpoint/2018/01/17/the-road-not-taken-in-vietnam. Max Boot, *The Road Not Taken: Edward Lansdale and the American Tragedy in Vietnam* (New York: Liveright, 2018).

128. Though largely seen by his colleagues as dated and eccentric in his later days in Vietnam, he often stands as either representative villain or ingenious hero of U.S. foreign policy in the cold war. Lansdale continues to feature in some extraordinary and baseless conspiracy theories that either glamorize or demonize spy culture. Jonathan Nashel, *Edward Lansdale's Cold War* (Amherst: University of Massachusetts Press, 2005). Marc D. Bernstein, "Ed Lansdale's Black Warfare in 1950s Vietnam," History.net, February 16, 2010, https://www.historynet.com/ed-lansdales-black-warfare-in-1950s-vietnam/?f. Sterling Seagrave and Peggy Seagrave, *Gold Warriors: America's Secret Recovery of Yamashita's Gold* (London: Verso, 2005). Jean Lartéguy offers a disparaging fictional portrayal of Lansdale in the 1962 novel *Yellow Fever* (Nashel, *Edward Lansdale's Cold War*, 197).

129. From 1945 to 1948, he was stationed with military intelligence in the Philippines, guiding the transition from Japanese occupation to Philippine independence. Edward Lansdale, *In the Midst of Wars: An American's Mission to Southeast Asia* (New York: Harper & Row, 1972), 5.

130. The Hukbalahap was a peasant resistance network concerned with land tenancy and fighting for economic justice. Huk nationalists had alternated guerilla combat with democratic mechanisms to promote their ends since 1930. Nashel, *Edward Lansdale's Cold War*, 38; McCoy, *Policing*, 374–79, 538.

131. He became well known from the Church Report on CIA activity and served as Kennedy's deputy assistant secretary of Defense for special operations. Michael McClintock, "Edward Geary Lansdale and the New Counterinsurgency: Lansdale in the White House," in *Instruments of Statecraft: U.S. Guerilla Warfare, Counterinsurgency, and Counterterrorism, 1940–1990* (New York: Pantheon, 1992), http://www.statecraft.org/chapter8.html.

132. McClintock, "Edward Geary Lansdale."

133. Bohannan had served as ethnographer at the Smithsonian and was a specialist in Navajo folklore. McCoy, *Policing*, 377.

134. Lansdale, *In the Midst*, 71; McClintock, "Edward Geary Lansdale," n.p.

135. Nashel credits Denis Warner for the anecdote. Nashel, *Edward Lansdale's Cold War*, 41.

136. As Nashel, *Edward Lansdale's Cold War*, points out, on important occasions, he was the only witness attesting to success.

137. Nashel, *Edward Lansdale's Cold War*, 42. Stephen T. Hosmer and Sibylle O. Crane, *Counterinsurgency: A Symposium, April 16–20, 1962* (1963; reprint, Santa Monica, Calif.: RAND Corporation, 2006), https://www.rand.org/pubs/reports/R412-1.html.

138. Nashel, *Edward Lansdale's Cold War*, 34–35.

139. Kuzmarov, "American Police Training," 4. Lansdale's ideas were also often grossly impractical and eccentric. Superiors denied his request to borrow a U.S. submarine, though he laid out a plan in which he and Bohannan would masquerade as Russian officers on the deck of a "Soviet" sub surfacing off the coast. He argued that Huk communist field commanders would find a "rendezvous" with a Soviet sub "irresistible" and could thereby be lured into capture. He had already begun practicing Russian phrases with Bohannan when the idea was rejected. He later lobbied to obtain a helicopter and train paratroopers—work he eventually abandoned. Lansdale, *In the Midst*, 62.

140. McClintock, "Edward Geary Lansdale."

141. A 1963 memo to National Security Council head McGeorge Bundy cited in McClintock, "Edward Geary Lansdale."

142. Nashel, *Edward Lansdale's Cold War*, 43.

143. In counterinsurgency, resistance is depoliticized, Owens argues, because the people are made objects of social administration, not political agents. Owens, *Economy of Force*, 37. Khalili and Lazreg see this as a function of racism; Khalili notes that race remains the unspoken axis of counterinsurgency theory today. Khalili, *Time in the Shadows*, 43; Lazreg, *Torture*, 51–52, 61.

144. William Tuohy, "'War Is Hell and, by God, This Is One of the Prime Examples'; A Big 'Dirty Little War,'" *New York Times Sunday Magazine*, November 28, 1965, https://www.nytimes.com/.

145. Tuohy, "War Is Hell."

146. Tuohy, "War Is Hell."

147. Tuohy, "War Is Hell."

148. Alberto R. Gonzalez, "Memorandum for the President, Decision RE Application of the General Convention Prisoners of War to the Conflict with Al Qaeda and the Taliban," January 25, 2002, in Mark Danner, *Torture and Truth: America, Abu Ghraib, and the War on Terror* (New York: NYRB, 2004), 84.

149. Chris Mackey and Greg Miller, introduction to *The Interrogators* (Boston: Little, Brown, 2004), xxiii.

150. Rejali, *Torture and Democracy*, 70–73.

151. Inspector General, Department of the Army, "Detainee Operations Inspection," July 21, 2004, 2, 46, http://www.globalsecurity.org/military/library/report/2004/daig_detainee-ops_21jul2004.pdf.

152. Inspector General, Department of the Army, "Detainee Operations Inspection."

153. Scheuerman offers a skeptical review of political science on "the new wars" but not the new war mythos itself. William E. Scheuerman, "Torture and the New Paradigm of Warfare," *Constellations* 15, no. 4 (2008): 561–75.

154. Elizabeth Gilbert, "Money as a 'Weapons System' and the Entrepreneurial Way of War," *Critical Military Studies* 1, no. 3 (2015): 202–19.

155. Bass, "Counterinsurgency and Torture."

156. See Bernard E. Harcourt, "Beyond the Counterinsurgency Paradigm of Governing: Letting Go of Prediction and the Illusion of an Internal Enemy," in *Reimagining the National Security State: Liberalism on the Brink,* ed. Karen J. Greenberg (Cambridge: Cambridge University Press, 2020), 141–53; Jordan T. Camp and Christina Heatherton, eds., *Policing the Planet: Why the Policing Crisis Led to Black Lives Matter* (London: Verso, 2016).

157. Galula, *Pacification in Algeria,* 119.

158. McCoy, *Policing,* 536.

159. The RAND Corporation began as a project of Douglas Aircraft that reorganized in 1948 as a private nonprofit. RAND hosted an influential 1962 conference, which drew an A-list of counterinsurgency theorists and practitioners.

160. McClintock, "Edward Geary Lansdale."

161. McClintock, "Edward Geary Lansdale."

162. McCoy, *Policing,* 379.

163. McClintock, "Edward Geary Lansdale"; Kuzmarov, "Modernizing Repression," 201.

164. Seigel, *Violence Work,* 56, citing a 1962 National Security Agency policy statement used to promote the creation of the Office of Public Safety.

165. Seigel, *Violence Work,* 56–57.

166. Stephen G. Rabe, *The Killing Zone: The United States Wages Cold War in Latin America* (Oxford: Oxford University Press, 2012), 11–112, 146. Notably, "Theodore Brown moves from director of the OPS in Brazil to head Operation Phoenix in Vietnam" (112).

167. McCoy, *Question,* 61. On Operation Phoenix, see Turse, *Kill Anything That Moves,* 190.

168. Trinquier, *Modern Warfare,* 35.

169. Seigel, *Violence Work,* 53, referring to Martha Huggins.

170. Mark Mazzetti and Tim Weiner, "Files on Illegal Spying Show CIA Skeletons from the Cold War," *New York Times,* June 27, 2007, https://www.nytimes.com/. They report on newly declassified CIA memoranda known as the Family Jewels. They note that secret CIA programs trained hundreds of thousands of people in twenty-five countries by the early 1960s, also including Laos, Cambodia, South Korea, South Vietnam, the Philippines, Thailand, and Iran, as well as Central and South American regimes. The documents suggest the Philippines would have been a recipient of Project X mail-order material or advisory training. They

also describe OPS bomb training in Dade County, Florida, in 1973. See also Rabe, *Killing Zone,* 111–12; Blum, *Killing Hope,* 74, 171, 385. The classified CIA inspector general's report (2004), addressing grievous interrogation abuses under Bush, also compared 2002–4 to the "resurgence of interest in teaching interrogation techniques" in the early 1980s "as one of several methods to foster foreign liaison relationships." CIA Inspector General John Helgerson, "Special Review: Counterterrorism Detention and Interrogation Activities," 2004, declassified 2008, available at the Torture Database, https://www.thetorturedatabase.org/.

171. Rabe, *Killing Zone,* 111–12.

172. McCoy, *Question,* 71. By the Pentagon's own admission, in 1996, courses in Latin America taught "torture, blackmail, murder, sabotage, bribery, extortion for political aims. Hypnosis and truth serum were recommended." Marguerite Feitlowitz, *A Lexicon of Terror* (Oxford: Oxford University Press, 1998), 8–10. On evidence of schools of torture, training, and manuals, see Rejali, *Torture and Democracy,* 427.

173. Quoting McCoy, *Question,* 86–87, 105–6. The army program Project X used an instruction course from the Phoenix program, among other "inappropriate" materials, to develop an exportable program for Latin America including "executions, beating, abduction of family, injections" (71, 78). See also Frederick H. Gareau, *State Terrorism and the United States: From Counterinsurgency to the War on Terrorism* (London: Zed, 2004).

174. The Nixon administration took the $347,000 cut from the OPS and directed it to counternarcotics work in Argentina. Kuzmarov, "Modernizing Repression," 220. See also Rabe, *Killing Zone,* 146. Blum, *Killing Hope,* 204. Alfred W. McCoy, *Torture and Impunity: The U.S. Doctrine of Coercive Interrogation* (Madison: University of Wisconsin Press, 2012), 99.

175. Seigel, *Violence Work,* 38–40. Seigel, *Violence Work,* and Schrader, *Badges without Borders,* draw this line directly through a wealth of archival documents.

176. Seigel, *Violence Work,* 40–41. The majority of funding went to U.S. police departments. Courts, prisons, and programs for victims were also recipients. At its height, the annual budget surpassed $1 billion per year.

177. Seigel, *Violence Work,* 57.

178. Molly Dunigan and Ulrich Petersohn, eds., *The Markets for Force: Privatization of Security across World Regions* (Philadelphia: University of Pennsylvania Press, 2015).

179. Anna Leander, "The Market for Force and Public Security: The Destabilizing Consequences of Private Military Companies," *Journal of Peace Research* 42, no. 5 (2005): 605–22, https://doi.org/10.1177/0022343305056237.

180. Rejali, *Torture and Democracy,* refutes a standard hypothesis that the United States has been a "universal distributor" of torture training with a wealth of data historicizing and tracking techniques regionally over time. He synthesizes the

argument against the hypothesis on pages 5–21. McCoy has written an indispensable book on the development of the CIA's "psychological paradigm" for torture. He at times approaches the universal distributor hypothesis, and his terminology unwittingly reinforces rhetoric that disguises stress to the body as simply psychological. McCoy, *Question*, 203.

181. McCoy, *Question*, 61.

182. Trinquier, *Modern Warfare*, 23.

183. Mitchell, Jessen & Associates received $81 million on contract from the CIA for this purpose. See the epilogue on the case of James Mitchell and Bruce Jessen and their debt to a torture network in the American Psychological Association. See also Stephanie Athey, "Psychology, Torture, Networks: Or, Structure as the Subject of Human Rights," in *Writing beyond the State: Post-sovereign Approaches to Human Rights in Literary Studies*, ed. Alexandra S. Moore and Samantha Pinto (London: Palgrave Macmillan, 2020), 175–98.

184. For astute histories of this process in Latin America, see Feitlowitz, *Lexicon of Terror;* Rabe, *Killing Zone;* and William Stanley, *The Protection Racket State: Elite Politics, Military Extortion and Civil War in El Salvador* (Philadelphia, Pa.: Temple University Press, 1996).

185. Reference is to the U.S. military presence in Iraq during 2003–11 and Afghanistan during 2001–21.

186. Scheuerman, "Torture and the New Paradigm of Warfare," 571.

187. See Khalili, *Time in the Shadows*.

188. On this process in the Iraq war, see Owens, *Economy of Force;* Khalili, *Time in the Shadows*.

189. Two U.S. installations receiving the most attention for detainee torture and abuse in this period provide a glimpse of the larger picture. At its height, the U.S. detention site at Guantánamo Bay, Cuba, held 779 men. The *Nation* noted that in a 2006 study, it was found that 86 percent of the first 571 detainees were not captured by troops but were handed over in an exchange for bounties. By August 2022, a total of 730 had been released, most uncharged with any crime. As of July 2023, thirty men remained. Of these, 16 are still detained despite having been cleared for release by the U.S. government. Eleven have cases pending, and three have not been charged. As to the second installation, Abu Ghraib, the Inspector General, Department of the Army, noted that Abu Ghraib alone held approximately 7,490 Iraqi detainees in March 2004. Red Cross monitors at Abu Ghraib reported, "Certain Coalition Forces military intelligence officers told the ICRC that in their estimate between 70% and 90% of the persons deprived of their liberty in Iraq had been arrested by mistake." Raids, roundups, and detentions continued for years. In 2006, a report accessed by *Salon* included the following summary of material recorded at Abu Ghraib: "A review of all the computer media submitted to this office revealed a total of 1,325 images of suspected detainee abuse, 93 video files of

suspected detainee abuse, 660 images of adult pornography, 546 images of suspected dead Iraqi detainees, 29 images of soldiers in simulated sexual acts, 20 images of a soldier with a Swastika drawn between his eyes, 37 images of Military Working dogs being used in abuse of detainees and 125 images of questionable acts." Other provisional numbers were among the military and state department cables and reports leaked in 2010: "The logs reveal that more than 180,000 people were detained in Iraq between 2004 and 2009. This is equivalent to one in 50 of the male population. In comparison, the number of people detained in Afghanistan, which has a similar population, was 7,500." See American Civil Liberties Union, "Guantánamo by the Numbers"; Edith M. Lederer, "Guantanamo Detainees Tell First Independent Visitor about Scars from Torture and Hopes to Leave," Associated Press, July 6, 2023, https://apnews.com. Moustfa Bayoumi, "Journey to Guantánamo: A Week in America's Notorious Penal Colony," *Nation,* July 11, 2022, https://www.thenation.com/. Inspector General, Department of the Army, *Detainee Operations Inspection* (Washington, D.C: Department of the Army, July 21, 2004), 23–24. International Committee of the Red Cross, "Report of the ICRC on the Treatment by the Coalition Forces of Prisoners of War and Other Protected Persons by the Geneva Conventions in Iraq during Arrest, Internment and Interrogation," GlobalSecurity.org, https://www.globalsecurity.org/military/library/report/2004/icrc_report_iraq_feb2004.htm; Salon Staff, "Abu Ghraib Files," *Salon,* updated March 14, 2006, https://www.salon.com/; Angus Stickler and Chris Woods, "Iraq War Logs: U.S. Troops Ordered Not to Investigate Iraqi Torture," The Bureau Investigates, May 23, 2011, https://www.thebureauinvestigates.com/2011/05/23/us-troops-ordered-not-to-investigate-iraqi-torture.

190. Schrader, *Badges without Borders,* tracks the similar connection of criminology and counterinsurgency in U.S. urban policy.

191. On exploiting division: Cassidy, "Long Small War." On human terrain mapping: McCoy, *Policing,* 45; Vanessa M. Gezari, "The Quiet Demise of the Army's Plan to Understand Afghanistan and Iraq," *New York Times,* August 18, 2015, https://www.nytimes.com/.

192. The U.S. military in the twenty-first century drew on a reissue of Rafael Patai's *Arab Mind,* an Orientalist work. Tony Lagouranis notes that MPs and MIs new to Abu Ghraib prison were instructed on Patai's "Arab phobias." The use of dogs was one result. Tony Lagouranis with Allen Mikaelian, *Fear Up Harsh: An Army Interrogator's Dark Journey through Iraq* (New York: New American Library, 2007).

193. Gilbert, "Money as a 'Weapons System,'" 212.

194. McCoy cites 3,257 killed and 35,000 tortured. McCoy, *Question,* 76.

195. McCoy, *Question,* 75–78.

196. Amnesty International, "Philippines, 2017–2018," https://www.amnesty.org/. Torture remains suspected in the 2021 disappearance of an Indigenous activist.

Amnesty International, "Philippines: Fears of Torture for Abducted Activist: Steve Abua," November 16, 2021, https://www.amnesty.org/en/documents/asa35/4997/2021/en/. UN Special Rapporteur on Human Rights Defenders, "Philippines: The Disappearance of Steve Abua (Joint Communication)," April 8, 2022, https://srdefenders.org/philippines-disappearance-of-steve-abua-joint-communication/.

197. McCoy, *Policing,* 454.

198. Steffen Bo Jensen and Karl Hapal, "Duterte's War on Drugs Led to Strong Changes in One of Manila's Poorer Districts," *Dignity,* August 3, 2022, https://www.dignity.dk/.

199. Amnesty International, "Philippines: Fears of Torture." Cecil Morella, "Philippine Torture Victim Relives Horror as Dictator's Son Rises," Agence France-Presse (AFP), updated February 23, 2022, https://news.abs-cbn.com/news/02/23/22/torture-victim-relives-horror-as-dictators-son-rises.

200. Meili Steele, "The Social Imaginary as a Problematic for Human Rights," in *Theoretical Perspectives on Human Rights and Literature,* ed. Elizabeth Swanson Goldberg and Alexandra S. Moore (New York: Routledge, 2012), 93.

3. Archetype

1. Nina Bernstein, "U.S. Is Settling Detainee's Suit in 9/11 Sweep," *New York Times,* February 28, 2006, https://www.nytimes.com/.

2. Under international law, rape of an inmate by staff is considered torture. Other forms of sexual abuse violate the internationally recognized prohibition on cruel, inhuman, or degrading treatment or punishment. Rape and sexual assault violate U.S. federal and state criminal laws. Allen J. Beck et al., "Sexual Victimization in Prisons and Jails Reported by Inmates, 2011–12—Update," Bureau of Justice Statistics, https://www.bjs.gov/index.cfm?ty=pbdetail&iid=4654. See Allen J. Beck et al., "Sexual Victimization in Juvenile Facilities Reported by Youth, 2012," Bureau of Justice Statistics, https://www.bjs.gov/index.cfm?ty=pbdetail&iid=4656; Amnesty International, "'Not Part of My Sentence': Violations of the Human Rights of Women in Custody," March 26, 2011, https://www.amnestyusa.org/reports/usa-not-part-of-my-sentence-violations-of-the-human-rights-of-women-in-custody/.

3. Orlando P. Tizon, "Assessing the Treatment of Torture: Balancing Quantifiable with Intangible Metrics," in *Witnessing Torture: Perspectives of Torture Survivors and Human Rights Workers,* ed. Alexandra S. Moore and Elizabeth Swanson (Cham, Switzerland: Palgrave Macmillan, 2018), 71–88 at 80.

4. Marcy Strauss, "Torture," *New York Law School Law Review* 48, no. 1/2 (2003–4).

5. Strauss, "Torture," 209.

6. That picture involves whipping or beating a suspect to secure confession, according to Strauss, "Torture." While she tests that picture against an array of varied

incidents drawn equally from Supreme Court decisions and from the highly imaginative speculative press I will discuss, the picture she arranges in the end reflects the familiar aspects of the archetype to be described here. In part, she says, because these definitions of torture remain "surprisingly blurry," she relies on the presumption of a shared mental image instead: "I will only use 'torture' as a generic term when a more precise delineation is *not necessary*. In those cases, the reader should simply bear in mind the type of abuse that most people would agree constitutes torture" (216).

7. See Human Rights First, "Command's Responsibility: Detainee Deaths in U.S. Custody in Iraq and Afghanistan," 2006, http://www.humanrightsfirst.info/pdf/06221-etn-hrf-dic-rep-web.pdf. The military identified thirty-four of these as suspected or confirmed homicides. Human Rights First identified eleven more cases in which physical abuse or harsh detention resulted in death, bringing its total to forty-five suspected or confirmed homicides in custody. Human Rights First, "Torture: Quick Facts," www.humanrightsfirst.org/us_law/etn/misc/factsheet (accessed December 7, 2009). See also John Sifton, "The Bush Administration Homicides," Daily Beast, May 5, 2009, www.thedailybeast.com/blogs-and-stories/2009-05-05/how-many-were-tortured-to-death/full.

8. Though investigative reporting stepped up in 2004, neither Hypothetical, Historical, nor Heart of Darkness strains in the news received extended comment in the press's own self-critical reflections following the Abu Ghraib revelations. For Hypothetical quizzes and surveys, see the prologue.

9. See Steve Chapman, "No Tortured Dilemma," *Washington Times,* November 5, 2001; Bruce Hoffman, "A Nasty Business," *Atlantic,* January 2002, 49–52, https://www.theatlantic.com/magazine/archive/2002/01/a-nasty-business/302379/; Michael T. Kaufman, "What Does the Pentagon See in 'Battle of Algiers'?," *New York Times,* September 7, 2003, https://www.nytimes.com/; Drake Bennett, "The War in the Mind," *Boston Globe,* November 27, 2005, https://www.bostonglobe.com/; and Mark Bowden, "The Dark Art of Interrogation," *Atlantic,* October 2003, 51–70. In variations on this France-and-Israel pattern, Hoffman discusses potential U.S. techniques in the war on terror in the context of the French campaign in Algeria and the Sri Lankans' fight against the Muslim Tamil Tigers, and Bowden discusses Israel and France and then reviews aspects of England's torture of Irish Republican Army suspects in the 1970s.

10. See Hoffman, "Nasty Business." Also see "Psychology and Sometimes a Slap: The Man Who Made Prisoners Talk," Word for Word, *New York Times,* December 12, 2004, https://www.nytimes.com/; Bowden, "Dark Art"; Joseph Lelyveld, "Interrogating Ourselves," *New York Times Magazine,* June 12, 2005, https://www.nytimes.com/.

11. Mary Louise Pratt, *Imperial Eyes: Travel Writing and Transculturation* (New York: Routledge, 2007); Daniel Cooper Alarcón, "John Stevens and the Ruins of

Manifest Destiny," in *Travel Narratives, Travel Fictions* (Lanham, Md.: Lexington, forthcoming).

12. Peter Maass, "Torture, Tough or Lite: If a Terror Suspect Won't Talk, Should He Be Made To?," *New York Times,* March 9, 2003, https://www.nytimes.com/.

13. Hoffman, "Nasty Business"; Bowden, "Dark Art."

14. Alan Dershowitz, *Why Terrorism Works* (New Haven, Conn.: Yale University Press, 2002); Alan Dershowitz, "Tortured Reasoning," in *Torture: A Collection,* ed. Sanford Levinson (Oxford: Oxford University Press, 2004). Sanford Levinson, "The Debate on Torture: War against Virtual States," *Dissent* 50, no. 3 (2003): 79; Sanford Levinson, "Precommitment and Postcommitment: The Ban on Torture in the Wake of September 11," *Texas Law Review* 81, no. 7 (2003): 2013–81; Sanford Levinson, "Contemplating Torture," in Levinson, *Torture: A Collection* (2004), 23–43. Richard Posner, "Torture, Terrorism, and Interrogation," in *Torture: A Collection, Revised,* ed. Sanford Levinson (Oxford: Oxford University Press, 2006), 291–98.

15. Eric Prokosch, "Amnesty International's Anti-torture Campaigns," in *A Glimpse of Hell: Reports on Torture Worldwide,* ed. Duncan Forest for Amnesty International (New York: New York University Press, 1996), 26–35.

16. Elaine Scarry, *The Body in Pain: The Making and Unmaking of the World* (Oxford: Oxford University Press, 1987).

17. Scarry, *Body in Pain,* 20.

18. Scarry, *Body in Pain,* 9.

19. For critics, see Judith Shklar, "Torturers," *London Review of Books,* October 9, 1986, https://www.lrb.co.uk/. Shklar praised Edward Peters's *Torture,* a legal and political history of torture predominantly in Europe, but she winced at the naïvety or mysticism behind Scarry's depiction of torture, declaring that it is not "a phenomenon that takes place in a chamber between two people, a victim and a torturer. It is always a part of a judicial and political system. To ignore that is to . . . make any effort to halt or impede it impossible."

20. David Luban, "Liberalism, Torture, and the Ticking Bomb" (2005), in *The Torture Debate in America,* ed. Karen J. Greenberg (Cambridge: Cambridge University Press, 2006), 35–83.

21. Luban, "Liberalism, Torture," 39.

22. Luban, "Liberalism, Torture," 39.

23. David Luban, *Torture, Power, and Law* (Cambridge: Cambridge University Press, 2014), 97–98.

24. David Sussman, "Defining Torture," *Case Western Reserve Journal of International Law* 37 (2005): 225–30.

25. David Sussman, "Torture, Self-Defense, and Fighting Dirty," in *Confronting Torture: Essays on the Ethics, Legality, History, and Psychology of Torture Today,* ed. Scott A. Anderson and Martha C. Nussbaum (Chicago: University of Chicago Press, 2018), 219–30 at 221–22.

26. This last quote is from David Sussman, "What's Wrong with Torture," in *The Phenomenon of Torture: Readings and Commentary,* ed. William Schulz (Philadelphia: University of Pennsylvania Press, 2007), 178–79.

27. Jeremy Waldron, "Torture and Positive Law: Jurisprudence for the White House," *Columbia Law Review* 105, no. 6 (2005): 1681–750 at 1727.

28. Waldron, "Torture and Positive Law," 1681–750.

29. Samuel Moyn, "On the Genealogy of Morals," *Nation,* March 27, 2007, https://www.thenation.com/.

30. Samuel Moyn, "Civil Liberties and Endless War," *Dissent,* fall 2015, https://www.dissentmagazine.org/article/civil-liberties-and-endless-war.

31. Samuel Moyn, "Torture and Taboo: On Elaine Scarry," *Nation,* February 5, 2013, https://www.thenation.com/.

32. Eric Schmitt and Carolyn Marshall, "In Secret Unit's 'Black Room' a Grim Portrait of U.S. Abuse," *New York Times,* March 19, 2006, https://www.nytimes.com/.

33. Human Rights Watch, "Leadership Failure: Firsthand Accounts of Torture of Iraqi Detainees by the U.S. Army's 82nd Airborne Division," September 22, 2005, http://hrw.org/reports/2005/us0905. Michael Hirsch, "Truth about Torture: A Courageous Soldier and a Determined Senator Demand Clear Standards," *Newsweek,* November 7, 2005, https://www.newsweek.com/.

34. Tim Golden, "Years after Two Afghans Died, Abuse Case Falters," *New York Times,* February 13, 2006, https://www.nytimes.com/.

35. Bernstein, "U.S. Is Settling Detainee's Suit."

36. Shafiq Rasul, Asif Iqbal, and Rhuhel Ahmed, "Detention in Afghanistan and Guantánamo Bay," Center for Constitutional Rights, July 26, 2004, http://ccrjustice.org/files/report_tiptonThree.pdf. James Yee, *For God and Country: Faith and Patriotism under Fire* (New York: Public Affairs, 2005).

37. Chris Mackey and Greg Miller, *Interrogator's War: Inside the Secret War on Al Qaeda* (Boston: Little, Brown, 2004), 3–6.

38. Moazzam Begg with Victoria Brittain, *Enemy Combatant: My Imprisonment at Guantánamo, Bagram, and Kandahar* (New York: New Press, 2007). Murat Kurnaz, *Five Years of My Life: An Innocent Man in Guantánamo,* reprint ed. (New York: St. Martin's Press, 2009).

39. Rasul, Iqbal, and Ahmed, "Detention in Afghanistan and Guantánamo Bay."

40. With six broken ribs, he was left hanging from wrists shackled behind his back. The cause of death was asphyxiation, "as in a crucifixion," according to Dr. Michael Baden, chief forensic pathologist for the New York state police. As a CIA official, Swanner avoided penalty or prosecution. See Jane Mayer, "A Deadly Interrogation," *New Yorker,* November 15, 2005.

41. Erik Saar and Viveca Novak, *Inside the Wire: A Military Intelligence Soldier's Eyewitness Account of Life at Guantánamo* (New York: Penguin, 2005), 46.

42. "Torture isolates and privatizes." "The world of the man or woman in bad pain is a world without relationships or engagements, a world without an exterior. It is a world reduced to a point, a world that makes no sense and in which the human soul finds no home and no response." Luban, "Liberalism, Torture," 39.

43. For other examples of mass numbers assembled for torture, see chapter 2, as well as discussion of torture in Algiers. For more on the ACLU work for photographic evidence, see chapter 4, as well as Eliza Relman, "A Picture of Torture Is Worth a Thousand Reports," ACLU National Security Project blog, April 28, 2015, https://www.aclu.org/blog/national-security/torture/picture-torture-worth-thousand-reports?redirect=blog/speak-freely/picture-torture-worth-thousand-reports.

44. Psychiatrist and torture survivor Arestivo's work is also discussed in the introduction. Arestivo, "Torture," 7–19 at 13.

45. Martha K. Huggins, Mika Haritos-Fatouros, and Philip G. Zimbardo, *Violence Workers: Police Torturers and Murderers Reconstruct Brazilian Atrocities* (Berkeley: University of California Press, 2002). Eric Fair, *Consequence: A Memoir* (New York: Holt, 2016). Tony Lagouranis with Allen Mikaelian, *Fear Up Harsh: An Army Interrogator's Dark Journey through Iraq* (New York: New American Library, 2007).

46. Yee, *For God and Country*.

47. Schmitt and Marshall, "In Secret Unit's 'Black Room.'"

48. See Danielle Celermajer, *The Prevention of Torture: An Ecological Approach* (Cambridge: Cambridge University Press, 2018), especially chaps. 3 and 4.

49. Tizon, "Assessing the Treatment of Torture," 80; Tizon is a sociologist and torture survivor. Laurence Ralph, *The Torture Letters: Reckoning with Police Violence* (Chicago: University of Chicago Press, 2020). John Conroy, *Unspeakable Acts, Ordinary People: Dynamics of Torture* (New York: Knopf, 2000). Flint Taylor, *The Torture Machine: Racism and Police Violence in Chicago* (Chicago: Haymarket, 2020).

50. Ervin Staub, "Torture: Psychological and Cultural Origins," in *The Politics of Pain: Torturers and Their Masters,* ed. Ronald Crelinsten and Alex P. Schmid (San Francisco: Westview, 1995), 99–112.

51. "How many IRFings did you do today?" Yee, *For God and Country,* 71–73.

52. "Acts that harm others, without restraining forces, bring about changes in perpetrators, other members of the group and the whole system that make further and more harmful acts probable. In the course of this evolution, the personality of individuals, social norms, institutions and culture change in ways that make greater violence easier. . . . the usual moral principles and values that prohibit violence and protect people from being harmed become inapplicable to the victims." Ervin Staub, "The Roots of Evil: Social Conditions, Culture, Personality and Basic Human Needs," *Personality and Social Psychology Review* 3, no. 3 (1999): 179–92 at 182–83.

53. Hazel Carby, "A Strange and Bitter Crop: The Spectacle of Torture," OpenDemocracy, October 11, 2004, http://www.opendemocracy.net/media-abu_ghraib/

article_2149.jsp. Allen Feldman, "Abu Ghraib: Ceremonies of Nostalgia," Open-Democracy, October 18, 2004, http://www.opendemocracy.net/media-abu_ghraib/article_2163.jsp. Susan Sontag, "Regarding the Torture of Others," *New York Times Magazine,* May 23, 2004, https://www.nytimes.com/. See also Joanna Bourke, "Sexy Snaps," *Index on Censorship* 1 (2005): 39–45.

54. See the Introduction, also Jared Sexton and Elizabeth Lee, "Figuring the Prison: Prerequisites of Torture at Abu Ghraib," *Antipode* 38, no. 5 (2006): 1009, https://doi.org/10.1111/j.1467-8330.2006.00490.x. "The chain of racialized torture that spanned slavery, lynching, and police whippings remains unbroken in the brutalization of black suspects and inmates routinely carried out in today's criminal justice system." Dorothy Roberts, "Torture and the Biopolitics of Race," *University of Miami Law Review* 62 (2008): 237.

55. See Celermajer, *Prevention of Torture,* for argument and bibliography; and Rebecca Gordon, *Mainstreaming Torture: Ethical Approaches in the Post-9/11 United States* (Oxford: Oxford University Press, 2014), especially 123–48.

56. On Enlightenment suffering: Luc Boltanski, *Distant Suffering: Media, Morality, and Politics* (Cambridge: Cambridge University Press, 1999). On symmetrical warfare in Clausewitz and the philosophical tradition on violence since: Idelber Avelar, *The Letter of Violence: Essays on Narrative, Ethics and Politics* (New York: Palgrave Macmillan, 2004), 1–23. For critiques of individualizing analyses of torture in particular, and the antistructural tendency of the legal imagination: Celermajer, *Prevention of Torture;* Mahmood Mamdani, *When Victims Become Killers: Colonialism, Nativism and Genocide in Rwanda* (Princeton, N.J.: Princeton University Press, 2002); Susan Marks, "Human Rights and Root Causes," *Modern Law Review* 74, no. 1 (2011): 57–78.

57. Greenberg, *Torture Debate.* Kenneth Roth and Minky Worden, eds., *Torture: Does It Make Us Safer? Is It Ever Okay?* (New York: New Press, 2005). Levinson, *Torture: A Collection, Revised* (2006). Schulz, *Phenomenon of Torture.* Anderson and Nussbaum, *Confronting Torture.*

58. Walter Pincus, "Silence of Four Terror Probe Suspects Poses Dilemma for FBI," *Washington Post,* October 21, 2001, https://www.washingtonpost.com/.

59. Lagouranis, *Fear Up Harsh,* 95.

60. This is not a fringe view among interrogation practitioners. See Intelligence Science Board, "Educing Information: Interrogation: Science and Art. Phase 1 Report" (Washington, D.C.: National Defense Intelligence College Press, 2006), https://fas.org/irp/dni/educing.pdf. Also see Mackey and Miller, *Interrogator's War;* and discussion by Michael Gelles of the Navy Criminal Investigative Service in Charlie Savage, "Split Seen on Interrogation Techniques: Navy Official Says Many Back Stance against Coercion," *Boston Globe,* March 31, 2005, https://www.bostonglobe.com/. The CIA's KUBARK counterintelligence interrogation manual says pain is counterproductive in interrogation, and FBI specialists hold that techniques

other than pain, so-called abuse, and coercion are likewise "ineffective, counterproductive and unlikely to produce reliable information" (*Boston Globe,* February 25, 2005, https://www.bostonglobe.com/). See also Paisley Dodds, "FBI Letter Alleged Abuse," *Boston Globe,* December 7, 2004, https://www.bostonglobe.com/.

61. Idelber Avelar, "Five Theses on Torture," *Journal of Latin American Cultural Studies* 10, no. 3 (2001): 253–71, https://doi.org/10.1080/13569320120090045.

62. John T. Parry, *Understanding Torture, Law, Violence, and Political Identity* (Ann Arbor: University of Michigan Press, 2010), 12. Jinee Lokaneeta, *Transnational Torture: Law, Violence and Power in the United States and India* (New York: New York University Press, 2011), 30.

63. Marnia Lazreg, *Torture and the Twilight of Empire: From Algiers to Baghdad* (Princeton, N.J.: Princeton University Press, 2007), 7.

4. Technique

1. The three persons quoted in epigraphs for this chapter appear, respectively, in the following three articles. Scott Shane and Mark Mazetti, "Tapes by CIA Lived and Died to Save Image," *New York Times,* December 30, 2007, https://www.nytimes.com/. Michael Mechanic, "Voluntary Confinement," *Mother Jones,* March 10, 2008, https://www.motherjones.com/news/feature/2008/03/voluntary-confinement.html. Victor Navasky, "Breaking the Barrier," *Columbia Journalism Review,* June 11, 2005, excerpt from Navasky's memoir, available at https://www.alternet.org/2005/06/breaking_the_barrier/ (accessed July 20, 2021). The Department of Defense authorized fifteen harsh techniques for use at Guantánamo Bay detention center in 2002. *Time* magazine revealed Mohammed al-Qahtani had been one of the first subjected to freezing temperatures, sexually explicit contact and images, and other degradations to the point he had begun talking to himself and pulling out his own hair. In a series of DOJ Office of Legal Counsel memos later produced for the CIA across 2004 to 2005, the waterboard was among thirteen other painful techniques "legally" permitted and kept secret until 2007. In this drowning torture, water is forced over and into the mouths and noses of captives. The practice had been prosecuted successfully as torture by the United States across the twentieth century. International Committee on the Red Cross reports and other documentation revealed approvals that subjected detainees to sleep deprivation, cramped confinement, wall slamming, slapping, "rectal feeding," and eight other "enhanced techniques of interrogation." A classified report by the CIA inspector general issued in 2004 was harshly critical of the CIA program, noting unauthorized techniques were being used, including guns, drills, threats, smoke, extreme cold, stress positions, "stiff brush and shackles," mock executions, and "hard takedown." In another arena, the Supreme Court in 2004 and 2006 delivered key decisions regarding the status of prisoners held at Guantánamo Bay, Cuba. These triggered

new legislation and executive orders to maintain executive control over detainee status and treatment in response. Meanwhile, court cases brought against the government and private contractors sought redress for torture. On the first fifteen techniques: Philippe Sands, *Torture Team: Rumsfeld's Memo and the Betrayal of American Values* (New York: Palgrave Macmillan, 2008), 3–6. On Al-Qahtani: Adam Zagorin and Michael Duffy, "Inside the Interrogation of Detainee 063," *Time,* June 15, 2005, https://time.com/. On rectal feeding: Dominic Rushe et al., "Rectal Rehydration and Waterboarding: The CIA Torture Report's Grisliest Findings," *Guardian,* December 9, 2014, https://www.theguardian.com/. Central Intelligence Agency Inspector General, "Counterterrorism Detention and Interrogation Activities," submitted by John Helgerson, 2004. Two declassified versions can be found at "What Were They Hiding? A Side-by-Side Comparison of the Bush and Obama Versions of the CIA Inspector General's Report on Torture," National Security Archive, George Washington University, https://nsarchive2.gwu.edu/torture_archive/comparison.htm. International Committee of the Red Cross, "Report on the Treatment of Fourteen 'High Value Detainees' in CIA Custody," February 14, 2007, http://www.nybooks.com/media/doc/2010/04/22/icrc-report.pdf.

2. Scott Shane, David Johnston, and James Risen, "Secret U.S. Endorsement of Severe Interrogations," *New York Times,* October 4, 2007, https://www.nytimes.com/.

3. Rajiv Chandrasekaran and Peter Finn, "U.S. Behind Secret Transfer of Terror Suspects," *Washington Post,* March 11, 2002, https://www.washingtonpost.com/.

4. Amrit Singh, "Globalizing Torture: CIA Secret Detention and Extraordinary Rendition," Open Society Justice Initiative, February 2013, https://www.justiceinitiative.org/publications/globalizing-torture-cia-secret-detention-and-extraordinary-rendition. Doug Jehl and David Johnston, "Rule Change Lets CIA Freely Send Suspects Abroad to Jails," *New York Times,* March 6, 2005, https://www.nytimes.com/. Stephen Grey, *Ghost Plane: The True Story of the CIA Rendition and Torture Program* (New York: St. Martin's Press, 2006), 39. Singh's investigation reports at least 136 individual rendition subjects have been identified to date, and others may still be classified. CIA officials, speaking anonymously in 2005, told journalists of a total of 100 to 150 "transfers." Investigative journalist Stephen Grey said his own research "would suggest total numbers ran into many, many hundreds," based on his own case files, a study of flight logs and itineraries for jets contracted to the CIA, and official numbers given to the press on different regions by Iranian intelligence, the Egyptian prime minister, and an expert on Sudan. Hoffman cites the European parliament count of 1,245 CIA flights during this period. Subjects were seized from locations in the United States and Europe as well as Middle East and Arab nations, and they were delivered incommunicado by off-the-books flights to countries with records well known to the U.S. State Department for torture, such as Egypt, Syria, Morocco, and Afghanistan. Singh's report identified twenty-five

governments as U.S. rendition partners in Europe, with fourteen in Asia and thirteen in Africa. Karen Hoffman, "Redress for 'Some Folks': Pursuing Justice for Victims of Torture through Traditional Grounds of Jurisdiction," *Georgia Journal of International and Comparative Law* 46 (2017): 97–128 at 100. See also Ian Cobain, "CIA Rendition Report Author Believes U.K. Could Face the Human Rights Court," *Guardian,* February 5, 2013, https://www.theguardian.com/.

5. That 1902 debate clearly acknowledged many diverse functions for torture in the United States and abroad, central among them white racial dominance.

6. Del Rosso's study refers to the rhetorical attempt to draw distinctions between "liberal and illiberal" violence. I am situating that distinction within a pattern of colonial and neocolonial thought on torture. Jared del Rosso, *Talking about Torture: How Political Discourse Shapes the Debate* (New York: Columbia University Press, 2015).

7. Del Rosso concludes that a common moral fabric that privileges instrumentality, rationality, and proportionality of violence marks congressional hearings of 2007 and 2008. Del Rosso, *Talking about Torture,* 145, 153–58.

8. Chris Mackey and Greg Miller, *The Interrogators* (Boston: Little, Brown, 2004), 428.

9. Michael Taussig, *Shamanism, Colonialism, and the Wild Man* (Chicago: University of Chicago Press, 1987), 121, 130–32.

10. Ann Laura Stoler, *Along the Archival Grain: Epistemic Anxiety and Colonial Common Sense* (Princeton, N.J.: Princeton University Press, 2009), 231.

11. Stoler, *Along the Archival Grain,* 253, 256, 255.

12. Stoler, *Along the Archival Grain,* 231.

13. Darius Rejali, *Torture and Democracy* (Princeton, N.J.: Princeton University Press, 2007), 31. Darius Rejali, "Modern Torture as a Civic Marker: Solving a Global Anxiety with a New Political Technology," *Journal of Human Rights* 2, no. 2 (2003): 153–71 at 157–59, https://doi.org/10.1080/1475483032000078152. Idelber Avelar, "Five Theses on Torture," *Journal of Latin American Cultural Studies* 10, no. 3 (2001): 261, https://doi.org/10.1080/13569320120090045.

14. Interview with Kayla Williams in *Interrogating // Torture,* dir. Jeff Stephens and Jay Boekelhide (Pushback Partners, documentary in production).

15. Congressional inquiries and media outrage circulated these events as they were captured primarily in photos curated for public release. Major General Antonio M. Taguba, *U.S. Army Report 15-6 of Abuse of Prisoners in Iraq,* December 2004, available at the Torture Database, https://www.thetorturedatabase.org/. The Taguba Report took the testimony of several men and women who witnessed or experienced rape. These were obtained by the *Washington Post* in 2004 and published as "Abu Ghraib: Male Rape Witness Statement from Taguba Report." See also Anthony R. Jones and George R. Fay, *Investigation of Intelligence Activities at Abu Ghraib* (Washington, D.C.: U.S. Army Public Affairs, August 23, 2004). Seymour

Hersh noted the existence of videotapes of boys being raped at Abu Ghraib; it is available as "Seymour Hersh's ACLU Keynote Speech Transcribed," July 14, 2004, http://www.informationclearinghouse.info/article6492.htm.

16. Erik Saar and Viveca Novak, *Inside the Wire: A Military Intelligence Soldier's Eyewitness Account of Life at Guantánamo* (New York: Penguin, 2005), 247. At Guantánamo, these group "disciplinary" beatings resulted in broken bones and traumatic brain injury. Walter Gilberti, "Former U.S. Soldier Speaks on Near-Deadly Beating at Guantánamo," World Socialist, June 24, 2004, https://www.wsws.org/en/articles/2004/06/guan-j24.html. Bruce Simpson, "The Beating of Lieutenant Sean Baker at Guantánamo Bay, Cuba: A Report of Findings and a Request for Relief," Center for the Study of Human Rights, University of California–Davis, December 4, 2004, http://humanrights.ucdavis.edu/projects/the-Guantánamo-testimonials-project/testimonies/testimonies-of-military-guards/the-beating-of-specialist-sean-baker-in-Guantánamo-bay-cuba.

17. Saar and Novak, *Inside the Wire*, 46.

18. Quoted in Mark Moyar, *Phoenix and the Birds of Prey: Counterinsurgency and Counterterrorism in Vietnam* (Lincoln: University of Nebraska Press, 2007), 91. Welcome trained and advised provincial reconnaissance units of South Vietnamese special forces in Binh Thuan province during 1968–69. CORDS and Phoenix destroyed homes, farms, and livelihoods to relocate hundreds of thousands, and killed 26,369 prisoners by 1972. Alfred McCoy, *A Question of Torture: CIA Interrogation from the Cold War to the War on Terror* (New York: Holt, 2006), 68, 225n29. This count falls below the tally reported by Vietnam's government.

19. Welcome omitted many extremities he might have named. Turse has documented that "abuse" unto death of this kind and worse was operational strategy in Vietnam. Nick Turse, *Kill Anything That Moves: The Real American War in Vietnam* (New York: Metropolitan, 2013).

20. Most examples in this chapter would rank as "interpretive denial" in Cohen's typology of denial. They accept the raw facts but quibble over their meaning. Stanley Cohen, *States of Denial: Knowing about Atrocities and Suffering* (Cambridge: Polity, 2001), 7–20.

21. Eliza Relman, "A Picture of Torture Is Worth a Thousand Reports," ACLU National Security Project blog, April 28, 2015, https://www.aclu.org/blog/national-security/torture/picture-torture-worth-thousand-reports?redirect=blog/speak-freely/picture-torture-worth-thousand-reports.

22. It was renamed the Protected National Security Documents Act. Jeff Zeleny and Thom Shanker, "Obama Moves to Bar Release of Detainee Abuse Photos," *New York Times*, May 14, 2009, https://www.nytimes.com/. Bill Mears, "Pentagon Bars Release of Photos Allegedly Showing Detainee Abuse," CNN, November 15, 2009, https://www.cnn.com/.

23. Justin Worland, "Pentagon Releases Detainee Abuse Photos after ACLU Lawsuit," *Time,* February 5, 2016, https://time.com/.

24. Lila Rajiva, *The Language of Empire: Abu Ghraib and the American Media* (New York: Monthly Review Press, 2005).

25. "There was . . . sadism that was certainly not authorized. It was kind of 'Animal House' on the night shift." "Report: Abu Ghraib Was 'Animal House' at Night," CNN, August 25, 2004, http://www.cnn.com/.

26. Saar and Novak, *Inside the Wire,* 247.

27. The U.N. Convention defines torture as "severe pain and suffering, mental or physical." But as already stated, torture marks the subject as an outcast or threat; the subject's experience is rarely sought and typically discounted. Even where perpetrator conduct may be visible, the latter must be "extreme and outrageous" and "specifically intended." Specific intent is "the intent to accomplish the precise criminal act that one is later charged with." Bryan A. Garner, ed., *Black's Law Dictionary,* 7th ed. (St. Paul, Minn.: West, 1999), 814. In the Bush OLC memos, the test for specific intention was posed this way: Could "adequately trained interrogators" be "expected to cause" or "reasonably be considered" to either "'consciously desire' or 'have knowledge or notice' that this act 'would likely have resulted in the proscribed outcome'?" See David Cole, ed., *The Torture Memos: Rationalizing the Unthinkable* (New York: New Press, 2009), 185, 150. The first is Steven Bradbury for John Rizzo, May 10, 2005: "Application of 18 U.S.C. 2340–2340A to Certain Techniques that May Be Used in the Interrogation of a High Value al Qaeda Detainee." The second is Daniel Levin for James B. Comey, December 30, 2004, "Legal Standards Applicable under 18 U.S.C. 2340–2340A."

28. David Luban, *Torture, Power, and Law* (Cambridge: Cambridge University Press, 2014), 281.

29. Eric Fair, *Consequence: A Memoir* (New York: Holt, 2016). Fair was a contract interrogator for CACI stationed at Abu Ghraib prison and Fallujah.

30. Josh White, "Documents Tell of Brutal Improvisation by GIs; Interrogated General's Sleeping-Bag Death, CIA's Use of a Secret Iraqi Squad Are among Details," *Washington Post,* August 3, 2005, https://www.washingtonpost.com/.

31. Evan Wallach, "Drop by Drop: Forgetting the History of Water Torture in U.S. Courts," *Columbia Journal of Transnational Law* 45, no. 2 (2007): 468–506. Democracy Now!, "Torture and Democracy," March 12, 2008, https://www.democracynow.org/.

32. Nance, "Waterboarding Is Torture . . . Period."

33. Nance, "Waterboarding Is Torture . . . Period," emphasis added.

34. Guy Debord, *Society of the Spectacle* (1967; reprint, New York: Zone Books, 1995).

35. Madelane Hron, "Torture Goes Pop!," *Peace Review* 20, no. 1 (2008): 22–30.

36. Mechanic, "Voluntary Confinement."

37. Hron, "Torture Goes Pop!," cites Parents Television Council data.

38. Sands, *Torture Team*, 62. See also Dahlia Lithwick, "The Bauer of Suggestion," *Slate*, July 26, 2008, https://slate.com/.

39. Heritage Foundation Conference, "*24* and America's Image in Fighting Terrorism: Fact, Fiction, or Does It Matter?," June 24, 2006, http://www.heritage.org/events/2006/06/24. The event featured Michael Chertoff, the secretary of Homeland Security; show cocreators Joel Surnow and Robert Cochran; actors; and conservative talk show phenomenon Rush Limbaugh. Also present were James Carafano, terrorism scholar for the Heritage Foundation, and David Heyman, terrorism scholar for the Center for Strategic Studies.

40. Intelligence Science Board, "Educing Information: Interrogation: Science and Art. Phase 1 Report" (Washington, D.C.: National Defense Intelligence College Press, 2006), https://fas.org/irp/dni/educing.pdf.

41. Human Rights First, "*Criminal Minds* Wins Human Rights Award for Portrayal of Interrogation," press release, October 15, 2007, https://humanrightsfirst.org/library/criminal-minds-wins-human-rights-award-for-portrayal-of-interrogation/.

42. One Prime Time Torture nominee shows rapport works better than torture to elicit information, yet breathes life into the ticking time bomb scenario, that stock figure of torture discourse decried by many seasoned interrogators as pure fantasy. In the winning episode of *Criminal Minds*, a man is tortured by one man, then treated kindly by the next, the show's hero. All the while, the subject suffers in timeless, incommunicado detention. The move from bad jailer to good and back, injury to care and back, is a classic rhythm of torture practice.

43. Elizabeth Swanson Goldberg, *Beyond Terror: Gender, Narrative, Human Rights* (New Brunswick, N.J.: Rutgers University Press, 2007), 51.

44. See Hron, "Torture Goes Pop!," 28; and Darius Rejali, "Torture Makes the Man," in *On Torture,* ed. Thomas C. Hilde (Baltimore, Md.: Johns Hopkins University Press, 2008), 165–83.

45. Jason Miller, "FBI Turns Troubled into Triumph with Sentinel System," Federal News Radio, August 1, 2012, https://federalnewsnetwork.com/ask-the-cio/2012/08/fbi-turns-troubled-into-triumph-with-sentinel-system/. Dan Eggan and Griff Witte, "The FBI's Upgrade that Wasn't: $170 Million Bought an Unusable Computer System," *Washington Post,* August 18, 2006, https://www.washingtonpost.com/.

46. See, e.g., the finale of *Missing* (dir. Costa-Gavras, 1982) and the media scene in *Battle of Algiers* (dir. Gillo Pontecorvo, 1966).

47. Stars included Jake Gyllenhaal, Reese Witherspoon, Alan Arkin, and Meryl Streep.

48. The citizen-wife's quest for justice collapses under the burden of pregnancy and rejection. In a heavy-handed visual metaphor, she buckles in fecund profile directly beneath the silhouette of the Capitol dome.

49. *Extraordinary Rendition,* in contrast to *Rendition,* devotes attention to the impact of torture on the survivor's return to everyday life, mental health, and marriage.

50. Monia Mazigh, *Hope and Despair: My Struggle to Free My Husband, Maher Arar* (Toronto: McClelland and Stewart, 2008).

51. Cole, introduction to *Torture Memos,* 4–35. See also Luban, *Torture, Power, and Law,* 261.

52. See discussion in the Introduction and chapter 2. The 2002 definition was written by John Yoo and signed by Jay Bybee for Alberto Gonzalez; see "Standards of Conduct for Interrogation under 18 U.S.C. 2340–2340A," in Cole, *Torture Memos,* 41–105. A second memo from that year is Bybee for Rizzo, August 1, 2002, "Interrogation of al Qaeda Operative," in Cole, *Torture Memos,* 107–27.

53. Yoo notes the revision was cosmetic: "Yeah, so when they rewrote the memo, they made the lines less clear. They deleted that sentence. But it's not all that different in what it actually says and what it actually allows." In Yoo, "Exclusive."

54. "Consideration [of the power to order torture in this memo] . . . would be inconsistent with the President's unequivocal directive that United States personnel not engage in torture." Levin for Comey, December 30, 2004, "Legal Standards," in Cole, *Torture Memos,* 130.

55. Cohen, in *States of Denial,* refers to this as magical legalism: we do not torture; therefore, what we do is not torture. On colonial strategies, see Stoler, *Along the Archival Grain.*

56. During the years the memos were secret, a changing team of lawyers continued evasive revision, attempting to keep techniques authorized despite leaks, new legislation to prohibit torture, and internal dissent. Jack Goldsmith, *The Terror Presidency: Law and Judgment Inside the Bush Administration,* reprint ed. (New York: Norton, 2009).

57. Cole, *Torture Memos,* 167, 184, 184.

58. Cole, *Torture Memos,* 184, 184, 186.

59. Cole, *Torture Memos,* 186, 185.

60. Cole, *Torture Memos,* 187.

61. These many sleepless hours "must be" followed by eight hours' sleep before beginning again.

62. Cole, *Torture Memos,* 187.

63. Cole, *Torture Memos,* all 117.

64. Cole, *Torture Memos,* 109.

65. Central Intelligence Agency Inspector General, "Counterterrorism Detention and Interrogation Activities." The inspector general found no evidence that "enhanced interrogation techniques," including the waterboard, aided in the search for intelligence.

66. Cole, *Torture Memos,* 191n51, emphasis added. The overzealous "psychologist/interrogators" were the subject of a landmark case pressed by survivors; Stephanie Athey, "Psychology, Torture, Networks: Or, Structure as the Subject of Human Rights," in *Writing beyond the State: Post-sovereign Approaches to Human Rights in Literary Studies,* ed. Alexandra S. Moore and Samantha Pinto (London: Palgrave Macmillan, 2020), 175–98.
67. Cole, *Torture Memos,* 191.
68. Cole, *Torture Memos,* 192.
69. Cole, *Torture Memos,* 193.
70. Cole, *Torture Memos,* 194n56.
71. Cole, *Torture Memos,* 194.
72. Cole, *Torture Memos,* 193.
73. "An application of water may not last for more than 40 seconds." Cole, *Torture Memos,* 168. In addition, there may be "no more than two 'sessions'" strapped to the board in a twenty-four-hour period for a total of four hours per day. Waterboarding can take place "no more than five days" during any thirty-day period (170, 193). The math here indicates that during those four hours each day, up to twelve minutes can be devoted to blocking the prisoner's airway with water. The memo allows twenty-four applications that last up to ten seconds and another twelve applications that last up to forty seconds. In other words, the prisoner spends four hours of the day restrained and anticipating drowning, and that prisoner can be choked with water thirty-two times during that period. This can continue for five days.
74. Cole, *Torture Memos,* 193n17.
75. Military trainees submit to the technique as a professional rite of passage, not as captives. Within this anomaly lurks a brief mention of testimony by the executive director for the Center for Victims of Torture, Douglas Johnson, who appeared in 2004 before the Senate Judiciary Committee.
76. Cole, *Torture Memos,* 236.
77. Senate Select Committee on Intelligence, *The Senate Intelligence Committee Report on Torture: Committee Study of the Central Intelligence Agency's Detention and Interrogation Program* (Brooklyn: Melville House, 2014). The top finding: "The CIA's use of its enhanced interrogation techniques was not an effective means of acquiring intelligence or gaining cooperation from detainees." According to CIA records, seven of thirty-nine detainees known to have been subjected to what the CIA termed "enhanced interrogation techniques" produced no intelligence. The committee examined the twenty most frequent and prominently cited examples of success and determined they were wrong in fundamental respects.
78. A five-year ethics review of this work made a formal finding of misconduct. That was laid aside in short order by DOJ superior David Margolis, who said the lawyers were guilty only of "poor judgment." See Luban, *Torture, Power, and Law,*

285. "Torture Lawyers," editorial, *New York Times,* February 25, 2010, https://www.nytimes.com/; Eric Lichtblau and Scott Shane, "Report Faults 2 Authors of Bush Terror Memos," *New York Times,* February 20, 2010, https://www.nytimes.com/.
    79. Shane, Johnston, and Risen, "Secret U.S. Endorsement."
    80. David Stout and Sheryl Gay Stolberg, "Schumer and Feinstein Back Mukasey," *New York Times,* November 2, 2007, https://www.nytimes.com/.
    81. Information on survivor experience is not in short supply. A 2016 count by Survivors of Torture International suggested the number of torture survivors living in the United States could be as high as 1.5 million. Survivors of Torture International, January 22, 2016, https://notorture.org/20160122numberof_refugee_torture_survivorsrising/. That number excludes, of course, those tortured as everyday practice in settings like prison, immigrant detention, and juvenile justice, as well as those tortured by policing. Treatment centers around the world have compiled a wealth of qualitative and quantitative data on all manner of torture for decades, including its long- and short-term effects; its conditions, techniques, and sequelae; and the regional and political contexts that give these meaning.
    82. See Clyde Haberman, "Bearing Witness to Torture," *New York Times,* October 30, 2007, https://www.nytimes.com/; "McCain Rebukes Giuliani on Waterboarding Remark," *New York Times,* October 26, 2007, https://www.nytimes.com/; Dana Milbank, "Logic Tortured," *Washington Post,* November 1, 2007, https://www.washingtonpost.com/; Marc Santora, "McCain's Stance on Torture becomes Riveting Issue in Campaign," *New York Times,* November 16, 2007, https://www.nytimes.com/. There is also one op-ed (Richard Cohen, "Rudy's Torture Talk," *Washington Post,* November 6, 2007, https://www.washingtonpost.com/) and one letter to the editor (by Larry Cox, *New York Times,* November 2, 2007, https://www.nytimes.com/). Dana Milbank's *Washington Post* story covered a press event organized by Physicians for Human Rights, Human Rights First, and Open Society Justice Initiative featuring testimony by survivors of water torture as well as historical background on waterboarding. Henri Alleg spoke of his own torture by the French in Algeria, and Vann Nath described his experience at the Khmer Rouge torture camp Tuol Sleng. Both addressed the meeting by telephone. Haberman's *New York Times* article "Bearing Witness to Torture" discusses the experiences of those who suffered water torture and received treatment for trauma at the Bellevue/NYU Program for Survivors of Torture.
    83. "The rag was soaked rapidly. Water flowed everywhere: in my mouth, in my nose, all over my face. But for a while I could still breathe in some small gulps of air. I tried, by contracting my throat, to take in as little water as possible and to resist suffocation by keeping air in my lungs for as long as I could. But I couldn't hold on for more than a few moments. I had the impression of drowning, and a terrible agony, that of death itself, took possession of me. In spite of myself, all the muscles of my body struggled uselessly to save me from suffocation." Alleg, quoted

in Leonard Doyle, "Waterboarding Is Torture, I Did It Myself, Says U.S. Advisor," *Independent,* November 1, 2007, https://www.independent.co.uk/. Nath appeared months later in a CNN story unrelated to the Mukasey hearings: "Yes, it is severe torture. We could try it and see how we would react if we are choking under water for just two minutes. It is very serious." Vann Nath quoted in Christiane Amanpour, "Survivor Recalls Horrors of Cambodian Genocide," CNN, April 7, 2008, http://www.cnn.com/.

84. Shane, Johnston, and Risen, "Secret U.S. Endorsement." On three detainees: Scott Shane, "Mukasey Calls Harsh Interrogation 'Repugnant,'" *New York Times,* October 31, 2007, https://www.nytimes.com/.

85. Drowning tortures were reported from Afghanistan, the shower block of Abu Ghraib in Iraq, and again after Abu Ghraib in Mosul and at Al-Asad air base. On Afghanistan: Murat Kurnaz, *Five Years of My Life: An Innocent Man in Guantánamo,* reprint ed. (New York: St. Martin's Press, 2009). On Iraq: Tony Lagouranis with Allen Mikaelian, *Fear Up Harsh: An Army Interrogator's Dark Journey through Iraq* (New York: New American Library, 2007). Lagouranis quoted in "Torture Nation," *Daily Dish,* February 13, 2007, https://dish.andrewsullivan.com/2007/02/13/torture_nation/. The Schlesinger report held that as specific personnel, companies, and special forces units moved across these theaters, they brought with them practical experience, example lists, and "word" of forms of coercion taking place elsewhere. These methods "migrated" across all three theaters. Department of Defense, *Final Report of the Independent Panel to Review DoD Detention Operations,* chairman James R. Schlesinger, August 2004, https://archive.org/details/DTIC_ADA428743, 9, 12, 14, 17, 86.

86. Del Rosso, *Talking about Torture,* 151.

87. The "ultimate": Shane, Johnston, and Risen, "Secret U.S. Endorsement." The lawyers describe the technique as "the most serious" and "most substantial" and the panic induced as "significant." Cole, *Torture Memos,* 191–92.

88. Shane and Mazetti, "Tapes by CIA Lived and Died to Save Image."

89. Brian Stelter, "How '07 ABC Interview Tilted a Torture Debate," *New York Times,* April 28, 2009, https://www.nytimes.com/. For an ABC interview conducted December 10, 2007, Kiriakou was introduced as a former CIA agent who participated in the capture of terrorist suspect Abu Zubaydah in Pakistan in 2002, "CIA—Abu Zubaydah," transcript of interview with John Kiriakou by correspondent Brian Ross, https://abcnews.go.com/images/Blotter/brianross_kiriakou_transcript1_blotter071210.pdf. See also "Brian Ross Interviews John Kiriakou about Waterboarding Abu Zubaydah," parts 1–3, on YouTube (https://www.youtube.com/).

90. Scott Shane, "2 Suspects Waterboarded 266 Times," *New York Times,* April 21, 2009, https://www.nytimes.com/. In April 2009, the newly declassified Justice Department memos confirmed the CIA had waterboarded Abu Zubaydah "at least

83 times" in August 2002 and Khalid Sheikh Mohammed 183 times in March 2003, using "greater volumes of water than permitted."

91. Scott Horton, "Kiriakou Recants," in "No Comment," *Harper's,* January 27, 2010, https://harpers.org/, citing Jeff Stein, *Foreign Policy,* January 2010, https://foreignpolicy.com/author/jeff-stein/.

92. Current TV Special Report, "Waterboard Demonstration," YouTube, https://youtu.be/y0SnqfFXc1k. See also "Getting Waterboarded," posted as Current TV, October 31, 2007, archived via the Wayback Machine (https://web.archive.org/) using the URL http://current.com/items/76347282_getting_water boarded. The footage of Larsen's waterboarding is all the more bizarre because it runs split screen against Larsen interviewing Alan Dershowitz, Mike Ritz (a former interrogator), and Juliette Kayyem of the Kennedy School about the torture debate.

93. This aired November 1, 2007. Transcript of *Special Report with Brit Hume,* Fox News, November 2, 2007, https://www.foxnews.com/.

94. "I wanted to prove it wasn't torture. They cut off our heads, we put water on their face. . . . I got voted to do this but I really thought, 'I'm going to laugh this off. . . . It is way worse than I thought it would be, and that's no joke. It is such an odd feeling to have water poured down your nose with your head back. . . . It was instantaneous . . . and I don't want to say this: absolutely torture." Erich "Mancow" Muller, "Mancow Waterboarded, Admits It's Torture," NBC Chicago, May 22, 2009, https://www.nbcchicago.com/.

95. "I held my breath for a while and then had to exhale and—as you might expect—inhale in turn. The inhalation brought the damp cloths tight against my nostrils, as if a huge, wet paw had been suddenly and annihilatingly clamped over my face. Unable to determine whether I was breathing in or out and flooded more with sheer panic than with mere water, I triggered the pre-arranged signal and felt the unbelievable relief of being pulled upright and having the soaking and stifling layers pulled off me. I find I don't want to tell you how little time I lasted. . . . I apply the Abraham Lincoln test for moral casuistry: If slavery is not wrong, nothing is wrong. Well, then, if waterboarding does not constitute torture, then there is no such thing as torture." Christopher Hitchens, "Believe Me, It's Torture," *Vanity Fair,* July 2, 2008, https://www.vanityfair.com/.

96. Marcus Baram, "Jesse Ventura Challenges Hannity on Waterboarding," *Huffington Post,* June 22, 2009, https://www.huffpost.com/.

97. Amnesty International Unsubscribe-Me campaign director MacNiece said she wants viewers to feel empowered and outraged. Amnesty International U.K., "CIA Interrogation Technique: Unsubscribe Campaign—Waiting for the Guards," YouTube, October 11, 2007, https://www.youtube.com/watch?v=TZ1NYizv2sw. Amnesty International, "The Stuff of Life," now entitled "Amnesty International: Waterboarding," YouTube video, April 25, 2008, https://www.youtube.com/watch?v=aJQCLzegDOo.

98. Ariel Kaminer, "Coney Island Sideshow Has Guantánamo Theme," *New York Times,* August 5, 2008, https://www.nytimes.com/.
99. Navasky, "Breaking the Barrier."
100. "The View from the Waterboard: A Former Justice Lawyer Did His Homework—And Raised a Red Flag," *Washington Post,* November 6, 2007, https://www.washingtonpost.com/. Scott Shane, "A Firsthand Experience before Decision on Torture," *New York Times,* November 7, 2007, https://www.nytimes.com/.
101. Arar had no ties to Syria. He emigrated with his family to Canada at age seventeen.
102. Luban, *Torture, Power, and Law,* 277. Mr. Arar's lawyers argued that he could prove his case without privileged information and that procedural safeguards could protect it. Center for Constitutional Rights, "*Arar v. Aschcroft et al.* Case Timeline," https://ccrjustice.org/home/what-we-do/our-cases/arar-v-ashcroft-et-al.
103. The "state secrets" defense is at times "just millimeters from cover up." Luban, *Torture, Power, and Law,* 282.
104. Singh, "Globalizing Torture," 2013. Doug Jehl and David Johnston, "Rule Change Lets CIA Freely Send Suspects Abroad to Jails," *New York Times,* March 6, 2005, https://www.nytimes.com/. Grey, *Ghost Plane,* 39.
105. Luban, *Torture, Power, and Law,* 284.
106. Similar routines for torture preceded the Bush administration; see chapter 1.
107. One case against the psychologists moved forward to a settlement. See Athey, "Psychology, Torture, Networks," as well as discussion in the Epilogue. A case against a contractor, *Al-Shimari v. CACI,* was moving through court challenges to plaintiff standing. The plaintiffs are Iraqi civilians Suhail Al Shimari, Salah Al-Ejaili, and As'ad Al-Zuba'e. In July 2022, CACI filed a new motion to dismiss on the bases of Supreme Court decisions issued in 2022. Judge Brinkema heard that motion on September 16, 2022, and denied it in July 2023. On October 2, 2023, the judge set the trial date for April 15, 2024. For updates, see the case timeline at https://ccrjustice.org/alshimari.

5. Perpetrators

1. Tony Lagouranis with Allen Mikaelian, *Fear Up Harsh: An Army Interrogator's Dark Journey through Iraq* (New York: New American Library, 2007), 137.
2. Physicians for Human Rights, "Leave No Marks," 2007, https://phr.org/our-work/resources/leave-no-marks/.
3. Lagouranis, *Fear Up Harsh,* 130.
4. Quotes from Leigh A. Payne, *Unsettling Accounts: Neither Truth nor Reconciliation in Confessions of State Violence* (Durham, N.C.: Duke University Press, 2008), 2, 19–20.

5. Martha K. Huggins, Mika Haritos-Fatouros, and Philip G. Zimbardo, *Violence Workers: Police Torturers and Murderers Reconstruct Brazilian Atrocities* (Berkeley: University of California Press, 2002), 202.

6. Philip Gourevitch and Errol Morris, *Standard Operating Procedure* (New York: Penguin, 2008), 75–76. The book is a companion to the film. Concerning al-Jamadi's corpse, Harman says, "His knees were bruised, his thighs were bruised near the groin, there were restraint marks on his wrists. It was obvious after you kept looking there's no way he died of a heart attack." Of the thumbs-up: "Whenever I'm in a photo I never know what to do with my hands, it just automatically happens." See also Philip Gourevitch and Errol Morris, "Exposure: The Woman behind the Camera at Abu Ghraib," *New Yorker,* March 24, 2008, http://www.newyorker.com/; Joel Roberts, "She's No Stranger to Grisly Images," CBS, May 10, 2004, https://www.cbsnews.com/.

7. Harman letter dated November 9, 2003; in Gourevitch and Morris, *Standard Operating Procedure.*

8. Lagouranis, *Fear Up Harsh,* 231.

9. Payne, *Unsettling Accounts,* 15.

10. In his book, Lagouranis admits fumbling that response, resorting to classic forms of torture denial: shifting blame and pointing to worse cases. Lagouranis, *Fear Up Harsh,* 130.

11. Interview with Alex Gibney, *All Things Considered,* conducted by Melissa Block, National Public Radio, January 18, 2008. Gibney seems taken aback and then returns to his point about the "overall context" and the larger chain of command: "I hope I didn't sanitize."

12. Lagouranis, *Fear Up Harsh,* 239.

13. Stephen Lewis, a fellow interrogator in the 513th Military Intelligence Brigade at Abu Ghraib, has also confirmed Lagouranis's account in interviews.

14. Lagouranis, *Fear Up Harsh,* 239.

15. Keith Brown and Catherine Lutz, "Grunt Lit," *American Ethnologist* 34, no. 2 (2007): 322–28.

16. Darius Rejali, *Torture and Democracy* (Princeton, N.J.: Princeton University Press, 2007), 21, 332, 426, 573–74.

17. Mark Bowden, "The Dark Art of Interrogation," *Atlantic,* October 2003, 51–70.

18. These methods of pain were used by the United Kingdom on Northern Ireland opposition, and they were deemed torture decades ago by the European Commission on Human Rights under highly politicized circumstances. They were later demoted to cruel treatment, also illegal, by the European Court of Human Rights. The European Commission on Human Rights, after seventeen months of deliberation and 119 witnesses, declared these techniques torture in 1976. The

European Court on Human Rights demoted them to "inhuman and degrading" on appeal in 1978. For the politics surrounding these cases, see John Conroy, *Unspeakable Acts, Ordinary People: Dynamics of Torture* (New York: Knopf, 2000). For decades, the U.S. State Department listed these techniques as torture and human rights abuses.

19. Lagouranis, *Fear Up Harsh*, 51.
20. Lagouranis, *Fear Up Harsh*, 51.
21. Lagouranis, *Fear Up Harsh*, 155.
22. Lagouranis, *Fear Up Harsh*, 230.
23. Lagouranis, *Fear Up Harsh*, 37–38.
24. Lagouranis, *Fear Up Harsh*, 39, 39, 50.
25. Seymour Hersh, the journalist covering the story of the Abu Ghraib torture photographs, uses an unnamed academic source to note that Patai is the "bible of the neocons" when it comes to Arab behavior. Seymour Hersh, "The Gray Zone," *New Yorker,* May 24, 2004. The book was denounced by Edward Said in his widely read *Orientalism* (New York: Pantheon, 1978) as a classic case.
26. Lagouranis, *Fear Up Harsh*, 17.
27. Lagouranis, *Fear Up Harsh*, 30, 74, 63.
28. Lagouranis, *Fear Up Harsh*, 54.
29. Lagouranis, *Fear Up Harsh*, 119.
30. Intelligence Science Board, "Educing Information." The Intelligence Science Board was chartered in 2002 as a scientific advisory group to the U.S. intelligence agencies. It was tasked by the director of National Intelligence to examine all existing social and behavioral studies on effective interrogation. It suggested that virtually no research indicates accurate information can be produced from unwilling sources through torture or coercive techniques. Moreover, technical research and development in this field has gone in the wrong direction, seeking how to achieve compliance not cooperation from unwilling sources. "In essence, there seems to be an unsubstantiated assumption that 'compliance' carries the same connotation as 'meaningful cooperation' (i.e., a source induced to provide accurate, relevant information of potential intelligence value)" (130). More astonishingly, given that the U.S. torture mythology has been fueled exclusively on anecdotes, when it comes to anecdotes and opinions on torture, the study states that even "the preponderance of reports seems to weigh against its effectiveness" (35) Another key finding: "Although pain is commonly assumed to facilitate compliance, there is no available scientific or systematic research to suggest that coercion can, will, or has provided accurate useful information from otherwise uncooperative sources" (35).
31. Human Rights First, "Command's Responsibility: Detainee Deaths in U.S. Custody in Iraq and Afghanistan," 2006, http://www.humanrightsfirst.info/pdf/06 221-etn-hrf-dic-rep-web.pdf.

32. Human Rights Watch, "No Blood, No Foul: Soldier's Accounts of Detainee Abuse in Iraq," July 22, 2006, https://www.hrw.org/report/2006/07/22/no-blood-no-foul/soldiers-accounts-detainee-abuse-iraq.

33. Lagouranis, *Fear Up Harsh*, 85.

34. Larry E. Cable, *Conflict of Myths: The Development of American Counterinsurgency Doctrine and the Vietnam War* (New York: New York University Press, 1986), 113–15; Marnia Lazreg, *Torture and the Twilight of Empire: From Algiers to Baghdad* (Princeton, N.J.: Princeton University Press, 2007). John D. Hutson, head legal counsel for the Navy from 1997 to 2000, puts it this way, "I know from the military that if you tell someone they can do a little of this for the country's good, some people will do a lot of it for the country's better." Scott Shane, David Johnston, and James Risen, "Secret U.S. Endorsement of Severe Interrogations," *New York Times*, October 4, 2007, https://www.nytimes.com/.

35. Lagouranis, *Fear Up Harsh*, 129.

36. Lagouranis's 2007 account of cousins differs slightly from that recorded by Human Rights Watch in 2006 as a story of two brothers. Lagouranis's Human Rights Watch testimony also differs in that he spoke of entering Mosul only to find an interrogation setting already using these techniques. Human Rights Watch, "No Blood, No Foul."

37. "I think they probably felt they were getting it pretty easy.... We were getting prisoners from the navy SEALs who were using a lot of the same techniques we were using, except they were a little more harsh. They would actually have the detainee stripped nude, laying on the floor, pouring ice water over his body. They were taking his temperature with a rectal thermometer. We had one guy who had been burned by the navy SEALs. He looked like he had a lighter held up to his legs. One guy's feet were like huge and black and blue, his toes were obviously all broken, he couldn't walk. And so, they got to us and we were playing James Taylor for them—I think they probably weren't that upset about what we were doing. Not that I'm excusing what I'm doing, but their reaction was not very severe to it." John Conroy, "Confessions of a Torturer," *Chicago Reader*, March 2, 2007, https://chicagoreader.com/.

38. Lagouranis, *Fear Up Harsh*, 131.

39. Lagouranis, *Fear Up Harsh*, 98, 90, 126.

40. Lagouranis, *Fear Up Harsh*, 116, 110, 127, 117, 128.

41. Lagouranis, *Fear Up Harsh*, 130.

42. Lagouranis, *Fear Up Harsh*, both 83.

43. Lagouranis, *Fear Up Harsh*, 95.

44. Lagouranis, *Fear Up Harsh*, 114.

45. Lagouranis, *Fear Up Harsh*, 136.

46. Sociologist del Russo offers analysis of the Senate discourse on Abu Ghraib; see Jared del Rosso, *Talking about Torture: How Political Discourse Shapes the Debate* (New York: Columbia University Press, 2015).

47. Eric Fair, *Consequence: A Memoir* (New York: Holt, 2016), offers another first-person torture confessional that is emotive and remorseful; however, it lacks Lagouranis's attempt to pursue internal and situational causes and culpability or analysis. Fair was received by interviewers and reviewers in much the same manner as Lagouranis, with a touch more skepticism from some corners but generally sympathetic reviews—for example, *Newsweek* and the *New York Times,* respectively. Hannah Gold, "Confessions of an American Military Torturer," *Newsweek,* August 20, 2016, https://www.newsweek.com/. Michiko Kakutani, "Review: Eric Fair's *Consequence,* a Memoir by a Former Abu Ghraib Interrogator," *New York Times,* April 4, 2016, https://www.nytimes.com/.

48. Lagouranis, *Fear Up Harsh,* 134.

49. Huggins, Haritos-Fatouros, and Zimbardo, *Violence Workers;* Conroy, *Unspeakable Acts;* Rejali, *Torture and Democracy.*

50. Lagouranis, *Fear Up Harsh,* 123.

51. Anthony Lagouranis, interview transcript, "The Torture Question," *Frontline,* PBS, October 18, 2005, https://www.pbs.org/wgbh/pages/frontline/torture/interviews/lagouranis.html. On this kind of "psychosis," see Celermajer's detailed description of the "dense worlds" of security services in Nepal and Sri Lanka within which torture came to seem rational. Danielle Celermajer, *The Prevention of Torture: An Ecological Approach* (Cambridge: Cambridge University Press, 2018).

52. For discussion of Stoler, selective attention, and not-knowing in the media and political landscape of the United States in 2007, see chapter 4.

53. Most notably, Staff Sergeant "Edwin," who had worked in Guantánamo, having seen the political and disciplinary fallout of interrogator frustration and escalating "enhancements," actually refused to use dogs and advised Lagouranis to "be very cautious about accepting orders" and to get anything questionable in writing. Lagouranis, *Fear Up Harsh,* 110.

54. Lagouranis, *Fear Up Harsh,* 94.

55. Lagouranis, *Fear Up Harsh,* 69–70, 46.

56. Lagouranis, *Fear Up Harsh,* 69–70. For example, during his first interrogations in Abu Ghraib, he is moved to report the prior abuse suffered by one prisoner, but not the severe beating suffered by another. He heard Ra'id was tortured in the hard site (49), but he filed no report. Someone did bother to do so; eventually, CID will come back and ask Lagouranis about Ra'id's treatment. At Mosul, Lagouranis filed no report concerning the nudity, ice water, anal thermometers, battered feet, and burned legs of Fadel, who detailed other appalling treatment at the hands of Navy SEALs on the base (80). Likewise, he reported a contusion on Mustafa caused by a guard. As an MP, the guard was immediately removed; meanwhile, Lagouranis points out, he was able to continue destroying that same prisoner's joints and mental health through stress positions, hypothermia, sleep deprivation, and dogs.

57. Lagouranis, *Fear Up Harsh,* 69–70.
58. See also Darius Rejali, "Torture Makes the Man," in *On Torture,* ed. Thomas C. Hilde (Baltimore, Md.: Johns Hopkins University Press, 2008); and Jasbir K. Puar, "On Torture: Abu Ghraib," *Radical History Review* 93 (2005): 13–38.
59. Amy Goodman, "Former U.S. Army Interrogator Describes the Harsh Techniques He Used in Iraq," Democracy Now!, November 15, 2005, https://www.democracynow.org/.
60. Twenty-seven-year-old civilian Fashad Mohammad died about seventy-two hours after capture, around April 5, 2004. The autopsy left cause of death "undetermined" but notes "multiple minor injuries, abrasions and contusions" and "blunt force trauma and positional asphyxia." Human Rights Watch, "No Blood, No Foul," found that three Navy SEALs were recommended for court-martial in association with his death but were not charged.
61. Lagouranis, *Fear Up Harsh,* 121, 164.
62. Payne, *Unsettling Accounts,* 130.
63. *Mediodia con Mauro,* 1997. He appeared on that program five times in 1997. Payne, *Unsettling Accounts,* 129, 131.
64. Harding cites Antjie Krog's *Country of My Skull: Guilt, Sorrow, and the Limits of Forgiveness in the New South Africa.* Jeremy Harding, "Picking Up the Pieces," book review, *New York Times,* May 30, 1999, https://www.nytimes.com/. Suzanne Daley, "Apartheid Torturer Testifies as Evil Shows Its Banal Face," *New York Times,* November 9, 1997, https://www.nytimes.com/.
65. Marguerite Feitlowitz, *A Lexicon of Terror* (Oxford: Oxford University Press, 1998), 193. Payne, *Unsettling Accounts,* 45–46.
66. Calls for legislation to ensure these survivors may never enter the United States to become a political force began in 2008. Eric Lichtblau, "Administration Calls for Action on Detainees," *New York Times,* July 22, 2008, https://www.nytimes.com/.
67. Berta Soley, "Engaging Torture Survivors in the Global Fight against Torture," *Torture Journal* 31, no. 1 (2021): 88–92, https://doi.org/10.7146/torture.v31i1.125764.

6. Networks

1. The first epigraph can be found in Stephen Grey, *Ghost Plane: The True Story of the CIA Rendition and Torture Program* (New York: St. Martin's Press, 2006), 22. The second is from the joint investigation by BBC Arabic/The Guardian: Mona Mahmood et al., "Revealed: Pentagon's Link to Iraqi Torture Centres," *Guardian,* March 6, 2013, https://www.theguardian.com/.
2. Stanley Cohen, *States of Denial: Knowing about Atrocities and Suffering* (Cambridge: Polity, 2001), 7–20.

3. Christina Nadler, "Denial: A Sociological Theory" (PhD diss., City University of New York, 2017), 42–43, https://academicworks.cuny.edu/gc_etds/2126/.

4. Nadler, "Denial," 43–48. Ruth Wilson Gilmore, "Globalisation and U.S. Prison Growth: From Military Keynesianism to Post-Keynesian Militarism," *Race and Class* 40, no. 2/3 (1999): 171–88. Loïc Wacquant, *Urban Outcasts: A Comparative Sociology of Advanced Marginality* (Cambridge: Polity, 2008), 46. Loïc Wacquant, "Deadly Symbiosis When Ghetto and Prison Meet and Mesh," *Punishment and Society* 3, no. 1 (2001): 95–133.

5. Mahmood et al., "Revealed: Pentagon's Link to Iraqi Torture Centres."

6. Journeyman Pictures, Guardian Films, and BBC World, *Terror TV,* YouTube, May 2005, https://www.youtube.com/watch?v=cC2s02OmqsU (no longer public).

7. Sometimes translated as *Terrorism in the Grip of Justice,* it later moved out from the detention-center set, taking prisoners to the scene of the crime, where the bomb-damaged community may confront them under the camera lights. France 24 English, "The Iraqi TV Show Where Victims Confront Terrorists," YouTube, September 30, 2014, https://www.youtube.com/watch?v=m2L7ZKYLH_o.

8. See Caryle Murphy and Khalid Saffar, "Actors in the Insurgency Are Reluctant TV Stars; Terror Suspects Grilled, Mocked on Hit Iraqi Show," *Washington Post,* April 5, 2005, https://www.washingtonpost.com/; Rory Carroll, "Trial by Television," *Salon,* March 28, 2005, https://www.salon.com/; Neil MacDonald, "Iraqi Reality-TV Hit Takes Fear Factor to Another Level," *Christian Science Monitor,* June 7, 2005, https://www.csmonitor.com/.

9. Dexter Filkins, "Sunnis Accuse Iraqi Military of Kidnappings and Slayings," *New York Times,* November 29, 2005, https://www.nytimes.com/.

10. Kirk Semple, "Over 3,000 Iraqi Civilians Killed in June, U.N. Reports," *New York Times,* July 18, 2006, https://www.nytimes.com/.

11. Babak Dehghanpisheh, "Iraq Death Squads Get Better at Hiding Handiwork," *Newsweek,* December 15, 2008, https://www.newsweek.com/.

12. U.S. Department of State, Bureau of Democracy, Human Rights, and Labor, "2007 Country Reports on Human Rights Practices: Iraq," March 11, 2008, https://2009-2017.state.gov/j/drl/rls/hrrpt/2007/index.htm.

13. Lila Rajiva, *The Language of Empire: Abu Ghraib and the American Media* (New York: Monthly Review Press, 2005); Jared del Rosso, *Talking about Torture: How Political Discourse Shapes the Debate* (New York: Columbia University Press, 2015).

14. Andrew V. Papachristos. "Murder by Structure: Dominance Relations and the Social Structure of Gang Homicide," *American Journal of Sociology* 115, no. 1 (2009): 74–128, https://doi.org/10.1086/597791.

15. Andrew Papachristos, "The Coming of Networked Criminology?," in *Measuring Crime and Criminality,* ed. John Macdonald (New York: Routledge, 2017),

101–40. It matters, for instance, whether most interact solely through their relationship with one centralized person, or whether everyone in a structure knows and interacts with most everyone else, as in a friendship clique, small working group, or street gang.

16. Papachristos, "Coming of Networked Criminology?," 114.

17. Papachristos, "Murder by Structure," 84.

18. Celermajer offers a careful analysis of the focus on individual agency in professional human rights practice and the "social imaginary of human rights." Danielle Celermajer, *The Prevention of Torture: An Ecological Approach* (Cambridge: Cambridge University Press, 2018), 199–230. Efforts to alter that focus must tackle the problem of uptake within the field. That is, any new frameworks must retain culpability for individuals (personal agency) yet must also be situated in material and relational factors that are active causal conditions. Frameworks must match with routines of practice (legal and activist) in human rights as well as with the common narratives about causes of torture (215).

19. David Corn, "From Iran–Contra to Iraq," *Nation*, May 6, 2005, https://www.thenation.com/. Dick Cheney, Donald Rumsfeld, and John Negroponte held U.S. administration positions during the 1980s war in El Salvador and were appointed to posts under George W. Bush. Several others in the Iraq planning circle were alumnae of Iran–contra illegal arms deal that funneled illegal trainers, arms, and military support to paramilitaries that were attempting to suppress a revolution in Nicaragua: Elliot Abrams, Robert Gates, Richard Armitage, and James Steele. Abrams was disbarred in Washington, D.C., for lying to Congress about U.S. support for the contras. Bush appointed him to the National Security Council. As ambassador to Honduras during the 1980s, Negroponte oversaw contra training that operated out of Honduras. He has been accused of widespread human rights violations by the Honduras Commission on Human Rights. Under Bush, he served as ambassador to Iraq from 2004 to 2005, then as U.S. national intelligence director, then transferred to deputy Secretary of State with responsibility for Iraq during the 2007 surge. Dahr Jamail, like Corn, notes Steele permitted Oliver North's smuggling flights to operate out of El Salvador, as documented in the final report of the Iran–contra special prosecutor. Dahr Jamail, "Managing Escalation: Negroponte and Bush's New Iraq Team," AntiWar, January 9, 2007, https://original.antiwar.com/jamail/2007/01/09/managing-escalation-negroponte-and-bushs-new-iraq-team/; Seymour Hersh, "The Redirection," *New Yorker*, March 5, 2007, https://www.newyorker.com/.

20. Under the heading "Denial as a Method of Counterinsurgency Warfare" and other sections of the Center for Strategic International Studies report by Anthony H. Cordesman, "The Developing Iraqi Insurgency: Status at End—2004," December 22, 2004, http://www.comw.org/warreport/fulltext/0412cordesman.pdf. Insurgent groups and militias were decentralized and were composed largely of

different ethnic and sectarian militias with disparate goals. Some were determined to influence the distribution of land and resources in a new Iraq; some wanted to fight Shi'ite control in an emerging Iraqi government; some wanted to oust the United States or simply feed on its missteps in Iraq. Some were independent and some were aligned with a growing collection of foreign fighters referred to by 2006 as AQI (al-Qaeda in Iraq). See Deborah Amos, *Eclipse of the Sunnis: Power, Exile, and Upheaval in the Middle East* (New York: Public Affairs, 2010); and J. Kael Weston, *The Mirror Test: America at War in Iraq and Afghanistan* (New York: Vintage, 2017). Remnants of AQI reassembled in 2011 and were calling themselves ISIS by 2013; it is also known as ISIL, Daesh, or the Islamic State. Repelling that threat in Iraq and Syria would engage competing militias, coalition forces, and the Middle East through 2019. The Islamic State now has decentralized affiliates in several nations, including many in Africa. Jeff Seldin, "Global Coalition Fears Islamic State Expansion in Africa," Voice of America, June 28, 2021, https://www.voanews.com/europe/global-coalition-fears-islamic-state-expansion-africa; "Diving Deep into the Origins of ISIS," Tony Blair Institute for Global Change, December 2014, https://institute.global/sites/default/files/articles/Diving-Deep-into-the-Origins-of-ISIS.pdf; Cameron Glenn et al., "Timeline: The Rise, Spread and Fall of the Islamic State," Wilson Center, October 28, 2019, https://www.wilsoncenter.org/article/timeline-the-rise-spread-and-fall-the-islamic-state.

21. Seymour Hersh, "The Coming Wars: What the Pentagon Can Now Do in Secret," *New Yorker,* January 24, 2005.

22. The United Nations report is: Commission on the Truth for El Salvador, "From Madness to Hope: The 12-Year War in El Salvador," 1993 report, https://www.usip.org/sites/default/files/file/ElSalvador-Report.pdf.

23. Stephen G. Rabe, *The Killing Zone: The United States Wages Cold War in Latin America.* (Oxford: Oxford University Press, 2012), 166–71. The United States spent $1 million from the State Department and $4 million from the CIA on elections. The salaried organizer was Colonel Nicolas Carranza.

24. Transcript, Cheney–Edwards vice presidential debate, October 5, 2004, https://www.debates.org/voter-education/debate-transcripts/october-5-2004-transcript/.

25. "Secretary of Defense Presides over Veterans Day Celebration," press release, U.S. Embassy in El Salvador, November 12, 2004, https://sv.usembassy.gov/.

26. Tim Weiner, "U.S.-Backed Rightist Claims Victory in Salvador Election," *New York Times,* March 22, 2004, https://www.nytimes.com/.

27. "President Bush Meets with President Saca of El Salvador," White House Archives of President George W. Bush, February 27, 2007, https://georgewbush-whitehouse.archives.gov/news/releases/2007/02/images/20070227-1_d-0044-2-515h.html; "IRI Honors President Saca," press release, International Republican Institute, November 29, 2007, http://www.iri.org/web-story/iri-honors-president-saca-2007-freedom-award.

28. Emphasis mine. They report an Iraqi general and director of Iraq's national intelligence estimated a sympathetic Sunni population of 200,000. Michael Hirsh and John Barry, "The Salvador Option: The Pentagon May Put Special Forces–Led Assassination or Kidnapping Teams in Iraq," *Newsweek,* January 10, 2005, available at Global Policy Forum, https://archive.globalpolicy.org/empire/intervention/2005/0110salvador.htm.

29. Trevor Bormann, transcript of "Searching for Steele," ABC News, February 4, 2013, https://www.abc.net.au/.

30. Peter Maass, "The Way of the Commandos," *New York Times Sunday Magazine,* May 1, 2005, https://www.nytimes.com/.

31. Thabit and Naqib were both Sunnis. While a large share of the commandos recruited were former Shi'ite Republican Guards, Naqib's Sunni leadership choices, and his own presence, were to signal a security effort free of religious rivalries. The next minister replaced them with Shia.

32. Hirsh and Barry, "Salvador Option"; Doug Jehl and Eric Schmitt, "Law Gives Spending Power to Special Operations Forces," *New York Times,* February 1, 2005, https://www.nytimes.com/. The CIA had vigorously rejected attempts by Defense to expand into clandestine intelligence operations without direct CIA approval. A single paragraph in an October 2004 Defense spending authorization bill approved Defense authority to pay informants and recruit foreign paramilitaries, up to $25 million annually through 2007.

33. Michael Moss, "How Iraqi Police Reform Became a Casualty of War," *New York Times,* May 26, 2006, https://www.nytimes.com/.

34. Paula Broadwell, *All In: The Education of David Petraeus* (New York: Penguin, 2012), 192–93.

35. Mahmood et al., "Revealed: Pentagon's Link to Iraqi Torture Centres."

36. Citing General Muntadher al-Samari. Mona Mahmood et al., "From El Salvador to Iraq: Washington's Man behind Brutal Police Squads," *Guardian,* March 6, 2013, https://www.theguardian.com/.

37. Broadwell, *All In,* 66–69. Referring to the president of El Salvador, Petraeus also speculated that success in Vietnam would have been impossible even with improved counterinsurgency techniques, given the "domestic unwillingness to stay for the long haul and given the absence of a Vietnamese Duarte" (68).

38. This is akin to the six degrees of separation structure in a small-world network. Qawi K. Telesford et al., "The Ubiquity of Small World Networks," *Brain Connect* 1, no. 5 (2011): 367–75, https://www.ncbi.nlm.nih.gov/pmc/articles/PMC3604768/. "Small-world networks have the unique ability to have specialized nodes or regions within a network (e.g., a computer network with a group of machines dedicated to a certain task) while simultaneously exhibiting shared or distributed processing across all of the communicating nodes within a network (e.g., all computers sharing the work load)." David Easly and Jon Kleinberg, "The Small World

Phenomenon," *Networks, Crowds, and Markets: Reasoning about a Highly Connected World* (Cambridge: Cambridge University Press, 2010).

39. Moss, "How Iraqi Police Reform Became a Casualty of War."

40. Moss, "How Iraqi Police Reform Became a Casualty of War."

41. Glenn Kessler, "Weapons Given to Iraq Are Missing," *Washington Post*, August 6, 2007, https://www.washingtonpost.com/. By 2007, Kessler notes, "the United States has spent $19.2 billion trying to develop Iraqi security forces since 2003, the GAO said, including at least $2.8 billion to buy and deliver equipment. But the GAO said weapons distribution was haphazard and rushed and failed to follow established procedures, particularly from 2004 to 2005, when security training was led by Gen. David H. Petraeus." James Glanz writes, "The weapons include rocket-propelled grenade launchers, assault rifles, machine guns, shotguns, semiautomatic pistols and sniper rifles." The special inspector general for Iraq reconstruction "found major discrepancies in American military records on where thousands of 9-millimeter pistols and hundreds of assault rifles and other weapons have ended up. The American military did not even take the elementary step of recording the serial numbers of nearly half a million weapons provided to Iraqis . . . making it impossible to track or identify any that might be in the wrong hands. Exactly where untracked weapons could end up—and whether some have been used against American soldiers—were not examined in the report, although black-market arms dealers thrive on the streets of Baghdad, and official Iraq Army and police uniforms can easily be purchased as well, presumably because government shipments are intercepted or otherwise corrupted." James Glanz, "U.S. Is Said to Fail in Tracking Arms Shipped to Iraqis," *New York Times*, October 30, 2006, https://www.nytimes.com/. See also James Glanz and Eric Schmitt, "Iraq Weapons Are a Focus of Criminal Investigations," *New York Times*, August 28, 2007, https://www.nytimes.com/.

42. Moss, "How Iraqi Police Reform Became a Casualty of War."

43. Mike Francis, "Ordered to Walk Away," *Oregonian*, October 30, 2010, http://www.oregonlive.com. See also Moss, "How Iraqi Police Reform Became a Casualty of War": the Iraqi Office of Human Rights decried a secret torture prison uncovered in 2004 operating outside of Baghdad. The Interior Ministry staged five inspections after this. According to Moss, no apparent action was taken.

44. Angus Stickler and Chris Woods, "Iraq War Logs: U.S. Troops Ordered Not to Investigate Iraqi Torture," Bureau of Investigative Journalism, May 23, 2011, https://www.thebureauinvestigates.com/2011/05/23/us-troops-ordered-not-to-investigate-iraqi-torture. Details on FRAGOs 242 and 039 were among the military and State Department cables and reports released by WikiLeaks in 2010. The order was made at the height of the Abu Ghraib revelations in May and June 2004. Stickler and Woods note the first mention in the Iraq logs of FRAGO 242 is on June 26, 2004: "Provided the initial report confirms U.S. forces were not involved in the

detainee abuse, no further investigation will be conducted unless directed by HHQ [Iraqi government]." "The second order, FRAGO 039, issued in April 2005 . . . modified FRAGO 242 and now requires reports of Iraqi on Iraqi abuse be reported through operational channels." In addition, "the logs reveal that more than 180,000 people were detained in Iraq between 2004 and 2009. This is equivalent to one in 50 of the male population. In comparison, the number of people detained in Afghanistan, which has a similar population, was 7,500." See also Greg Mitchell, "On the Tenth Anniversary of the U.S. Invasion of Iraq: When WikiLeaks Exposed 'The War Logs,'" *Nation,* March 19, 2013, https://www.thenation.com/.

45. In 2010, WikiLeaks published the cable Rumsfeld had received from Steele. Mahmood et al., "Revealed: Pentagon's Link to Iraqi Torture Centres."

46. Bormann, "Searching for Steele." The Pace and Rumsfeld televised press conference took place November 29, 2005, and is featured in the documentary film *James Steele: America's Mystery Man in Iraq* (BBC Arabic/The Guardian, 2013).

47. Stickler and Woods, "Iraq War Logs."

48. Mahmood et al., "Revealed: Pentagon's Link to Iraqi Torture Centres."

49. Mahmood et al., "Revealed: Pentagon's Link to Iraqi Torture Centres."

50. Bormann, "Searching for Steele."

51. Transcript of interview with Brigadier General Karl Horst conducted by *Frontline,* PBS, February 9, 2007, https://www.pbs.org/wgbh/pages/frontline/gangs ofiraq/interviews/horst.html. See also Robert F. Worth, "Iraq Interior Ministry Looks into Reports of Death Squads," *New York Times,* February 17, 2006, https://www.nytimes.com/.

52. Joel Roberts, "Iraq Downplays Torture Charges," CBS News, November 17, 2005, https://www.cbsnews.com/.

53. David Cloud and Greg Jaffe, "The Bunker in Jadriyah," in *The Fourth Star: Four Generals and the Epic Struggle for the Future of the United States Army* (New York: Crown, 2010).

54. David H. Petraeus, "Letter from Headquarters, Multi-national Force—Iraq," May 10, 2007, https://www.washingtonpost.com/wp-srv/nation/documents/petraeus_values_051007.pdf.

55. Petraeus asked lawmakers to consider crafting an exception "beyond normal techniques" into law. Spencer Ackerman, "Petraeus (Kinda, Sorta) Re-opens the Torture Debate," *Wired,* June 23, 2011, https://www.wired.com/2011/06/petraeus-kinda-sorta-re-opens-the-torture-debate. Adam Serwer, "Did General Petraeus Change His Position on Torture?," blog entry, *Washington Post,* June 24, 2011, https://www.washingtonpost.com/.

56. Mazan Taha compiled the names of some seven hundred Sunni men who had disappeared or been killed in four months: "How did these killers get police uniforms?" . . . "How was it that they were operating freely after curfew? That they had police cars?" In Filkins, "Sunnis Accuse." See also Dexter Filkins, "Where the

Shadows Have Shadows," *New York Times,* February 5, 2006, https://www.nytimes.com/; Damien Cave, "Gunmen in Police Uniforms Kidnap 5 British Civilians," *New York Times,* May 30, 2007, https://www.nytimes.com/; John F. Burns and Michael Luo, "Dozens Arrested in Brazen Raid on Iraq Ministry," *New York Times,* November 15, 2006, https://www.nytimes.com/. In contrast, Moore lays police torture directly at the Interior Ministry's feet and implicates the United States. Solomon Moore, "Police Abuses in Iraq Detailed," *Los Angeles Times,* July 9, 2006, https://www.latimes.com/.

57. Petraeus is an avid fan of Lartéguy and conducted a correspondence of decades with Marcel Bigeard, a French general known for torture in Algeria; see chapter 2.

58. Maass cites the draft report by Cordesman, "Developing Iraqi Insurgency."

59. Worth, "Iraq Interior Ministry Looks into Reports of Death Squads." MacDonald reported in 2005 that the Iraqi Ministry of Human Rights had asked the Judicial Council to review the legality of the commando's television program. MacDonald, "Iraqi Reality-TV Hit Takes Fear Factor to Another Level."

60. For contrast, see a 2005 article by Josh White printed three months after Maass's appears. White describes the 2003 murder of Iraqi major general Abed Hamed Mowhoush, accomplished by sixteen days of extraordinary beatings by a sequence of U.S. Army members, U.S. Special Forces, CIA advisors, and an Iraqi paramilitary Scorpion team. While reporting on murder charges in this one incident, White is clear the work was collaborative and had happened before. Mowhoush had entered the base on foot to request the release of two sons. He finally died smothered in a sleeping bag with crushed ribs and straddled by a U.S. soldier. The murder was in the Qaim region near the Syrian border. Four U.S. soldiers were court-martialed. Charges were eventually dismissed for three, and the last was convicted of negligent homicide. He received a reprimand but no prison time. Josh White, "Documents Tell of Brutal Improvisation by GIs; Interrogated General's Sleeping-Bag Death, CIA's Use of a Secret Iraqi Squad Are among Details," *Washington Post,* August 3, 2005, https://www.washingtonpost.com/. Josh White, "Sentence in Death of Iraqi Angers Son; Soldier's Reprimand 'Is Not Justice,'" *Washington Post,* January 25, 2006, https://www.washingtonpost.com/.

61. In 2007, Petraeus returned to a combat post as a five-star general, with great public fanfare and a new and widely read *Counterinsurgency Field Manual* to his name. This was the doctrinal imprint he had dreamed of for "small wars," the vision that excited him as a young man in El Salvador observing Steele's methods. He followed the first wave of Salvador-style counterinsurgency in Iraq that he had helped to implement and expanded it, leading a second wave that added another thirty thousand U.S. troops to work on infrastructure, policing, and combat. Petraeus rebranded this wave of counterinsurgency as COIN, as if the years from 2003 to 2006 had been something else. This clever repackaging was said to be a return to

"classic" counterinsurgency and a departure from the disreputable mess of Vietnam (and El Salvador and now Iraq). In 2012, Petraeus became a partner in the venture capital firm KKR as chairman of their new Global Institute. Pascal Houzelot, "David Petraeus: Ex-CIA Chief, New Media Mogul in Eastern Europe—The Complete Investigation," *Observatoire de journalisme,* April 10, 2018, https://www.ojim.fr/david-petraeus-ex-cia-chief-new-media-mogul-in-eastern-europe-the-complete-investigation/.

62. Moore, "Police Abuses in Iraq Detailed." Without irony, the U.S. response "declared 2006 the year of the police" and vowed a renewed effort to "expand and professionalize Iraq's civilian officer corps."

63. "Engineer Ahmed" led an intelligence directorate within the Interior Ministry and was a senior officer within the Badr Organization. In 2006, other militias came to control other vital sectors of society, operating, for instance, within the ministries of transportation, health, and agriculture. Colonel Joel D. Rayburn and Colonel Frank K. Sobchak, eds., *The U.S. Army in the Iraq War, Volume 1—Invasion–Insurgency–Civil War, 2003–2006* (U.S. Army War College Press, 2019), 496, 587, 590–91, https://press.armywarcollege.edu/monographs/386.

64. Jadriyah was said to be "the first indisputable evidence" that the Interior Ministry, not simply rogue Shia militias, had institutionalized torture. Rayburn and Sobchak, *U.S. Army in the Iraq War,* 496. Ned Parker's 2015 review of unpublished reports on Jadriyah by the Interior Ministry and the United States noted that the United States consistently overlooked such evidence in order to defeat Sunni insurgents and stabilize the country. The United States relied on Shi'ite militia to fight ISIS. Ned Parker, "Rise of the Militias: Torture by Iraqi Militias: The Report Washington Did Not Want You to See," Reuters, December 14, 2015, https://www.reuters.com/. On the symbiosis through 2021, see Zack Kopplin, "How the Pentagon Accidentally Funnels Millions to Iraqi Militia Groups It's Also Fighting," *American Prospect,* March 25, 2021, https://prospect.org/.

65. Of Steele's relationship to Petraeus, Maass says, "I talked to both of them about each other and it was very clear that they were very close to each other in terms of their command relationship and also in terms of their ideas and ideology of what needed to be done. Everybody knew that he was Petraeus's man. Even Steele defined himself as Petraeus's man." Mahmood et al., "Revealed: Pentagon's Link to Iraqi Torture Centres." Ben Emmerson, "Reconciliation in Iraq Is Impossible without U.S. Truth about Its Dirty War," *Guardian,* March 7, 2013, https://www.theguardian.com/.

66. Ewen MacAskill and Mona Mahmood, "Pentagon Investigating Link between U.S. Military and Torture Centres in Iraq," *Guardian,* March 7, 2013, https://www.theguardian.com/; United Nations, "Towards the Prevention of Torture in Iraqi Detention Facilities," October 5, 2021, https://www.ohchr.org/en/stories/2021/10/towards-prevention-torture-iraqi-detention-facilities-0.

Epilogue

1. This phrasing on acknowledgment, accountability, and healing is courtesy Mariame Kaba, *We Do This 'til We Free Us: Abolitionist Organizing and Transforming Justice* (Chicago: Haymarket Press, 2021).

2. Alex Emmons, "Historic Settlement Reached on Behalf of CIA Torture Victims," *Intercept,* August 17, 2017, https://theintercept.com/2017/08/17/cia-torture-settlement-aclu-mitchell-jessen/.

3. The indemnification contract was to last through 2021. Senate Select Committee on Intelligence, *The Senate Intelligence Committee Report on Torture: Committee Study of the Central Intelligence Agency's Detention and Interrogation Program* (Brooklyn: Melville House, 2014), 16–17.

4. Emmons, "Historic Settlement Reached."

5. "Physicians under Threat, Warns WMA President," World Medical Association press release, June 23, 2003, http://web.archive.org/web/20030715220823/http://www.wma.net/e/press/2003_9.htm. See also Kenneth S. Pope, "A Human Rights and Ethics Crisis Facing the World's Largest Organization of Psychologists: Accepting Responsibility, Understanding Causes, Implementing Solutions," Articles, Research, and Resources in Psychology, August 27, 2018, https://kspope.com/apa/crisis.php.

6. If psychologists' ethical responsibilities posed an unresolvable conflict with law, regulations, or other legal authority, then psychologists may adhere to the authority's requirements. See Article 1.02 of that code, discussed in Mark Burton and Carolyn Kagan, "Psychologists and Torture: More than a Question of Interrogations," *Psychologist* 20, no. 8 (2007): 484–87.

Mitchell and Jessen cited Nuremberg-era defenses in their motions to dismiss the trial. Stephanie Athey, "Psychology, Torture, Networks, or Structure as the Subject of Human Rights," in *Writing beyond the State: Post-sovereign Approaches to Human Rights in Literary Studies,* ed. Alexandra S. Moore and Samantha Pinto (London: Palgrave Macmillan, 2020), 175–98. This essay discusses the APA support for torture in detail; it also considers the value of network thinking for human rights organizing, for prosecuting violence networks, and for reinventing justice beyond law. Not until 2010 and 2017, under persistent membership pressure, was the Nuremberg line in the APA ethics code removed. It was replaced with this: "Under no circumstances may this standard be used to justify or defend violating human rights." American Psychological Association, "Ethical Principles of Psychologists and Code of Conduct," http://www.apa.org/ethics/code/index.aspx (accessed August 17, 2018).

7. David H. Hoffman et al., "Report to the Special Committee of the Board of Directors of the American Psychological Association; Independent Review Relating to APA Ethics Guidelines, National Security Interrogations, and Torture,"

American Psychological Association, 2015, 178, https://www.apa.org/independent-review/revised-report.pdf.

8. Gretchen Borchelt, "Break Them Down: Systematic Use of Torture by U.S. Forces," Physicians for Human Rights (PHR), 2005, 43–47, https://phr.org/our-work/resources/break-them-down/. Neil A. Lewis, "Broad Use of Harsh Tactics Is Described at Cuba Base," *New York Times,* October 17, 2004, https://www.nytimes.com/; Neil A. Lewis, "Red Cross Finds Detainee Abuse in Guantánamo," *New York Times,* November 30, 2004, https://www.nytimes.com/; Scott Shane, "Chinese Inspired Interrogations at Guantánamo," *New York Times,* July 8, 2008, https://www.nytimes.com/.

9. Stephen Soldz, Nathaniel Raymond, and Steven Reiser, "All the President's Psychologists: The American Psychological Association's Secret Complicity with the White House and U.S. Intelligence Community in Support of the CIA's 'Enhanced' Interrogation Program," *New York Times,* April 30, 2015, https://www.nytimes.com/; also available at https://www.transcend.org/tms/2015/05/all-the-presidents-psychologists/. The independent review is Hoffman et al., "Report to the Special Committee of the Board of Directors of the American Psychological Association."

10. On the corporate side, the circle is far wider than just the business associates named in the legal case: "According to a document filed with the state of Washington in 2008, the seven owners of Mitchell, Jessen & Associates were: James Mitchell, John Bruce Jessen, David Ayers, Randall Spivey, James Sporleder, Joseph Matarazzo, and Roger Aldrich. Records show Mitchell, Jessen & Associates became inactive in October 2009. However, four of the company's owners appear to work at other firms that currently consult with the U.S. government. Three of them, Spivey, Sporleder, and Aldrich, are still working together at a company called the Center for Personal Protection & Safety, which counts both the Department of Defense and FBI among its clients." Hunter Walker, "These Seven Men Owned the Company Linked to CIA Torture," *Business Insider,* December 11, 2014, https://www.businessinsider.in/These-7-Men-Owned-The-Company-Linked-To-CIA-Torture/articleshow/45469806.cms.

11. Scott Selisker, *Human Programming: Brainwashing, Automatons, and American Unfreedom* (Minneapolis: University of Minnesota, 2016), 103, 99.

12. John Marks, *The Search for the Manchurian Candidate: The CIA and Mind Control* (New York: New York Times Books, 1979), 157–58.

13. As with cybernetics, the Defense and university collaboration on command, communication, and control gave rise to the global information networks that now connect our social and economic worlds. For a discussion of the evolution of network thinking as a possibility for more emancipatory projects within indigenous feminism, feminist physics, social science, and human rights, see Athey, "Psychology, Torture, Networks."

14. Alison Howell, "The International Political Sociology of Psychology and Mental Health," *International Political Sociology* 6, no. 3 (2012): 3, https://doi.org/10.1111/j.1749-5687.2012.00166_7.x.

15. Brinton M. Lykes and Erin Sibly, "Liberation Psychology and Pragmatic Solidarity: North–South Collaborations through the Ignacio Martín-Baró Fund," *Journal of Peace Psychology* 20, no. 3 (2014): 211–12.

16. Burton and Kagan, "Psychologists and Torture," 486.

17. For example, using Martín-Baró's model, a refugee project focused on the persecuted Shan ethnic community of Burma. They used international human rights conventions to claim a right akin to structural analysis. See Lykes and Sibly, "Liberation Psychology and Pragmatic Solidarity," 221.

18. Fireweed Collective, "Our Framework," https://fireweedcollective.org/our-framework/. The Audre Lorde Project is "a Lesbian, Gay, Bisexual, Two Spirit, Trans and Gender Non-Conforming People of Color center for community organizing, focusing on the New York City area. Through mobilization, education and capacity-building, we work for community wellness and progressive social and economic justice. ALP is committed to promoting multi-racial coalition-building, advocacy and community organizing activities among LGBTSTGNC people of color, and with allies in struggles for equality and liberation" (https://alp.org/about). BEAM describes itself as "a national training, movement building, and grant making institution that is dedicated to the healing, wellness, and liberation of Black and marginalized communities" (https://beam.community/).

19. Dr. Ximena E. Mejia directed me to coalition-based innovations that grew from the work of Martín-Baró. Fireweed emerged from the ashes of the Icarus Project, which disbanded in 2019 after intense struggle over oppressive relationships within the organization.

20. Kaba, *We Do This 'til We Free Us*, 61.

21. A public sigh of relief seemed to accompany a few events that were partial and relevant only to torture in the war on terror. These were announced as bookends to a period of U.S. torture, as if that had ended. One of these events occurred with the release of the Senate's report, which was narrowly focused on CIA involvement in torture. An earlier case was the newly inaugurated President Obama's ban on torture targeting war on terror detentions in 2009. Despite this, he kept international capture and rendition networks open. Obama also limited interrogation to the techniques permissible in the revised Army Field Manual of 2006. That manual eliminated some CIA techniques, yet it also removed restrictions on "abnormal sleep deprivation," stress positions, and "chemically induced psychosis." Its appendix M also contains directives for the use of isolation, sensory deprivation and overload, sleep deprivation, and dietary and environmental manipulation. The manual retained the requirement of medical supervision during interrogation as a fig leaf for these techniques. Jeffrey Kaye, "U.N. Cites Torture and Ill-Treatment

in U.S. Army Field Manual's Appendix M," ShadowProof, November 28, 2014, https://shadowproof.com/2014/11/28/un-review-cites-torture-ill-treatment-in-u-s-army-field-manuals-appendix-m/.

22. As Celermajer argues, the criminalization of torture is simply insufficient. Most work against torture has attended to the legal level (criminalization, prosecution, and admissibility of evidence, with some attention paid to conditions of detention). Her book is an astute articulation of why recourse to criminalization is an incomplete strategy for the normative and institutional change required to end torture. Danielle Celermajer, *The Prevention of Torture: An Ecological Approach* (Cambridge: Cambridge University Press, 2018), 188–98.

23. Kaba, *We Do This 'til We Free Us,* 14.

24. Micol Seigel, *Violence Work: State Power and the Limits of Police* (Durham, N.C.: Duke University Press, 2018), 7.

25. Seigel, *Violence Work,* 7.

26. Kaba, *We Do This 'til We Free Us,* 14–15.

27. Kaba, *We Do This 'til We Free Us,* 59–60.

Index

Abadilla, Rolando, 255n62
abolition: of prisons, 16–18, 222–23; of slavery, 222
Abrams, Elliot, 292n19
Abu Ghraib prison: archetype of torture versus, 101, 113–16; *Ghosts of Abu Ghraib* (film), 162, 164–67, 179–80, 184; key literature on, 17; number of detainees at, 112, 266n189; plural nature of torture at, 110–11, 271n40; racialized science and, 267n192; reporting of, xiv–xv; *Standard Operating Procedure* (film), 29, 162, 164–66, 286n6; Tools of torture at, 130–31, 132
Aceh insurgencies, 126–27
African Americans: BEAM (Black Emotional and Mental Health Collective), 221, 301n18; Chicago police department's torture of, xiii, 4, 14–16, 27–28, 112, 227n5, 231n5; incarceration of, 17–18, 222; lynching of, 15, 58, 60, 62, 253n36, 273n54; systemic police violence against, 3–7, 50–51, 100–101, 221–23. *See also* racial capitalism; racialization
Aguinaldo, Rodolfo, 255n62
Al-Asad airfield, Mosul, 160, 174, 283n85
Aldrich, Roger, 300n10
Al-Ejaili, Salah, 285n107

Alexander, Michelle, 16
Algerian war for independence: Larteguy's account of, 77–80; racialized science in, 95–96; torture as terror in, xiii, 10–11, 76–77, 260n102; Trinquier's writing on, 69, 71–77; U.S. delegations sent to observe, 71, 257n76
al-Jamadi, Manadel, 110, 164, 166–67, 174, 271n40, 286n6
Alleg, Henri, 149, 282nn81–82
Allen, Henry T., 64, 250n10, 253n31
All the President's Psychologists, 219
Almarabh, Nabil, xvi
al-Naqib, Falah, 200, 294n31
al-'Owhali, Mohamed, 248n54
al-Qaeda, xvi, 33, 85, 103, 292n20
al-Qahtani, Mohammed, xi, 274n1
Al Shimari, Suhail, 285n107
Alter, Jonathan, xvii, 41, 105, 229n24
Al-Zuba'e, As'ad, 285n107
American Psychological Association (APA), complicity in torture, 30, 147, 217–23, 266n183, 299n6, 300n10
Amnesty International, 29, 96, 105, 141, 151–52
Anderson, Warwick, 66
anecdotes: assessment of torture practice in, 43–47; common premises in, 40–43; as crafted delivery mechanisms for national security

303

rationale, 33, 34–37; dimensions of state torture illustrated by, 47–55, 245n28; facts of case, 31–34; formulaic and folkloric distortions in, 37–43, 245n21; implications for torture discourse, 55–56; Lansdale's use of, 82–83. *See also* Lansdale, Edward; Mohammed, Khalid Sheikh; Murad, Abdul Hakim, case of
anthrax, xv, 228n15
AQI. *See* al-Qaeda
Aquino, Corazon, 96
Arab Mind, The (Patai), 172
Arar, Maher, 121, 124, 139–41, 156–57, 285nn101–2
archetype of torture: in antitorture scholarship, 100–101, 104–9; certainty and doubt generated by, 130–31; challenges to, 109–16; concept of, 7, 28–29, 99–102; consequences of, 102, 111–16; fixation on interrogation in, 101, 111–12; iconic scenario of, 102–9, 269n6; national security rationale supported by, 101, 111–12; police brutality versus, 5, 50, 100–101; in speculative press debate, 100–104; symmetry of force in, 116–18; unseating, 102, 118–20
Arestivo, Carlos Alberto, 10, 21, 113, 233nn21–22
Argentina, challenges to perpetrator performance in, 185–87
Argoud, Antoine, 71, 75
Armitage, Richard, 292n19
Atlantic Charter of 1941, 256n69
Atlantic Monthly, speculative articles published by, xi–xii, 5–6
atrocity, denial of: official/organizational, 203–7; public, 207–13; social phenomenon of, 190

Audre Lorde Project, 221, 301n18
Aussaresses, Paul, xiii
Australian Times, xvi
Avelar, Idelber, 118
Ayers, David, 300n10
Azmath, Mohammed Jaweed, 229n18, 229n20

Bacevich, Andrew J., 256n73
Baden, Michael, 271n40
Badr Organization, 202, 298n63
Bagram Airbase, Afghanistan: archetype of torture and, 110–11; eyewitness accounts of, 128; numbers of detainees at, 112; perpetrators at, 168
Bandholtz, Harry H., 65
Banks, Dennis, 4
BEAM (Black Emotional and Mental Health Collective), 221, 301n18
Beaver, Diane, 136
Bell, Derrick, 247n50
Benzien, Jeffrey, 186
Bigeard, Marcel, 71, 77–78, 260n111, 297n57
Bigelow, Kathryn, 43
Bilibid prison, 66, 81
bin Laden, Osama, 36
Black Panther activists, 4
boarding schools, American Indian, 4–5, 13, 28, 232n6, 232n8, 235n36
Body in Pain, The (Scarry), 105–6
Boer war, 69
Bohannan, Charles, 81, 262n133, 263n139
Bojinka plot. *See* Murad, Abdul Hakim, case of
Boot, Max, 81
borders: border security regimes, 1–2, 13, 16–17, 23–26, 51, 200, 215, 237n54; Chinese immigrants and,

INDEX • 305

15, 236n42, 238n55; *Egbert v. Boule,* 237n54; frontier wars, 61, 69; immigrant detention, 5, 17–18, 50–52, 226n4, 238n55, 242n1 (*see also* Metropolitan Detention Center, Brooklyn)
Bouhired, Djamilia, 261n123
Bourne trilogy, 135, 137
Bowden, Mark, 105, 170
Bowman, John, 4
Bradbury, Stephen, 155
Broadwell, Paula, 201
Brooke, John R., 251n17
Brzezinski, Matthew, 38
Burge, Jon, xiii, 227n5, 231n5
Burton, Mark, 221
Bush, George W.: appointments of, 292n19; legal memoranda on enhanced techniques, 123, 141–48, 280n56, 281n73, 281n78; Office of Legal Counsel, xi, 121, 148, 218. *See also* U.S.–Iraqi network
Byrne, John, 231n5

CACI, 167–68, 278n29, 285n107
Cambodia, 2, 230n2, 264n170. *See also* Nath, Vann
Camp Nama, 110, 114
Cannon, Darrell, 231n5
Carafano, James, 279n39
Carranza, Nicolas, 292n23
Cassell, Douglas, 24, 27
Casteel, Steve, 200, 202, 208, 210
Castoriadis, Cornelius, 24
Castro, Fidel, 81
Celermajer, Danielle: on criminalization of torture, 302n22; on definitions of torture, 8–9, 232n14, 233n16; ecological diagnosis of torture, 48, 238n64, 242n94; on interagency contexts, 114; on organizational settings, 48–53, 247n45; on political logics of torture, 18; on social imaginary, 27
Center for Personal Protection & Safety, 300n10
Central Intelligence Agency (CIA): American Psychological Association's association with, 217–23, 299n6, 300n10; creation of, 256n75; engagement in El Salvador, 197–99; interagency and interpersonal relationships of, 113–14; KUBARK interrogation manual, 273n60; in legal memoranda on enhanced techniques, 146; psychological paradigm for torture, 249n55, 265n180; transnational torture relationships, 45–47, 91–94, 255n62, 264n170, 266n183. *See also* extraordinary rendition; Tools of torture; torture networks
Chandrasekaran, Rajiv, xiv
Chauvin, Derek, 222
Cheney, Dick, 198, 225n1, 292n19
Chertoff, Michael, 136, 279n39
Chicago police, torture of African American residents by: historical foundations of, 14–15; impact on justice system, xiii, 4, 231n5; key literature on, 16; numbers of victims, 112; organizational goals of, 27–28, 227n5
Chinese Americans: immigrant detention, 238n55; lynching of, 15, 236n42
Churchill, Winston, 256n69
CIDTP (cruel, inhuman, and degrading treatment or punishment), 9
civic discipline model, 50–51, 248n51
Clark, Mark, 231n5
Clausewitz, Carl von, 74

Coffman, James, 200–202, 213
Cohen, Stanley, 190
COIN, 255n66, 256n73, 297n61
COINTELPRO, 4, 231n4, 231n5
Cole, David, xvii, 229n21
collaboration in terror: American Psychological Association (APA), 30, 147, 217–23, 266n183, 299n6, 300n10; characteristics of, 20, 215–16; public–private, 24, 26, 28, 50, 64–65, 94, 122, 156–57; U.S.-Philippines (*see* Philippines, colonial violence and control in); Washington–Baghdad, 189–203, 209–14
Colombia, implements of torture exported to, 2, 230n2
colonial violence. *See* counterinsurgency; Philippines, colonial violence and control in
community building, 3, 7; archetype of torture and, 114–16; counterinsurgency and, 87–97; social and organizational setting, 48–53, 113, 161, 174–76, 288n37; social benefits of torture, 176–79; social functions of torture and, 19–22, 53–54, 129–130, 174–79; through torture discourse, 21–22, 42; Tools of torture and, 123–24
complicity in torture, 215–23
Condon, Richard, 259n92
confessions: as performance, 162–68; overreliance on, 49–50, 247n47
Conroy, John, xiii, 45, 114, 288n37
continuum of violence, 9, 119, 125
control of space, 64, 75, 88, 95
Convention Against Torture (CAT), 8–9, 142, 232n12, 278n27
coordinated denial/disregard, U.S.-Iraqi network: official denial and organizational disregard, 203–7, 295n44; public disregard, 207–13
Corn, David, 292n19
counterinsurgency: colonial-to-counterinsurgency continuities, 94–96; control of space in, 64, 75, 88, 95; discourse about torture in, 6–7, 15–16, 28, 63; evolution and infrastructure in delivery of violence in, 88–90; formation of, 68–71, 256n72; key literature on, 15–16, 236n44; Lansdale's support of, 80–83, 262n131, 262nn128–29, 263n139; Lartéguy's support of, 77–80, 260n106; mobilization for war in, 94–96; overview of, 87–88, 255n65; peacekeeping in, 91–94, 264n170, 265n173; Philippines torture outcomes and, 96–97; Trinquier's support of, 71–77. *See also* racial capitalism; racialization
Crenshaw, Kimberlé, 247n50
criminalization of torture, 222, 242n94, 302n22
critical race theory, 241n87, 247n50
cybernetics, 219

Daesh, 292n20
"Dark Art of Interrogation, The" (Bowden), 170
Davies, Jeremy, 260n108
Davis, Angela Y., 16, 18
Davis, Ken, 167, 180
death penalty, 233n15
death squads. *See* U.S.-Iraqi network
Debord, Guy, 134
Defense Language Institute, 172
Delgado, Richard, 247n50
denial, U.S.-Iraqi network: official/organizational, 203–7, 295n44; public, 207–13

Dershowitz, Alan: archetype of torture used by, 105; impact of speculative news on, xii; Murad case cited by, 34–35, 38, 42
Detainee Photographic Record Protection Act, 129
Devine, Richard, 4, 231n5
Dignan, Peter, 231n5
dimensions of state torture: organizational setting, 48–53; social functions, 53–54; torture discourse, 54; torture practice, 48
Discipline and Punish (Foucault), 11
disregard, U.S.–Iraqi network: official/organizational, 203–7, 295n44; public, 207–13. *See also* Stoler, Ann
Division of Military Information, Manila, 65
"Does torture work?" question, xii, 35–36, 135–36
dominance personae of violence workers, 162, 182–84
Drug Enforcement Agency (DEA), 92, 190
Duarte, José Napoleón, 198
Du Bois, W. E. B., 252n27
Duffy, Kevin Thomas, 31–32, 37, 46, 52, 245n28
Dugan, Tony, 167–68

effectiveness of torture, xii, 35–36, 135–36, 239n66
Egbert v. Boule, 237n54
Einolf, Christopher, 61
Eisenhower, Dwight D., 71
Elmaghraby, Ehab, xiii, 29, 99–101, 110, 112, 118
El-Masri, Khalid, 157
El Salvador, U.S. engagement in, xiii, 197–99, 220–21, 292n19. *See also* Salvador Option

emergency model, 51
Emmerson, Ben, 213
ending torture, 215–23
England, Lynndie, 163, 167
enslavement. *See* slavery
entrepreneurial way of war. *See* counterinsurgency
Estonia, implements of torture exported to, 2, 230n2
executive power, torture in, 22–23
extraordinary rendition: Maher Arar case, 140–41, 156–57, 280n49; numbers of, 275n4; origins of, 33, 53; torture networks required for, 29
Extraordinary Rendition (film), 122, 140–41
eyewitness accounts, 128–31

Fainaru, Steve, 37–38
Fair, Eric, 132, 289n47
Fall, Bernard, 73, 258n86
Farabundo Martí National Liberation Front, 199
Fay, George R., 113
Fear Up Harsh (Lagouranis and Mikaelian), 29, 160, 168–69, 182. *See also* Lagouranis, Tony
Federal Bureau of Investigation (FBI): COINTELPRO, 4, 231n4, 231n5; collaboration in Murad torture, 31–33, 45–47; historical foundations of, 14; interagency and interpersonal relationships of, 113–14; interrogation techniques of, 273n60. *See also* Murad, Abdul Hakim, case of
Feinstein, Diane, 148
Feitlowitz, Marguerite, 186
Ferro, Alberto, 47
film: confessional performance in, 162–68; Tools of torture in, 123, 134–41. *See also individual films*

Finn, Peter, xiv
Finnegan, Patrick, 136
Fireweed Collective, 221
Floyd, George, 222, 247n50
Forrestal, Michael, 240n73
Forward Operating Base Mercury, Iraq, 110–11
Foucault, Michel, 11
four-dimensional framework for state torture: benefits of, 47–48; organizational setting, 48–53; social functions, 53–54; torture discourse, 54; torture practice, 48
Francia, Luis H., 38
Freeman, Doug, 140
Front de libération nationale (FLN), 69
frontier wars, 61, 69
funding, U.S.–Iraqi network, 202–3, 295n41

Galula, David, 75–76
Galvin, Jack, 201
Gannon, John, 149
Gates, Robert, 292n19
Gellman, Barton, xiv
gender: feminism and femininity, 183; gender-based violence, 9, 233n16; gender-making functions of torture, 7, 21, 51, 116; LGBTQ population, 18, 221, 301, 301n18; masculinity performance, 182–83; race oppression and, 231n3. *See also* misogyny; rape; sexualized violence
Geneva Conventions, xi, 172, 175
Ghosts of Abu Ghraib (film), 162, 164–67, 179–80, 184
Gibbs, Wm. J., 251n17
Gibney, Alex, 168, 286n11
Gilbert, Elizabeth, 87
Gilmore, Ruth Wilson, 16, 17, 190
Glanz, James, 295n41

Glenn, Edwin, 251n16, 252n18
Gloria, Glenda, 37–38
Godard, Yves, 71, 77
Golder, Andrew, 135
Gonzalez, Alberto R., 85–86, 148, 225n1, 280n52
Grenier, John, 13
Grey, Stephen, 275n4
groupthink, 24
Grunhard, Charles, 231n5
Guantánamo Bay detention site: aggressive protocols, spaces, and personnel in, xi; archetype of torture and, 112–13, 115; eyewitness accounts of, 128; national security rationale for, 85; number of detainees at, 112, 266n189; Tools of torture at, 41, 110, 274n1, 277n16

Hampton, Fred, 4, 231n5
Hannity, Sean, 151
Haritos-Fatouros, Mika, 183
Harman, Sabrina, 29, 163–67
Harrigan, Steve, 151
Heart of Darkness narratives in speculative news, xii, 102–5, 153, 170–71. *See also* Lagouranis, Tony
Heiser, Victor, 66–67
Hendrickson, Dan, 204
Heritage Foundation Conference, 136, 279n39
Herrington, Stuart, 136
Hersh, Seymour, 197, 201
Heyman, David, 279n39
Hiatt, Lincoln, 135
historical narratives in speculative news, xii, 102–5
Hitchens, Christopher, 151, 284n95
Hoffman, Bruce, 105, 269n9, 275n4
Hood, Gavin, 139–40
Horst, Karl, 206, 213

INDEX · 309

Horton, Scott, 166–67
Huggins, Martha, 113, 183
Huk rebellion, 58, 80–83, 90, 262n130
Human Rights First, 136, 140, 169, 269n7
Human Rights Watch, 169
Hume, Brit, 151
Hunt, Lynn, 108, 109
hypothetical narratives in speculative news, xii–xiii, xvi–xviii, 102–5, 225n2

Icarus Project, 301
immigration bans and detention: detainee deaths, 242n1; *Egbert v. Boule*, 237n54; mass protest of, 5; torture claims in, 17–18, 50–52, 226n4, 238n55. *See also* Metropolitan Detention Center, Brooklyn
incarceration, 17–18, 222
incentives, U.S.–Iraqi network, 202–3, 295n41
Indigenous land, theft of, 13
Indigenous populations. *See* Native Americans
Indochina, 69, 71–72, 260n105
Initial Reaction Force (IRF), 115, 128
Innocence Project, 247n47
Intelligence Science Board, 136, 173, 242n1, 287n30
interagency/interpersonal relationships, 113–14, 175–76
interrogation, 225n1; archetypal depiction of, 28–29, 42, 103–5, 109–10, 117–18, 134; as distinct from torture, 19–20, 111–12, 273n60; national security rationale of, 68, 73–74, 79–80, 97, 101–2; noncoercive, 249n55, 273n60, 287n30; plural nature of, 20, 101–2, 110–11;

questioning, 118, 273n60; standards of conduct for, 225n1, 301n21
Inventing Human Rights (Hunt), 108
Iqbal, Javaid, 29, 99–100
ISIS, 8, 292n20, 298n64
Islamic State, 292n20

Jabr, Bayan, 206
Jadriyah torture bunker, 206, 298n64
Jamail, Dahr, 292n19
Jessen, Bruce, 217–19, 299n6, 300n10
Johansen, Andrew, 209
John Paul II (Pope), 36, 43
Johnson, David, 246n31
Jones, Anthony R., 113
juridical model, 49–50

Kaba, Mariame, 16, 222
Kagan, Carolyn, 221
Kandahar, Afghanistan: eyewitness accounts of, 128; numbers of detainees at, 112; torture at, 110–11, 128
Karpinski, Janis, 163
keeping the peace, 91–94, 264n170, 265n173
Kendi, Ibram X., 235n33
Kennedy, John F., 90, 256n76
Kennedy, Rory, 164
Kenya, 1998 embassy bombings in, 53, 248n54
Khalili, Laleh, 15
Khan, Ayub Ali, 229n18, 229n20
King, Martin Luther, Jr., 4
Kiriakou, John, 149–50
KKR, 297n61
Komer, Robert, 91
Krog, Antjie, 186
KSM. *See* Mohammed, Khalid Sheikh
KUBARK interrogation manual, 273n60
Kurnaz, Murat, 157

310 · INDEX

Lagouranis, Tony, 29, 117; counternarratives to, 184–87; dominance personae of, 182–84; impact of speculative news on, xii; interagency and interpersonal relationships of, 175–76; mass-mediated culture and, 168–74; media attention to, 159–62; moral positioning of, 179–82, 289n56; performance of, 162–68; personal background of, 159–60; psychological needs and social rewards of, 161, 176–79; quest for professionalism, 171–74; on racialized, militarized science, 267n192; silence concerning survivors, 184–87; social and organizational setting of, 174–76
Lance, Peter, 41, 245n21
Langguth, A. J., 15
Lansdale, Edward: popularity of, 97, 262n131, 262nn128–29; security imagining of torture, 28, 69, 80–83, 88–90, 263n139
Larsen, Kaj, 150–51
Lartéguy, Jean: impact of, 97; Petraeus's admiration for, 77–78, 297n57; popularity and credibility of, 260n106; security imagining of torture, 28, 69, 77–80, 261n123, 261nn121–22
Latour, Bruno, 239n68
Law Enforcement Assistance Administration (LEAA), 92, 265n176
Lawrence, T. E., 211
Lazreg, Marnia, 10–11, 16, 64, 71, 119, 175
Lee, Elizabeth, 17
legal commentators: impact of speculative news on, xii, 229n22; Murad case cited by, 34–35
legality of Tools, 123, 131–32

legal memoranda, narratives of Tools of torture in, 123, 141–48, 280n56, 281n73, 281n78
Léger, Christian, 76–77, 260n105
Les Centurions (Lartéguy), 77–80, 261n123, 261nn121–22
Levin, Daniel, 142, 155
Levinson, Sanford: archetype of torture used by, 105; impact of speculative news on, xii; Murad case cited by, 35, 42
Lewis, Stephen, 286n13
LGBTQ population, 18, 221, 301n18
Lodge, Henry Cabot, 60
Lokaneeta, Jinee, 119
Lost Command (film), 77
Louima, Abner, xiii
Luban, David, 35, 106, 112, 132, 156, 272n42
lynching: in colonial and neocolonial expansion, 13, 62, 102; in United States, 15, 58, 60, 62, 236n42, 253n36, 273n54

Maass, Peter, 40–41, 105, 207–14, 298n65
MacArthur, Arthur, 88–90
Mackey, Chris: doubt and certainty in account of, 125–26; eyewitness appraisal of, 128–29; interagency and interpersonal relationships described by, 113; national security rationale used by, 86; performance of, 163; plural and collaborative nature of torture described by, 110
Malcolm X, 4
Manchurian Candidate (Condon), 259n92
Mao Zedong, 69
Marcos, Ferdinand, 45, 68, 255n62
Marcos, Ferdinand "Bongbong," Jr., 96

INDEX · 311

Margolis, David, 281n78
Marks, John, 260n108
Martín-Baró, Ignacio, 220
masculinity performance, 182–83
mass-mediated culture, role of, 168–74
Massu, Jacques, xiii, 71, 75
Matarazzo, Joseph, 300n10
material infrastructure, 114
Matsuda, Mari, 247n50
Matus, Victorino, 41, 243n3
Mazigh, Monia, 141
McChrystal, Stanley, 77
McClintock, Michael, 262n131
McCoy, Alfred, 15, 64, 66, 89, 96, 249n55, 255n62, 265n180
McNamara, John, 256n76
Means, Russell, 4
Mejia, Ximena E., 301
Melzer, Nils, 233n19
Mendoza, Rodolfo "Boogie," 47
Mesmer, Pierre, 256n76
Metropolitan Detention Center, Brooklyn, xiii, 52, 99, 112, 226n4. *See also* Elmaghraby, Ehab
Meyers, Richard, 204
Mikaelian, Allen, 160
Milgram, Stanley, 164–65, 179
misogyny: at Abu Ghraib, 172, 183; hierarchies of, 215; torture as engine of, 5, 11, 18, 21, 102, 113
Mitchell, James E., 217–19, 299n6, 300n10
Modern Warfare (Trinquier), 23, 72–77, 90
Mohammad, Binyam, 157
Mohammad, Fashad, 184, 290n60
Mohammed, Khalid Sheikh, 36–37, 42–43, 146, 245n25
moral positioning of violence workers, 161–62, 179–82, 289n56
Morris, Errol, 29

Morris, George B., 251n17
Mossad, in Murad anecdote, 39–41, 44–45, 93, 243n3, 245n21
Moussawi, Zacarias, xvi
Movement for Black Lives, 5, 51
Mowhoush, Abed Hamed, 297n60
Moyn, Samuel, 108–9
Mufti, Basr, 194
Mukasey, Michael, 121, 148–49, 151, 156
Muller, Erich Mancow, 151, 284n94
Murad, Abdul Hakim, case of: assessment of torture practice in, 43–47; as crafted delivery mechanism for national security rationale, 28, 33–37; dimensions of state torture illustrated by, 47–55, 245n28; facts of, 31–34; formulaic and folkloric distortions in, 37–43, 245n21; implications for torture discourse, 55–56; premises of, 40–43

Nadler, Christina, 190
Nagel, Thomas, 107
Nagl, James, 255n66
Nance, Malcolm, 132–34, 140, 148
Naser, Ali, 29
Naser, Jafar Ali Abdul, 184
Nashel, Jonathan, 82
Nath, Vann, 149, 282n81
National Security Act of 1947, 256n75
national security imagination: alteration of, 217–23; concept of, 1–8; as example of social imaginaries, 3, 24–28, 215; historical grounding of, 22–24; shared and characteristic orientations of, 26–27. *See also* archetype of torture; networks; perpetrators; rationale; Tools of torture
national security rationale, 7, 28, 87–88; colonial violence and, 57–68;

counterinsurgency theory formation and, 68–71; definition of, 33; evolution and infrastructure in delivery of violence, 88–90; Lansdale's support of, 80–83; Lartéguy's support of, 77–80; market perspective on, 92–94; mobilization for war in, 94–96; Murad anecdote crafted to support, 28, 33–37 (*see also* Murad, Abdul Hakim, case of); peacekeeping in, 91–94; Philippines torture outcomes and, 96–97; premises of, 40–43; in torture discourse, 54, 83–87; Trinquier's support of, 71–77; in Vietnam War, 84–85; in war on terror, 85–87. *See also* racial capitalism; racialization

Native Americans: boarding schools for, 4–5, 13, 28, 232n6, 232n8, 235n36; capture and confinement of, 13–14; enslavement of, 13–14; lynching and massacres of, 15, 58, 60, 62–63, 253n36, 273n54

Navy SEALs, 111, 176, 180, 288n37, 289n56, 290n60

Negroponte, John, 292n19

Nelson, Tauren, 235n33

Neocleous, Mark, 15

networks. *See* torture networks

news anxiety and addiction, as context of speculative press debate, xv–xviii, 228n13

Newsweek, speculative articles published by, xi–xii, 5–6, 225n2

New York, Metropolitan Detention Center, xiii, 52, 99, 112, 226n4

New Yorker, speculative articles published by, xi–xii

New York Times, speculative articles published by, xi–xii, xviii, 5–6, 225n2

9/11 Commission, 38
Nixon, Richard, 265n174
North, Oliver, 292n19

Obama, Barack, 156–57, 301n21
Odeh, Mohammed Saddiq, 248n54
Office of Legal Counsel (OLC), xi, 121, 148, 218
Office of Public Safety (OPS), 90–94, 255n62, 265n174
official denial and disregard, U.S.–Iraqi network, 203–7, 295n44
organizational setting: archetype of torture versus, 113; in Murad case, 48–53; perpetrators and, 161, 174–76, 288n37
Osty, Jean Pierre Lucien. *See* Lartéguy, Jean
Othman, Sadi, 205
Owens, Patricia, 15, 236n44, 256n72

Pace, Peter, 204–5
Papachristos, Andrew, 195–96
paramilitary policing structures: Philippine Constabulary, 59, 63–68, 250n10, 253n31, 254n45; Philippine National Police, 67, 96–97. *See also* Murad, Abdul Hakim, case of
Parents Television Council, 135–36, 148
Parry, John T., 9, 119, 238n55
Patai, Raphael, 172, 267n192, 287n25
Patterson, Thomas, 62
Payne, Leigh, 163–64, 185–86
peacekeeping, 91–94
Pellegrino, Frank, 32–33, 46, 53
perpetrators, 7–8, 29; American Psychological Association as, 217–23, 299n6, 300n10; confessions of, 162–68; counternarratives to, 162, 184–87; dominance personae

of, 162, 182–84; exaggeration and boasting by, 44–45; fascination with, 159–62; interagency and interpersonal relationships of, 113–14, 175–76; mass-mediated culture and, 161, 168–74; moral positioning of, 161–62, 179–82, 289n56; performance of, 162–68; psychological needs and social rewards of, 161, 176–79; quest for professionalism, 171–74; silence concerning survivors, 184–87; social and organizational setting of, 113, 161, 174–76, 288n37

personnel, Washington–Iraq network, 199–202, 294n31, 294n38

Petraeus, David: Bigeard and, 77–78, 260n111, 297n57; Lartéguy's influence on, 77–78, 297n57; later career of, 297n61; position on torture, 189, 201–2, 205–7, 296n55, 298n65; Steele and, 298n65; U.S.–Iraqi network and, 200–208, 213, 255n66

Philippine Constabulary (P.C.), 59, 63–68, 250n10, 253n31, 254n45

Philippine National Police (PNP), 31, 67, 96–97. *See also* Murad, Abdul Hakim, case of

Philippines, colonial violence and control in: colonial-to-counterinsurgency continuities, 94–96; control of space, 64, 75, 88; evolution and infrastructure in delivery of violence, 88–90; historical context of, 58–61; Huk rebellion, 58, 80–83, 90, 262n130; independence movement, 59–61; Lansdale's tactics, 80–83, 88–90; overview of, 6, 28, 57; Philippine Constabulary, 59, 63–68, 250n10, 253n31, 254n45; Philippine National Police, 67, 96–97 (*see also* Murad, Abdul Hakim, case of); racialized context, 57–60, 62–68, 95–96, 252n27, 254n48; Tools of torture in, 61, 124–27, 251nn16–17, 252n18; torture outcomes in, 96–97. *See also* counterinsurgency

Physicians for Human Rights, 149, 282n81

Pincus, Walter, xvi–xvii

Pinochet, Augusto, xiii

plurals of torture, 20, 101–2, 110–11

policing structures: credibility of, 44–45; historical foundations of, 14–15; key literature on, 15–18; Law Enforcement Assistance Administration, 92, 265n176; market perspective on, 92–94; OPS and CIA association with, 91–94, 255n62, 264n170, 265n174, 266n183; Philippine Constabulary, 59, 63–68, 250n10, 253n31, 254n45; Philippine National Police, 67, 96–97 (*see also* Murad, Abdul Hakim, case of); police brutality concept, 5, 50, 100–101; replacement and reform of, 221–23; roots in slavery/enslavement, 16, 240n83, 273n54; sex with persons in custody, 233n15; torture as civic marker in, 50–51, 248n51; use-of-force continuum, 16–17. *See also* Chicago police, torture of African American residents by

political coverage, waterboard in, 123, 148–50, 282nn81–82, 283n85

Posner, Richard: archetype of torture used by, 105; Murad case cited by, 35, 42

Powers, Steve, 152

Praeger, Frederick, 90

press debate. *See* speculative press debate
Priest, Dana, xiv
Prime Time Torture Project, 136, 140, 279n42
Prisoner without a Name, Cell without a Number (Timerman), 154
prisons: abolition of, 16–18, 222–23. *See also* Abu Ghraib prison
process, torture as, 4, 19–20
Project X, 264n170, 265n173
Protected National Security Documents Act, 277n22
psychological torture: CIA paradigm for, 248n55, 265n180; eyewitness accounts of, 130–31; as indistinguishable from physical torture, 41–42; premises in torture anecdotes, 40–41
public denial and disregard, U.S.–Iraqi network, 207–13

Question, The (Alleg), 149
questioning, 118, 273n60. *See also* interrogation

racial capitalism: concept of, 7, 11, 235n33; incarceration and, 17–18; relationship of torture to, 109, 222
racialization: in Algerian war for independence, 79; in colonial violence and control, 57–60, 62–68, 95–96, 250, 252n27, 254n48; emergence of, 235n33; gender oppression and, 231n3; in interrogator training, 172–74; racialized, militarized science in, 64–68, 95–96, 254n48; torture as tool of, 248n51; white supremacy and, 58, 252n22; World War II era, 73, 258n84. *See also* lynching; national security rationale; Philippines, colonial violence and control in
racialization and racial capitalism: in colonial violence and control, 6; domestic examples of, 3–7; key literatures on, 16–18; racialized, militarized science in, 57; torture as tool of, 12–14, 50–51
Rahman, Gul, 217
Ralph, Laurence, 16, 114, 237n49
RAND Corporation, 76, 82, 90, 218, 264n159
rape: in Algerian war for independence, 79, 261n123; incarceration and, 16; in Metropolitan Detention Center cases, 99–100; in Murad case, 32, 42; plural nature of, 110–11; as torture, 9–11, 99–100, 268n2
rationale. *See* national security rationale
Reagan, Ronald, 209
reenactors, waterboard, 150–56, 284nn94–95
Rejali, Darius, 12, 265n180; on apprenticeship of torturers, 170; on civic doubt, 127; on organizational setting, 48–53
remorse, in perpetrator confessions, 163–64
Rendition (film), 122, 139–40, 148
Rice, Condoleezza, 156
Road Not Taken, The (Boot), 81
Roberts, Dorothy, 17
Robinson, Mary, 4
Rorty, Richard, 109
Rumsfeld, Donald, 159, 174, 198–202, 204, 209, 292n19

Saar, Erik, 111, 128–31, 163
Saca, Elias Antonio, 199
Sachs, Jack, 248n54

INDEX · 315

Salim, Suleiman Abdullah, 217
Salim v. Mitchell, 217
Salvador Option: funding and incentives, 202–3, 295n41; overview of, 8, 29–30, 195–97; personnel and structure of, 199–202, 294n31, 294n38; shared schematic for, 197–99, 292n20, 293n23
Samar massacre, 62–63, 250n10
Sanchez, Ricardo S., 174
Sand Creek massacre, 62–63
sand cure, 62, 124
Sands, Leonard, 248n54
Sands, Philippe, 136
Scarry, Elaine, 29, 105–6, 108–9, 112, 270n19
schematic, Salvador Option, 197–99, 292n20, 293n23
Schlesinger, James R., 130, 283n85
Schrader, Stuart, 15
Schumer, Charles, 148
Scilongo, Adolfo, 186
Scilongo Effect, 186
Score, Gina, 232n6
Scott, Ruben, 4
security rationale for torture. *See* national security rationale
Seigel, Micol, 15, 92
Senate: 1902 debate over torture, 61–63; Mukasey hearings, 148–49, 151; Senate Select Committee intelligence report on enhanced interrogation, xviii
Sentinel project, 138
settlement, historical accounts of, 12–14
Sexton, Jared, 17
sexualized violence: eyewitness accounts of, 130–31; Lagouranis's distancing from, 183. *See also* rape
Shah, Wali Khan Amin, 36, 246n30

Shi'ite Badr Brigade, 204
Shi'ite death squads, 8
Shklar, Judith, 270n19
Sifton, John, 169
Simbulan, Roland, 68
Simmons, F. M., 62
Simón, Julio, 185
Singh, Amrit, 275n4
Skier, Stephanie, 152
Slahi, Mohamedou, 157
slavery: abolition of, 222; Abraham Lincoln test for moral casuistry and, 285n95; of Native Americans, 13–14; relationship of torture to, 13–15, 107, 116; roots of U.S. surveillance and policing in, 16, 240n83, 273n54
small-world networks, 294n38
Smith, Andrea, 190
social functions of torture, 19–22, 53–54, 129–30, 174–79
social imaginaries, 215; alteration of, 217–223; concept of, 1–8, 24–28. *See also* national security imagination
sodium pentothal, xvii, 91
Solitary (TV series), 135
solitary confinement, xvi, 109, 226
Soud, Mohamed Ahmed Ben, 217
South Africa, challenges to perpetrator performance in, 185–87
South Dakota State Training School, 4–5, 28, 232n6, 232n8
space, control of, 64, 75, 88, 95
spectrum of violence, 9, 119, 125
speculative press debate: archetype of torture in, 102–5; context of, xv–xviii, 228n13; impact of, xii; launch of, xi, 225n1; omissions in, 5–6; patterns in, xii–xv, 5–8; War Is Hell–style reporting in, 84, 207–8, 211–12. *See also* story types

spiked batons, manufacture and export of, 1, 230n2
Spivey, Randall, 300n10
Sporleder, James, 300n10
Standard Operating Procedure (film), 29, 162, 164–66, 286n6
state violence: mosaic of, 9, 233n15; role of torture in, 8–10
Staub, Ervin, 115
Steele, James, 198–204, 208–10, 213, 292n19, 298n65
Steele, Meili, 97
Stewart, Douglas, 23
Stoler, Ann, 126, 146, 190
story types, xii–xiii
Strauss, Marcy, 111, 269n6
stress and duress, xiv
Struck, Doug, 39
structural evolution of U.S. violence, 88–90
Stuff of Life, The (film), 152
surveillance, colonial-to-counterinsurgency continuities in, 94–95
survivor perspectives, 148–49, 282nn81–82
Survivors of Torture International, 148–49, 282nn81
Sussman, David, 107
Swanner, Mark, 111, 271n40
Syria, implements of torture exported to, 2, 230n2
Syriana (film), 135

Taguba, Antonio M., 113, 159
Taha, Mazan, 296n56
Tajikistan, implements of torture exported to, 2, 230n2
Taliban, 85
Tanzania, 1998 embassy bombings in, 53

Taussig, Michael, 126, 146, 192
Taxi to the Dark Side (film), 168
Taylor, Charles, 24
Taylor, Flint, 114
Taylor, Harold, 4
Taylor, Maxwell, 84
techniques. *See* Tools of torture
terror: in Algerian war for independence, 76–77, 260n102; definition of, 10–11; torture as instrument of, 3–11
Terrorism in the Hands of Justice (TV series), 192–93, 205, 208, 291n7
Terror TV, 192–95
Thabit, Adnan, 199–200, 205, 208, 210, 294n31
Thoburn, James Mills, 63
Thornburgh, Richard, xvii, 117, 229n22
thumbscrews/thumb cuffs, manufacture and export of, 1–8, 230n2
ticking time bomb argument: as archetype of torture, 105–6; Lartéguy's depiction of, 77; Murad anecdote crafted as, 33, 43; origins of, 260n108; Petraeus and, 296n55; in public conversation on torture, xvii, 27
Tillman, Ben "Pitchfork," 62
Time, speculative articles published by, xi–xii, 5–6
Timerman, Jacobo, 45, 154–55
Tizon, Orlando, 114
Tools of torture: Maher Arar case, 139–41, 156–57, 280n49, 285nn101–2; authorization of, 274n1; certainty and doubt generated by, 123–32; colonial violence and control, 61, 124, 251nn16–17, 252n18; consequences of, 156–57; eyewitness accounts of, 128–31; legal memoranda narratives of, 123,

141–48, 280n56, 281n73, 281n78; legal preoccupation with, 123, 131–32; limits of, 153–56; manufacture and export of, 1–2, 230n2; political narratives of, 123, 148–50, 282nn81–82, 283n85; public preoccupation with, 122–23; survivor perspectives of, 148–49, 282nn81–82; symbolic weight of, 121–23; TV and film narratives of, 123, 134–41. *See also* extraordinary rendition; waterboard
torture, definition of, 8–11, 100
Torture and Democracy (Rejali), 12, 48
Torture and the Twilight of Empire (Lazreg), 16
torture anecdotes. *See* anecdotes
torture dimensions, 47–55
torture discourse: community building and positioning through, 42–43; in counterinsurgency theory, 6–7, 15–16, 28, 63; in Murad case, 54; torture anecdotes in (*see* anecdotes)
Torture Letters, The (Ralph), 16
torture literatures, 11–19
torture lore, definition of, 7, 232n10. *See also* anecdotes
torture networks, 7–8, 29–30; American Psychological Association and, 217–23, 299n6, 300n10; archetype of torture and, 115–16; colonial thinking in, 209–13; complicity in, 215–23; concept of, 189–92; investigation into, 213–14; legal memoranda narratives of, 123, 141–48, 280n56, 281n73, 281n78; market perspective on, 92–94; official denial and organizational disregard in, 203–7, 295n44; personnel and structure of, 199–202, 294n31, 294n38; public disregard in, 207–13; shared schema, 197–99, 292n20, 293n23; *Terror TV* analysis of, 192–95; withdrawing support for, 216–17. *See also* U.S.–Iraqi network
torture practice: definition of, 31–32; in Murad case, 43–47, 48; in Philippines, 59–68
Torture Victim Protections Act, 142
transgender. *See* LGBTQ population
transnational torture relationships, 20, 53, 91–94, 249n55, 264n170. *See also* counterinsurgency; Murad, Abdul Hakim, case of
Trinquier, Roger: impact of, 97; popularity of, 259n92; security imagining of torture, 28, 69, 71–77, 90, 240n73
Truman, Harry S., 23, 70–71, 256n75
Truth and Reconciliation Commission, South Africa, 186–87
Tuohy, William, 84–85, 208
TV series, Tools of torture in, 123, 134–41
24 (TV series), 135–40

Under the Crescent Moon (Vitung and Gloria), 37, 45
United Nations Convention Against Torture (CAT), 8, 142, 232n12, 278n27
Universal Declaration of Human Rights, 256n69
universal distributor hypothesis, 93, 265n180, 266n183
"unnecessary body cavity search," 99–100, 110–11, 118. *See also* rape
U.S. Commerce Control List, 1, 3, 230n2
U.S.–Iraqi network: colonial thinking in, 209–13; concept of, 189–92; investigation into, 213–14; overview of, 195–97; personnel and structure

of, 199–202; Salvador Option, 195–203; shared schematic for, 197–99; *Terror TV* analysis of, 192–95; U.S. responsibility and participation in torture, 195–203
U.S. News and World Report, speculative articles published by, 5–6

Ventura, Jesse, 151
Verbitsky, Horacio, 186
V for Vendetta (film), 135
Vietnam War, 81, 83–87, 128, 277n18
violence workers. *See* perpetrators
Virtual Case File project, 138
Vitug, Marites, 37–38

Wacquant, Loïc, 16, 190
Waiting for the Guards (film), 151–52
Wald, Mark, 210
Waldron, Jeremy, 107–8, 116
Waller, Littleton, 62
Wall Street Journal, speculative articles published by, xi–xii, 5–6, 225n2
War Is Hell–style reporting: colonialist conventions in, 207–8, 211–12; in Iraq war reporting, 207–8; Lartéguy's impact on (*see* Lartéguy, Jean); origins of, 84
Washington Post, speculative articles published by, xi–xii, xvi, 5–6, 225n2
waterboard: authorization of, 274n1; certainty and doubt generated by, 124–32; foundational narrative of, 132–34; legal memoranda narratives of, 123, 141–48, 280n56, 281n73, 281n78; legal preoccupation with, 131–32; limits of, 153–56; political narratives of, 123, 148–50, 282nn81–82, 283n85; public preoccupation with, 29, 122–23; symbolic weight of, 121–23; TV and film narratives of, 123, 134–41; waterboard reenactors, 150–56, 284nn94–95
Waterboard (multimedia), 152
water cure, 61, 124, 251nn16–17, 252n18
Welcome, Richard, 128–29, 277nn18–19
Wells-Barnett, Ida B., 59–68
White, Josh, 297n60
Whitehouse, Sheldon, 148
Why Terrorism Works, 34
Williams, Kayla, 128, 130
Williams, Kristian, 10
Winik, Jay, 37–40
Wolfe, Patrick, 14
women, incarceration of, 18
World Conference against Racism, 4
Wren, Christopher, 37–38
Wyden, Ron, 204

Yee, James, 113, 115, 163
Yoo, John, 22–23, 27, 166, 239n72, 280n53
Yousef, Ramzi Ahmed, 36, 39, 42, 54

Zero Dark Thirty (film), 43
Zimbardo, Philip, 183
Zubaydah, Abu, 144–46, 150

STEPHANIE ATHEY is professor of cultural studies at Lasell University in Boston and editor of *Sharpened Edge: Women of Color, Resistance, and Writing.*

www.ingramcontent.com/pod-product-compliance
Lightning Source LLC
Chambersburg PA
CBHW060752200525
26707CB00020B/7